Acting Magic

The Complete Guide to the Art of Acting

DESLIE MCCLELLAN

PB
Playhouse
Books

Emmaus, Pennsylvania

Published by Playhouse Books
For more information, please contact:
sales@playhousebooks.com

All possible efforts were made by Playhouse Books to secure permission and ensure proper credit given for every quote used in this book. To the best of our knowledge, all illustrations are copyright free.

For a full description of other Playhouse Books products, please visit:
www.playhousebooks.com

Library of Congress Control Number: 2006937341

ISBN 978-0-9790089-5-5
Printed in the United States of America.

First Edition

To my husband and children,

the stars in my life…

Acknowledgements

A life's work is a rainbow of many colors, which God illumines by His grace. With deepest love and gratitude, I would like to thank those who brought their exceptional skills and loving hearts to this work:

My mother, who insisted that I go to my speech and drama lesson, my singing lesson, and my dance lesson every week—rain or shine.

Mrs. Barbara Dare, my dramatics teacher, who taught me to respect the art of acting and pursue it with excellence.

Mr. John Miles-Brown, Examiner at the Trinity College of Music, London, who inspired in me the romance of theater.

Patricia Spadaro, for her impeccable editing skills.

Not least of all, the students I have taught, and their priceless gift of joy.

5   Unit Study Five: Sense Awareness and Memorization 119

6   Unit Study Six: Mime and Pantomime   135

Introduction

Acting Magic is a professional acting course designed to acquaint students with the beauty and magic of theater—to take them from beginning voice, stage movement, and role-playing exercises to a level of performance excellence and repertory disciplines. The program trains the students to express themselves confidently and joyfully, to create a character role with genuine emotion, and to portray it with technical skill. *Acting Magic* also helps nurture self-esteem, reinforce oral language skills, and inspire a real enthusiasm for classical literature—and the students have fun.

This curriculum is based on my experience as an actress, singer, director, and a trainer of young actors for the professional theater. I received my teaching degree in the theory and practice of speech and dramatic art from the Trinity College of Music, London. When I first started teaching, the only instructional materials available were British books on elocution (not easily understood by American students brought up on Hollywood movies). With the translations of Russian director Constantin Stanislavski's revolutionary writings on the art of acting, a more introspective approach to training began to evolve that rivaled the classical school. Later followers would call it "method" acting—absent the ethics and idealism of its founder.

Though splendid and penetrating in their insight and originality, Stanislavski's concepts have never been easy to apply practically in a drama classroom filled with school-aged children. Today, alternate texts on method acting abound in the Hollywood and New York studios. Finding them geared towards adults, nuanced in psychological complexity, and inadequate in their instruction of a clear and well-formed technique, I decided to write my own curriculum. The result is *Acting Magic,* a classic and complete guide to the art of acting that combines the best of the English tradition and the vital components of American theater.

What Is Acting Magic?

When I was just three years old, I gave my first public performance at an Eisteddfod (an English competition for the performing arts). That debut earned me a silver medal and the applause of an audience charmed by a precocious little girl who spoke every line of her poem with perfect, if somewhat exaggerated, diction. Though it was many years ago, I can still vividly recall the experience and the way I felt when I recited the words of the poem upon what seemed to me at the time to be the biggest stage in the world. I also remember the smiling faces of the people in the audience as I carefully walked off the stage and returned to the seat next to my mother. The event was and still is bright in my imagination because it was magical. The stage had power over my heart from that day forward. It is a magic that cannot be defined in words, for it must be felt. Therein lies its transforming joy. That old acting magic has kept me in its spell all these years, and it is always my hope that I can transfer it to each of my students.

The ways by which actors arrive at experiencing that magic onstage and conveying it to their audience vary according to their temperaments and the individual practice of their craft. Ultimately, an actor must work with his own tools, and rely on his own inspiration as his best guide. One thing is certain: to quote visionary artist and composer Tom Miller, "There is no great art of any kind without magic."

What is this transformative magic but the love affair between the character and the audience. How the actor brokers such a love affair, how he makes the life of his character leap out of the script, onto the stage, and into the hearts and understanding of his audience, is what constitutes his art. My temperament has favored the more stately and graceful acting styles of artists belonging to a more romantic era—those of the distinguished repertory tradition such as Laurence Olivier, Ronald Colman, Greer Garson, Leslie Howard, John Gielgud, Dame Edith Anderson, Dame May Whitty, Robert Donat, Gladys Cooper, Claude Rains, Alec Guinness, Irene Dunne, and C. Aubrey Smith—actors who combined the perfect balance of skilled vocal technique, imaginative rendering, and an easy, dignified stage presence. With seeming effortlessness, they created a lucid and exalting theater experience, whether on the stage or the screen. Never wildly passionate, but always intensely true, they wedded technical skill to the intuitive, suffusing their characters and their art with a spiritual light and loveliness that never failed to touch the beauty in our hearts.

Through their artistry, the drama spoke to us. Whether they played characters from the plays of Sophocles, Shakespeare, Sheridan, and Chekhov, or from the great classical novels of Dickens, Austen, Alcott, and Bronte, they contributed a polish and elegance to the art, personifying Hamlet's prototype actor in every way. No matter the madness or sanity, the humility or haughtiness, the gentleness or cruelty of the roles portrayed, these actors had a high sense of theater. With a noble intention, they conveyed to the audience the true soul of their characters and the true glory of dramatic art. They brought to their work the command and integrity of their own hearts and the belief that when art appeals to the highest and best in men, it is an irresistible appeal.

Can we go wrong in affirming what the actors of this earlier golden age of acting understood: that theater is all about expressing the hope of something purer and better than what man lives and experiences in the real world? That was the noble intention and "grace" they brought to their characters. Author and journalist Peggy Noonan, in a December, 2006 article for the Wall Street Journal, described grace as "a sensitivity, mercy, generosity of spirit, [and] a courtesy so deep it amounts to beauty." No more fitting definition could apply to these cherished actors of a time gone by.

In his book *A Rose for Mrs. Miniver,* author Michael Troyan quotes Greer Garson in her advice to young actors: "Have faith in your star and follow your dream, not for any thought of fame or fortune, but simply because, as an actor, you can be a great and powerful influence for good. So much of what we see on the stage today is hopeless and despairing. Producers should have more courage. People will respond to stories with beauty, romance and idealism and happy endings. Films should speak to the best in us—of hope, courage, persistence in adversity, and generosity in triumph....I think the mirror should be tilted slightly upward when it's reflecting life—toward the cheerful, the tender, the compassionate, the brave, the funny, the encouraging—and not tilted down to the troubled vistas of conflict."

Theatrical life must be larger than real life—brighter and more glorious. Real life is not lived on a stage; it is lived in the arena of one's own personal experience. We go to the theater not to experience actuality but to transcend it. The actor's job is to lead us by the grace and genius of his art to that higher revelation of life. As Stanislavski himself stated, art should lend beauty and nobility to life, and "whatever is beautiful and noble has the power to attract." That is the true magic of theater.

Who Will Benefit

In observing the works of great painters, composers, and playwrights, each has followed his own artistic instincts, and hence is master of his own school. As with these other disciplines, so with acting. I do not present the instruction that follows in this book to experienced artists who have already proven their own school, but to the student who is searching for the heart of the dramatic experience.

While this curriculum is often used to prepare children and young adults for a professional career, it also serves richly for more avocational purposes. It is fully packaged and customized for school and college theater programs and homeschool drama enrichment as well as for regional and community repertory groups that present several different plays or musical productions in the course of a season. The curriculum is laid out with clearness and simplicity so that even the most inexperienced English teacher or homeschool mom will feel up to the task. Whether taught on an amateur or professional basis, the benefits of the course are rich and lasting.

The unit studies are meant to be taught to all age groups. Where necessary, I have simplified the material for younger children. You may wish to pick and choose what "chunks" you feel are appropriate and engaging for your little ones. Theatrical games and dramatic exercises that demonstrate the various skills taught in each of the unit studies, are also arranged according to age and performance difficulty.

I suggest that the drama classes be divided into the following grade levels:

Kindergarten through 2nd grade: ages 3 to 7

3rd through 7th grade: ages 8 to 12 (If your age 8 to 12 group consists of more than 12 students, establish two separate classes: ages 8 to 10 and ages 11 to 12)

8th grade and above: teens/adults

What Students Will Learn

The acting curriculum consists of 12 individualized unit studies that introduce the fundamentals of acting that a professional actor spends a lifetime refining and perfecting. Every lesson offers incremental opportunities to develop the many skills of the actor's art. Students learn through theater games and progressive exercises how to develop their imagination and memory, increase their sense awareness, concentration, powers of observation, ease of movement, vocal expressiveness, and presence of mind. They have lessons in breathing and relaxation techniques, stage geography and blocking, deportment, mime, improvisation, character building and interpretation, and voice for the stage (including a thorough selection of speech drills). The course also offers a detailed overview of the history of acting, an extensive glossary of theatrical terms, and an in-depth analysis of the classical elements that constitute good drama.

Our training is "craft-oriented" with major emphasis on developing a flexible and skilled vocal technique, a controlled and expressive countenance, and an ability to bring a character to vivid life. Unit 10 is an authoritative study in voice because voice is the most important component of an actor's technique. Just as a successful musician, singer, or ballet dancer must master both the theory and practice of his art until he can demonstrate control of his instrument, so the actor must comprehend the physiological laws underlying the production of his voice and its dynamic expression. A complete vocal technique is not something an actor can learn overnight. To develop your voice into the best possible physical instrument for the stage requires training new habits and applying them in performance until they become second nature.

Whenever I use the terms "craft" or "technique," I am not referring to some mechanical application of technical correctness, but to a stage presence that is assured, natural, and rich in feeling and imagination. Too many actors of the method school disregard the importance of a practiced vocal technique, with the result that the speech of many of our current popular stage and film actors is slovenly, lacking the essential elements of a beautiful voice: power, flexibility, expressiveness, sensitivity, responsiveness to emotional nuance, and mobility for caricature and dialect. In contrast to the stars of an earlier era, they rely almost exclusively on their personal charisma and sex appeal to define the roles they play. There is a vast difference between an actor who suits the role to his own personal (and uncultivated) mannerisms of voice and movement, and the actor who captures and renders the essence of his character through vocal mastery.

The exercises and theater games that accompany each unit study are graduated in difficulty so that the students can internalize the skills at their own pace. As drama is the concentrate of life, we cannot teach it without intersecting the political, social, and spiritual life of our culture. Therefore, I have discussed the impact of these changing cultural dynamics on the growth and development of theater throughout the ages, as well as their direct influence in molding acting styles up to the present day. This material is optional and suitable only for the older students.

Scheduling the Lessons

As a working textbook, the curriculum is a complete teaching kit that can be adapted to traditional school quarters or college semesters (also typical of an acting studio schedule) of one 14-week fall session and a longer 22-week to 24-week winter/spring session with recital.

I suggest class periods of 45 minutes for those aged 3 to 7, one and a half hours for those who are 8 to 12 years old, and a minimum of two hours for teens and adults.

There is enough teaching material in the units to provide at least 2 years of classes and some have used it for an even longer period of time. Each unit study contains a wealth of detailed information. Do not panic if you don't cover everything you want by the end of class. Since each drama component has several levels of difficulty built into it, you, as the director, can choose to spend as long as you want on one particular component, especially if the students show an earnest desire to continue gaining skills in that one area of development. Each unit study is like a well. The director can keep coming back to draw from that well, raising the skill level each time and incrementally building the students' familiarity with and confidence in the material. In this way, the students can revisit the more challenging levels once they have shown some proficiency in the fundamentals.

Sometimes you will have to be flexible and flow with the needs and interest curve of the class. You may have an enthusiastic, talkative bunch who like to take an idea into original tangents. This is a valid way to draw out from each student his or her own personal gifts. Although you have a structure to follow, there is room and time for creative latitude. As long as drama is an experience of joy for your students, you are succeeding.

The Quality of the Aspiring Actor

As a course in the dramatic arts, the first goal is to encourage self-expression, and thus reveal those unique qualities in each student that form the basis of individual artistry. The second and complementary goal is to develop the theatrical skills which the student can apply to create an artistic product that has integrity and beauty. The teacher cannot superimpose an artistry; the student can only produce it from within. The unit studies are the stimulus and structure to draw it forth and keep it on course towards its mature unfolding. Your goal as a teacher is to motivate the student to show you what he is learning and how well he is learning it. In this way, the student teaches the teacher what to teach. Until a child shows you what he can do, what his strengths and weaknesses are, you cannot help him do any better.

The goal of teaching drama is to transfer to the student the joy of performing. That joy finds its ultimate expression in the happy and grateful applause of the audience. But the path that leads to that high attainment at curtain call is one that requires hard work and persistence. Nineteenth-century Italian actor Tommaso Salvini summed it up in his personal motto: "I must study, study again, study always." Stanislavski fervently impressed the same advice upon his company of actors at the Moscow Art Theater: "An actor must work all his life, cultivate his mind, train his talents systematically, develop his character; he may never despair and never relinquish this main purpose—to love his art with all his strength and love it unselfishly."

Perhaps if I could choose three qualities that every aspiring actor should cultivate, they would be self-discipline, the will to excel, and an endless patience that takes the good and bad reviews (the praise and the blame) with equal thanks. Success, with or without its attendant fame and wealth, is rarely achieved without these chief virtues. The glamor and excitement that seems to glow like a halo around the actor who has "made" it is a crown earned and not lightly.

If the student resolves to be an actor, then he must begin at the beginning, performing even the lowliest of tasks and the least of roles with an earnestness and zeal. Each step he takes in the classroom should lead him onward and upward. Remind your students that the climb to the top requires that they step on every rung of the ladder so that if and when they are cast upon the giddy heights of stardom, they will be in full possession of the balance, humor, and good sense that they gained with such care on the way up, starting with their first drama class.

Working with the Curriculum and the Role of Director

The curriculum describes each lesson in detail and provides teacher's "keys" throughout that summarize and track the concepts taught in the lesson. They are printed in bold in their own angel box for easy location. The amount of time needed to cover some lessons will vary according to the number of students and the proficiency sought. Throughout the curriculum, I use the terms director and acting teacher interchangeably given that the director of a children's theater or school program not only directs all the plays, but is usually the primary acting teacher.

The lessons are descriptive rather than outlined. With the exception of the Introductory Lesson, "Getting to Know You," the 12 units are written like a script that you can read from to teach the key points in the lesson. Where I have referred to my own personal experiences, I frame the comments under a title in bold called "Author's Story."

Each unit study also includes notes that describe what materials you should prepare before class, clear and simple instructions to help you guide the students through the interactive classroom exercises, stories that illustrate key points in the lesson, and special guidelines for various age groups. In addition, the voice exercises that accompany Unit Study 10, and which are printed on the voice handout sheets located at the back of the book, have been recorded on a CD to show you how to execute the voice drills correctly. You can order this CD directly from either the publisher's web site at www.playhousebooks.com or from our theater's web site at www.familyplayhouse.com.

The curriculum is so easy to understand and so carefully laid out that even the most unimaginative teacher will feel confident and up to the task. At the same time, the format allows for personalization of the material and originality in its presentation according to the changing classroom dynamics.

I recommend that the children refer to you as the director. This gives you a theatrical authority and your own role to play. Teaching acting is a unique challenge. You cannot approach it as you would a math problem or even an artistic pursuit such as piano. It is the one discipline of the arts that requires all of your enthusiasm and empathy. Acting deals with the expression of emotions and feelings. That, for many children, is quite a chore. Your role is to lovingly guide them in that self-expression so that acting class is something they will always look forward to. When a child joyfully proclaims during the course of his study that he "loves" drama, it means that he feels confident and worthy to be a participant. You have done your job and all the rest will follow with practice and performance.

Throughout the lessons, I use the word actor to refer to both males and females. If your class is composed mainly of girls, you may choose to refer to the girls as actresses. Art, as a discipline and as an artistic product, is androgynous. As the girls will eventually be performing with the boys in scenes, it is important from the beginning to create an atmosphere of mutual respect and camaraderie. At the same time, there are obvious distinctions between the sexes and you should not try to ignore them. It has always been my policy to expect plain gallantry from the boys and feminine modesty from the girls.

Recitals

I have published six different recital collections that are complementary to our teaching curriculum. Since the curriculum is based on family values, our selections are glimpses into the lives of people who make choices for truth and goodness. The boys like our action-packed scenes of swashbuckling musketeers, knights on noble quests, rope-twirling cowboys, and soldiers fighting for great causes. Our younger girls love the heroines out of early America and Victorian England, while our teens enjoy the adventure, romance, and chivalry offered by the world's great literary classics.

Many of our scenes are based on famous men and women in history who overcame great obstacles and endured suffering to accomplish a noble work. I've found that the teens enjoy putting on the moccasins of the luminous figures of the past whose lives seem much graver and more deeply felt than the lives of modern man or woman. The examination of such people under a dramatic microscope helps strengthen the student's discernment and appreciation of the finer and more subtle aspects of our life experience.

Though most of our scenes are adapted from period classics, historical fiction, or biographical data, I've written a few contemporary work pieces for students who feel more comfortable playing characters close to their age and experience. I have also adapted some musical scenes from the nostalgic past and Broadway classics to suit the more musically inclined. All the roles are challenging, adventurous, and inspiring. It is best to introduce Shakespeare after the students have mastered a higher skill level of characterization and technical execution. Character roles involving a more complex understanding of human evil or human weakness require a level of emotional maturity as well as an intellectual grasp of the values of life under examination.

Our *Golden Treasury of Acting Scenes* offers abundant selections of recital scenes for new students having their first drama performance. The collection contains dramatized Aesop Fables as well as tried-and-true scenes adapted from period classics, including *Heidi, A Little Princess, Jane Eyre, Anne of Green Gables, Rebecca of Sunnybrook Farm, The Adventures of Tom Sawyer, The Secret Garden, The Little Colonel, Ivanhoe, Pollyanna, Pride and Prejudice,* and *The Three Musketeers.* The collection also includes nostalgic musical scenes as well as modern-day pieces that illustrate lessons in friendship, courtship, and brotherly love. With over 450 pages of scenes, each accompanied by a story summary and character notes, you will have fun customizing a recital with the perfect scene for every child in your class. Other dramatic scene collections include *Love and Courtship, For the Love of Shakespeare, Christmases of Long Ago,* and *Fireworks: A Patriotic Tribute to the Brave and the Free.* Once the students have gained skill and confidence in performing scenes, they are ready to act in any of my full-play productions, including *The Secret Garden, Little Women, Anne of Green Gables, Anne of*

Avonlea, Saint Bernadette, Meet Me In St. Louis, and *The Three Musketeers* as well as our many abridged Shakespearean plays for both teens and the "littlest players."

The first quarter of instruction should not include a recital program. The students need these 12 to 14 weeks to effectively digest all the new information and to build up self-confidence. Stage a recital at the end of your second quarter, but do not introduce the dramatic selections any earlier than six to eight weeks before the scheduled performance date. As beginner students, the children get bored if given their scenes too early. If your student actors are adults, they will have the focus and attention span to work on their performance pieces for a more extended period of classroom time. Teen and adult students are more capable of assimilating instruction in fundamentals and applying it to the roles they take on for study and/or performance.

Arrange a field trip with a local college or community theater to tour their facility so the students can gain firsthand knowledge of a real theater and stage. If you live near a major metropolis like New York or Los Angeles, schedule an event with your students and their family members to attend a play or musical in one of the first-rate professional playhouses. There is nothing more exciting or inspiring to a young drama enthusiast than to experience a live theatrical performance by professional actors.

You can also suggest to your students that they get involved with a local theater company, particularly one that stages shows for families, and volunteer time to help out in any way that is needed, whether selling tickets at the box office, moving around props during a show, or simply handing out flyers before a production. The more hands-on experience that a student has in a real theater, the richer will be his learning and the more quickened his advancement. He will also absorb something of the stardust of fascination that seems to settle on everyone connected with making magic happen on the stage.

The Noble Task of Art and the Artist

The world of the arts has come to a time of critical ferment and flux, more marked than any since the early Renaissance. Artists have at their fingertips state-of-the-art technology to bring their theatric life to a global audience and in the most technically expert way. If, however, the actor does not use his art to communicate a vision of something higher and nobler, then what purpose is all this technology? It might be said that the Elizabethan players on their bare stage in front of their motley audience contributed more true magic to the world than some of what is daily being churned out on our television and movie screens.

As actors we must keep faith with the highest and best traditions of the theater. To do that, we must know why we are performing on the stage (or screen). Is it to remind our audience of the depressing realities of their lives? When we do that, when we confine the theatrical experience to the domestic struggles of man, without reference to hope, to faith, or to some rainbow hue of promise, we destroy the possibility of transcendence, which is what defines the very purpose of theater and creates its glory.

Wouldn't we serve our profession more meaningfully if our performances brought to the hearts of men, not sadness and anxiety but beautiful memories of the value and graciousness of life—its joys, its wonders, its blessings—that make us feel heart-whole? For if anything in life can lend wings to the spirit and help it find its way to the heart's ideal, it is theater. When one of Stanislavski's students questioned the high ethical standards his teacher expected of him personally, pointing out that no such theater existed in the world, Stanislavski replied: "It is all the more reason why you should be the ones to discover the right, the high minded significance of the theater and its art.... Unless the theater can ennoble you, make you a better person, you should flee from it." If there is to be a new flowering of drama in our time with joy and hope in it, we cannot forget the transcendent realities that are the foundation of all true art.

If the artist is to do no more than track the common man's footsteps as he trudges through life, how can beauty and truth survive? Leonardo da Vinci wrote, "In life beauty perishes, but not in art." Only in true art can beauty and truth live on, which is why people look to the arts to provide the vision of what life can be in its highest and purest expression. In the theater district of New York, in one evening alone, hundreds of thousands of theatergoers attend an opera, a symphony, a ballet, or a Broadway play to capture the excitement and glamor of what they hope will be an emotional and spiritual adventure. That is the ancient magic of the stage—the promise of living actors intensifying and concentrating life in its essential beauty and glory.

If this century has failed us, and the arts proven craven and sordid, it is because the vision and the thinking of the age have been so. With a renewed faith in the divine ideals that always bring moral beauty to the world stage, we as artists can capture once again what was in Greece or in Shakespeare's Globe, and we can do it no less nobly and even more perfectly. It is the responsibility of the arts to remold life into its nobler form and utterest beauty. This is especially true of theater, which is the most human of the arts and the nearest to the soul.

The artist's study and portrayal of man must be a noble one and not an intoxication with the worst manifestations of human nature. Freedom, wisdom, and beauty only come into our lives when we climb life's initiatic ladder to virtue and fineness. Stanislavski believed that "every human being deep down within himself possesses a natural longing to bring out all that is best within him." Shakespeare's Hamlet spoke of that "best" with unforgettable eloquence: "What a piece of work is man! how noble in reason! how infinite in faculty! in form and moving how express and admirable! in action how like an angel! in apprehension how like a god! the beauty of the world! the paragon of animals!"

Despite the evil that man has done and still continues to do, as actors we must draw from the concentrate of goodness and not merely dwell on the evil, unless that evil is framed against an eternal backdrop. Only then can we illumine the stage with our hope. As it's true in life, so it's true in drama—only through the climbing, not the leveling, can our best selves be realized. Our task is to reveal the startling beauty behind life's masks of comedy and tragedy and so build those "great bases for eternity" that Shakespeare told us about. Illustrating and unfolding the drama of the soul, with all its heroic struggle and overcoming, is the true substance of character study and the noble task of art and the artist.

"The actor," Stanislavski wrote, "is the standard bearer of what is fine. Remember this from the very beginning of your term of service to art and prepare yourselves for this mission. Develop in yourselves the necessary self-control, the ethics and discipline of a public servant destined to carry out into the world a message that is fine, elevating, and noble." Can we do anything else, and dare to call ourselves artists?

"The mountaintop of the Ideal is never shaken." These words of Francis Bacon—Elizabethan statesman, philosopher, and foremost contender for authorship of the Shakespearean plays—must describe the actor's faith. The breath of inspiration comes to the artist not only from the subconscious but also from the spirit at Beauty's urge (thus the inner meaning of the word inspiration: the action of the inner spirit).

Belief in the ideal is therefore our dearest possession as actors. Without it, we have no wings to fly heavenward and draw down the subtle fire that can transform our creative labor into something that can make the world seem fair, no matter the season. This explains why even child actors like Freddie Bartholomew or Shirley Temple could beguile their audiences with their acting magic. The more attuned we are as actors to that spirit within, the more inspired—and thus more magical—will be our performance, irrespective of how old we are or how imperfect our technique might be. When the actor's art inspires others to live their lives more beautifully, he fulfills the ancient alchemy of his craft.

The ideal of beauty has been set forth by the great artists of centuries past. Their priceless works are there to remind us that beauty, as a moral principle, cannot be destroyed. We can keep beauty in place in our lives if we have the vision of the ideal. Vision is having the noble goal in sight, if only with the inner eye, and faithfully pursuing it. To remain faithful to an ideal, wonder and awe are essential, and these have been effectively eroded in our society. There no longer dwells in our youth the innocence, the guilelessness, or the ability to wonder because the ideal is never set before them. And it is the pure instincts born of idealism that make youth beautiful. Children instinctively want to model themselves on the role of the hero and all that is positive, joyous, and uplifting. We have to nourish this, for aren't our children our most important hope?

If we, as a society, have lost sight of the spiritual cause behind existence and the need to strive upwards beyond our mortal lot, then it is the artist, with his deep creative sense, who must bring alive the virtuous life that has become invisible to so many in our materialist culture. As artists, we can create the acting magic that makes tangible the intangible and visible the invisible. It is our appointed mission and quest. When, as an artist, you become a transparency for the noblest, purest, and most beautiful thoughts that uplift the heart, you are truly a star.

Perhaps never has the stage been farther from the divinity with which it was marked in other eras. It has dug down into human experience not in a way that uncovers divinity, but in a way that shows humanity its weaker face, that lays bare deformities and perversities and flea-bites. It has become a narrow, prying, gossipy-minded theater, with the bigness and fineness gone out of it. Only once in a hundred visits do we glimpse rapture or high nobility or sheer purging beauty.

And yet each one of us, in his collective experience, has known that other divine theater. In the playhouses of our time we have been stirred by the old expectant excitement, have revelled in being part of a responsive crowd, have felt our nearness to the gods in the hushed auditorium, when everything on the stage and in the world fell into a unison, stilling the conscious mind; have been miraculously purged by tragedy, have been healed with the tonic of laughter at comedy, have felt pleasantly sinful, have been revolted, have been lifted again to the realm of beauty, wisdom, and perfect understanding.

—Sheldon Cheney (Art and theater historian)

Getting to Know You

An Introductory Lesson

Class materials needed: Handout, *To Be a Star!*
Personalized folders (with pockets)
Optional treasure box for young children
containing their names typed in a large font

Before the class, prepare a folder for each student. Use separate colors to distinguish the folders for the boys and the girls. Create an orientation sheet that summarizes your recommended dress and snack requirements and any other guidelines for the semester, and place a copy inside each folder. Personalize your orientation sheet based on your group's needs. You may also include in the folder a summary of those sections of the curriculum that you intend to teach in the first quarter, although you may not always follow it as prescribed. For the young children, you can also prepare a little treasure box containing slips of paper with their names typed in a large plain font.

The goal of the first lesson is to get to know your students and make them feel comfortable with you and with each other. You also want to create a high level of interest and enthusiasm. An acting course always stirs up more pre-class anxiety than any other instructional program in the arts. From the very beginning, your presence needs to be warm and reassuring. Greet each student personally when he or she arrives, be generous with your smiles, and let your class know how excited you are about teaching them drama.

Introduce yourself, briefly share your goals for the course, and describe what they will be learning. If you intend to stage a recital as part of the curriculum activities, explain that each student will be assigned two performance pieces, one of which will involve working with another actor. Let them know that you will try and match those who wish to do scenes together, but that you, the director, will make the final choices in casting. You can field some questions, but don't take too many. You have a lot to cover in the first class.

Ask the students to introduce themselves while remaining seated in their chairs, rather than standing up. The first class is not a good time to make them feel awkward or nervous in front of their future classmates. With younger children, you can use the treasure box. Call upon the littlest ones to pick a name from the box. Ask whosoever's name was picked to introduce himself next. Be aware that some children at this age may not read well or even read at all. Be ready to help. Make sure each child states his name, age, and grade level. You can encourage the process by gently asking questions such as, What is your favorite subject? Do you play any musical instrument? What is your favorite activity in the summer? Do you have any brothers or sisters? Have you ever been in a play?

Let the students know that everyone feels self-conscious during the first few weeks—even the director—and the best way to overcome this feeling is to *do* something. Encourage them to volunteer for the games and exercises and to stay active. The wonderful benefit of drama is that it teaches the student to escape from his shy self, his unconfident self that worries about how he will measure up to everyone else. He can share the best of himself with others in a safe and joyful way and become a valuable part of a team in the process.

Optional Quiz: The Handout *To Be a Star!* is a fun way to learn something about your students and to discover how they perceive themselves. The handout asks students to respond to a list of 15 questions that define the qualities an aspiring actor should possess. The more *yes* responses, the better the score. Scores are calculated as follows:

7 or less	=	Fair Actor
8-11	=	Good Actor
12-14	=	Great Actor
15	=	*Star*

Tally the answers in class or collect them and return them scored the following week. Though the qualities listed are indeed the prized attributes an actor can bring to his profession, make it clear that even if some only scored themselves as fair, you think of them all as stars, and that your job is to help them shine more brightly. By studying hard and participating actively in class, each one can become a star. The shiest of your students will need extra encouragement and sometimes more personal attention to achieve your expectations. Explain to the class that an actor should not feel that he is in competition with anyone except himself. When an actor enters the dramatic race for coveted acting roles, as with every other profession or sport, his goal is to keep surpassing his *own* best, even as he makes every effort to outshine his colleagues in performance excellence. In the same way, swimmers in the Olympics strive to beat their own personal and world records as well as do their utmost to win the Gold.

Next, pass out to each student his own personalized folder and explain what is inside. Ask each child to put his name on his folder. The younger children can decorate their folders at home.

A common question asked by the parents of beginner students is, Can I sit in on the first class? I don't recommend this. Usually there are two reasons parents want to monitor the first class. Either they fear that their child needs them or they want to be sure that the material you present is proper and age-appropriate. Though these are natural concerns, to placate them does not benefit the child. Trust between the student and the teacher is the first requirement of progress, so it's important that the teacher have the students all to herself for the first few classes to establish a bond of trust. If a parent is present, the child will automatically gravitate to the strongest emotional tie. A child may also interpret the situation to mean that her parent does not trust the teacher, so why should she?

Explain to parents that they are welcome to attend after the third or fourth class. By that time, the child will have bridged a happy level of trust with you. Whenever a parent sits in, she should participate as your assistant and not as an observer. You can generally avoid any difficulties by stating the rules up front when a parent first expresses an interest in enrolling his or her child in the course.

If you have large classes, encourage a few of your older students or a couple of the parents to be regular assistants. They will always provide a stabilizing influence. Parents who express a willingness to be actors or production helpers in the recitals and plays that you hope to stage later on are the best choice to be assistants, and they will personally enjoy and benefit from the class instruction. You would be surprised how many parents (and grandparents) are frustrated thespians who are only too delighted to add their joy and enthusiasm to your efforts.

KEY: Getting to the heart of the issue

When you resolve to be a shining light, you *can* be!

Unit
Study
One

Theater Is Magic

1

Theater Is Magic

What Makes Something Magic?

Who likes magic shows? How many of you have watched a magician perform magic tricks? Did you ever wonder if the magician's tricks were not tricks at all but real magic? Did you ever wonder if the white rabbit that popped out of his black hat really *did* appear just because the magician used a special wand and spoke some strange words?

A good magician makes his tricks look real. He makes us believe something is real when it isn't. It seems like magic to us because of our imagination. You can think of imagination as the place where our minds can travel and create a world of "magic ifs"—a term that the great Russian director Constantin Stanislavski made up to describe the creative imagination or, as he called it, the inner creative state. It is our creative imagination that invents things and makes them happen as we wish them to happen, much like producing our own motion picture film, where we are the writer, director, *and* starring actor. Every true artist, whether he is a painter, a composer or a dramatist, must have a great imagination so that he can visualize wonderful subjects for his art and share them with the rest of us. Magic happens when we enter the world of the imagination, suspend our disbelief for a little while, and feel and act as though what we are experiencing is actually taking place.

Theater is magic for the same reason. Nothing in theater is true or real, but it appears absolutely true and real. Sitting in the theater and watching actors onstage makes our imagination come alive—so alive that we forget it's all a show.

What comes to your mind when you hear the word *theater*? [*Usual answers: A place where we see a play or movie, famous actors, Broadway, putting on makeup, getting dressed up in costumes, playing someone else, being a star, etc.*] Every one of these answers describes different aspects of theater, but they all have one thing in common: they deal with make-believe, with a world created of the stuff of dreams—a world that kindles our imagination and brings delight and enchantment because it takes us away from the worries and concerns of our real lives and lifts us into a rarer atmosphere.

The magic of acting comes about when an actor uses his theatrical skills to create life out of illusion. The life he creates onstage is a magic presence that can transform the thoughts and feelings of his audience. With the help of the playwright and the director, the actor interprets his character, applies his art to portray that character on the stage or screen, and convinces you, the audience, that his character is just as alive and real as you are—in fact, more intensely alive because his theatrical role is larger than life. Let's look at the different ways we feel the magic of the theater.

The Magic of the Theater

How many of you have seen a play in a real theater? Did you feel a sense of excitement when you walked in and sat down in one of the tiered velvet seats? It feels different inside a theater than it does to walk in a mall, for instance, because the theater is not the real world. The theater is a world of magic, and when you enter that world you take on the part of being an audience member or a maker of that magic (either onstage or behind the scenes). To make the magic happen, the people in the audience have to open their hearts and be willing to believe in what the actors want to share with them. That is the first part of the magic—the magic of trusting the actor and all that he or she creates onstage. Nowhere in life, except in houses of worship or other sacred places, do we so willingly take in with such perfect trust what is shared with us in a theater.

The theater, with its hushed darkness and beautiful dance of lights on the arched, velvet curtains creates a perfect environment for that special flow of attention from the audience to the actors. It is an interactive communion that is sustained automatically once the play starts and will continue as long as there is nothing extraneous to interrupt it. In this electrically charged atmosphere, the audience is the intimate friend of the character onstage. No one has as much access to the interior life of that character than the audience—and no one has as much access to the interior life of each audience member than the character.

The theater includes the entire building where a play takes place, but the stage or playing area is where the magic of the actor's creation is seen and felt.

The Magic of the Actor

The actor is a magician because he is able to convince the audience that what he does and says has the "ring of truth." During the time you are onstage as an actor, you must make the audience forget that it's you playing a role. The audience should be aware only of the reality of your character moving, thinking, feeling, and interacting with other characters as the playwright intended him to. Actor Ben Kingsley described it this way: "The trick is to try and justify every word on the page [of the script] and make sure my character is the man who would say that." When the actor accomplishes this task, he is practising "the art of acting."

An actor on a stage can do extraordinary things and be believed. However, if he attempted the same thing in front of his friends at the local mall, it would hardly be "cool." Yet in that magic place of the theater, he has a captive audience who is willing and wanting to believe anything. Because he has the power to influence his audience in a way he could not do anywhere else, it is important that the actor take responsibility for making every moment of his character's life onstage true and inspired.

A painter, a poet, a writer or a composer can take time to alter and perfect his work of art before presenting it to his public. An actor on the live stage must imbue every one of his performances with the magic of his genius because each performance is an original work of art created just for that particular audience. If his performance one night lacks the quality of his magic, then it is too late for that audience: he can't make it up to them if he acts better the next night. Whatever the actor creates in the short time he is on the stage is what will live in the memory of that audience.

Despite the power of film to make permanent the great offerings of an actor's art, it is only in live theater that the audience can experience firsthand the inspired warmth of the actor's passion and the glow of his genius in all its creative moment. Only in the theatrical medium can the audience be an active and integral part of that magic, since the actor draws from them the energy (immediate and potent) that fuels his creativity. When the actor creates magic on the stage, he is taking the rainbow colors of his inspiration, forming them into an artistic creation by means of his craft, and fixing those colors in the hearts and minds of each and every one of his captive listeners.

It is because he is given such an awesome responsibility and privilege that the actor must be mindful of the kind of material he presents to theatergoers. If an actor performs plays that convey a view of life that is hopeless and despairing, or takes the audience into a bewildering world of inverted moral values and visceral sensory experience, he may not be an influence for good but an influence for darkness. This doesn't mean an actor should always play heroes, or that his plays should only deal with sunny subjects with happy endings. An actor learns to play all sorts of people in all sorts of life situations, but it is very important that the audience understands why a character is good or why he is evil and sees the consequences of the right or wrong choices of that character.

The plays of William Shakespeare teach us that striving toward the highest expression of moral beauty is the lesson that great art teaches. When there is not a clear line between the hero and the villain and between good behavior and bad, we can confuse the audience. The actor must always make enlightened choices about what roles are good for him to play *and* good for an audience to experience. My litmus test is: Would I invite Mother Teresa or the Dalai Lama to see me perform this role? *(Director can choose someone else in the place of these world-respected figures.)*

The Magic of the Role

Because audiences trust you, the actor, so intimately, the roles you play can profoundly affect their lives. Obviously, we want to influence people in a positive, constructive way so they go away from the theater cheered up and perhaps thinking more deeply about life. We want to give to the audience the best of ourselves and the best of our creative choices. An actor who lives his life with integrity will imbue his roles with that same integrity, for the actor ultimately draws from his personal belief system to invest his performances with sincerity and truth. What you draw from the deepest and truest part of your being is what will touch and live in the hearts of your audience long after the curtain comes down.

As an actor, you should decide wisely what roles you will play. Acting in plays and films that have taste, discretion, and artistry, with roles that are uplifting to an audience, is what will make your work beautiful and meaningful. Ben Kingsley, who won an Academy Award for his portrayal of the martyred spiritual leader Mahatma Ghandi in the 1982 film, *Ghandi,* spoke about the personal benefits of playing a man of such hallowed purpose and honor: "I think I'm more bonded, emotionally and in a craft sense, to films that tell extraordinary stories about extraordinary destinies." Think of yourself not just as an actor applying the tools of his craft in the common mode of any workman, but as an artist serving the best and highest traditions of his art and the best and highest expectations of his audience. The role you play is the way you spread the magic dust of the richest and sweetest part of yourself.

Before the advent of realism in the style and content of plays and screen scripts, the worth of an actor's art was greatly judged by the roles he played. It was an intrinsic relationship: the more noble the role he brought to life onstage, the more esteemed was his reputation. To play, and play well, the Shakespearean tragic heroes was the highmark of an actor's achievement, and thus the truest expression of his art.

In "Life and Art of Edwin Booth," author William Winter wrote of this American actor: "In all characters that evoked his [Booth's] essential spirit—in characters which rested on spiritualized intellect, or on sensibility to fragile loveliness, the glory that fades, and the beauty that perishes—he was peerless. Hamlet, Richelieu, Faust, Manfred, Jaques, Esmond, Sydney Carton, and Sir Edward Mortimer are all, in different ways, suggestive of the personality that Booth was fitted to illustrate. It is the loftiest type that human nature affords, because it is the embodied supremacy of the soul, and because therein it denotes the only possible escape from the cares and vanities of a transitory world."

In other words, the great actors of the nineteenth century were expected to bring to the stage the noblest representation of man, for only roles that were larger than life could elevate the hearts of a world-weary audience. It was the sole purpose of their art, and the guarantor of their immortality. They relied on a complete theatrical technique, especially a vocal mastery that demonstrated shading of tone, use of vibrato, and creative pitch, to move their audience's emotions, and so achieve the goals of their interpretive art on the stage.

Today, bringing moral beauty to the stage is no longer the artistic imperative of the actor. Most roles, both in live theater and on the screen, play to the commonplace of everyday existence without the fine touch of romance or pathos to soften or ennoble the view of life presented. It is not easy for a young actor to find roles that have moral boundaries or a proper context in which to lead the audience to something better.

Author's Story: I knew of a young actress who earned her way up through regional theater to be awarded the coveted leading role in what later became one of the longest-running musical shows on Broadway. As is customary, before the play could premiere in New York, the cast had to take the show to other cities to try it out first. The musical was performed in repertory—that is, the actors were required to play additional roles in other plays that were staged on alternate nights to the main production. The young actress in question was cast in one of these secondary plays in a role she found uncomfortable playing because it promoted a social message that was objectionable to her. When she asked if someone else could take that role, she was given an ultimatum of playing all roles assigned to her or being fired. She chose to leave the company. To get to Broadway, and in a major role, had been her cherished dream. After many years of dedicated study and hard work, that dream was now within reach, but she made her choice based on what she felt was right for her. She wanted to remain true to the highest and best in herself and in her profession.

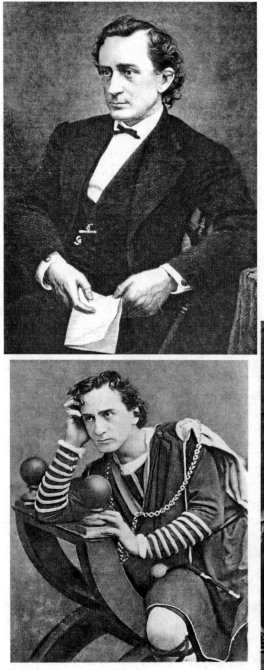

Edwin Booth, American actor (1833-1893)
Edwin's younger brother John Wilkes Booth, also an actor, assassinated Abraham Lincoln. In an ironic twist of fate, Edwin Booth saved Abraham Lincoln's son, Robert, from injury and possible death by pulling him up onto a train platform after Robert had fallen.

Edwin Booth as Cardinal Richelieu

As Hamlet

*"It is a far, far better thing that I do, than I have ever done;
it is a far, far, better rest that I go to, than I have ever known."*

Sydney Carton, the hero of *A Tale of Two Cities*, was another dramatic part brought to life on the stage by Edwin Booth. The coveted role was later portrayed on the screen by acclaimed British actors, Ronald Coleman and Dirk Bogarde.

Young actors always have the choice to decline roles that would or could embarrass them, roles that do not meet the moral standards they have set for themselves or meet aesthetic standards of goodness and beauty. Such a choice can be summed up in one word: integrity. This does not mean, however, that an actor should shy away from a role that requires the searching out of the deeper, more complex issues of life and the human condition. Character roles that have true humanity built into them are the most riveting and genuine and can inspire every audience member to want to be a better person. Sometimes, by playing a role that demands the embodiment of a negative emotion, such as fear, hate, jealousy, anger, guilt, or self-loathing, an actor can help provide catharsis and healing for his audience as well for himself.

The same holds true of scripts that deal with difficult and heartrending issues, such as racism, child abuse, rape, murder, or even the horrors of genocide. This kind of subject matter, however, should be framed in a proper context whereby the character grows in understanding of himself and of his life experience. There is never any good purpose served when the tragedies of life are presented without the light of hope or personal overcoming. Moreover, young actors should not be troubleshooting issues in class that are personally invasive or directly challenge their moral or spiritual beliefs. Even with teenage students, the teacher should always defer to the parents before introducing subjects that touch upon personal morality or are controversial in nature.

If a child is cast to play a part that deals with a sensitive issue, the parents need to be very sure that their child can handle the difficult if not overwhelming emotional and spiritual demands of such a role, and that the director of the play or movie will carefully prepare their child, respectful of his or her age and innocence. Young children should not appear in a stage or film production that has violence and horror (whether physical or psychological) as its end. Such products only exploit the actors and the audience, and serve no artistic or aesthetic purpose.

The Magic of the Moment

Perhaps the greatest magic of all in theater is when actor and audience share a transcendent moment together, a moment that is alive and radiant in the heart because it touches the inner world of the Spirit. How does this moment happen? You can only prepare for it as a farmer prepares his crops for the harvest—by lovingly planting the seeds of noble intention (the desire to bring something fine and elevating to your audience) and practising every component of your technique with an ardor and belief that makes it second nature. By nourishing your own inner spark, you stimulate the inner genie of your inspiration. Let's imagine that "magic moment."

You have finally been given a role that you know you can carry to the hearts of your audience. The alchemy of forging this character's life has challenged all of your artistry, all of your skill. And now, opening night has arrived. You share the expectant excitement of the crowd that fills the auditorium. The house lights are down. The stage manager calls "Places!" You stand in the wings, the lights go up, and the stage is aglow. Then slowly the curtain opens and the play begins.

You watch as the other actors bring to the opening scenes the excitement and rhythm you had all hoped for and worked so hard to achieve. Now it is your turn. You make your entrance. Just seconds ago, you were more nervous than you can ever remember being in your life, but now that you are onstage, you feel alive, joyous, and perfectly content. The audience is with you. You have perfect possession of your character as you become part of the integral flow of the play, scene after scene.

Then, before you even know it, you are playing out the climactic scene—that fragile, wonderful scene you rehearsed over and over again. You feel yourself larger than life, as though you had wings and could take the audience with you anywhere. You have entered deeply into your character. Ever so carefully, with your voice, your gestures, and your movements, you conduct the emotion that floods your being. You feel as if you are the only one onstage. You command the hushed attention of every spectator. The "moment" has come. You know that at this moment, the entire audience is suspended. The slightest thing you do or say can bring the thousand watchers to joyful tears, to a healing of their grief, or to perfect understanding.

This moment somehow transcends time and space. There *is* no time and space, only a living flame within that you experience as a cessation of the outward life of the world. You have entered into an intensification of the life of the spirit, one with its beauty and clarity, yet you are fully conscious, fully in control, fully cognizant. Ensconced in that flame, you know that you are sharing this moment of beauty and clarity with your audience. It is the moment of acting magic.

This is the moment toward which all drama tends, the artist's highest mode of communication. It is the moment of healing and of resolve because your spirit has addressed the spirit of your audience. It is the moment that brings to both actor and audience a higher revelation of life. This magic moment is the true experience and end of theater.

KEY: Getting to the heart of the issue

> Strive to give the gold of your self—the highest and best expression of your skill and inspiration—and not the silver of your second best.

Unit

Study

Two

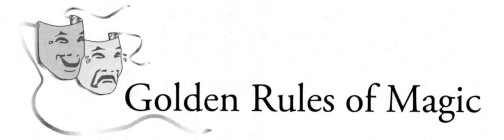

Golden Rules of Magic

2

Golden Rules of Magic

Class materials needed:

Velcro or masking tape
Handout #2-1A, 1B *Stage Geography*
CD player and two of the following musical
selections, one a waltz and the other a march:

Edward Elgar: "Pomp and Circumstance"
Franz Lehar: "The Merry Widow Waltz" *(The Merry Widow)*
Edvard Grieg: "Wedding Day at Troldhaugen" *(Peer Gynt)*
Any of Tchaikovsky's waltzes from *The Nutcracker*
Armed Forces Songs: "Marines' Hymn," "Air Force Hymn,"
"Anchors Aweigh," "The Caissons Go Rolling Along"

How to Make a Stage

If your teaching facility does not have a real stage, mark off a space at one end of your room as the designated stage or playing area. This will be used as your workplace stage. If you can obtain platforms that will elevate your playing area, even if only 6 inches above the floor, the illusion of a "real" stage will be increased. If you build platforms from wooden planks, remember to carpet them to help absorb, and thus dampen, the sound on the boards. Make your outline of the stage area using Velcro or a masking tape that does not leave glue marks on the floor and is easily removed.

Mark your stage space according to Handout #2-1, *Stage Geography*. This 2-page handout represents the ground plan for a conventional, picture frame proscenium stage. The outline of the stage floor is shown by the trapezoid shaped lines. This defines the stage or playing area that is visible to the audience when the actors are performing their roles. You may optionally choose to add in the two (dotted) vertical and the two (dotted) horizontal lines that are not present on a real stage but are included in the handout only to help the student visualize the actor's areas.

To help guide the students in the first few classes, use additional small pieces of tape in the shape of a plus sign (+) to represent the central point in each of the nine major stage areas (described under Golden Rule Two) where the students will be directed to stand. The individual pieces of tape should be symmetrically placed. The name of the stage area, such as DC (Downstage Center), should not be written on the tape, as the students will be asked to memorize where all the playing areas are located. Many teachers do not have a real stage to work with so a workplace stage is the next best thing to get the students familiar with their performance area. Allow at least two feet of free space all around the stage floor to allow entrance and exit room. This free space, not visible to an audience in a real theater, would normally be part of the *wings*.

How to Make Magic

Just as a magician follows certain rules to make his tricks work, so an actor must be obedient to certain rules if he wants his audience to believe that he is someone else. Look at the person sitting next to you. Look at how he or she is dressed, how he is sitting, the expression on his face and in his eyes, how tall or short he is, how he wears his hair or folds his arms. How long would it take to study that person's way of speaking, way of walking, way of acting with other people and all the mannerisms that make up his personality before you would feel comfortable enough playing that person onstage? It might take months of being a private detective and shadowing all he does and says before you would feel up to the task—and you would only be informed about his external habits! The person you hope to imitate also has a complex psychological or inner world that you must tap into and try to understand, so that you can render all of his character truthfully and compellingly.

Searching out the character you are to play is like going on a treasure hunt. You need a clearly drawn map that has on it all the necessary clues. You need to solve each clue in order to continue on to the next one. If just one clue is missing, you will not have a complete picture of your character. Your goal is to present a total understanding of your character to the audience so they can connect all the theatrical dots (which are the clues that you give them) and bring that character to life in their imaginations.

Everything we do when we are just being ourselves is natural. We don't really think about how we act most of the time. It is an unconscious process. When we have to act in the role of another person, even if it's someone we know very well, suddenly we become self-conscious and awkward. It's like learning to walk and talk all over again, but without the defects that stage lights or a film camera lens will inevitably highlight. The actor cannot merely reproduce a person as he is in ordinary life. He must render his character in a way that will be theatrically convincing and artistically pleasing to the audience. He cannot miss a step in the process of his training if he wishes to accomplish this goal.

There are special rules or disciplines that must be followed in every profession, whether you are a lawyer, an architect, a doctor, an accomplished pianist, or an actor. In acting, there are special rules that help you bring a character to life, and make that character live intensely in the imagination of your audience. I call these the golden rules of acting, and you can make magic onstage when you follow these rules. You cannot play Rachmaninoff's *Concerto No. 2 in C Minor Op. 18* unless you have mastered playing the piano as your instrument, which takes many years of committed study and application in the theory and practice of the laws of harmony and rhythm. Even then, you must have the interpretive skills that allow you to translate your technical expertise into artistic performance. In the case of acting, *you* are the instrument that must be finely tuned before you can bring a character off the pages of your script and into the world of your audience.

KEY: Getting to the heart of the issue

To make your character live onstage, you
must follow the golden rules of acting.

The Golden Rules

GOLDEN RULE ONE: A relaxed mind and body enable optimal performance.

Relaxation is the key to unlocking the natural flow of our physical and mental energies. Only when the actor starts with a relaxed mind and body can the body respond strongly and freshly and the mind create spontaneously. Those of us who are shy and constrained are usually not as relaxed as those who are naturally outgoing, but all of us can benefit from relaxation exercises, which are an essential part of every class.

Professional actors develop regimens of stretching, breathing, and relaxation, which they incorporate into their rehearsals and performances. We will learn more about breathing exercises in later sessions on voice.

Since much of our mental tension comes from thinking about ourselves (and how we measure up to everyone else), placing our thoughts on something or someone other than ourselves helps us release mental anxiety. One of the best ways to achieve this in acting class is to thoroughly take in the details of everything around you. What color are the walls of the room and the carpet on the floor? How many students are in the class? Who wears glasses and who wears contact lens? All these ways of focusing away from yourself will help you respond more openly and spontaneously to others.

Relaxation in acting class should never be confused with "hanging out," "getting some shuteye," or being in a state of mental stupor (or nonthinking). Relaxation is a state of openness and alert receptivity to your surroundings, a state unmarked by worry or thoughts about yourself. When you turn your attention to people and things outside of yourself, you will more richly appreciate the special and wonderful qualities in your fellow actors, qualities that will make you prize them as lively dramatic companions. This habit of consciously taking pictures, with your eyes and with your ears, of everything that is going on around you develops in you the skill of being an expert observer and listener. Being able to vividly record with your senses the physical images that make up your immediate setting is the first step to successfully visualizing imaginary objects—an important element of stimulating the creative imagination.

Director's Notes: In some schools, young actors are encouraged to relax by giving each other physical massages or back rubs. In my experience, this can force an unnatural intimacy between the students. Physical contact in the classroom setting, especially between those of the opposite sex, should only reflect the requirements of the dramatic context—in other words, what the training exercises or scenes ask for. This does not apply to little girls who may be best friends and who like to hold hands and do scenes together or to groups of boys who love to wrestle or climb trees during every class break! The exercises in this curriculum will help students accomplish trust and rapport gradually and naturally.

Author's Story: Many years ago, when my son was a mere six years of age, he was playing the role of the "beau" in a musical scene that we adapted using the song "Alice Blue Gown." The little girl who played Alice was a stunning beauty, as was her sister, who was a year older. Unfortunately, both girls had a very obvious crush on my son. During rehearsal breaks, they would chase him all over the lawn in front of our studio, trying to plant a kiss. They never did catch him, as he was fast and fleet of foot. It was a year later that the little beauty proved triumphant. She was playing the role of Constance opposite D'Artagnan (played by my son) in our Littlest Players performance of *The Three Musketeers*. In the scene where Constance sends him off to England with a secret letter from the Queen, one of his stage directions was to kiss the hand of Constance. Though he refused to do so during all rehearsals, it took the opening night performance for the beautiful little Rachel to receive her first stage kiss, albeit on her hand, but a kiss, nevertheless!

EXERCISE 2-1 Simple Warm-Ups

The following familiar stretching exercises will help to get your body relaxed, your muscles toned, and physical tensions released. We will do at least a few of these simple warm-ups every week before class. Try and develop the habit of practicing them daily at home, so that relaxing your muscles becomes a natural thing to do. We cannot get results if we only do these exercises during the special time set aside for class every week. Most of them can be performed in a standing position with feet apart, and repeated several times:

- Slowly rotate your head from the neck in large circles clockwise and then counterclockwise. Try and do this without moving your shoulders.

- Rotate your right shoulder and then your left shoulder in a circular pattern.

- With hands on your waist, as if hula-hooping, make large circles with your hips both clockwise and counterclockwise.

- Intertwine fingers, then stretch the arms above the head, while turning palms upwards. With your head between your outstretched arms, stretch your body to the left and then to the right. Then rise on your toes and hold the stretch for a few seconds.

- Alternate between a closed fist and spreading open the five fingers on your right hand. Do this at least ten times. Repeat with left hand.

- Rotate each hand from the wrist in circular or figure-eight patterns, keeping the fingers relaxed. Rotate your forearms from the elbow, both clockwise and counterclockwise, then from the shoulder in the same way, then each foot at the ankle, followed by the lower legs from the knee. Finish by alternately stretching and squeezing your toes.

- Shake both hands vigorously, while keeping the lower arms and wrists relaxed.
- Jump rope (especially good for the little ones).

EXERCISE 2-2 Breathing Warm-Up

The simple breathing exercise below can continue for several weeks as an optional warm-up before class begins. Though it involves deep breathing, it is used here as a relaxation exercise, and is not designed to instruct the students in proper breathing habits. More detailed breathing exercises will be introduced in Unit Study 10:

- Take a deep, full breath.
- On the outbreath, students see how far they can count (to a regular rhythm of counting) until they have no breath left.
- Don't force the count by speeding up the rhythm. This will only increase the stress and tension on the throat. The idea is to increase our capacity to use less breath as we speak and therefore control our breathing more easily. (Practiced every week at the top of each class, the little ones can easily reach a count of 12, the younger ones a count of 20, and the older ones up to 40 on their outbreath.)

EXERCISE 2-3 The Body Flop

This exercise introduces deep, rhythmic breathing. It demonstrates the importance of measured and controlled breathing in helping to physically relax the student. Once again, the emphasis is on consciously reducing tension rather than learning how to breathe correctly:

- Stand up, away from your chairs, leaving enough room to extend arms in a circle without touching anyone else. Keep feet apart.
- Gently flop forward from the waist with slightly bent knees (not straight) and arms loosely extended in front like a rag doll.
- As I count to 8, slowly breathe in as you draw your bodies up to a standing position with arms to the side. Remember to keep arms and shoulders perfectly relaxed. Breathe out normally.
- Gently flop forward again, but this time, as I count to 8, wave your arms around like rag dolls as you slowly straighten up, breathing in as you do.

- Now, with feet apart, bend your knees and place your hands on your knees as if you were in a football stance. Blow out all the air in your lungs and then hold your breath (out) for three seconds. Then slowly and deeply breathe in to the count of 8 as you draw your body up to a standing position. Breathe out normally.

Director's Notes: Some children can find it scary to hold their breath out when there is no air in the lungs. To alleviate any anxiety, you can suggest an optimal 3 seconds, but tell them that 1 or 2 seconds is also acceptable until they get better at it with practice. Encourage them not to make a dramatic gasp once they do begin to breathe in again.

You can adapt this exercise for the younger ones in the following fun way:

Imagine you are

...a rubber inflatable toy and that someone is blowing air into you until you are nearly bursting. Then the air is let out and you collapse.

...a stuffed animal and that an imaginary child pulls out your stuffing one chunk at a time—then stuffs you up again.

...a balloon and someone starts blowing you up. Then, very quickly, he lets go of you and all your air fizzles out.

...a character in a wax museum. The janitor turns the heat on instead of the air conditioning. The place becomes hotter and hotter until you melt.

EXERCISE 2-4 The Floor Angel

This exercise consists of lying on your back on the stage or classroom floor and relaxing all the tense muscles of your body. Just as you lie on the snow or sand perfectly relaxed when you want to make a snow (or sand) angel, we can use this exercise—absent the daring back dive—to achieve the same results:

- Lie down on the floor, leaving enough room to extend arms in a circle without touching anyone else.

- Extend arms and legs out according to individual comfort. (Some students prefer a full extension like a starfish; others will only slightly separate their arms and legs.)

- Consciously try and locate all the muscles throughout your body that may be tense and relax them one by one. Start with the neck, then move down to the shoulders, shoulder blades, arms, hands, back, waist, base of the spine, thighs, knees, ankles, and feet. Make sure that as you continue the process of relaxing one muscle, you don't tighten up another. Be aware that your facial muscles, especially the forehead and eyebrows, have a tendency to contract from concentrating so hard.

- Imagine every part of your body sinking into and making contact with the floor—much like a cat or a baby sinks heavily onto a soft cushion when laid there to sleep, leaving a fully sculptured bodily imprint when lifted up.

- You will feel a state of relaxation when not a single muscle is tense, and all parts of the back of your body are touching the floor.

Homework: The students can practice this exercise on their beds, just before going to sleep at night. They can also try it out at the beach. If they have a cat, they might also lie down with the animal on a sofa and observe how relaxed its muscles are in rest.

Relaxing the muscles not only promotes the flow of physical (and thus emotional) energy, it also makes possible the balance and adaptability of the body—qualities that are necessary for any actor who wishes to perform on the stage. Stanislavski believed that relaxation of the muscles created *plasticity* of the body, which he believed was foundational to the body's equilibrium and center of gravity. This, in turn, allowed the actor to spring into action with both agility and artistic ease whenever required. In other words, the more supple the body, the more responsive and expressive it can be.

Stanislavski pointed out that when we are given an isolated action to perform, such as raising our right hand like a stop sign, other muscles in the body, be they neck, shoulder, arm or back, might tense up or contract to compensate for the movement of the raised hand. When executing such a singular action, it is necessary, therefore, to make sure that all other parts of the body remain free and without tension. In his book *An Actor Prepares,* he writes: "In raising one's arm by the aid of shoulder muscles and contracting such [muscles] as are necessary to the movement, one must let the rest of the arm, the elbow, the wrist, the fingers, all these joints hang completely limp."

The more relaxed an actor is, the more efficient is his apportionment of energy. Stanislavski used the example of a cat to show the benefits of freeing the muscles. A cat passes instantaneously from complete repose to lightning motion because it does not waste any energy in superfluous muscle contractions. The cat saves up all its strength in a state of relaxed alertness to strike more quickly and more effectively when and where that strength is needed. That is why a cat's movements are so precise, well-defined, and powerful.

These same qualities describe many sports champions. If we look at a game like tennis, players who stay free and loose throughout a match can respond to their opponent's plays with greater quickness and agility. A tennis champion like Roger Federer exemplifies this kind of fluidity that enables him to adjust his plays with lightning speed and make brilliantly executed defensive and offensive shots that other players can only dream about.

Complete muscular control, with its freedom from all tension (and thus unnecessary expenditure of energy), gives a competitor like Federer the swiftness and pounce of a cheetah, which is why professionals in the tennis world call him the Federer Express. Even more significantly, Federer's perfectly relaxed demeanor allows him to make use of a large variety of adaptations of play to suit the changing circumstances of a match— such as an indoors or outdoors setting, what court surface it is played on (grass, clay, or hard court), the physical fitness of the opponent, the weather conditions, injuries, the dynamic shifting mood of the crowd, bad calls by the linesman, etc.

As actors, we need that same power of adaptability, given that we are also constantly making fine and subtle adjustments in ourselves and in our technique when playing a part before a live audience. Relaxation is the first and the most necessary requirement of a successful actor.

KEY: Getting to the heart of the issue

A relaxed actor is free to move and create artistically. A tense actor is a prisoner of his own constraint.

GOLDEN RULE TWO: Know the theater.

Director's Notes: Distribute Handout #2-1A and 1B, *Stage Geography*. All common theater terms discussed below will appear in italics.

The theater is the actor's home. He must know it as well as a captain knows his ship. If your goal as an actor is to share your character with your audience, you need to feel comfortable on your home turf and navigate it blindfolded. You must know exactly where you are and how you are affecting your audience at any point during the performance. That kind of natural instinct comes not just from learning how to act, but from having a practical, working knowledge of all the artistic and technical elements that unite to produce a play. We start with the theater building itself.

When we say we are going to the *theater,* we are referring to the building used for the presentation of plays or entertainment events. This building includes the auditorium (or *house*) where the audience sits to watch the show, the box-office where the tickets are sold, the lobby and refreshments bar, all public service areas out in front of the stage, all storage areas backstage (or behind the stage), and the stage itself. It is the *stage* where the actors perform their magic that interests us the most. Though the need to provide more advanced technical support for the actor has increased the complexity of the theater and its stage, the essence of good drama is the relationship between the actor on the stage and the audience in the house.

Although there are many different kinds of theater stages, including *thrust* and *arena* (also known as theater-in-the-round), we will mainly deal with the three-walled stage with a proscenium arch (a curved or rectangular frame enclosing the stage). The term *proscenium* refers to the invisible fourth wall, architecturally framed, that separates the audience from the stage playing area. The magic of the theater is projected over and through the proscenium, which is usually represented by a tableau curtain—a pair of stage curtains, typically velour, that are drawn open and closed or that rise and descend at the beginning and end of a play. We must always respect this framed wall, for it is the window through which the audience enters into our world of magic. While in character, for the duration of the play, the actor should never step beyond this invisible wall because he will destroy the magic of make-believe that the wall preserves between his character and his audience. The proscenium wall makes sure that the characters on the stage remain in their own separate world and never interact directly with the audience.

The design of the proscenium stage dates to the seventeenth-century Italian Renaissance when artists used painted scenery (often elaborate and panoramic in its spectacle) to create the illusion of a real setting for a play or musical performance. Since the set design was viewed as a huge painting, it seemed only natural to frame the painting, and so the Italians developed the proscenium to sustain the illusion created by the scenery while hiding from the audience those aspects of technical production that helped make the magic happen. This architectural frame would later develop into the *box set* as we know it today, consisting of three walls that enclose the acting area, in imitation of a room from which the fourth wall has been removed, and through which the audience views the play once the tableau curtains are opened. The side walls have openings or gaps between them, which allow for the entrances to and exits from the stage. The box set, with variations in size and depth, is the most commonplace theater design today for opera, ballet, and drama.

The proscenium picture frame or box set stage, with its focused viewing angle through the imaginary fourth wall, provides the theater artist with control over what his audience sees and how they react to his character at any given point during the performance. Since all of the artistic and technical elements of the performance can be presented within the frame of the proscenium, while *masking* the offstage space and overhead machinery, the theatrical illusion can be more easily maintained.

The *thrust* stage does not have the fourth wall to act as the magical "open sesame" between the actor and the audience. A direct descendant of the *open stage* of medieval times, and later the Elizabethan stage of the inn yards, the acting area is projected or thrust out into the audience, thus breaking through the proscenium, with the rear of the stage available for entrances and exits and any permissible decor. The original inn yard stage was surrounded by covered balcony or gallery seats, usually occupied by the wealthier patrons, while the poorer playgoers stood in the open yard or pit to watch the plays. Thrust stages are popular today because of the flexibility they offer in staging and the emotional exhilaration that the audience can experience because of its physical closeness to the actors. Because of the absence of the proscenium, the actors have to work even harder to sustain the *aesthetic distance*—the separation of audience and actor by means of the proscenium to preserve the illusion created on the stage.

No part of the proscenium model is present in an *arena* theater because the stage is out in the middle of the house with the audience seated all round. This 360 degree viewing angle entirely eliminates the aesthetic distance. Entrances and exits are made through gangways between the audience. Though the actors have a more "intimate" proximity to the arena audience, the wide-angle sightlines expose other audience members who might sit across from you or to the left and right of you, in effect becoming the backdrop scenery to the moving play action.

The traditional proscenium stage provides for the representation of more aesthetically consistent and realistic interior sets. Clearly, audience sightlines prohibit this in the other stage designs. You cannot build a wall, for example, on an arena stage, as it would block at least part of the audience's ability to see the play. What furniture and stage properties *(props)* are used on either a thrust or arena stage have to be *set* and *struck* (removed) within the full view of the audience. The *grid* (or structural support that holds the equipment to hang scenery and lights) is also visible to an arena audience instead of being masked behind the proscenium. Unlike the theatergoers of Shakespeare's day, who relied on the playwright's descriptive words to paint the glory of a sunrise or the violence of a battle, today's audiences are not so unquestionably accepting of or as responsive to the spoken word unaided by scenic art.

Just as actors in a movie do not break out of the cinema screen and talk to the audience directly, so the theater actor plays his character *to* the audience but never assumes familiarity *with* them. In line with traditional theatrical convention, the actor should not engage the spectators at any time during the performance, though his character may address them in dramatic *asides* (private words spoken to the audience that are not audible to the other characters onstage). The television or movie screen doesn't allow the audience to talk to the characters, and the same is true in live theater. The proscenium wall is just like the television screen; it keeps the magic of the make-believe characters intact. Even if the stage is thrust or arena, the actor should still observe the same golden rule.

Some interactive dinner theater shows and children's plays ignore the proscenium discipline, while the more experimental practitioners have tried to fuse the actor's space with the audience's space, thus removing the traditional separation entirely. These attempts are generically referred to as *environmental* theater, which places the audience into the "environment" or "event" of the play, requiring the audience to interact with the actors—much like a guest at a dinner party would interact with the principal hosts—even getting up out of their seats and following the actors to another room or part of the stage. Most directors and actors, however, find that respect for the proscenium ensures a greater performance integrity.

Why do some theater companies prefer open stages—that is, thrust, theater-in-the-round or arena—to the conventional picture frame proscenium? There are both financial and artistic reasons. The business of theater is a costly one. Among nonprofit theater companies, community ensembles, and educational groups there is keen competition for grants of monies and corporate sponsorship. A proscenium stage, with its reliance upon scenic spectacle, is an expensive and cumbersome proposition, whether using one permanent box set, several different sets that are struck after each scene or act, or a multiple set that has all the individual scene settings built into it and from which the action moves uninterrupted through skillful lighting. The only options to these traditional arrangements are either a simple curtained setting or the even more economical open stage with its limited or hoisted scenery.

A director may choose the open stage because he wants to preserve the sense of intimacy between actors and audience, and thus more powerfully engage the spectator in experiencing, up close and personal, the revealing moments of dramatic conflict and catharsis in the play. Though the proscenium stage can more easily focus these magical high points because of its pictorial depth and force of theatrical illusion, the trend in ensemble theater is the thrust platform stage with multi-tiered fully sighted seats as in the new Courtyard Theater of the Royal Shakespeare Company in Stratford-Upon-Avon. Such a theater house allows highly flexible design adaptations offering exciting technical and spatial possibilities in direction, as well as leaner set budgets. The growing use of improvisation among actors instead of total reliance upon scripted lines during actual performances, especially in social-issue related plays, is another factor that weighs heavily in favor of the open stage.

A Renaissance stage with a typical "picture" scene behind a proscenium frame. This kind of theater emphasized scenic display and was the beginning point of the courtly staging that persisted from about 1600 to 1900.

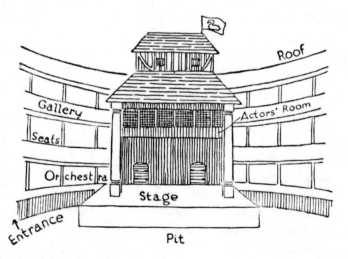

An Elizabethan playhouse modeled on an Inn Yard where plays were formerly performed. Note the square stage "thrusting" out into the yard. Poorer playgoers stood in the open pit for a penny to watch the play. The balcony or gallery seats, reserved for wealthier patrons, cost a penny or two more.

The Proscenium Stage

The area marked off in our rehearsal room matches the one drawn on your handout sheet. This area is called the *stage* or *playing area*. The stage is the centerpiece of the theater, for it is here that the actor creates his character and brings his drama to life before his audience. This is where the actor performs his magic. The actor is *onstage* when he is anywhere on the playing area in view of the audience or house. The actor is *offstage* or *behind the scenes* when he is out of view of the audience or house.

The *wings* are situated on either side of the stage. The wings are where actors wait to make their entrances onto the stage and where they go when they make their exits from the stage. The term *wings* also has a general meaning, referring to any place bordering the stage to the right and the left sides where the audience cannot see you during a play. It includes the place where the *prop table*, containing all the stage properties (or props) needed during the play, is set up for easy access. On the left side of the wings, down near the audience, sits the *prompter,* though he may move depending upon where the actors are speaking their lines. He is the person who, during the performance, feeds actors lines if they forget them. You will also find in the wings an actor who speaks *offstage lines* (those meant to be heard as if from another room).

The wings are usually delineated by border curtains or vertical strips of fabric called *legs.* Typically black, and about four to six feet wide, legs reach down to the stage floor and are used mainly for masking the left and right sides of the stage. Legs can usually be angled so that they completely enclose the acting area or they can be turned at right angles to form wing entrances, while still masking the wing areas.

When the tableau curtains are drawn back, there is usually a gap between the sides of the proscenium arch and the ends of the set of curtain draperies, thus allowing the spectators to see into the downstage wings. To mask the gap, left and right *returns* are used. Returns (sometimes called tormentors) are usually permanent canvases stretched onto a wooden frame, and painted flat black, which may explain why they are called *flats.* Theatrical flats can also be made up of just plywood boards (usually eight feet by four feet) with a framework of timber to support them. Flats are not just used to close off the side view of the downstage wings to the audience. You can make whole units of sets out of flats by nailing them together and painting scenery on them. A standard box set stage design almost exclusively uses eight by four feet flats for its interior settings, as well as cut-out (carefully shaped) flats designed and painted to give a realistic sense of perspective and space when more of an open air exterior setting is needed.

In *Speech Training and Dramatic Art,* John Miles-Brown describes a typical realistic box set found on the conventional stage. It consists of flats constructed from canvas stretched on a wooden frame. The flats are nailed or lashed together and supported by stage braces, the ends of which are either screwed to the stage floor or held down by heavy stage weights like sand bags. The flats, painted to represent a real setting like the interior of a living room, can be fitted with life-sized doors and windows with backings behind them painted and/or lighted to represent an exterior view, like a sunset or a mountain. Doors, windows, or decorative features like fireplaces are constructed as a single unit which fits into the space provided in the canvas flat and is secured into position. Stairs, steps, and archways are all constructed as units which fit into the set in the same way. A box set might also have a ceiling consisting of a very large canvas flat painted white resting on top of the walls of the set.

The *back wall* refers to the back line of the visible stage area. Here we place a *back curtain* and/or *back (scenery) drop* called a *cyclorama* or *sky-cyc* for short. Made of heavy canvas or muslin and painted a white or sky blue, the sky-cyc, when illuminated from below and above by skillful lighting, can create the impression of a variety of interior and exterior settings to include various times of the day and night, as well as the seasons. Many large theaters have multiple back drops (or *back cloths* as they are sometimes called), which can be raised and lowered according to changing scenes. An open air setting, such as a seaside coast or woodland meadow, will often use a cyclorama in combination with cut-out flats painted to look like rocks, trees, or other natural features suggestive of an outdoor scene.

A stage with curtained legs might also have additional *traverse* curtains (sometimes called *travelers*) which can be pulled horizontally across the stage when needed. A rear traverse curtain is drawn in front of the cyclorama, and can be parted to provide rear entrances or reveal certain scenic perspectives of the cyclorama. A center traverse curtain is situated between the rear traverse and main tableau curtains. With the addition of these extra curtains, action can now take place at three levels of stage depth. Actors can appear on the apron stage in front of the closed tableau curtains, downstage in front of the center traverse, upstage in front of the rear traverse, or the action can be silhouetted by the cyclorama when the rear traverse has been parted.

Following the innovative practices of early twentieth-century set designer Gordon Craig, some directors prefer masses of sheer white curtains that compose the entire set to a cyclorama or a realistic box set made of flats. Capturing something of the simplicity of ancient Greek theater, curtained settings can create beautiful variations of stage depth, as well as a more flowing and elegant ambiance, especially with the different lights dancing on them.

Directly behind the cyclorama is a walkway passage connecting the two sides of the stage. (Alternatively, the connecting passage can be below the stage.) Beyond this is the *backstage* area. *Backstage* refers to the offstage areas which are not visible to the audience. Though backstage can refer to all offstage areas, including the wings, it usually applies directly to the administration offices, dressing rooms, costume, lighting, and prop storage rooms, actors' restrooms, and spaces for operating the lights and backdrops.

With the exception of the sound (and sometimes lighting) technicians, who often occupy a booth above the far end of the auditorium opposite the stage, the production staff and technical crew are positioned backstage. The cast members remain backstage until they are called for an entrance. Some actors prefer to stand in the wings when they are not onstage instead of going backstage to the dressing rooms, especially if they do not have costume changes. When an actor leaves the stage or playing area, he goes offstage. During a performance, offstage refers to somewhere backstage, out of sight of the audience. During rehearsal or when there is no audience present, offstage refers to anywhere in the theater building, other than the stage.

While the term *stage* refers specifically to the performance or playing area, it is sometimes used to include the immediate offstage areas behind the proscenium arch that directly relate to the artistic or technical production of the play. The more accurate term, however, is *stage house*. The *stage house* comprises both the stage where the actors perform their parts and the work areas where the technical crew and machinery are placed in order to make the production happen. Stage house, or *skene*, is a term that was used in ancient Greek theater. It referred to a rectangular building, situated opposite the audience, which functioned as a dressing room and architectural background, while concealing the actors who entered the stage through its three doors.

The ground plan of the stage shown in the handout and the description (above) of theatrical terms applies to a conventional, proscenium box set or curtained setting stage. Many small stages, school auditoriums, and church halls will not have an unbroken length of wall at the back to use as a cyclorama, or any back drops at all, let alone machinery like swivels, joists, and pulleys from which to hang them. Small stages might also lack a rear exit/entrance, apron, dressing rooms, storage rooms, or even a tableau curtain. Sometimes, however, the most inadequate stage conditions can be overcome if the actors and crew have ingenuity and imagination. After all, good theater is all about sustaining the magic between the character and the audience, and that power resides, more than anywhere else, in the actor himself.

Director's Notes: You will likely not be conducting your classes on a real theater stage with a proscenium curtain. Nevertheless, even if your "stage" is a marked-off space in your rehearsal room, you can remind students that from the moment they make their entrances onto the stage until they exit out of view, they should respect the playing area as much as a veteran actor respects it while performing on the most technologically-equipped Broadway stage. Moreover, even in the humblest community hall, the power and magic of the proscenium (fourth) wall is the same, and the students can demonstrate their understanding of that power and magic by staying in character and not relating directly to the audience.

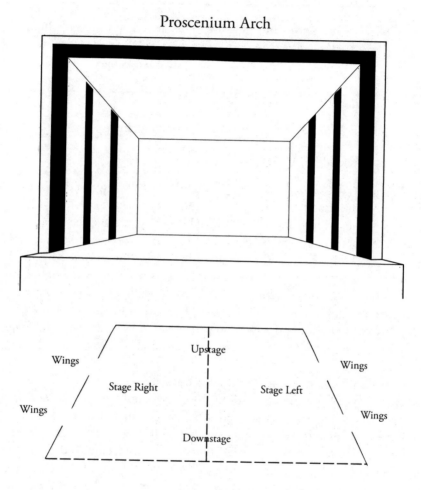

Elevated Box Set Proscenium Stage (above)
Ground Plan of Box Set Proscenium Stage (below)

KEY: Getting to the heart of the issue

 The proscenium is the invisible screen through which the audience experiences the magic of your character. Respect it every moment you are onstage.

GOLDEN RULE THREE: Know the stage or playing area.

Description of Stage or Playing Area

The 2-page *Stage Geography* handout shows the layout or ground plan of a simple stage with the conventional proscenium arch and main tableau curtains, which separate the stage from the auditorium. For comfortable acting, a stage requires a minimum space of 18 feet across and 15 feet deep, but we have to do our best when we have a wee space to work our magic. When an actor is onstage, he is given *stage directions* by the director, who in turn received his stage directions from the playwright who wrote them into his script. *Stage directions* tell the actors when and where to move during the performance, and sometimes his character's mood or intent. Stage directions also instruct the technicians and other working crew members where sets and props are to be placed on the stage in relation to the players, and how the actors and the set objects need to be lighted.

If we were to imagine the main curtains opening, so that we could see into the picture frame stage from the auditorium, the view would show nine major playing areas where the acting takes place as well as six designated or exact spots. In the handout, two imaginary (dotted) lines parallel to the curtain line have been drawn across the stage creating three equal divisions: *center*, *downstage*, and *upstage*. We call the middle area of the stage *center*. The area below or in front of the center section is the *downstage* or *down position* for the actor. The area above or behind the center is the *upstage* or *up position* for the actor. (In the diagram shown on the previous page, the four terms indicated are meant to be directional positions, not playing areas.)

Downstage describes that part of the stage nearest to the audience and nearest to the curtain line. It does not include the part of the stage that extends in front of the curtain line, called the *apron* or *apron stage*, since footlights (in older theaters) or floor microphones are often placed there. The apron is anything from one to six feet deep. A narrator or a character performing a monologue will sometimes utilize this space in front of the closed curtains. At operas, principal singers take bows on the apron stage during intermissions between Acts. Downstage also does not include the sunken area in front of the proscenium called the *orchestra pit*, where the musicians who make up the orchestra play during a musical performance, such as an opera or ballet. Sometimes the ground floor seating in a theater auditorium is referred to as the *orchestra*, which should not be confused with the orchestra pit.

Upstage describes that part of the stage furthest from the audience and furthest from the curtain line. In other words, an actor who is upstage is away from the audience, and an actor who is downstage is near the audience. The reason these two terms, downstage and upstage, are used is that historically the stage was not flat like it is in modern theaters, but was "raked." A *raked* stage had a floor that sloped or tilted slightly from its highest point, at the rear, down to the part of the stage where the footlights used to be. It was designed this way so the audience could see the actors more clearly, especially the stars, who usually remained upstage of the other actors. This showed that they had a higher position than the supporting cast, while allowing them to be more easily viewed by the audience.

A raked stage floor also gave a more picturesque perspective to the settings. Theaters today have flat stages but raked auditoriums to aid visibility. The term *above* is used as a synonym for "upstage of," as when an actor crosses "upstage" or behind (from the point of view of an audience) another actor or piece of furniture. The term *below* is used when an actor crosses downstage of—or in front of—another actor.

If the actor stands at center stage (CS), facing the audience and the auditorium, and extends his arms straight out toward the wings, his right arm will point to *stage right* and his left arm will point to *stage left*. Therefore, stage left is on the actor's left hand but on the audience's right hand as the audience is sitting facing the actors. Stage positions are determined from the actor's point of view as he faces the audience. What is right to the actor is left to the audience.

When a director uses the terms stage right or stage left, he is not referring to a designated spot on the stage. He is merely indicating a directional positioning on the left or the right side of the stage that includes anywhere from the downstage to the upstage area. Moreover, a director may tell an actor who is standing on the extreme edge of downstage right (DR) to move one step stage left. After executing the move, the actor is still situated downstage right but he has directionally moved one foot to the left of the stage, or stage left. If an actor, whose back is to the audience, is asked to move one step stage right, he will move one step to his left, and thus the audience's left, but the actor's right.

As we learned in Golden Rule Two, the term *onstage* refers to an actor moving onto some part of the stage or playing area, in visible sight of the audience, and in response to the director's instruction. When the actor moves away from the stage, so that he is no longer seen by the audience, he is *offstage*.

Major Stage or Playing Areas

To help distinguish the main playing areas on the stage where the director positions or "blocks" his actors, the stage (as depicted on the handout) has been vertically divided into three parts, referred to as right (R), center (C), and left (L). With the two imaginary horizontal lines and the two imaginary vertical lines, we now have a stage divided into nine *major* stage or playing areas for the actor, each having the name indicated on the handout sheet. The nine major acting areas are as follows:

DC	Downstage Center
C	Center or Center Stage (CS)
UC	Upstage Center
DR	Downstage Right
R	Right or Center Right (CR)
UR	Upstage Right
DL	Downstage Left
L	Left or Center Left (CL)
UL	Upstage Left

Designated Stage or Playing Positions

In addition to the nine major stage or playing areas, there are six designated stage positions between the major stage areas. These are often used to specify more exact placement. These subdivisions are written on the dotted lines on the handout:

DRC	Downstage Right Center
DLC	Downstage Left Center
RC	Right Center (Right of Center)
LC	Left Center (Left of Center)
URC	Upstage Right Center
ULC	Upstage Left Center

Director's Notes: Sometimes an "S" (for stage) is added to the downstage and upstage symbols. For example, DC will be written DSC. Some texts also list only six major acting areas, dividing the stage into three downstage and three upstage positions (DSR, DSC, DSL, USR, USC, USL), with an imaginary horizontal center line delineating an additional three designated stage positions: Center (C) RC (Right of Center) and LC (Left of Center). As an actor, you will need to adjust to your director's personal use of these stage terms.

E X E R C I S E 2-5 Navigating the Stage

- Choose a student to walk to all of the nine major stage areas, stopping where the plus sign (+) piece of tape has been placed as the central point in each of these areas. Repeat until every student has had a turn.

- Choose a student or ask for a volunteer to serve as the director to assign another student to walk the major stage areas. Repeat as long as the enthusiasm is high, and everyone has a chance to be the director.

- Once the students become familiar with the nine major areas, repeat the exercise using only the six designated stage positions.

- Once again, encourage each of the students to be the director to guide another student to the various positions.

- As students become more proficient at identifying all the fifteen areas of the stage, they execute the director's orders in a stage run, moving from stage area to stage area as rapidly as possible. The director should not wait until the actor reaches his position to give him the next order. This rapid pace forces the student to think ahead.

- To add some fun, ask the students to move to their positions with different *character attitudes*—for example, with a happy and lively step, as shy and hesitant, as bold and soldierly, etc. (This also prepares students to think in terms of taking on roles rather than just being themselves when they perform an exercise.)

Homework: The younger students can play the director as they direct their favorite action figure onto the various stage areas on their handout sheet. They might also like to create a stage in their backyard with washable chalk and practice their stage positions. (Make sure they ask permission of their parents first!) They can also invite their siblings or neighborhood friends to make it into a game.

KEY: Getting to the heart of the issue

> The actor, not the audience, has the right of way in theater. Every stage direction is given from the actor's point of view.

GOLDEN RULE FOUR: Learn to execute every movement with ease and grace.

Just as good posture is important to your health and personal appearance, it is essential for stage performance. You need to be able to stand properly and move gracefully. A well-schooled technique in deportment, movement, and gesture rests on the fundamental disciplines of balance, grace, strength, flexibility, and endurance. These elements need to be mastered in all the performing arts, but especially in theater acting, where the challenges of playing many different roles can be strenuous.

EXERCISE 2-6 Simply Standing

The ideal posture for standing is to hold your body in an upright position with shoulders back, the chest relaxed, and your chin lifted up (but not pointing to the stars). The back should be flat with the hips pushed or curved ever so slightly forward (especially for women). At no time should the actor stand with the trunk of his body tilted forward and his hips and bottom pushing backward. Arms should hang loosely (gracefully in the case of women) by the side, and legs should be straight with knees relaxed and not locked. The feet can be spread comfortably apart or one foot can be placed slightly in front of the other. In either position, the weight should be centered over both feet. The following exercise should be practiced regularly until a perfect posture becomes natural.

- Students line up and stand squarely with shoulders back and feet slightly apart (will vary with height and build of each student) and barely turned out. Keep the stomach taut but not "sucked in," which will cause muscle tension. The weight should be centered on the balls of the feet. Keep the center of gravity over the two feet and do not rest the weight on either of the hips—a common temptation.

- While remaining relaxed, bend all the way forward as if you were a rag doll, with arms hanging loosely to the floor. Keep knees relaxed, not stiff.

- Raise your body slowly to an erect position, keeping arms relaxed and loose by your side, your head high and your chin perfectly straight so that it is perpendicular to your throat.

- Stand with feet comfortably apart or move your right foot slightly forward and out, keeping the center of gravity over the two feet. Make sure you do not lean forward or sway back, thus shifting the axis of your body and losing balance. Remain straight but relaxed.

- Think of yourself as "standing tall" with strength and confidence.

EXERCISE 2-7 Simply Walking

Walking straight ahead with eyes looking forward, and your weight falling on the balls of your feet, is the natural and easy way to walk both on and off the stage. The spring of your movement comes from the balls of the feet, even though the heel touches the ground first. Your body should swing easily from your hips, with your arms following suit in opposition to your legs—that is, when your left leg is moving forward, your right arm is swinging back.

- Clear the chairs and create a walkway from one end of the room (or stage) to the other.

- Choose one student at a time to perform the following:

- Assume a "standing tall" position.

- As you prepare to take a step, shift the weight of your body onto the ball of the left foot, which will act as a spring for the step forward with your right foot—the heel striking the ground just before the ball and toes.

- Keep walking, feeling the spring from the balls of your feet. Walk rhythmically. Though the size of your steps will vary according to your build, try not to take either large strides or little steps. Don't "try" to walk. Your muscles know exactly what to do. You are simply getting your body into the optimally best position to carry out a very natural activity.

- Don't look at the ground as you walk. Keep your eyes forward.

- When you reach the end of the room (or the stage), turn with your whole body in one smooth motion of head, shoulders, and hips. Make your turn by rotating on the ball of the foot that is leading (the right foot on a right turn and the left foot on a left turn), shifting your weight to that foot as you do so. Be careful not to fall back on your heels and lose your balance, or to cross one foot over the other, which not only closes off your body to the audience but can trip you as well.

- If you have stairs in your rehearsal space, have the students practice walking up and down the stairway, keeping their eyes straight, and one hand resting lightly on the bannister.

- Do NOT:
  ◊ Shift the weight of your body to the hip as you turn
  ◊ Hold one shoulder higher than the other
  ◊ Look at your feet as your walk

◊ Drag your feet

◊ Sway back, thus walking on your heels

◊ Walk with feet too far apart, creating the impression of a swagger or bowlegged appearance, like a cowboy

◊ Be stiff and tense

EXERCISE 2-8 The Soldier's Stride and the Step of Grace

Make your entrances and exits in character and with proper deportment. First and last impressions count the most onstage. When entering the stage, always lead with the upstage foot so that your body is open to the audience. For example, if you enter from stage left, start with the right foot. If you enter from stage right, start with the left (or upstage) foot.

The goal of all movement is controlled and graceful coordination. The relaxation exercises are designed to free up any tight muscles so that your body can be flexible when you walk, sit, turn, or execute any unusual action of the body, such as a stage fall. When gesturing to the waltz music (below), keep in mind that the arms and hands should always move in a curve, extended in one, continuous line from the chest through the shoulder, elbow, wrist, and completing itself in the ends of the fingers.

- Students line up along the backstage wall, the girls in one group (entering upstage right) and the boys in another (entering upstage left).

- Play a slow march like "Pomp and Circumstance" as a student from each group takes turns walking (1 step per beat) diagonally across the stage from UR (upstage right) to DL (downstage left) or from UL (upstage left) to DR (downstage right). Keep the back straight, head up, and eyes forward. Walk with a natural arm swing. Repeat at least three times.

- Play a waltz piece to practice grace and balance. Each step is equal to three beats. Students advance diagonally to their respective downstage positions in step with the slower 3/4 time of the music while using these gestures:

  ◊ If starting with the right foot (from UL), slowly extend the right hand from the level of the heart out to stage right during the course of your walk, bringing the arm down to your side as you complete the walk.

  ◊ Repeat the same when entering from UR with the left foot, extending the left hand out from the heart to stage left. Keep gestures smooth and the arms extended in a graceful arc above the waist or heart.

  ◊ You can visualize taking a gift from your heart and extending it to another person to the right or left of you.

Director's Notes: Though these gestures of extending the arm are considered theatrical cliches in modern theater, they are excellent trainers in graceful deportment. It is helpful to have a real ballet teacher or older dance student assist you with these exercises. They may have a more practiced eye in coaxing grace and balance from the students.

EXERCISE 2-9 Simply Sitting

Sitting is not so easy on the stage, especially when the way we sit is greatly governed by the motive and attitude of the character we play. Slovenly habits that we can get away with in our ordinary lives will not do under stage lights or the camera's eye. We must follow certain rules to make sitting look theatrically pleasing to the audience.

- Set up a chair or bench center stage.
- The student waits CL in the wings and performs the following:
- Memorize (or visualize) the exact position of the chair.
- Enter CL, leading with your upstage (or right foot) and walking straight to the chair. Try not to look at the chair directly, but keep its position in view out of the corner of your eye.
- As soon as you arrive in front of the chair, turn your body front so that the back of your leg (the calf of the right or upstage leg) touches the chair.
- With the weight shifted to the upstage foot, lower yourself into the chair, keeping the head and back straight. Do not shimmy towards the back of the chair or lean against it. It is usual to sit somewhat forward in a chair onstage, unless you are directed to do otherwise. On the other hand, make sure you are not sitting on the front edge, where your weight will tip over the chair.
- Let your hands rest lightly in your lap, either clasped or folded together, or one hand over the other, unless directed otherwise. Men often rest the palms of their hands against their thighs or knees. You may also rest your hands on the arms of the chair, if it has arms. Your goal is to look relaxed and composed, so don't cross your arms or fold them in any way. When you do that, you restrict your breathing and look tense. Don't fidget with jewelry or any part of your clothing. Don't dig your fingers into your arms or scratch your skin.

- If you are a male, your legs will naturally spread several inches apart, according to your height and build. Place one foot slightly in front of the other. If you are a female, keep your feet (and legs) close together. You can slide both legs to one side, placing one foot behind the ankle of the other (a typical model's pose). Don't cross or spread your legs, or move them in a way that would distract the audience, such as stretching the leg or tapping the foot nervously. While sitting, keep your back straight. Don't lean over or slouch. And don't rest your elbows on your knees.

- In rising, keep your back as straight as you can without looking stiff. Lead with your upper body and not with your head. Center your weight on the balls of your feet, making sure that one foot is slightly forward of the other. Use your rear foot (the one closest to the chair) to push yourself up—keeping your center of gravity intact. Don't use the arms of the chair to push up from. Breathe in as you lift up. This relaxes you and helps to keep your chest reasonably high as you stand.

EXERCISE 2-10 Simply Falling

The act of falling on the stage is an art. The way to fall safely and still make your fall look real to your audience is to (1) completely relax your body and then let each individual unit—ankles, knees, legs, hips, thighs, upper body, arms, and head—be gently lowered, one part at a time; (2) be able to control your body so that you are as close to the floor as you can get before you actually touch the ground; (3) make sure that the flesh parts of your body (the forearms, thighs, and legs) absorb the impact with the hard surface.

- Choose one student at a time to perform the following:

- Stand and relax the body completely.

- Sway the body a little to the side, forward, then backward—making sure the arms are hanging loose.

- Feel as though your whole weight is sinking to your ankles. Let the knees bend first as you pivot in the direction of your fall, getting closer to the floor as you do so. Lower the left or right shoulder according to the direction you are falling, and allow your whole body to sink into the fall.

- Land on the calf of your leg, absorbing the fall with your thigh, and then roll with your hip. Your forearm should catch the weight of your body, as you gently lower your head to the ground.

- After the fall, ask the student if any part of his body felt sore or if he was aware of any part of his body tensing up before or during the fall. Have the rest of the class observe and comment on how the fall looked.

- Have the students think up various situations onstage where a fall might be needed—for example, becoming faint and dizzy, receiving a gunshot or knife wound, slipping on some object, etc.

- Discuss how to fall safely and convincingly in the situations suggested.

- Ask for volunteers to try these situation stage falls.

- The rest of the class should critique each stage fall attempted.

KEY: Getting to the heart of the issue

 Everything you do onstage creates a lasting impression. From the moment you enter, you are painting a living picture of your character that cannot be erased.

GOLDEN RULE FIVE: Think like a director.

Acting areas constitute your designated work space. The director must *block* the characters or *block* the play within this work space. This means that he will move or choreograph all the actors into various positions (or arrangements) on the stage according to what the playwright wrote in his script and the kind of stage being used. If your goal is to share your character with the audience in the most effective way possible and to be aware of your character's stage relationship with other characters at all times during your scenes, you must think like a director. This means that you have to understand, even anticipate, where your character should be when he delivers a certain line or engages in a particular action, reaction, interaction, or non-action.

Acting areas differ in their strength as playing positions for the actor. In terms of the vertical plane positioning of the actor onstage (center, right or left), center area placement is the strongest, right area placement is strong, and left area placement borders on weak. Let's discuss why. Downstage Center (DC) is the closest position to the audience, allowing them to see and hear the actor more clearly than anywhere else. The people in the front row can even tell the color of the actor's eyes or the color of the lipstick the actress is wearing. The closer the audience members are to you, the more clearly they can see your facial expressions, and the more strongly they will feel the emotion you are portraying. Of course, a truly skilled actor can project the power of his emotion to the entire house, from any position onstage.

The next most desirable positions are also lined up in the center area, even those designated upstage. Being positioned center and upstage from the audience is still more advantageous than being downstage right or downstage left. This is because when you are positioned in the center area, the whole span of the audience has a larger, clearer view of you. Standing in the center brings you closest to the largest number of audience members at any given time during the performance. Moreover, if the actor stands anywhere on an imaginary center line that divides the stage vertically into two halves, the distance between the actor and the audience is equidistant, whether the audience is sitting on the left or right side of the auditorium. For example, someone sitting on the right far edge of the seating stalls has an equal view of the actor (in terms of distance) as his counterpart sitting on the extreme left edge of the seating stalls. In a standard proscenium stage, with its U shaped audience viewing, this same audience/actor distance ratio exists for every seat in the house. For this reason, center stage is where most of the dramatic action is concentrated.

Any of the actor's positions in the right area of the stage are stronger than the counterpart positions in the left area. Downstage Right (DR), for example, is stronger than Downstage Left (DL). We naturally look or read from left to right, so as the curtain rises the audience inevitably looks to their left (stage right) to take in their first impression of the stage setting. Thus, in a scene with two people, the actor standing on the spectator's left (or stage right) has the advantage. In Chinese theater, it's the opposite. Why? (*The answer is that the Chinese read from right to left.*)

At the same time, when dealing just with right and left stage placements (as opposed to center), downstage will always trump upstage. For example, Downstage Left (DL) is stronger than Right (R), which is further upstage and therefore weaker. All other factors being equal, the relative strengths of the acting areas diminish as the actor moves from downstage center and away from the audience—that is, in this order: DC (the strongest), DRC, DLC, C, RC, LC, UC, URC, ULC, DR, DL, R, L, UR, UL. Both UR and UL are common entrance points to the stage, but are too weak to be used for blocking important scenes unless there are other factors involved, such as a raised level, to strengthen the physical presence of the actor.

A director blocks his characters according to how he wants to focus his audience's attention. When two characters are sharing a scene, the principal character will be blocked in a more visible, dominant position than the minor character. Sometimes a director may build an upstage balcony to give more visibility to an actor when other characters are positioned in the same scene downstage. For example, in the celebrated love scene of *Romeo and Juliet*, Romeo is in the garden below and Juliet is on her balcony above. Although she has the disadvantage of an upstage blocking, her height above Romeo balances the audience's focus between the two characters. This is exactly what the scene requires if the audience is to fully experience the youthful earnestness and romantic charm of the immortal lines they speak to each other as the world's most eloquent lovers.

EXERCISE 2-11 *Stage Dominance*

- Choose a student to stand downstage center with a full-front position of the body.

- Have the student retreat backwards (upstage) one step at a time, as far as the back wall, while keeping his body full front.

- Ask the other students in the audience to observe how the actor's degree of dominance is reduced each time he or she takes a step backwards, away from them, as he withdraws his presence upstage.

- Repeat the same exercise but this time reverse the position—that is, the student stands upstage and advances one step at a time downstage, while the students observe his changing degree of dominance.

- To demonstrate the relative strength of each stage area, choose two students and assign them different stage areas, with both standing full front to the audience.

- Have the other students decide which of the two stage areas is more dominant.

Director's Notes: Some of the acting positions can be confusing so it is important to be consistent in the way you name them. If you decide to call the center stage area Center (C), instead of Center Stage (CS), make sure you refer to it that way each time. I personally refer to the center stage area as Center (C) and use the term Center Stage (CS) when referring specifically to the (imaginary) centerpoint of the stage. In other words, when I direct an actor to Center Stage (CS), I am directing him to an exact (central) spot on the stage rather than somewhere within the major acting area known as Center (C). The same applies to the stage areas Right (R) and Left (L). If you choose, instead, to call them Center Right (CR) and Center Left (CL), as many teachers do, be careful not to get them mixed up with the similar sounding but distinctly different designated positions of Right of Center (RC) and Left of Center (LC).

EXERCISE 2-12 Stage Entrances and Exits

- Students take turns entering the stage from the following stage positions: UR, UL, R, L, DR, DL.

- Each time, the student walks to center (C), faces full front, turns and then exits at the same position from which he entered.

Director's Notes: Optional terms for *enter* are *make your entrance* or *cross in*. For example, "cross in upstage left" means to enter from the upstage left position.

KEY: Getting to the heart of the issue

 The actor on the stage is like a piece on a chessboard. He is moved about to gain the greatest overall advantage, and to achieve the best overall result.

GOLDEN RULE SIX: Know the stances of your body.

Working within the proscenium frame stage, the actor's position onstage must relate both to the other characters sharing the scene with him and to the audience.

Traditional bodily stances are listed below:

1. *Full front.* The body and head directly face the audience. This position is very strong. Feet should be slightly apart to avoid locked knees or an appearance of stiffness.

2. *One-quarter (right or left).* This position is also called *quarter right* or *quarter left*. The body is turned 45 degrees towards stage right or stage left. If turning to his right, the actor turns about halfway between full front and right profile. If turning to his left, the actor turns about halfway between full front and left profile. With three quarters of the face and body to the audience, this position is strong but less so than full front. If turning *quarter right*, the right (or upstage) foot should be ahead of the downstage (left foot). Reverse the directions for *quarter left* turn.

3. *Profile (one-half to right or left).* The body is turned 90 degrees, facing right or left, so that the side of the body is toward the audience.

4. *Three-quarter (right or left)*. The body is turned halfway between profile and full back, facing toward upstage right or upstage left. This is the only really weak position for the actor, since most of his face and body are closed to the audience.

5. *Full back*. The body is turned, facing upstage, with the back directly to the audience. Feet are slightly apart to maintain balance. This position is as strong as a profile position.

The reason for the intrinsic strength and weakness of these bodily positions is that the greatest emotional contact with the audience comes from the full front body and face. That is the standard from which all other positions are derived. The emotional impact diminishes as the position of the body closes away from the audience. Bear in mind, however, that other factors—such as level (the height of the actor above the stage floor as he is sitting, lying down, or standing), color of costume, lighting, and an actor's place onstage in relation to the other actors—all play their part in modifying the relative strength or weakness of the bodily stances. In addition, a director may want to create a certain emotional response from the audience by placing a character in a non-standard position. In many open stage productions, where the proscenium is not in play, the actors are blocked in relation to each other more than to the audience. Moreover, some directors give their actors the freedom to improvise during the live performance in order to create a more spontaneous mood.

A Director's Stage Terms:

In order to convey the shifting layers of character subtext (underlying meaning) and story emphasis, a director may choreograph or block many different changes in the positions of one actor or a group of actors in a scene. Like a good chess player, however, he never loses sight of the big picture. Below are the common phrases the director uses to relate an actor's position to other actors and to the audience:

1. To *open* or *open up* is to turn more of the body toward the audience. An actor, for example, may be standing profile and when told to "open up" will shift to a quarter but more often a full-front position.

2. To *turn in* or *close in* is to turn away from the audience and toward upstage.

3. To *turn out* is to turn more of the body to the audience toward downstage. In *turning out*, an actor *opens up*.

4. An *open turn* is when the actor turns (usually to make an exit), sharing more of his face and body with the audience. This is the long way out to the exit.

5. A *closed turn* is when the actor turns in a more tightly woven movement that exposes more of his back to the audience. This is the short way out to the exit.

6. To *move in* is to cross towards the center of the stage.

7. To *move out* is to cross away from the center of the stage.

8. To *move downstage* (or *down)* is to move toward the audience or the curtain line (no more than two feet unless directed) while maintaining the same bodily position.

9. To move *upstage* (or *up)* is to move away from the audience or the curtain line, maintaining the same position.

10. To *cross in* means to make an entrance (from the wings) onto the stage.

11. To *cross out* means to make an exit from the stage (into the wings).

12. To *cross above* is to move upstage or behind a person or object.

13. To *cross below* is to move downstage or in front of a person or object.

14. To *cross to* is to move from one position on the stage to another.

15. To *move forward* is to walk in the direction in which you are facing.

16. To *move back* is to step back from the position in which you are standing.

17. To *give stage* is to take a weak position so another actor can have focus.

18. To *take stage* is to move into a more prominent position on the stage or put more energy into a scene and so strengthen your stage presence.

19. To *cheat out* is to speak your lines to the audience either in a full-front or quarter position when the actor you are addressing is situated profile or in a position upstage of you.

20. To *steal* is to move so quietly and unobtrusively on the stage that the audience doesn't even see it.

21. To *blend in* is a general direction describing subtle changes in the position of the body to achieve a better relationship to the other actors.

22. To *throw away* is to underplay a moment in a scene. To *throw away a line* is to play down or render a more casual or less energetic reading of a line (or a piece of stage business).

Director's Notes: Some of these stage terms can be confusing when first introduced, so do not expect the students to remember them all. Once they start practically applying them in performance, the directions will become meaningful to them.

EXERCISE 2-13 Bodily Stances

- On a bare stage, an actor stands downstage center, full front.
- Direct him or her to the following positions, asking the student to return to full front position after completing each direction. For example, if the direction is to turn quarter left, after the student completes the move, he then returns to full front in preparation for the next direction:
  ◊ turn quarter right
  ◊ turn profile left
  ◊ make one step forward
  ◊ turn three-quarter right
  ◊ turn full back
  ◊ turn three-quarter left
  ◊ turn full front
  ◊ turn quarter left
  ◊ turn profile left
  ◊ turn profile right
  ◊ turn full back
  ◊ make one step back
- Repeat the same directions as above. This time the student does not return to full front each time but executes the next direction from where he is last positioned.
- Repeat exercise until the entire class is familiar with every position.

Director's Notes: The exercise above can be tiring because it involves quick thinking and concentration. If you sense that the students are losing interest, or are having difficulty remembering each move, try and make a game of it by splitting up the class into girls and boys, or redheads, blondes, and brunettes. It doesn't really matter what your criterion is to create separate groups, so long as you stimulate interest by encouraging competition.

EXERCISE 2-14 Comparative Stage Positions

- Three students are standing in the same stage area—for example, DR.

- To test the comparative strength of different heights or levels, direct them to take varying positions, for example:

  ◊ all stand
  ◊ all sit on the floor
  ◊ one sits and two stand
  ◊ one sits on a chair and two sit on the floor
  ◊ one sits on the floor, one sits on a chair, and one stands.

- The other students rearrange the three who are onstage in different levels and comment on the relative strength of the arrangements.

- To test the comparative strength of bodily positions, areas, and levels in relation to one another, have three students at a time assume different positions—for example, two actors stand in a profile position of equal strength and the third actor sits on the floor full front. Which actor is the most dominant or are they equal? Does a three-quarter position DC have the same strength as a full-front position UR?

Director's Notes: When comparing the relative strengths of juxtaposed positions of actors, it is often difficult to know for certain which is the strongest or weakest. A full front is the strongest bodily stance, but a weak UR placement of the actor will cancel out some of the full-front strength. The questions are meant to make students think about the critical importance of positioning vis-a-vis placement, where the effect on the audience can be largely subjective, especially when lighting and costuming are thrown into the mix. A good director applies both his theatrical reason and his intuitive sense when blocking a play. In other words, he never forgets that his ultimate end is to create magic.

KEY: Getting to the heart of the issue

Behind every placement and positioning of the actor is good theatrical sense and a pinch of magic dust.

GOLDEN RULE SEVEN: Learn your shop talk.

Throughout the theater's long history, a vocabulary of stage terms has been passed down, as well as unique and picturesque phrases that have added to the special charm and glamor of acting in the theater. Stage actors have their own "shop talk" just like any profession. Once the newcomer becomes familiar with this language, he will feel at home, and part of a magical fellowship.

Director's Notes: You can introduce some of these terms each week, or ask the students to design a quiz to test each other.

Traditional Terms Belonging to the Stage: (In alphabetical order)

ACT: A major subdivision of a play. A short play is often a "One-Act" play. Most plays have three or four Acts. Acts are subdivided further into scenes.

ACTOR: A theatrical performer who acts out a role in an artistic production. Besides playing dramatic roles, actors may also sing, dance, work as a stand-up comic, a voice artist (for radio), or as a voice-over actor for animated film roles. Actor is a gender-neutral term, though a female actor is commonly called an actress. An actor works in live (or legitimate) theater, movies, television, radio, or as a street entertainer.

ACTORS EQUITY ASSOCIATION: The American labor union established to represent actors, directors, designers, and stage managers working in live theater. The American union started in 1913 in New York City. The British "Equity" counterpart was founded in 1920 after a strike by actors. *Equity Waiver* refers to small, professional theaters seating 99 or less that do not have to comply with most of the union's equity contract provisions—thus the term "equity waiver." Originally, an equity waiver theater referred only to small theaters in Los Angeles. However, even in New York, some of the threadbare off-off-Broadway theaters are equity waiver. Actors usually work in these theaters in order to showcase themselves for movie work, which is why equity waiver theaters are also referred to as operating under "showcase code."

AD LIB: To make up a line or action during a performance that is not part of the original script or director's blocking. An actor usually ad libs when he forgets the real line or when another actor onstage misses a line or fails to enter on cue. Ad libbing is sometimes called improvising.

AESTHETIC DISTANCE: The distance between the audience and the action on the stage that allows the theatrical illusion to be maintained, and thus the audience's emotional involvement.

AMATEUR: A member of a theater company that is not professional. The word can also refer to an actor who has not had any professional training and/or is not paid for his performance in a show.

ANGEL: An individual (or company) who financially backs the commercial production of a play or musical. Because of the spiralling costs of mounting a commercial play or musical (which may cost anywhere from two to ten million dollars), producers more commonly look to corporate investors rather than to individual "angels."

ASIDE: Lines delivered by a character directly to the audience, and which are not supposed to be overheard by the other characters onstage. The thoughts expressed in an aside are meant to be like the unspoken thoughts of the character. As such, the actor is not directly engaging the audience.

AT RISE: Refers to the action taking place as the curtain rises.

AUDITION: A competitive tryout for an actor who is seeking a role in a theater production. At an audition, the actor usually performs a prepared monologue or a short scene for the director or casting director of the show. Generally, many actors turn up at an audition so that the director can find the most suitable person for a particular role. Sometimes an actor may be asked to do a *cold reading*. A cold reading tests your ability to perform a piece from a script that you have never seen before. The director may also interview an actor at an audition or ask him to improvise a scene that he (the director) describes.

AUDITORIUM: The part of the theater where the audience sits during a performance. From the Latin *Audio*—"I hear." Sometimes known as the *house*.

BACKING: A scenic piece which goes behind an opening in the set, such as a window, to mask the technical work area behind it. Also known as a *Backing Flat*.

BALCONY: The term that refers to the upper level in the auditorium. A balcony usually has tiered seating. In English theaters, the balcony is known as the Circle, with further distinctions such as Upper Circle, Dress Circle, or Grand Circle. Many of America's opera houses, such as the Metropolitan Opera House, have seating arrangements that include a Family Circle (the highest and least desirable), the Balcony, the Dress Circle, and the Grand Tier.

BEAT: A deliberate pause by the actor in his delivery of a word or line of dialogue for dramatic or comic effect. A beat is also used as a measure of time when cueing. For example, the technical script might say, "Lighting Cue#5 needs to go three beats after Danny exits."

BEGINNERS: Those members of the cast who are onstage when the curtain goes up. The stage manager may also give a "Beginner call" to bring those actors who appear in a particular Act to the stage. For example, "Act Two Beginners on the stage, please."

BIO (Short for biography): A short narrative about an actor that states the most important facts concerning his work, such as the plays he has performed in or any acting awards he has won. A bio is usually written by the actor himself and is used in theater programs or in press releases. A bio also provides personal information (called personal stats) such as where and when he was born, and if he is married or not.

BIT PART: A small role. (Original meaning: a small piece of artwork.) Most actors start off their careers appearing in bit parts. *Cameo* refers to a bit part in a film played by a well known actor who would normally not take such a small part. There were many cameos of famous actors in the 1956 movie production of *Around the World in 80 Days*.

BLACK HOLE: An accidentally unlit portion of the stage. There is a t-shirt that became popular several years ago that said, "If All the World's a Stage, I Want Better Lighting!" An actor, by natural instinct, will never retreat to a part of the stage that is unlit.

BLACKOUT: An extinguishing of all stage lights, often at the end of a scene or Act, so that nothing can be seen on the stage. Sometimes abbreviated BO. A blackout can take place very quickly, or by a "slow fade" of the lights. Though there is no onstage light during a blackout, the blue working lights backstage remain on as do the exit signs and other emergency lighting.

BLOCKING: The physical movement of an actor or actors from point to point in a scene. In film and television these points are called "marks" and consist of two pieces of tape on the floor in the shape of a "T." An actor hits his mark when he stops at the "T." On a live stage the actor must memorize where he goes. It is the job of the stage manager to record all the movements (or blocking) of the actors during a play in his *Prompt Book,* such as "Alan X DL" meaning that Alan crosses to Downstage Left.

BOARD: The main control for the stage lighting. Originally known as the lighting console or dimmer board. The lighting technician for a show is said to be "on the board." In the early twentieth century, a director would refer to his cast as being "on the boards," meaning that they were listed as *dramatis personae* for an ongoing production. This cast list often took the form of a small chalkboard posted backstage which had the names of the actors and the parts they played written on it in chalk. It also referred to the billboard with the names of the players on it, that was left outside the theater to advertise the show to passers-by. Sometimes a photo of the starring actor might be attached to the board. When directors in the nineteenth century spoke of actors "on the boards," they referred to the cast of actors in a currently running play—that is, those working on the stage, the floor of which was made of wood floor boards. The actor did not want to hear that he was "off the boards"—that is, out of a part!

BOOKING: A specific job or acting role that a performer is contracted to do.

BOX OFFICE: Part of the theater lobby area where people can buy tickets to see a play. Most box offices are now computerised, and offer phone or online internet reservations, though reserved tickets can still be picked up at the box office.

BOX SET: Realistic setting (set) of a complete room with three interior walls built from flats and a missing fourth wall (proscenium) through which the audience views the play.

BOOTH (Also known as the *Control Room*): The room at the rear or above the rear of the auditorium (in a proscenium theater) where sound and sometimes lighting is operated from. The control room is usually soundproofed from the auditorium so that communications between the technicians and the backstage crews cannot be heard by the audience. The control room has a large viewing window as well as a communications relay to the stage. The booth technician must be able to hear the performance as the audience hears it so that he can correctly balance or "mix" the sound.

BREAK A LEG: A traditional and popular good luck wish exchanged by theater performers who feel that saying "good luck" is a jinx. Many explanations have been offered as to how this phrase first came about. One of the most picturesque is that theaters were known to be favorite places for ghosts or sprites to haunt. These mischievous spirits were believed to enjoy wreaking havoc and causing trouble, such as making the curtain come down at the wrong time, or tripping an actor as he makes an entrance onto the stage. If the sprites heard you ask for something, they would surely try to make the opposite happen. Telling someone to "break a leg" therefore was an attempt to outsmart the sprites and in fact make something good happen.

BREAKDOWN: A detailed description of a character role in a play.

BRING UP: A lighting term that means to increase the intensity of the lights or lamps.

BROADWAY: That area of New York City on and adjacent to the street named Broadway where America's most popular commercial theater is concentrated.

CALL: A notification to actors and crew of a work session or performance time, as in "Full cast rehearsal is tomorrow at 3 p.m." The term also describes a request for an actor to come to the stage for his (imminent) entrance, as in an *Actor's Call*. The word also means an acknowledgment of applause by the audience at the end of the play, as in a *Curtain Call*. A call given to the actors one half hour before showtime is a *Half Call*. A *Casting Call* is a notice or advertisement of auditions to be held for casting roles in a play. Normally these auditions are only open to actors who have been submitted by an agent, and who belong to Actor's Equity Association. An *Open Call* is when auditions are open to all actors whether or not they have been submitted by agents. A *Cattle Call* is an open audition for anyone and everyone (including untrained hopefuls) to try out for a production.

CALLBACK: A second or third audition used to further narrow the field of actors competing for a particular role in a play. Also called a "Follow-Up" audition or interview.

CALLBOARD: A place backstage in the theater where company rules, announcements, notes, and messages are posted for those involved in the production.

CALLING A SHOW: The process of calling the lighting, sound, scene-change cues, as well as the actor's timed entrances during a performance. This is the job of the stage manager using a headset. He uses a *Prompt Book* which contains a copy of the script and all production cues annotated. Calling the show means giving the signal to execute these production cues (or changes). Each cue is assigned a number or letter and the respective technicians know what they must do for each cue, and when. Each kind of technical cue has its own abbreviation—for example, a sound effects cue is abbreviated SFX. The prompt book would have SFX#4 to mean Sound Cue#4. The stage manager will give a warning signal about half a page before the cue is meant to be executed. Then a few seconds before, he will signal with a *Stand by*. Finally, when the technician hears "GO" from the stage manager, that particular cue is executed.

CAST: The performing members of the acting company. They act out all the characters that are in the play.

CASTING: The process of the director choosing the right actors to play the character roles in a script.

CAT WALK: A narrow platform or walkway built or suspended above the stage to permit ready access to the ropes, the lights, the hung scenery, and other stage equipment and service areas. In English theater it is called the *Bridge*. In the movie, *Phantom of the Opera*, the masked phantom makes his many escapes along the cat walk of the Paris Opera House.

CHARACTER: A person in a play created by the playwright. An actor represents, acts out, or "plays" a character onstage, or in front of movie or television cameras.

CHOREOGRAPHER: The person who creates and teaches the dance elements for a show. A choreographer is usually needed for a musical, but rarely for a drama.

COLD READING: The reading aloud of a script (usually at an audition) by an actor with little or no time to prepare. "Cold" also describes the fear and anxiety that an actor experiences when asked to do a cold reading. The more an actor is familiar with his script, the more he "warms up" to it.

COMEDY: A type of play genre which offers a light, humorous view of life or which makes its point through sharp ridicule and satire. A comedy usually has a happy ending.

COMPOSITE: A resume comprising several photos of an actor in different situations, and with different "looks"—thus showing his versatility. A composite is used to solicit modeling work, as well as acting jobs for commercials, television, and film. Though stage actors normally secure a role through a live audition, and only need a *glossy* (8x10 headshot), some do send composites to agents, who then send them out to casting directors.

COVER LETTER: A letter that you write when you send a publicity photo, composite or resume to an agent or director. A cover letter personalizes the correspondence and is considered a professional courtesy.

COSTUME FITTING: The fitting of the actor for his or her costume/s. The wardrobe staff must make sure that the costume fits, and that the actor can move freely in it. When an actor has a *Costume Change,* he changes into a different outfit. An actor may have several costume changes during the course of the play. If an actor has to do a quick costume change, a *Quick Change Area* will be set up backstage. Depending upon how many changes are required, this area may include a costume rack and mirror.

COSTUME PARADE: A review by the director, designer, wardrobe, and lighting technician of all the costumes worn by each actor in the play. The actors walk onstage, one at a time, wearing their costumes under stage lighting. The parade is designed to show not only the costumes, but the actors *in* those costumes. Any ill-fitting garments or lighting problems are noted and corrected before the first *Dress Rehearsal*.

CONTACT SHEET: The list of addresses, phone numbers, email addresses and other contact information of the cast and crew. The list is used to keep track of everybody's whereabouts during the production period, or to get in touch with them in a timely manner in case of unexpected or last-minute production changes.

CONTINENTAL SEATING: An arrangement of theater seating without a center aisle.

CRITIC: A journalist who writes reviews for theater productions—that is, they tell the public what was good (or worked) in the play and what didn't. The review also assesses how each of the actors performed their roles. Because many theatergoers decide if they should attend a play based on how good or bad the reviews are, a good critic should have a sound knowledge of and love for theater, so that his reviews are fair, unbiased, and informative to the public and to the players. Obviously, a good review attracts bigger audiences, and that's what everyone wants. A good review of a play can also be helpful in drawing attention to the playwright, the actors, and the theater company itself. Good reviews are often posted in the lobbies of theaters, and used to promote good PR (public relations) for that theater. Sometimes actors will stay up all night to wait for the reviews. Over the span of his career, a professional actor will probably earn good, mixed, and bad reviews. Reviews teach an actor to have a thick skin.

CURTAIN (Also called the *House Curtain*): The main tableau curtain or drapery in a proscenium theater that moves up and down or opens from side to side at the beginning and ending of Acts in the play, or at the beginning and end of the play itself. They are called *draw* curtains if they are drawn from side to side. If they are pulled up into or lowered from the flies, which are situated along the inside top of the proscenium arch, then the curtains are said to be *flown*. The curtain separates the stage from the audience.

CURTAIN CALL: Actors taking a bow in front of the audience at the end of a show. The curtain call is a time when the audience can show their appreciation for (or displeasure with) the players.

CURTAIN SPEECH: An announcement given by the director (or his representative) in front of the closed curtain, just before the performance starts. In most theaters the announcement is recorded, such as, "Good evening, ladies and gentlemen, and welcome to the (insert name) Theater. Please switch off all cell phones and pagers as a courtesy to our performers and to other members of the audience. Flash photography is not permitted. We hope you enjoy the show."

CURTAIN UP: The beginning of the show when the curtain rises. Also called *Curtain Time*.

DEUS EX MACHINA: Originally a theatrical device in ancient Greek theater where a god would appear above the scenery at the end of the play and resolve all the conflicts. In modern theater it refers to any event happening late in the play that, in a miraculous way, resolves everybody's problems.

DENOUEMENT: The resolution or wrapping up of the story of the play during which all conflicts between the characters are resolved. (From the French word meaning to *unknot* or *unravel* the plot or complications in a story.) The denouement always occurs in the final scene of the play and is the play's conclusion.

DIALOGUE: The lines or words spoken by the characters in a play. Originally, dialogue referred to a verbal exchange between at least two characters, but today it refers to any words spoken by an actor—even a monologue.

DIMMER: A lighting term. Electrical or electronic device which controls the amount of electricity passed to a lamp, and therefore the degree of intensity of that lamp. Dimmers are employed more often to soften the intensity of the lighting on the stage when the scenes or actors require it.

DIRECTOR: The person who has the ultimate responsibility for staging the script, directing the actors, and making the final decisions on all artistic and technical aspects of the production. The most important role of the director is to unite all the elements of a play for the purpose of communicating the playwright's intention to the audience. It is the director who must bring the play script to theatrical life. A *Technical Director* coordinates all the technical elements of the show, from organizing the crew to ensuring equipment is ordered, to making sure that the lighting, sound, set, and costume designers are all working to help realize the artistic vision of the play. In English theater, a technical director is usually called the *Production Manager*.

DRAMA: A literary art form or play genre that probes the more serious issues of life and the conflicts thereof. A good drama tries to offer hope in the face of life's challenges or tragedies.

DRAMATIS PERSONAE: A Latin phrase that refers to the dramatic persons of the play—in other words, the cast of characters.

DRAMATURG: A person who works as an advisor and research assistant to the director on the background and historical context of the play being produced. He can also act as a liaison between the director and the playwright, especially when it comes to script changes or revisions.

DRESS THE SET: Add the decorative items to the set, such as curtains, furniture, props, etc.

EIGHT BY TEN (8x10): A photograph, 8x10 inches, used by actors for audition and promotional purposes.

ENSEMBLE: An acting group where the actors see themselves as part of a company working together rather than as individual "stars."

ENTR'ACTE: A musical interlude between the first and second acts of a performance. Usually found in a musical production rather than a drama.

ENTRANCE: An opening in the wings or on the set through which the actor makes his appearance onto the stage. The word also refers to the action of an actor walking onto the stage, as in "make an entrance." The term also references the point in the script when an actor is directed to appear onstage.

EPILOGUE: A speech to the audience by a character in the play after the formal action of the play is concluded. The speech is meant to provide some moral insight or final comment on the action. Examples are Rosalind's epilogue in Shakespeare's *As You Like It* and Puck's epilogue in *A Midsummer Night's Dream*.

EXIT: An opening in the set that is used for leaving the stage. Also, the act itself of leaving the stage, as in "make an exit" or "exit the stage." The term also refers to the point in the script at which an actor leaves the stage. *Exeunt:* Stage direction meaning "they exit." In every theater auditorium there are *exit signs,* usually illuminated in red, which tell the audience where to leave the auditorium when the play is over.

EXTRA: An actor who is onstage but has no speaking lines. His role might be to fill out a crowd scene, and so may only speak or react as part of a group. The term is more commonly used in the film industry.

FADE: A fade is an increase, diminishment, or change in lighting or sound level. To *fade up* or *fade in* is to bring the stage lights up (or increase) gradually. *Fade down* or *fade out* is the reverse.

FALSE STAGE: A special stage floor laid 2 to 3 inches above the real stage floor. A false stage allows the running of steel cables in the shallow void between the false floor and the original stage floor. A false stage is needed for putting a *revolve* or turntable onto a stage.

FEEDBACK: A high-pitched squeal heard from the sound system when a sound is picked up by a microphone and is amplified through the speaker to which it is connected. The microphone then picks up the amplified sound and it is sent through the system again. Feedback can be avoided by careful microphone positioning, and can be reduced by use of equalization to reduce the level of the frequency band causing the feedback.

FIRE CURTAIN: A heavy fire-proof curtain that is dropped during a fire emergency, thus sealing the stage from the auditorium and from the spread of flames. A fire curtain is designed to block the spread of an onstage fire until the audience can be evacuated.

FLASHBACK: A theatrical convention in which the audience is able to see scenes acted out from the past through the memory of one of the characters in the play. The audience is literally taken back in time to experience some moment in the past that helps to explain the present situation the character finds himself in. A flashback also provides the audience with a greater insight into the mind and emotions of the character himself.

FLY: The space above the stage in which scenery and lamps are hung so that they are not seen by the audience. *Fly bars* refer to the metal bars to which scenery and lamps are attached for *flying* above the stage.

FOOTLIGHTS: A row of low-wattage and varied colored lamps mounted on the apron of the stage floor that provide general illumination. Footlights are rarely used today except for special effects, or in old theaters. The earliest use of footlights was in England in 1672. In 1758 footlights became very popular when the famous actor and theater manager, David Garrick, installed them at the Drury Lane Theater in London. This was before the time of electricity, so the lamps were burning live flame.

FORESHADOWING: This occurs when the dialogue or action in one part of a play gives a hint to the audience of something that will happen in a later part of the play.

FREELANCING: Refers to an actor who is working without being contracted to an exclusive agent. With the exception of the big stars, most actors are freelance. When we hear in the sports world that a player is a "free agent," this means the same thing as being freelance or self-employed (and thus able to work for a number of employers) in the theatrical world.

FREEZE: To stop all movement by the actors on the stage. A classic example in theater tradition of a freeze is a tableau, when all the actors hold their positions to suggest a picturesque grouping. Such a grouping is held until the lights fade down.

FRENCH SCENE: A scene division within a play marked (as in French drama) by the entrance and exit of a principal actor. Sometimes when rehearsing a play, the director will "french the scenes"—that is, have each scene start with the entrance of the main or principal character and then cut everything in between until that character exits. It is an expedient way to rehearse the continuity of entrances and exits for the main character or characters without having to go through the whole play.

FRESNEL (Pronounced "Fre-nell"): The Fresnel is a common lighting lamp which produces an even, soft-edged beam of light through a Fresnel lens. The lens has concentric circles on the front and is pebbled on the back. It is named after its French inventor, Augustin Jean Fresnel (1788–1827). The lens was originally developed for French lighthouses so that they could be seen further out to sea and could achieve a longer focal length with less glass.

FRONT OF HOUSE (FOH): Every part of the theater in front of the proscenium arch. Includes auditorium, foyer, and other areas open to the public. The backstage areas of the theater are known as *Rear of House* (ROH). Starting with the first preview performance, the stage manager must be in constant communication with the *Front of House Staff.* The FOH staff are all the people who work out front of the proscenium, including those who sell the tickets, prepare the refreshments, hand out the programs, seat the patrons, market and advertise the show, etc.

FULL UP: A lighting term that refers to a bright lighting of lamps at "full" (100%) intensity.

GENRE: A way of categorizing different types of literature or drama.

GLOSSY: An 8x10 headshot of the actor. A "glossy" refers to the shiny finish of the photo.

GLOW TAPE: Luminous yellow self-adhesive tape used to mark floors so that the stage crew can see where to place set pieces of furniture when changing out a scene during a blackout. The tape also helps to guide actors off and on the stage during the blackout.

GREASEPAINT: Refers to a special makeup supplied in stick form, used by actors for performing on the stage. Greasepaint is applied to the face or body and needs special removing cream.

GREEN ROOM: A small room or lounge adjacent to the stage where the actors in a play meet and relax, and get ready to go on. One explanation for 'green' is that in medieval days, when strolling players gave performances on the village green, a tent was set-up for them to change costumes in. One of the most famous green rooms is at Drury Lane Theater in London. Tradition holds that it was originally draped or painted in green, which some believe explains the true origin of the term.

GRID (Short for Gridiron): The scaffolding structure used to support the rigging necessary for *flying* scenery. The grid is constructed from steel or wooden beams.

GRIP: A member of the stage crew responsible for moving items of scenery during the show. A grip, like most of the stage crew, usually wears black. In the film industry, a grip handles and sets up camera equipment and lighting.

HAM: A genial term that applies to an actor who overplays his part to the point that his acting is considered a comic absurdity. To *ham it up* is to play up the part for all its worth, even to the point of overacting.

HAND PROP: Any prop handled by an actor during a performance, such as letters, books, walking cane, policeman's whistle, cigarettes, etc.

HEADSET: General term for theater communication equipment that allows the stage manager and stage crew to speak to each other. The stage manager always wears a headset.

A HEAVY: The role of a villain or a "bad guy." The term is used more in films than for the stage.

HOT SPOT: The brightest part of the beam from a lamp. And the actor does feel very hot under it!

HOUSE: Another term for the audience, as in "How big is the house tonight?" The house also refers to the auditorium itself with its rows of seats in which the audience sit to watch a performance, as in "The house is now open."

HOUSE LIGHTS: Refers to the lights that illuminate the auditorium of a theater. The house lights do not include the "exit" lights. House lights are controlled from the light booth. They are commonly dimmed or faded out when the performance starts, and are faded up during intermission or after the play ends.

INGENUE: From the original French "ingénue." It referred to the fresh and innocent young girl unawakened as yet to the wickedness of the world—a character French authors were fond of drawing, and therefore frequently found in French romantic literature from the time of Molière. Today, it is simply an old fashioned term for the female juvenile lead.

INNER STAGE: A part of the acting area which can be masked off and revealed only during certain scenes. The Elizabethan theaters, like the Globe Theater, had an "inner stage" set back in the rear, which was used for bedchamber and banquet scenes.

LANTERN: General term that refers to a unit of lighting equipment. The term has been replaced by the internationally recognized "luminaire" or "instrument." Different kinds of lanterns include flood, fresnel, spotlight, and profile.

LEGITIMATE ACTOR (Stage actor): An actor who has received training for acting on the stage in contrast to acting for television and film. A legitimate actor works in legitimate theater, also known as "live theater." Legitimate actors are expected to bring a more disciplined presence to their performances, whether stage or screen, than actors without stage training or stage experience.

LIBRETTO: The part of a musical score that contains only the lyrics or words that are sung and spoken. It is like the text or script of a musical or opera.

LIGHTING PLAN: A scale drawing that details the exact location of each lantern used in a production and any other pertinent information.

LIGHTING PLOT: The recorded information about the lighting for all the scenes. This information may be recorded in a script with the lighting cues written in and highlighted. These days, the lighting configurations are already pre-recorded into the memory of a computerised lighting board for subsequent playback as the lighting cues in the script call for them.

LIMELIGHT: An obsolete source of intensely bright light, most recently used in *followspots*. When an actor is *in the limelight* it means he is the focus of the audience's attention. This term is also used to mean that an actor has achieved a level of stardom (or notoriety).

LINE: This is what an actor calls out when he has forgotten a line. This cues the prompter (usually sitting stage left) to immediately give the actor his line.

MAKING THE ROUNDS: When an actor goes from place to place, dropping off "glossies" and "composites" to agents and casting directors.

MATINEE: A theatrical performance held during the daytime. From Latin roots, meaning "of the morning" (though most matinees take place in the afternoon). The French word "matinée" referred to the break that French workers traditionally took during a work day to attend a lecture, read the sports results, or pause for a cup of coffee, usually in the mid afternoon.

MONOLOGUE: Uninterrupted speech delivered by one character in a play, with or without the presence of other characters listening.

MORE SKIN OFF YOUR NOSE: Theatrical greeting originating in the nineteenth century when makeup was very coarse and crude, and would peel skin off the face. It is said that you could identify actors at that time by their blotchy facial appearance. So the greeting meant that the person hoped the actor would keep working and thus lose more skin off his face!

MUGGING: Using exaggerated, often excessive facial expressions.

NARRATOR: One who tells the story, while speaking directly to the audience. If the storyline has to span many years, narration can be used to summarize major events without the actors having to take time to act them all out, and thus create an overlong play. A narrator is an important component because he sets the mood and also the pace of the story, though he is not an actual character in the play. He keeps the story on theme, while sometimes acting as the direct conscience or voice of the playwright. In some cases, the narrator can be one of the main characters in a play, like Jane in *Jane Eyre*, who looks back in time and tells her story.

NOTES: Following a rehearsal, and up through the dress rehearsal, the director will give notes to the cast and crew about where to make changes, and how to improve the overall play. In repertory theaters, the director might choose to give notes through the early performances of the *run* of the play.

OFF-BROADWAY: Smaller, professional New York theaters of less than 500 seats located outside the central theater district of Broadway.

OFF-OFF-BROADWAY: Small, often eclectic experimental theaters found throughout New York City, that have a 99 or less seating capacity and operate under Equity's "Showcase Code," where actors work for free in order to get seen. These theaters can be set up in barn lofts, warehouses, or churches, and tend to stage productions that are original or push social agendas.

ONION AT THE END: An old English music hall term referring to the moment or action at the end of the play that makes the audience cry.

ON THE BOOK: An actor who needs to refer to the script during a rehearsal is said to be "on book." An actor should try to memorize his script quickly so that he can get "off book."

ON THE STAGE: A term used to refer to the acting profession, as in "What does your daughter do for a living?" "My daughter is *on the stage*."

OPENING NIGHT: If there has not been a preview show, opening night will be the first time the play is performed before an audience. The house is usually packed with friends and family, as well as one or more critics. Opening night is the most exciting time for everyone involved with the production. Opening night performance is often followed by a formal reception, a cast party, and/or an all-night vigil waiting up for the "reviews" hot off the press.

ORIENTATION: The initial gathering of the cast to make introductions, explain policies, hand out rehearsal schedules, and discuss the interpretation of the play.

OUT FRONT: A reference to the audience sitting out front, or out in front of the stage actors.

OVERTURE: The orchestral beginning of a musical play or opera. In an overture, we hear all the main themes or keynotes of the songs that make up the music score.

PLACES: A call given by the stage manager to bring those actors who appear at the beginning of the play to the wings, or onto the stage if those characters need to be preset. This call is traditionally given five minutes before curtain time.

PAINT SHOP: The room backstage where scenery is painted or decorated.

PAPER THE HOUSE: This refers to a theatrical marketing technique, where tickets for a show are given away, such as on opening night, to make a show seem to be selling better than it actually is. Free tickets may also be given to well-known celebrities with the intention to generate publicity for the show and thus create public interest.

PICK-UP: To speed up or shorten the time between a cue and the next line. This will in turn pick up the tempo of the scene.

PLAYWRIGHT: The author of the play. In theatrical tradition, the playwright was considered the most important person in the making of a theater production. Today, the leading actors in the play and/or the director share that celebrity. In musicals, the authors include the writers of the music and its lyrics.

POLISHING REHEARSAL: A rehearsal that concentrates on tightening up the timing of the actors in their delivery of lines and stage business with the intent to perfect the overall rhythm or tempo of the play.

PREPRODUCTION: A planning phase of production before the actors rehearse or are even cast. Such meetings bring together the production team in determining the staging of the play, the budget, the possibilities of set design, etc.

PREVIEW PERFORMANCE: A special performance aimed at helping the director judge the response of the audience once the play is open to the public. Usually the audience members who watch a preview show are all personally invited. Sometimes the critics attend the preview show instead of opening night. Amateur companies often provide free tickets for a preview performance to groups like handicapped children or seniors in nursing homes. Other theaters attract preview audiences with reduced admissions.

PRESET: Anything in position on the stage before the beginning of a scene or Act. Includes actors as well as set pieces and props. Stage lights are also part of the preset. Preset also refers to the lighting configurations worked out for certain scenes, which are already recorded in the memory of the computer as part of the lighting plot.

PRINCIPALS: The main actors in a show with the lead speaking roles. The principal characters in a play are responsible for advancing the conflict and storyline.

PROLOGUE: A speech or a short scene preceding the main action of the play that sets the mood or offers an introduction to the play. Some prologues can be more like expositions to the play. An example of such is the Prologue in Heaven from the First Part of Goethe's *Faust*. In this prologue, Mephistopheles wagers with God that he can lead Faust, a loyal servant of God, astray. God accepts the wager, declaring that Faust will follow "the right path."

PROMPT BOOK: This is the stage manager's production book containing the script as well as a detailed record of all cues (blocking, sound, lighting, music, etc.) used for staging the performance. It is sometimes referred to as the *Production Bible* or *Production Book*. The stage manager (or sometimes the assistant stage manager) is responsible for putting together the prompt book, and will use it to "call" the show from during performances. The prompt book is also used to provide lines to actors who forget them, or to correct blocking if the actors move incorrectly. A prompt book should be legible so that if the stage manager is unable to call the show, his notes can be understood by any of the technical crew. A show can be recreated from the information in the prompt book.

PROMPTER: This is generally the job of the stage manager during rehearsals, once the blocking is set and the actors know their lines. During performance, the prompting may be delegated to an assistant stage manager who sits on the prompt side (the position from which he prompts—usually a downstage position). The prompter may need to move around depending upon where the longer scenes are being played and where there is the best opening in the set so that he can be heard by the actors.

PROPERTY MASTER OR MISTRESS: The person responsible for the acquisition and/ or building of the stage properties (props). A property master has a master list of all items that are used in the production.

PROPS (Properties): Any moveable items used on the set of a play or handled by an actor. These might include furnishings, set dressings, and other miscellaneous items, large and small, which cannot be classified as scenery or wardrobe. Props handled by actors are known as hand props. Props which are kept as part of an actor's costume are known as personal or costume props, such as a small purse or a handkerchief.

PROP TABLE: A table placed in a convenient offstage area on which all the props are placed when not in use during the performance. The actors take their props from this table when needed, and return them to the table after use. If an actor cannot get to the prop table easily before an imminent entrance, one of the *prop crew* (or stagehands) will be responsible for taking it to the actor. Sometimes there are two prop tables, one in the stage left wings and the other in the stage right wings.

PUBLIC DOMAIN: A literary manuscript, such as an opera, play, musical, or song, that is not under copyright protection—that is, can be used freely without the user having to obtain permission from the author and/or pay him royalties.

PROSCENIUM ARCH: The opening between stage and auditorium in some theaters. Also called the *fourth wall*. Because this invisible wall is architecturally framed (like an arch), it is sometimes referred to as the picture frame through which the audience sees the play. In some older theaters, especially in Europe, the proscenium arch is ornately painted to contrast with the surrounding walls so that it will stand out. Everything that happens behind the proscenium arch is integral to the production of the show.

PUNCHLINE: A line from a play that is intended to get a laugh.

READ-THROUGH: The cast read through the play to become acquainted with the story, the characters, and the dialogue flow. A read-through also offers the opportunity for actors to ask questions, clarify meanings and pronunciations, and gain insight into the director's interpretation of the play.

REGIONAL THEATER: Also called resident theater. A term applied to nonprofit professional theater companies that are situated outside the major theater centers. Regional theaters bring a high level of performance to a region. They can offer training workshops to nurture local talent and encourage new plays of special regional interest.

REHEARSAL: From its Latin root, rehearse means "re-harrow" or to "go over again." Rehearsals are work sessions for actors and technical crew that take place continuously up to the opening of the play. Rehearsals give actors the opportunity to practice their dialogue and movement, and explore character interpretation, while the technicians can experiment with and set the lighting, sound, costuming, and other technical elements of the show. Rehearsals are needed to give cast and crew the opportunity to perfect their contributions to the production. A *Work* or *Working Rehearsal* has the objective of exploring, then setting and practicing, the artistic directions for the play. This includes not only the *blocking* of the actors, but decisions about character interpretation and line readings. A *Walk-Through Rehearsal* requires actors to walk through entrances, moves, and exits to make clear if any changes or alterations are necessary. Character lines are not spoken during a walk-through. *Line Rehearsals* take place when actors are expected to be "off book" and line perfect. A *Technical Rehearsal* is the first time the technical elements (lighting, set, etc.) are combined with actors. A *Run-Through Rehearsal* is when the actors perform long sections of the play (either an Act or the entire play) without interruption, usually to improve the sense of continuity. A *Dress Rehearsal* is a performance of the show as it will be on opening night.

REPERTOIRE: An entire stock of theatrical material, whether dramatic or musical, that is already known and can be performed by a company of actors. Sometimes a community or regional theater, for example, will stage one of its popular repertoire shows every two or three years. This is especially the case with companies that specialize in particular kinds of musicals, such as Gilbert and Sullivan operas, or standard Rodgers and Hammerstein favorites.

REPERTORY (Rep): A permanent theater company of actors that presents performances of different plays within one season, each production having a limited run, and using the same actors. At any one time in a repertory season, there is normally one production in performance, another in rehearsal, and several others in varying degrees of preproduction.

RESUME: Professional information which an actor attaches to his 8x10 headshot, including credits, training, personal information, etc.

REVOLVE (Revolving stage): A large turntable which turns the set so that, even though two or more scenes may be on the revolve, only one is visible to the audience at one time. The turntable is built into the stage floor and then driven into view. Actors can perform on a turntable and appear as though they are moving. Usually requires a false stage floor to hide steel cables that would drive it.

RISER: Any platform on the stage. The series of platforms for choral presentations are called choral risers. Risers provide varying heights on a stage. They can be covered over with canvas and then painted so that a series of risers can look like rocks or hills.

ROYALTIES: The prescribed fee paid to an author (or his agent) for the right to perform his work.

SCENARIO: An outline of the story of the play.

SCENE: Divisions within an Act of a play, usually denoting a change in time or place. A *Scene Breakdown* is a list of scenes showing which characters are in which scenes.

SCRIPT: The text or written form of the play that tells the story. The script includes all the dialogue, as well as information about the characters, stage directions, time and locale of scenes, costumes, and other details provided by the playwright to aid the cast and crew in their interpretation and staging.

SEGUE: Originally a musical term for an immediate follow-on from one section of music to another. The term is now used generally to mean any immediate follow on.

SET: The complete stage setting or decoration for a scene or Act.

SILHOUETTE: A lighting effect when you light the performer from upstage, or when you light a backdrop behind him or her.

SOLILOQUY: Lines delivered by an actor as if talking to himself. A soliloquy is spoken alone onstage and is used as a theatrical device to express the inner, most private thoughts of the character. The purpose of a soliloquy, therefore, is to let the audience know what the character is thinking and feeling. A soliloquy is always introspective and usually highly emotional, as in Hamlet's "To be or not to be..." speech.

SOUND EFFECTS (Abbreviated SFX): These are sounds not produced by the actors on the stage, but are created to add to the atmosphere of a scene. Sound effects can be prerecorded or may be performed live offstage. If recorded, Digital Audio Tapes (DAT's) or Compact Discs (CD's) work well. The *Sound Technician* can find many sources for his sound effects, including downloading an infinite selection from the internet. Some plays require no sound effects, others require hundreds. In a play like

The Secret Garden, a variety of recorded sound effects are needed, such as the action of an old train arriving at and departing from a railway station, heavy rain, thunder and lightning, the wind on the moor, a child's ghostlike cry in the night, as well as numerous and varying robin chirps. Some sound effects are more effective when performed live, like a gunshot, a door slam, a scream, or offstage voices talking.

SPECIAL EFFECTS: Technology-produced effects that add moments of splendor and spectacle to the play, or provide a shocking or moving impact. Although "special effects" is a technical term for the manipulation of filmed images, many modern theaters, equipped with multi-media audiovisual systems, can create quite dazzling special effects that heighten the experience of the play for the audience. Special effects are essential in fantasy productions, such as *The Wizard of Oz*, where the magical power that the Wizard holds over Dorothy and her friends can only be conveyed to the audience by the use of specific technologies such as robotics and mechanical illusions. Special effects applied to the traditional stage can never be as technologically overpowering as those created in films such as *Armageddon, Star Wars*, and *King Kong*, but they can and do worthily contribute to the magic of the theater experience.

SPOTLIGHT (Spot): A type of lantern whose beam is focused through a lens or series of lenses to make it more controllable. When we *spotlight* an actor, we focus a strong light on him. A spotlight is often used for a soliloquy (or musical solos or duets) in order to attract the audience's attention to the most important person or people onstage.

STAGE BUSINESS: Small pieces of action performed by actors on the stage to establish a character presence, fill a pause in dialogue, or create some realistic action in a scene. Stage business can be scripted or unscripted (improvised), and is often comic in intention.

STAGE CREW: Members of the production staff who are responsible for moving props and/or scenery during the show, and for ensuring that these items are working correctly and are properly maintained. Stage crew are also known as *Stagehands*.

STAGE DOOR: The backstage door to the theater through which the director, actors, and technical crew enter and exit. The stage door is not open to the public. Large theaters normally have a *Stage Door Keeper*, who takes messages for performers and acts as a security guard at the door entrance. The stage door keeper is traditionally held in high regard as he knows everyone, guards and preserves the privacy of the actors, deals with unauthorized people who feel entitled to meet the "stars" of the show, and expertly manages the press.

STAGE MANAGER: The person responsible for the artistic integrity and smooth execution of a show for the duration of its scheduled run. He is also responsible for the safety and security of the entire production staff. He attends all rehearsals and meetings, coordinates all the production elements, and knows the show forwards and backwards. The stage manager puts together the prompt book, which contains a copy of the script annotated with all production cues. He uses it to "call the show"— that is, to give the signals to actors and technical crew to execute their cues. He is also the person who takes over from the director and runs the show after it opens. A stage manager is never recognized for the amount of work he does.

STEAL A SCENE: To attract attention that should be on another actor. A *Prima Donna* (the principal woman soloist in an opera production) or a *Star* (the leading actor of a show) is often accused of stealing scenes from supporting actors when both are on the stage (or screen) at the same time. A prima donna is sometimes used to describe an artist who is demanding and difficult to please—as in, "She's a real prima donna."

STOCK SCENERY: Scenery that is stored and used over and over again for many different productions, such as flats and risers or a standard sky-cyc.

STRIKE: To remove or strip from the stage its sets and props. The stage crew do this either in between scenes or in between Acts, depending upon the need to change an existing set and replace it with another. After a show has finished its run, the actors often help the stage crew strike the entire set and all the properties from the stage area.

SUBTEXT: The implied or unspoken thoughts that accompany the text or dialogue delivered by an actor. When actors learn to express subtext in their characterizations, they help achieve more truth and subtlety in their performance, as long as the subtext matches the author's original intention.

SUMMER STOCK: Theater companies that operate in regional areas, outside the accepted theatrical centers. They mount productions during the summer months and produce an intensive season of plays. Summer stock provides a great opportunity for actors to work hard and improve their technique, as well as invite agents and/or directors to come and see them perform in a variety of roles.

TABLEAU: A suspended moment onstage in which a living picture is created and held by the actors without motion or speech as the lights fade down or the curtain falls.

TAG LINE: A final line of a scene or Act, or the exit line of a major character. When it is the final line of an Act, it is also called a *Curtain Line*.

TAKE FIVE: A slang term used to indicate that you are going to take a break from working for five minutes. Directors, stage managers, and choreographers use it a lot. Quite often the break is never exactly five minutes, but more like ten or fifteen.

TECHNICAL REHEARSAL (Tech Rehearsal): The first time the show is rehearsed in the *venue* (the place where the performance will take place) with lighting, scenery, and sound. Costumes are sometimes incorporated in a tech rehearsal when there is concern about an actor needing to do quick costume changes. Technical rehearsals are needed for perfecting the integration of all the technical elements of the show with the actors onstage. These rehearsals are very important to the smooth running and proper tempo of the production. A *Dry Tech* is a technical rehearsal without the actors present. Its purpose is to rehearse all the technical elements together—lighting, sound, scenic changes, etc. It follows that a *Wet Tech* is a full technical rehearsal with actors present. A *Paper Tech* is a work session without the set or actors when the technical and design team talk through the show ensuring everything's going to work as planned. The stage manager often uses this session to make sure all the technical notes are written correctly in his prompt book.

TEMPO: The pace of a scene. Tempo depends largely on cue pickup, the delivery speed of the lines, the intensity and energy level of the actors, and the overall rhythm of the technical elements working together with the artistic.

THESPIAN: Named after the Greek poet and actor, Thespis, considered to be the founder of Greek tragedy. A thespian is a follower of Thespis—in other words, an actor.

THESPIS: A Greek poet and actor who is said to have been the inventor of Greek tragedy. He was the first prize winner at the Great (or City) Dionysia, a religious festival held in Athens, Greece in 534 BC. He was an innovator for the theater, who introduced the idea of the independent actor, as opposed to the choir. The word for actor, "thespian," comes from his name.

TIMING: A more specific term than tempo, timing refers to the choosing of the exact moment to say a line or to execute an action onstage in order to elicit from the audience the desired response.

TONY: Awards given annually by the American Theater Wing for Excellence in the Theater. Officially called the Antoinette Perry Awards, they cover 25 categories of artistic and technical performance, including Best Play, Best Performance by a Leading Actor in a Play, Best Performance by a Leading Actress in a Play, Best Musical, Best Original Score, Best Scenic Design of a Play, Best Choreography, etc.

Antigone and Ismene

Two of the most beloved character roles from the play *Antigone* by Sophocles

Electra

From the *Electra* of Sophocles, Electra laments over the urn containing her brother's ashes, and plots her vengeance. One of the great tragic heroines of Greek theater, the character of Electra grows from deep despair to spiritual exaltation.

Phedra and Hyppolytus

The tragic Phedra from Jean Racine's play, *Phedra*, is considered the greatest female acting role in dramatic literature.

The Sacrifice of Iphigenia

The character of Iphigenia, a coveted acting role, was immortalized in *Iphigenia in Tauris* by Euripides, and in the poem *The Sacrifice of Iphigenia* by Aeschylus.

TORMENTORS: Narrow masking flats adjacent and sometimes at right angles to the proscenium arch. The term is used interchangeably with *Returns*. Tormentors are so named because they stop you from being able to peep into the secrets of the wings.

TRAGEDY: A play genre or type of drama that deals with the issues of human suffering. In classical (or ancient) tragedy, the protagonist is noble, whose suffering and death are brought about by a tragic flaw in his character, or by circumstances outside his control. The most famous of the Greek tragedies are the *Oedipus* plays of Sophocles, and *Oresteia* (a trilogy) of Aeschylus, which deal with man in conflict with the gods as he struggles toward self-perfection. *Hamlet, Othello,* and *King Lear* are the most beloved Shakespearean tragedies. Modern tragedy generally deals with the domestic struggles of ordinary people in situations of human conflict, which lead to defeat and death. Their realistic content largely explains why they are written in prose rather than the more uplifting poetic verse.

TRAP: An opening through the stage floor that is often used for special stage effects, such as having scenery or performers rise from below. A trap also allows the construction of a staircase which ostensibly leads to a lower floor or cellar. A *Grave Trap* is a lowered rectangular section used in a churchyard scene, such as the one in *Hamlet,* when Hamlet discovers the skull of Yorick, the King's jester, and recalls the merriment of the fellow.

TRAP ROOM: The area directly below the trapped part of the stage.

TRAVELER: A horizontally drawn curtain. Can be referred to as a *Traverse* curtain.

TURN: An antiquated name for an actor. The term was used in earlier centuries most often by the technical crew, as in "The new turn will give us some problems."

TYPECAST: An actor who is regularly cast in the same kind of role due to physical similarity (rather than acting skill) to a certain dramatic or comedic type. An actor can also be typecast because he is known to play that kind of role effectively and so is a safe bet for the director. Actors are more often typecast in films than in stage productions, since stage actors are trained to take on diverse roles. If an actor is cast in a completely different role to what he normally plays, he's said to have been cast *Against Type*, and that his character is *Out-of-Type*.

UNDERSTUDY: An actor who has learned and rehearsed the part of one of the leading actors, and who is therefore prepared to take over the role in the event of illness or some other emergency. Often the understudy already has a (smaller) role in the play. In true theater tradition, some understudies have gone on to become stars by outshining the actors they replaced. An example is Catherine Zeta-Jones. When just 17, while living in London, she signed on for the chorus of the musical *42nd Street*. She became second understudy to the lead. One evening, both the lead and the first understudy were sick, leaving Catherine to fill in as the lead, Peggy Sawyer. That night the show's producer, David Merrick, who had never attended any of the previous performances, happened to catch this one. He was so impressed that he gave her the lead full-time, and she played it for nearly two years.

UPPER CIRCLE: Highest balcony in the auditorium. Also known as the *Gods*. Normally has a very steep view down to the stage, and the seating is highly raked. The term is a carry-over from English theater.

USHERS: Members of front-of-house staff who guide the audience to their seats. Ushers often sit in the auditorium during the show in case of any emergency, or to prevent latecomers from trying to find their seats once the performance has begun—an activity that can be distracting to the actors on the stage.

WARDROBE: General name referring to the costume department, its staff, or the costumes themselves. A *Wardrobe (Costume) Designer* is the person who designs and usually makes the costumes needed for a play. She also supervises the *Wardrobe Mistress*, whose job is to make sure all the costumes are available for the actors when needed and remain in good order for the duration of the run of the play. The wardrobe mistress also helps the actors get dressed and takes care of any minor mending or alterations. In smaller theaters, the costume designer *is* the wardrobe mistress. A wardrobe mistress normally prepares a *Wardrobe Plot:* an actor-by-actor, scene-by-scene inventory of all the costumes in a production, with a detailed breakdown into every separate item comprising each costume.

WARM UP: A work session in which the actors prepare their bodies through a number of physical and mental exercises. Singers warm up with voice scales, while dancers limber up with stretching and dance steps.

WASH: A lighting term referring to a large spread or "wash" of softly focused light that covers the entire stage, as in "We'll use the violet wash for the love scene."

KEY: Getting to the heart of the issue

For an actor, the language of the theater speaks to the heart.

GOLDEN RULE EIGHT: Critique, not criticize, the efforts of your fellow actors.

When an actor works in a classroom with other students, he wants to feel assured that what he does in front of his colleagues is not ridiculed, and that his efforts are evaluated fairly and intelligently. He wants to be critiqued and not criticized. An actor exposes his personal vulnerabilities when he performs, since what he creates in the classroom or on the stage is expressive of himself. This is especially true when the actor is just beginning to learn his craft. The greatest fear of an actor is that he or his abilities are not thought well of.

When you critique, you point out what worked theatrically and what didn't work, and why. You offer suggestions for how to make it work better next time. When you criticize, you demean the actor's abilities, which he can interpret as a personal attack. Critiquing involves a considered, intelligent, and respectful analysis of the creative work performed and the person who performed it; criticizing places the emphasis on finding and pointing out what was wrong or bad. As a form of censure, it is not constructive, since it promotes discouragement, self-consciousness, and sometimes bad will. Know the difference between the two.

Director's Notes: This rule is especially important when working with little children, who are very sensitive to criticism. Every big and little effort by them should earn lavish praise. If you see a poor effort, say something like, "What a wonderful job you did. Do you think you could make it even more wonderful?" If the student answers "no," ask the other students if they can think of any way the performance could be made even better than it was.

KEY: Getting to the heart of the issue

**It only takes a moment to crush a tiny bud.
Always be kind and helpful to other actors.**

THE GOLDEN RULE: Do unto others as you would have them do unto you.

Unit
Study
Three

The Theatrical Cue

3

The Theatrical Cue

Class materials needed: Handout #3-1, *Theatrical Cue*
Handout #3-2, *Do Not Upstage*
Two medium-sized sponge balls

Instructions: Some of the exercises performed in previous units will be repeated from time to time as a pre-class workout, in some cases with more progressive skill levels added, which will be indicated by the words *Level Two Action, Level Three*, etc. Since students are often anxious or excited when they come to class, it's good to start off with Exercise 2-2 or optionally Exercise 2-1. The whole class should participate in these exercises, as they are necessary for building fundamental relaxation skills.

Repeat Exercise 2-2: The Body Flop or Exercise 2-1: Simple Warm-Ups

Repeat Exercise 2-3: Navigating the Stage

> *Director's Notes:* Make sure that every student can easily navigate all the stage blocking positions on the playing area. Students take turns giving the directions (as the director) and receiving directions (as the actor).

Read out loud more "theater talk" definitions from Golden Rule Seven, or have the students quiz each other.

Repeat Exercise 2-6: Stage Entrances and Exits, *Level One Action*

EXERCISE 2-6 Stage Entrances and Exits

Level Two Action:

- Place a chair CS (center stage).

- Choose two students and direct them, one at a time, according to the sample stage directions given below. The first student will be Actor #1. The second student will be Actor #2.

Director's Notes: When you give the stage directions listed below to the students, make sure you speak what the letters stand for. For example, say "enters downstage right" rather than "enters DR."

1   Actor #1 enters UR, Xs (crosses) to chair C, sits.
2   Actor #2 enters UL, Xs to LC, turns quarter right and looks at Actor#1.
3   Actor #1 rises from chair, looks over at Actor #2, then Xs to DC.
4   Actor #2 Xs to DR, looks out as if through a window.
5   Actor #1 turns quarter right and looks at Actor#2.
6   Actor #2 looks across to Actor #1, does open turn and Xs out UL.
7   Actor #1 Xs out DR.

Because the spectator's eyes move left to right, an actor crossing from stage left to stage right has a stronger presence than an actor moving from stage right to stage left.

Level Three Action: Remove chair from stage for this level. Ask two actors to volunteer. Give each actor four consecutive directions to execute. Actor #2 enters only after Actor #1 completes his blocking. For example:

- Tell Actor #1 to enter UL, X (cross) to CS, count to ten, exit UR.

- Tell Actor #2 to enter UR, X to DL, count to five, exit UL.

Level Four Action: Make the directions to one actor dependent on what the other actor does. For example:

- Using the directions given in Level Three, tell Actor # 1 to enter UL, X to CS.

- Tell Actor #2 to enter UR and X to DL.

- When Actor #2 reaches his DL position, Actor #1 should count to ten.

- When Actor #1 is finished counting to ten, Actor #2 should start counting to five.
- When Actor #2 reaches the count of three, Actor #1 turns and exits UR.
- Once Actor #2 completes his count of five, he makes his exit UL.

Level Five Action: This time use three actors.

- The students themselves make up a scenario of interconnected moves.
- Each student takes a turn at being either director or actor.
- You can increase difficulty by asking students to add simple lines of dialogue instead of counting.

Director's Notes: The Stage Entrances and Exits exercise makes the student aware that the directed moves of each actor onstage are the building blocks that make up a complete stage action. Critique the accuracy with which each actor follows his specific directions, the proper sequence of his interactions with the other actors, and his walking, turning, sitting, and standing positions. Remind the students not to look down when they walk. Keep head up at all times, especially when they speak lines.

The Theatrical Cue

Director's Notes: Distribute Handout #3-1, *Theatrical Cue.*

A stage production must follow a preconceived blueprint, like any construction project. Each building block used to assemble a home is placed, secured, and sealed before the next one can be applied. Likewise, a theatrical play is composed of building blocks called *cues.* When an architect designs a home, he knows exactly what materials he needs to build it, and the builder knows exactly how to put all the materials together to make it look and stand as the architect envisions. Each building block, whether a 2x4 block of wood, a concrete slab, a brick, a steel girder, a piece of siding, a sheet of glass, or even a small nail has a special role to play if the house is to be successfully put together according to the original design. In theater, the *playwright* is the architect, the *producer* is the company or individual financing the project, the *director* is the builder, the *stage manager* is the foreman, and the *actors* are the workmen.

A *theatrical cue* is the term we use to describe all the individual building blocks that go together to make up the play. Every stage direction is chosen by the director to enhance a more truthful performance by the actor and to further the storyline of the play as the author intended. Every light, sound, scenery, special effects, music, and curtain cue, every line of dialogue, action, interaction, and reaction, every movement, gesture, and facial expression of the actor is a theatrical cue. Together, they make up the tapestry of the theatrical experience. Together, they make magic.

E X E R C I S E 3-1 Imagine the Play

Director's Notes: Use a real headset with a built-in microphone for this exercise.

- Ask the students to imagine that they are seated in a theater about to watch a live play. Ask them: What would you be doing while you are waiting for the show to begin? Reading the program? Chatting to the person next to you? Looking around the auditorium? Finishing a cough drop? Calling a friend on the cell phone?

- Position yourself by a main light switch and begin *stage manager's* monologue: I want you to imagine that I am the stage manager of the play you are about to watch. It is *The Secret Garden*. As stage manager, I am responsible for making sure that all the director's cues written into my prompt book are executed properly. I am wearing a headset with a built-in microphone so that I can communicate with my actors and all the technical crew backstage. Sometimes I like to "call" the show from the lighting booth at the back of the house where I have good sightlines of the stage. Sometimes I prefer to call the show from the wings of the stage. If I do so, I use a mini-light to read my prompt book, since it is dark backstage. I am now ready to start the show.

- *(Speak quietly into the headset microphone.)* Front-of-house, stand by house lights. Ushers hold latecomers. "House lights down GO" *(Turn off all the lights in the room.)* "Stand by light cue 1. *(Wait three seconds.)* Light cue 1 stage lights up GO." *(Turn the stage lights on, or if there is not a separate switch for that part of the room, leave as is.)* "Stand by music cue 1. Is Mary preset on bed? Is Ayah waiting DL? Music cue 1 GO. Stand by curtain cue 1. Listen for change of tempo in bar 6. *(Wait four seconds.)* Curtain cue 1 GO. Stand by music cue 2. Fade out when Mary steps up to window. *(Wait six seconds.)* Music cue 2 GO. Stand by Ayah enter DL on Mary's word cue "Jamila." *(Wait five seconds.)* Ayah enter DL GO. Are Rose and John UL? Is Rose's champagne glass on prop table? Stand by music cue 3 when Ayah exits DL. *(Wait four seconds.)* Prop crew stage left, place glass in Rose's hand. Music cue 3 GO. Stand by Rose and John enter UL. Stand by sound cue 1—waiting for Mary's word "Mother." *(Wait five seconds.)* Sound cue 1 GO. Rose and John enter UL GO.

- Remove the headset.

And so it continues. Before we have completed the very first scene of the play, the stage manager has already executed dozens of cues. There are thousands of theatrical cues programmed during the life of a play. The actors, lighting and sound technicians, set and property assistants, and all coworkers in the production share the responsibility for the theatrical cues, but it is the stage manager who signals the execution of the cues by the operative word, GO.

With experienced technicians, the director does not need to describe what the cue is as I did in the exercise above. Usually only the cue number is sufficient, as in "Light cue 1 GO" instead of "Light cue 1 stage lights up GO."

The cues given by the stage manager signify when certain things should happen either onstage or behind the scenes. During the show, a stage manager will follow the performance as it unfolds line by line or, if there is no dialogue, by whatever the actors do in their blocking. The stage manager uses his prompt book, which contains all the cues, to call the show. The first thing he does is to give the technicians the signal of warning for the cue coming up. In the scenario above, I left out the warning signal in order to compress time. Normally it is called a half (script) page before the cue is meant to be executed. Saying, for example, "Warning light cue 8" tells the light board operator to be aware that light cue 8 will be coming up soon. Following the warning signal, the stage manager gives a stand by signal, usually several seconds before the GO of that cue. Saying, "Stand by light cue 8" tells the technician that light cue 8 will happen in just a few seconds. The key signal is the GO. When the stage manager calls the word GO, as in, "Light cue 8 GO," the technician executes that particular cue.

The stage manager's cues are invisible to the audience. No matter how many there are, or how heavy some sets might be to move in between scenes or Acts, everything must flow smoothly and effortlessly, or at least give that impression to the audience. All theatrical cues should be executed without the audience being aware of them happening on the stage or behind the scenes. The only time an audience might be aware of these cues is if something goes wrong and the rhythm of the play is disrupted—for example, an actor might forget his line, a stage set might fall down, a character might miss his entrance cue, the lighting technician might hit the Blackout cue by mistake, or the CD with the sound cues might create a discordant static during a scene. In these cases, the stage manager, in communication with the director (if he is still around) and technical crew, has to make on-the-spot decisions to remedy the situation or mask the errant cue so that the stage magic is sustained.

It is important to know that some technicians are not in a position backstage to either see or hear what is happening onstage. In other words, they are blind as to when their cues should be executed, and thus are totally dependent upon the stage manager to tell them. Therefore the word GO must not be used under any circumstances except by the stage manager as the critical signal to execute a cue.

In many community and children's theaters, the stage manager delegates the execution of the cues to the individual technicians, as long as they are familiar with the production and are in a position to see and hear what is taking place on the stage. This frees up the stage manager to concentrate on other aspects of the performance, such as helping any children prepare for their entrances and exits, which is quite a chore, especially in large dramatic and musical productions.

Unless they are traveling troupes, such as the Missoula Children's Theater, who mount a prepackaged show, most children's theaters rely heavily on volunteers to work the technical aspects of a show. In many cases, the technicians are the older students who are not in the production, or who have parts that allow them to do double duty both onstage and behind the scenes as well.

Every theater production is a team effort. The director, the actors onstage, the stage manager and technical assistants working under him, the ushers, and even the box office helpers out front work together as equal players on the team. The director is responsible for the choice and proper sequence of each and every cue to create a seamless theater experience. The stage manager is responsible for executing each and every one of these cues to ensure that the director's artistic vision is realized. Just as the builder's goal is to assemble the house so that everything fits together and no single component stands out, the director's goal is to mount the play as one cohesive piece. The director is not concerned about making one actor shine as the star. No team can achieve its goal without the cooperation and synchronization of all players.

KEY: Getting to the heart of the issue

A theatrical cue grows out of the truth or theatrical life of the play. We do not think, we do not feel, we do not act on the stage without a theatrical cue.

THEATER GAME 3-1 Magic Cue Ball

Set-Up:

- Students form a large circle. (For more than 12 to 15 students, create two smaller circles, in which case you will need two sponge balls.) The circle represents the cast in a play, and each student represents an actor in that cast.

- Hold up one of the sponge balls and announce: "You may think this is just an ordinary sponge ball. Well, it is not. It is a magic cue ball. It represents a theatrical cue."

- Appoint a team captain and give him or her one of the colored balls.

- Explain that each time the ball is thrown to a player, it's as if an actor is giving a cue to another actor onstage. That actor responds to the cue by catching the ball, and then he sends his own cue on to yet another actor, and so forth.

Goal of Game: To send the ball around to each player in the circle, following a prescribed pattern of throwing, in order to complete one round or as many rounds as possible without anyone dropping the ball. This is a *magic* cue ball because without the successful execution of the cue from actor to actor, in a proper and ordered timing sequence, there can be no completion of dramatic action.

Level One Action:

- The captain creates and originates the course of the ball. He throws it to the person opposite him in the circle.

- Then the captain directs that person to throw the ball to someone else in the circle, usually the person farthest away from him.

- The captain then directs the person who has received the ball to throw it to a fourth player and so on until everyone has thrown and received the ball once and the ball returns to the captain.

- The captain needs to memorize the route that he sets in motion, as some players may forget who their ball partner is.

- The ball should be thrown under the arm in softball pitching style and not over the shoulder as in baseball. It should be thrown carefully and with a steady rhythm to provide the maximum opportunity for the receiving partner to catch it.

- Each player focuses on only two things and nothing else: the person he is receiving the ball from and the person he is sending the ball to. If any player drops the ball, the ball is returned to the captain and the round starts again from the beginning.

Goal of Level One: To complete three uninterrupted rounds. By the end of Level One, all players should have the route memorized.

Director's Notes: The game's success is built upon the concentration of each player in the circle. One lapse by one player aborts the round. Make sure each player stays in the circle and throws the ball gently underarm. The student should not be watching other players throwing or receiving their balls. His entire attention should be locked on the person who will be throwing the ball to him. The little ones may never move beyond Level One using only one ball. Their coordination and concentration skills are less developed and they are more easily distracted. Make it easy for them to complete one round by having them stand in a small, tight circle feeding the ball to each other.

Level Two Action:

- When three uninterrupted rounds have been accomplished, add a second ball and appoint a second team captain. (You will need four balls if you have two circles.)

- As soon as the person who captain #1 throws the ball to catches it, captain #2 starts off the second ball, throwing it along the same route.

- For this level, both balls should be thrown along the same course so that each player has the same partners for both balls.

Goal of Level Two: To complete one to three uninterrupted rounds.

Director's Notes: The cues have now been doubled and a higher level of concentration is required. Remind students to remain silent during the exercise. There should be no embellishment of cues (such as a student making a dramatic dive for the ball or yelling out when someone misses a ball). The cues should be delivered by each player silently and efficiently, without a lot of show. If a player forgets where he is supposed to throw the ball, only the captain should remind him, not one of the other players.

The cue is the building block of the scene. Anything unnecessary or "extra" that is added to a cue will force the other actors to react and thus distract their focus from the original and essential cue. Throwing a ball carelessly is like throwing a line away or delivering it so inaudibly that both the audience and the other actor waiting for that cue will miss it or have to strain to hear it. In addition, a player who gets distracted by the ball cues of other players is like the actor who forgets his lines when his cue comes because he is too concerned with the other actors' lines or is simply not concentrating hard enough on his own job. You could compare this to an outfielder in a baseball game who misses an easy flyball because he is not paying attention, or because he is too interested in watching one of the other players react to the hit.

KEY: Getting to the heart of the issue

> Concentration simplifies the most complicated task.
> Distraction complicates the simplest task.

THEATER GAME 3-2 The Roadrunner Cue

Set-Up:

- Students set up two lines of chairs vertically from one end of the room to the other. Each chair in the line should be touching the one next to it. The chairs in the two lines should face each other and be about two to three feet apart. The knees of opposite players shouldn't touch.

- Place an extra chair at the top of the lines facing in toward the players. This is called the Victory seat.

- Appoint a team captain.

- All students except the captain sit in the chairs. (If there are not enough students to fill two equal rows of players with one assigned as a captain, the director should be the captain.) The captain stands at the bottom end of the two lines, opposite the Victory seat at the top end. The students represent two competing teams, Team A and Team B.

Goal of Game: To see which team is the fastest to send the roadrunner cue to the Victory seat.

Action:

- Each player joins hands with the player next to him. The two players at the top of the line next to the Victory seat rest their free hand on their knee. These two are chairmen of their respective teams.

- Players at the bottom end of the lines join their free hand with the left and right hands (respectively) of the captain.

- The roadrunner cue is a squeeze of the hand. The captain initiates the first squeeze simultaneously to both Team A and Team B and each of the seated players passes it on in order to the person next to him.

- When the last player (the chairman) of each team feels the squeeze, he slaps the Victory seat with his free hand.

- The first team that slaps the Victory seat wins the game point.

- The captain keeps score, and the team that first earns 10 game points wins the match.

- Repeat the game at least three times, mix players each time, and give other students the opportunity to be captain or chairman of a team.

- The captain should mix up the rhythm of his squeeze cues—for example, the first time he sends the cue, he may only wait a few seconds. Another time, he may wish to wait 5 or 10 seconds, thus keeping the players in a state of anticipation.

Director's Notes: Be sure the captain changes the rhythm of his squeeze cues. When a team can predict a steady rhythm, the players will often jump the gun and pass on a cue that hasn't been given. If that happens, the team should be penalized a point. Impress the importance of receiving and passing on the cue silently and quickly without a great show. It can be distracting if a player excitedly jumps out of his seat when he receives the cue. Extraneous behavior lessens everyone's concentration.

KEY: Getting to the heart of the issue

No player is more important than another in achieving the goal. Be a team player!

Do Not Upstage

Director's Notes: Distribute Handout #3-2, *Do Not Upstage.*

Upstaging means to draw the audience's attention away from the actor who is speaking or around whom the action is centered in a particular scene. Upstaging results in a weakened stage presence of the actor who is upstaged.

There is a right time to diminish a character's presence as well as a wrong time, depending on the character, line of dialogue, and emotional or dramatic context of the scene. The only right time to upstage is when a director *intends* a weakened stage presence of one character in order to enhance the dramatic moment for another character in the scene. The wrong time to upstage is when an actor upstages either himself or another actor through poor technique or inexperience.

An actor gains a *strong* presence by stepping forward (downstage), speaking lines full front, straightening up, placing the weight of his body on the forward foot, cheating the body out to the audience when speaking a line, rising from a chair (lower to higher stage level), raising an arm, or walking (toward) downstage.

An actor creates a *weak* presence by stepping backward (upstage), slouching, looking down at the floor, placing the weight of his body on the rear foot, sitting down, lowering an arm, walking (toward) upstage, or turning around and walking away from another actor or object.

Do not upstage yourself (unless specifically directed to) by:

1. Turning your body upstage (away from the audience) when speaking lines

2. Speaking lines directly to another actor instead of cheating out to the audience

3. Standing directly behind another actor or standing upstage of him when you are speaking your lines

4. Lowering yourself or sitting down on a chair when speaking lines

5. Stepping or leaning backward while delivering a line or during action.

Do not upstage another actor (unless specifically directed to) by:

1. Standing in front of or downstage of the actor who is speaking

2. Moving or making a gesture while another actor is speaking or is the focus of the dramatic action

3. Creating any kind of sound that competes with the other actor's lines

EXERCISE 3-2 Upstaging
_____

•   Students practice different ways of upstaging themselves and other actors, as listed above.

Simplified Explanation for Little Children

Instructions: For the younger children, use the term *The Naughty No's* when referring to things that we should *not* do when we are onstage. To make it easier for the children to remember, you may wish to type out in a big font the following list of the *Naughty No's* and provide them as handouts or post them somewhere in the classroom. Keep adding to the list as you and the children discover more things *not* to do onstage.

The Naughty No's

1. Do not talk out loud backstage or in the wings. Whisper everything!

2. Do not eat or drink (unless it's a sip of water) just before you go onstage.

3. Do not chew gum before you go onstage. You might forget to take it out of your mouth!

4. Do not peek through the main curtain to see the audience.

5. Do not let the audience see your makeup and costume until you walk onstage. You want it to be a surprise!

6. Do not stand in front of another actor so that the audience can't see him.

7. Do not turn your face or body away from the audience when you speak.

8. Do not speak at the same time that another actor is speaking.

9. Do not move around, sing, or dance when another actor is speaking.

10. Do not run around another actor or anywhere on the stage.

11. Do not scratch yourself when you are onstage, especially when another actor is speaking his lines.

12. Do not touch or tickle another actor just because you feel like it.

13. Do not laugh at another actor when he says or does something onstage that you think is funny or silly.

14. Do not whisper another actor's lines to him if he forgets them.

15. Do not decide to sit or lie down onstage just because you feel tired.

16. Do not call out or wave to your mom and dad in the audience when you are on the stage.

17. Do not tell the audience you have forgotten a line. It must be a secret!

KEY: Getting to the heart of the issue

Your character lives a short life onstage. Never upstage a single moment of it!

Unit
Study
Four

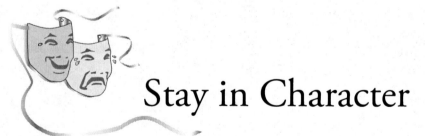

Stay in Character

4

Stay in Character

Class materials needed: Handout #4-1, *Stay in Character*
Three sponge balls, one a different color
A thick, soft-fibered rope at least six feet long
Two thick oven mitts

Repeat Theater Game 3-1: Magic Cue Ball

Director's Notes: After the completion of three uninterrupted rounds, introduce Level Two Action. If that goal is accomplished, introduce Level Three.

THEATER GAME 3-1 Magic Cue Ball

Level Three Action: Level Two required the successful passing of two balls around the circle. The balls were the same color and followed identical courses.

- For Level Three, replace one of the balls with a different-colored ball.

- After the two team captains are appointed, the first captain sets a course and starts the game. After the players become familiar with the course, the second captain begins his round, but instead of following the same course as the first captain, he reverses that course. For example, if the second captain normally receives the ball from Susie in the original round, he would start his course by throwing the ball to her. In other words, whoever you send the first ball to, you will receive the second ball from.

- Give the students a few practice rounds to get used to the two different courses. Only after the players successfully complete one or two rounds of each course separately should the students start passing the two balls at the same time.

- When both balls are thrown, both captains should start at the same time so that the two different courses run simultaneously. The players are essentially juggling two balls that are being passed around at the same time but going in reverse directions.

Goal of Level Three: To complete one uninterrupted round.

> *Director's Notes:* The cues have not only been doubled but mirror image each other. The players need to concentrate and keep extraneous cues to a minimum. The captains alone should remind players who their partners are if they forget.

Stay in Character

> *Director's Notes:* Distribute Handout #4-1, *Stay in Character.*

The most important rule in acting is to *never break character.* Making your part believable from the moment you appear onstage to the moment you make your final exit is your first priority. You should be true to your character—no matter what!

In this handout, you see the actors standing in a circle, which we call "the Magic Presence." This is where your character lives. Around this circle are "slings and arrows of outrageous fortune," which the character Hamlet spoke of in Shakespeare's play of the same name. All extraneous cues (that is, cues that do not grow out of the life of the character or do not contribute to the unfolding of the play) are like slings and arrows that try to penetrate the circle of your character attitude and destroy your concentration and thus your stage presence. Remember that your convincing stage presence is what creates magic for the audience.

The same rules help us get through life. Once we decide what we want to accomplish, it is important not to let extraneous influences distract us from our course. As in life, we must be prepared onstage for unexpected "slings and arrows" and never let them overcome us. It sometimes requires quick thinking and ingenuity to outsmart the distractions. In theater we practice exercises in improvisation to develop the ability to spontaneously invent new cues that absorb or cover over the interruptions of the disrupting, extraneous cues.

Countless stories from both World War I and World War II speak of how American GI's improvised in life-threatening situations to outsmart the German and Japanese strategies of offence. It was more than good command leadership and technology that won the war; it was good old Yankee or GI ingenuity—the ability to adapt to a difficult situation with a practical and clever resourcefulness. As actors, we must employ that same kind of spontaneous quick thinking to ensure that we, too, can stay focused against all opposition and achieve our goal. Ingenuity is the stuff of heroes. It is also the stuff of great actors.

E X E R C I S E 4-1 The Extraneous Cue

An extraneous cue is a cue that is not essential or pertinent to the dramatic action. The term also refers to movement or dialogue coming from without that may distract from the real action. (This exercise is not dependent on whether or not the students complete Level Two or Level Three of the Magic Cue Ball game.)

- The students form the same kind of circle as in the Magic Cue Ball game.

- Prepare to play Level One of the Magic Cue Ball game.

- Appoint an opposition player whose role is to stand in the middle of the circle and prevent the ball from getting to its destination, much like a goalie in soccer.

- The players should throw only one ball in a designated course, as in the Level One Action of the Magic Cue Ball game.

Goal of Level One: To complete one round without the ball being diverted or stolen.

Director's Notes: This exercise teaches students to connect their cues, sustain the steady rhythm of the game, and accomplish the goal without responding to extraneous cues, represented by the opposition player. Because the opposition player will have to do more than just stretch his arms to steal the ball, expect a greater amount of physical action and emotional engagement by all the players. Even so, remind the students to keep their concentration and not contribute to the distraction by shouting or making extraneous movements themselves. Repeat this exercise at least three times using different opposition players.

KEY: Getting to the heart of the issue

No matter what extraneous happenings occur inside the theater house or on the stage, stay in character and remember that the show must go on.

The Magic Presence

Beginner actors are usually at sea when they go out onstage, and the audience is the first to spot it. A stage presence is a learned art and a student actor rarely possesses it before at least one or two years of training. It takes practice and experience to create and sustain a stage presence where the level of emotion expressed by the actor onstage can move an audience. With each classroom exercise, with each character he plays, the student advances one more step towards developing that *magic presence*. Concentration is the key.

When you miss a cue (forget your line) or give it incorrectly (say the wrong line), you have to summon your concentration and dive deeper into your character to maintain the circle of your stage presence. The great test of an actor occurs when he is the victim of an extraneous cue that comes right out of the blue.

> **Author's Story:** Once I was playing the role of Lily, Colin's mother, in *The Secret Garden*. I made my entrance onstage wearing a shimmering gown. Beautiful music was playing and the scene was dramatic. My son, who was two years old at the time, was in his daddy's arms watching the play from the back of the theater house. Days earlier my son had seen the movie *The King and I* on television and was fascinated with the music and costuming. As soon as I walked out onstage, I (and everyone else in the scene) heard an excited and perfectly clear voice echo across the audience, "Mommy. King and I." My little boy had recognized me and to him I looked just like Anna in *The King and I!* Normally an extraneous cue is not difficult to ignore, but this interruption was especially challenging because it was personal to me. Moreover, some members in the audience knew that it was my son who had cried out and were watching me carefully for any sign of breaking out of character. I had to make a very determined effort to stay in character and not lose my concentration.

A second story also demonstrates the significance of staying in character at all costs. In my theater company's premier performance of *The Secret Garden* in Montana, the prop mistress had neglected to preset an item of clothing on the set of Misselthwaite Manor, where Mary Lennox is brought to live with her uncle. In the first scene, Mrs. Medlock, the housekeeper, must undress Mary and put a nightgown on her. When she turned to gather the nightgown, it was not there. The actress playing Mrs. Medlock thought quickly and loudly called out the name "Martha." As the character of Martha was in the next scene, the actress was already waiting in the wings to make her entrance. Comprehending that something was amiss, she entered in character and was scolded by Mrs. Medlock for not having the nightgown placed on the sofa as she was told to. She was then ordered to find the nightgown and bring it in immediately. The actress playing Martha left the stage, located the nightgown from the prop table, and reappeared with it onstage, improvising a line of apology to Mrs. Medlock. The scene went on without a hitch, and the audience did not know that anything had been out of its proper order.

Yet a further example of an extraneous cue occurred during a performance of the same play but with a different cast. In one of the scenes between Colin, the crippled boy, and Mary Lennox, there is a pillow fight, after which Mary tells him that there is really nothing wrong with him and that he should turn over and let her look at his back. The young actress who played Mary pushed the actor too hard and Colin rolled off the bed. Since Colin is meant to be a cripple, he could not simply get up and hop back into bed. The actress playing Mary had to think quickly on her feet. Realizing the difficulty for her fellow actor, she continued her taunts while lifting him up as a dead weight and pushing him back onto the bed. The extraneous cue of Colin rolling off the bed was so effectively covered up by these young actors that parents in the audience who knew how the scene had previously been rehearsed commented on how much more effective the *new* blocking was!

Professional actors understand the importance of staying in character, and the concentration and commitment it requires. There is an implicit trust between the actor and his audience that no outside interference can disrupt. Only the actor can destroy that trust by breaking out of character. The actor himself is the only one who can cut the magic tie that enables the audience to enter into the heart of the dramatic experience. An actress who understands such a noble trust is Anna Marie Pearce, whom we all knew many years ago as Patty Duke.

A Wonderful Story: In 1959, Patty Duke was a 12 year-old actress playing the role of Helen Keller in the New York Playhouse Theater production of *The Miracle Worker*—a role she would reprise with the same cast in the 1962 film version, for which she would win an Academy Award. During one of the scenes in which Helen is blocked downstage, sitting all by herself, one of the large columns belonging to the stage set shifted and fell diagonally across the stage floor, shocking the audience. The column missed Patty Duke by inches. What is remarkable, however, is that Miss Duke did not react. Because she was supposed to be playing a blind mute, she did not flinch or scream in the normal way a person would if a column came toppling down right next to her. She *stayed in character* completely and continued on with the scene as though nothing had happened. Following her example, the rest of the cast sustained their character attitudes and did likewise. At the end of the scene, the curtain was drawn so that the stage crew could remove the column. The audience members were so enamored of the bravery and professionalism of the young actress that they stood and gave her a ten-minute standing ovation until the director himself had to come out in front of the curtain and beg them to please be seated so the play could continue.

"The play's the thing," as Hamlet told us. Miss Duke demonstrated that an actor must give his unconditional commitment. "The show must go on" is an often-heard cliché, but that should not detract from its serious application in the theater world. Theater is not a casual activity. It is an artistic discipline, and the intensity of the theatrical experience can only be realized by the dedication of theater artists to work fully and responsibly with each other on a consistent basis. Discipline creates someone who can be counted on. There is no better place to start learning artistic disciplines than in an acting class.

Director's Notes: Though audiences are always willing to laugh at little children who break out of character when they are on the stage and do funny (and sometimes endearing) things, it is still important to convey to your littlest actors how especially wonderful it is if they can stay in character when they are onstage. Tell them how proud they can be of themselves if they don't let anything or anyone make them forget their magic role. Remind them that you think of them as "stars" and that "stars" never lose their magic presence.

KEY: Getting to the heart of the issue

 Forgetting your lines or your blocking can be excused. Breaking out of character cannot. The audience will forgive you everything onstage as long as you do not break the magic of their make-believe world.

E X E R C I S E 4-2 Tug of War

Level One Action:

- Create a cleared space, at least 12 feet long (horizontally).
- Mark a (vertical) center line.
- Two students stand opposite each other, toe to toe.
- Give them each an oven mitt and one end of a thick, soft-fibered rope.
- They may turn one end of the rope around their respective mitts if they choose, but no more than that.
- Once they are set, call out "Begin!"
- The students play tug of war to see which student can pull the other over the center line to his side.
- Repeat the exercise with several pairs of students.

Director's Notes: Do not allow the students to go to extremes in their enthusiasm to win. A student should back off if he experiences pain. The students are out of control if they burn their hands with the rope (even with the mitts on) or are catapulted backwards or forwards when they let go of the rope.

Generate a discussion with these questions:

How much physical strength was required to achieve the goal?
How much discomfort were you willing to suffer?
How much psychological commitment was needed to win?
Why did one student succeed and the other lose?
What is the difference between physical strength and psychological commitment?

All of our physical energy must be exercised to have any real chance at the tug of war. Often, however, it is not physical strength that is the winning factor. A person of weaker strength can win his goal if he has a higher level of psychological commitment.

Now compare this to acting. Physical *strength* is not a changing dynamic but a static attribute of the actor. In other words, the actor can only be as physically strong onstage as he is in person. There is nothing on the stage that is going to suddenly transform him into a Hercules. Psychological *commitment,* on the other hand, is dynamic—it can change and grow once the actor takes on his role. Only through commitment can you give a lifelike energy and believability to the character you create on the stage. Only with the most focused concentration and follow through of willed action can you draw from your character the drama and pathos that can move even the hardest of hearts.

Level Two Action:

- Repeat the exercise above. This time, however, a new motivational factor is added to the simple action of tug of war.

- In the Level One exercise, the rope was just a physical object. Now the students will visualize the rope as the last lifeline to their family dog. They should imagine that they are pulling the dog to their side with this rope to save it. This would be the moment of crisis in a storyline and possibly the climax.

- Afterward, students discuss how they approached the Level Two exercise differently from the Level One exercise.

Director's Notes: In the Level Two Action, you have upped the ante and raised the level of emotional risk for each actor to achieve his goal.

KEY: Getting to the heart of the issue

When you commit yourself as an actor to a role, you are investing that role with a life of its own and a will to live.

EXERCISE 4-3 Star in the Magic Circle

- Choose a student to be the star in the Magic Circle.

- All the other students sit cross-legged in a circle around him.

- The star does something that the others imitate exactly. (For example, if the star claps his hands, all the students do likewise. If he moves his head to the left, all the students do the same, and so forth.)

- The students should do nothing but what the star does.

- If a student adds any of his own movement or sound, he has to leave the circle.

Director's Notes: This is a "Simon Says" type exercise for the younger children. Make sure all the students have a chance to be the star. Explain ahead of time that even if a student moves or makes a sound inadvertently, such as sneezing, he still has to sit out. Whether he means the distraction or not, the circle can only sustain its magic when there are no competing or extraneous cues.

EXERCISE 4-4 Follow the Director

Level One Action: Students line up in a circle with the director at the head of the circle.

- The director initiates an action, such as walking on tip toe, hopping on one foot, or skipping—all the while keeping the circle moving.

- The rest of the students follow and do exactly as the director does.

- The director stops suddenly and freezes, and the students must do the same.

- Those who do not respond quickly enough or who lose their balance in the freeze, sit out.

- The director continues the circle moving with another action.

- Repeat until there is only one student left in the circle with the director.

- That student can be the leader in the Level Two Action.

Level Two Action:

- The students line up in a circle as before, but this time the winner of the previous Level One is the leader. If there is no winner, the director can assign a student to be the leader.

- The same rules apply.

Director's Notes: This is a really fun exercise. Expect laughing and silliness from the age 3 to 6 group. Keep in mind that it is hard for them to hold their balance, so be encouraging and not as exacting as you would be with older students.

EXERCISE 4-5 Slings and Arrows

- Each student takes a turn sitting center stage facing out to the audience with a serious character attitude.

- Choose another student to do whatever he or she can to break the player's concentration and thus his character attitude.

- The student attempting to break the player's concentration can say or do anything (within propriety) except physically touch the player.

- If a student is particularly strong in his concentration skills, two interference players at a time can attempt to distract him or disrupt his circle of concentration and thus his character presence.

EXERCISE 4-6 Drop the Book

- Each student takes a turn walking across the stage from downstage left to downstage right balancing a book on his head.

- Assign a student to be the interference player to try and cause the actor to lose his concentration and drop the book before reaching the other side.

- The interference player can use any tactic of intimidation he chooses, short of yelling and screaming, or direct physical contact.

- If the interference player touches the actor, the game is forfeit to the actor.

- If the actor drops the book at any time before reaching the other side, the game is forfeit to the interference player.

Goal: For the actor to get to the other side of the stage with the book on his head.

Director's Notes: In order to achieve his goal, the actor must concentrate on two levels. The first level requires that he physically balance the book while in motion. The second level involves resisting the bombardment of extraneous cues from the interfering player. If the interference player stands directly in front of the actor to block him from crossing the stage, the burden is upon the interference player not to make physical contact with the actor. In other words, the interference player needs to move and get out of the way if the actor keeps coming forward.

KEY: Getting to the heart of the issue

An extraneous cue is like a pebble thrown into a pool of water. Ever-widening circles ripple from the center out to the circumference of the water surface. An actor must learn to neutralize and absorb all extraneous cues into the circle of his magic presence.

The Power of Concentration

Stanislavski believed that the power to concentrate your attention is the key not only to staying in character and avoiding distraction but to penetrating to deeper levels of your character so that you can make your characterization more truthful. He was concerned that young actors were content to merely pretend to be their characters— an activity that does not require much concentration or talent. An actor, he wrote, cannot enter the creative process of *finding* his character if he has not cultivated the power to fully focus his attention. If you are interested enough in your character and the scene onstage in which your character lives, you will not be distracted by anything outside that theatrical life. To paraphrase Stanislavski, from the very moment that an actor concentrates on something behind the footlights, he ceases to think about what is going on in front of them.

The actor's goal is to build and sustain the circle of his magic presence. Without the habit of concentration, the actor cannot enclose himself in this magic circle in which he creates his character's life. He develops this power of concentration by developing his powers of observation. This means looking at an object, not in an absent-minded way, but with penetration. The actor can practice this not only on the stage but in real life, where he can photograph with his mind a clear, sharp impression of whatever is going on around him.

Stanislavski developed the concentration of his actors by having them direct their attention to the nearest object onstage, examining it with the most intense focus. Then those actors expanded their concentration incrementally to other objects or persons that were further away. Stanislavski wrote: "As the circle grows larger the area of his [the actor's] attention must stretch. This area, however, can continue to grow only up to the point where you can still hold it all within the limits of your attention, inside an imaginary line. As soon as your border begins to waver, you must withdraw quickly to a smaller circle which can be contained by your visual attention."

Exercises in developing the power of concentration are necessary not just to build a reliable attention span but to hold on to it under difficult conditions. If you lose concentration on the stage, for whatever reason, you must be able to collect it again so that you are not in danger of either breaking character or failing to reach a level of characterization beyond pretension. That is why Stanislavski suggested to his actors that they find one single point or object within that circle of attention and hold fast to it as one would a single light in the darkness. Keep expanding the circle of concentration so that fewer and fewer distractions will cause your mind to lose focus on the intrinsic theatrical action.

E X E R C I S E 4-7 Object of Attention

- Have all the students sit on the stage, while you (the director) sit in the classroom (or auditorium) opposite them. Ask them to look down at the stage floor and concentrate very hard on observing its physical details.

- While the students are busy working at their task, get up from your seat, walk to the back of the classroom, pick up an object (such as your purse or a book), and return with the object to your seat.

- As soon as you sit down again, stop the exercise and ask the group if any of them noticed what happened out in the classroom while they were concentrating on their task. (Every student will be able to relate what you did, with at least some detail.)

- Then ask: "Would all of you please look very carefully again on the stage, as I believe one of my contact lenses fell on the floor somewhere."

- While they are busily absorbed in examining every square inch of the stage for the object, get up from your seat and go over to the window and look out for several seconds, then return to your seat and write something in your notebook.

- Then say: "You can stop looking now. Did anyone notice what happened out here in the classroom (or auditorium) while you were busily searching for my contact lens?" (Most, if not all of the students, will tell you that they didn't notice anything because they were absorbed in searching for the object.) Tell them what you did, then ask them why they think they were not distracted the second time by your movements in front of the stage area.

Director's Notes: Make sure you tell the students that you did not lose a contact lens. It was only a theatrical cue.

The reason why you were not distracted the second time by my classroom movements is that you were totally caught up in what you believed to be a real life action onstage of searching for a lost object—a task that totally absorbed your attention. To use Stanislavski's own words: "In order to get away from the auditorium (audience distraction) you must be *interested* in something on the stage."

This exercise demonstrates that every performing artist, whether a singer, musician, or actor, must have a point of attention on the stage so that he is not distracted by any activity outside the stage. In real life, it is easy to fix our attention on an object or a person with whom we are interacting. On the stage, the conditions are entirely artificial and therefore we have to make a very conscious and determined effort to concentrate our attention on an object in a meaningful and real way.

In our ordinary lives we do everything naturally and unconsciously, from walking, sitting, and talking to moving about and interacting with other people. As Stanislavski reminds us, when we do these same things in front of an audience, we have to be taught to do them all over again—even those that are the simplest and most familiar to us. It is a re-education to look and see, to listen and hear anew.

EXERCISE 4-8 Point of Light

Level One Action:

- Have all the students sit on the stage. Place a single candle with holder on a small table near where the students are sitting. Add at least two other objects near the table, such as a book and an item of clothing.

- Turn the lights off on the stage (or in the building if there are not separate switches) so that the room is dark.

- Light the candle so that it is the only bright, visible object on the stage.

- Have the students concentrate their whole attention on the light. Tell them to observe and try to memorize all the physical characteristics of the lighted candle—its height, color, the way the burning wax drips down the side, the movements of the flame itself, etc.

- After a minute or two, add another lighted candle so that the other two objects on the stage can be seen within the circle of illumination, if only in a shadowy form. Tell the students to concentrate, once again, only on the first lighted candle.

- After a minute or two, turn the stage (or main room) lights on again so that both the stage and the auditorium are fully lighted. For the third time, ask the students to focus their attention on the details of the first candle only.

- After another short period, stop the exercise and ask them which situation offered the best setting for concentration on the lighted candle: (1) when all was dark and only the single candle was visible, (2) when the second candle was lit and the other objects on the stage were also visible, or (3) when all the lights were turned on and the entire stage and room were clearly visible.

You will find that it is much easier to fasten your attention on the candle flame when it is surrounded by darkness. As soon as other objects come into view, they compete for your attention. The quality of the concentration is also more intense when there is only one object clearly in sight, especially if that object is the nearest one to you. The more distant the object or person onstage, the less easy it is for you to hold them in the center of your attention.

The more intense the concentration, the more the mind is able to block out all other stimuli. Only then can the actor start to build an imaginary relationship with the object—that is, invest something of his feelings and not just his thoughts in the object. Concentration is therefore a necessity for establishing your circle of attention *and* entering into the creative process of building your character.

In time, you will learn to establish a larger and larger circle of attention and not move outside it while onstage. A well-trained actor is able to establish his circle of attention every moment he is performing—whether on a real stage with stage lights or on a street in front of passers-by, as along Kalakaua Avenue in Waikiki, Hawaii, where dozens of highly costumed and brilliantly painted street entertainers remain frozen in a character attitude for 45 minutes or more at a time, without a single flicker of movement or change in facial expression. They continue their unmoving pantomime for upwards of 5 hours every night, 7 days a week and provide some of the most professional entertainment in Honolulu.

The magic presence represents the moving center of attention that the actor has to learn to carry around with him and enclose himself within. Your magic circle is your most essential and practical possession as an actor.

Level Two Action:

Level Two of this exercise can be performed at home.

- Place a single candle with holder on a small table in your bedroom. Make sure you have your parent's permission to use a live candle flame.

- When it is nighttime, light the candle and turn off the lights in your room so that the light is the only visible object.

- Concentrate with your full attention on the flame. For the first few minutes, consciously observe and memorize every physical detail of the candle light. If you feel your attention waning, draw it back to the flame.

- After you are able to hold a concentrated circle of attention, let your mind build some imaginary story around the object. Perhaps the lighted candle is the object that leads to a discovery of a treasure, or the means of a daring escape, or the singular light that saves someone's life.

- You can present your story at the next class.

The action of looking at an object to examine its physical details helps us to develop our concentration and to fix our attention. We can also develop our "inner attention" by using our imagination (or inner eye) to create a picture story around the object. In building a story around the lighted candle, we are focusing our attention on the candle not just as a physical object but as something that we can invest our feelings in. By creating story images, we are endowing the candle with an imaginary life. We can create a fictional history around it and write for ourselves a romance, an adventure story, a thriller, or just a simple poem.

Attention, therefore, is built in many layers. The more layers that an actor can explore and master, the richer, finer, and deeper will be his acting experience.

Simplified Exercise for Little Children

Level One Action:

- Bring several plastic Hula-Hoops to class (one for each child) and have the children put the hoops around their waists.

- Ask the children to take turns walking from one side of the stage to the other, holding the hoop around their waists.

I want you to imagine your magic circle to be just like the Hula-Hoop. Only *you* are allowed in your own magic circle. The character you play onstage goes everywhere you go, just like the hoop, because the character lives inside the hoop and nowhere else. It is a magic circle because that is where you perform your *acting magic.*

Level Two Action:

- Take the hoops from half of the children and ask those without hoops to share a hoop with one of the other students.

- Have the children (now grouped in pairs inside one hoop) take turns once again walking across the stage. Ask them if they liked sharing a hoop with someone else or having their very own. *(Every child likes to have his own.)*

An actor concentrates better on what he has to do and where he has to go when he controls his own magic circle.

KEY: Getting to the heart of the issue

 When you can sustain the circle of your attention onstage, you will have achieved the first step towards developing your magic presence.

Unit

Study

Five

Sense Awareness and
Memorization

5

Sense Awareness and Memorization

Class materials needed: Three medium-sized sponge balls, one a different color
A warm sweater and a book (either the New Testament or
the Works of William Shakespeare)

Repeat Exercise 2-2: The Body Flop

Repeat Theater Game 3-1: Magic Cue Ball at the last level reached

Sense Awareness

Everything created in theater is larger than life, so your sense awareness—that is, the degree of responsiveness of your five senses to the environment around you—must be greater than that of the average person. As we learned in earlier lessons, your stage setting must be as comfortable and familiar to you as your own bedroom because it is where your character lives. What you bring alive in your mind, and give emotional authority to, is what the audience will experience.

In the last unit we learned to fix our attention on physical objects. On the stage, these objects make up the external setting in which we place our character. The actor must educate his senses so that the unfamiliar stage setting in which he plays out his character's life becomes a believable setting to himself. Only then will it be believable to the audience. An actor must be alert to every sense experience onstage, yet deftly dismiss extraneous cues that are not an intrinsic part of the action.

In ordinary life we use our senses unconsciously. On the stage, everything we do is self-conscious, yet it must appear perfectly natural and effortless. We define our theatrical environment by our five senses. We need to sharpen them, therefore, in order to transform the artificial setting on the stage into a setting that comes alive to us, and therefore alive to the audience. The film and television actor does not have to work as hard as the stage actor in making his world look real because screen sets *are* real, for the most part. They are not framed by a proscenium arch or limited by sky-cycs. As stage actors, we must strengthen and intensify our sense experience. By so doing, we increase not only our own visualization skills but those of the audience. Senses that are alive and palpable onstage open the door to the world of the imagination for those watching through the proscenium wall.

If you can create a vibrant sensory environment onstage, the audience will be able to enter into the inner life of your character. The outer senses—what the character sees, hears, tastes, touches, and smells—are the door to that inner life. In a theater setting, the well-trained actor only has to indicate that inner life by connecting the sensory dots of his character and the audience will fill in the rest. Unlike film and television acting, it is not necessary for the theater actor to create "actual" life on the stage in all of its "lived" intensity. The stage actor's purpose is to create theatrical life. If he does so, convincingly, he will inevitably draw the audience into his character's world and invite their emotional and psychological participation in that world. That is part of the excitement of live theater. The spectator enters in through the magic of the milieu created by the actor.

Obviously, the more vibrant and colorful the theatrical environment, the deeper and more meaningful the audience's experience will be. That is why the actor must also develop what Stanislavski called "inner attention," which deals with the experience of the five senses in imaginary circumstances. "Material things around us on the stage call for a well-trained attention," he wrote, "but imaginary objects demand an even far more disciplined power of concentration." Those "imaginary objects" are the building blocks that bring the emotional and spiritual life of the character into focus for the audience. Because we are creating an imaginary (inner and outer) life on the stage—a life that is to be intimately shared with the audience—we must develop our imaginary senses of seeing, hearing, feeling, tasting, and smelling.

KEY: Getting to the heart of the issue

**Your character will come alive onstage
if you bring to it rich sensory experience.**

The Power of Observation

Anyone who possesses the ability to form an astute, vivid, and detailed impression of whatever he places his attention on—remembering what is most essential, striking, or significant in the object of his attention—is gifted with the power of observation. It is a skill that every actor needs to cultivate if his senses are to successfully paint the portrait of his character onstage. All the exercises below are designed not only to increase the power of observing accurately and well but also to heighten the ability to visualize how to respond with the five senses in imaginary situations.

EXERCISE 5-1 The World of Sight Sense

- The students sit in chairs in a circle.
- Choose one student and ask him to close his eyes.
- Ask the first student, who has his eyes closed, to describe in detail the appearance of a second student you choose at random.
- The first student should not open his eyes at any time until he has completed his task, remembering as much as he can.
- After the student has answered to the best of his ability, ask him to open his eyes and check how accurate he was.
- Have the same student repeat the process—that is, close his eyes and recall, for a second time, the other student's appearance. (This time, there should be a marked improvement in the recall of those same physical details.)
- Repeat the exercise two or three times with different students.

Goal: For the actor to increase his power of observation and his ability to recall as many visual details as he can regarding another's appearance.

Director's Notes: Generally the first student will remember little about the person he is asked to describe, so you might need to coach him along with questions like: What is the color of her hair? Eyes? Is she wearing a t-shirt or a turtleneck? Is there a design on the shirt? Is the material denim, corduroy, wool? Is she wearing any jewelry? Any watch? Cover every detail from head to foot. The students will observe and describe more accurately with each attempt. Remind the students that you will call upon anyone at any time in the weeks ahead to describe the appearance of any other student, so they should be aware and consciously memorize the details of each other's outer appearance (including the director's). If you have a class calendar, choose some class dates and write yourself a reminder to include this exercise.

Homework: When traveling in a car, eating at a restaurant, shopping in a grocery store, or going for a walk in the woods, consciously observe all details of passing scenes, objects, and people. As a specific exercise, select a room in your home, memorize it in every detail, and be able to describe it if called upon in class.

E X E R C I S E 5-2 The World of Sound Sense

- The students close their eyes and listen to all the sounds they hear, both nearby and far away, for about two minutes.
- Insist on perfect silence during the time allowed and then call on different students to tell you what they heard.
- Students describe how the quality, pitch, or intensity of different sounds affected them physically and emotionally.
- Repeat two or three times.

Goal: Increase hearing astuteness and the ability to visualize how different kinds and intensities of sound impact our senses.

Director's Notes: Normally, by the third time around, the students are concentrating enough to hear sounds that they did not catch the first or second time. Nearby sounds such as a cough, a sniffle, the scraping of a chair leg on the floor, are obvious. The challenge is to isolate sounds, both near and afar, that we have all gotten into the habit of listening to unconsciously, and therefore take for granted.

E X E R C I S E 5-3 The World of Taste Sense

Instructions: Explain to the students that they are not meant to merely "pretend" that they are eating a certain kind of food. The purpose of the exercise is to stimulate their remembrance of the physical and emotional sensations associated with tasting different foods, and thereby conveying that remembrance vividly in their facial and bodily expressions, such as tensing up the muscles, quivering, clenching the hands, frowning, lifting an eyebrow, pursing the lips, grimacing, smiling, licking the lips, etc. Similarly, the emotions expressed should match the physical reactions. For example, the toasted marshmallows might conjure an emotional mood of perfect contentment and pleasure, while the cold, boiled cabbage may elicit profound aversion or even horror at the thought of having to chew and swallow it.

Level One Action:

   While seated in their chairs, have all the students imagine themselves eating the following foods. They can hold an imaginary cup or utensil, if they choose. The emphasis, however, is not on how accurately they mime, but how their sense of taste responds to an imaginary food and is conveyed expressively. Call each food item out in order:

> A sweet pickle
> Cotton candy
> Hot chocolate
> Sour warheads
> Marshmallows cooked over a fire
> A juicy lemon
> Sweet, ripe strawberries
> Cold, boiled cabbage
> A sugar cube

Level Two Action:

- Choose two students to act out the eating of foods that have opposite tastes. This will show each student reacting very differently to the imagined food. Have the pair of actors decide between themselves what foods they want to imagine eating. For example, one may act out eating a lemon and the other a strawberry. The students do not have to choose from the list above.
- The rest of the class guesses what imaginary foods they are eating and if the reactions of the body and face are convincing.

Goal: Increase taste awareness and the ability to visualize (and recall) how different qualities of taste affect our senses.

Director's Notes: For Level One, before the students act out the imaginary tasting of the different foods in the list, you may want to discuss with them the common physical and emotional reactions to such foods. For example, when eating a lemon, not only do the lips, tongue, and cheeks shrivel, but the nose often wrinkles up, especially if juice gets squirted. Just the expectancy of tasting a sour food can affect sensory reaction. Do not expect more than a general response from the little ones as they tend to caricature—that is, represent in broad strokes, the situations and characters they are asked to act out. Sometimes "pretending" is all they can manage.

EXERCISE 5-4 The World of Smell Sense

For many, the sense of smell is the most compelling and evocative of the five senses. Helen Keller wrote: "Smell is a potent wizard that transports you across thousands of miles and all the years you have lived." Smells (or scents for the more romantic among us) can have very powerful effects on people. They can vividly call to life memories that are buried deep in the subconscious. Just the imaginary thought of the smell of certain objects can be a very emotional experience. Of all the senses, smell is the open sesame to our emotional memory and to our inner spirit, both of which can provide a bountiful source of experience, real or imagined, from which an actor can draw to give texture, depth, and truth to his characterizations.

Boys and girls differ markedly in their responses to smells. Favorite smells that often pop up for the boys include new tires, sawdust, smoke from a gun shot, a mechanic's shop (with its odors of oil and grease), a baseball glove, paint, a horse barn (with its hay, grass, and grain), and a basement (with its tools and faint aroma of mildew). Favorite smells for girls often include vanilla, flowers and fruit blossoms, lavender, soap, perfume, the salt spray of the ocean, baby's powder or shampoo, and fruit, such as strawberries. Boys tend to have strong dislikes, such as dog poop (especially if they have to clean it up), while the girls can't tolerate the smell of gasoline, for example.

Some smells are so bad and so strong that you can taste them in the back of your mouth. Other smells are more easily described than acted out. A lemon, for example, has a refreshing and lively smell, though its taste is tart and sour. An orange blossom's scent is strong and lingering—so real that you feel you could touch it. An object can have an even more pungent smell in certain conditions. Honeysuckle, for example, smells extra strong after a heavy rain, especially in humid climates.

Particular memories can be associated with smells. The smell of the fresh, salt-sprayed air off the sea might remind you of the first time you glimpsed the ocean. A bar of Palmolive soap might recall the smell of a baby sister or brother after a bath or the feeling of being clean and safe and cared for. Fresh-baked bread or cookies often evoke scenes of "visiting grandma." A wood campfire is often associated with boy scout days, of friends and camaraderie, and of the beauties of nature and the outdoors. For someone who was brought up on a farm, the smell of freshly mowed grass or alfalfa and clover awakens memories of home. The smell of wood floor wax might conjure school days at a college dorm, or getting married in a church. Suntan lotion is evocative of summer holidays spent at the beach. The smell of horse's sweat and leather can key in reminiscences of rounding up sheep or cattle with your dad or competing in equestrian shows. The smell of antique books might recall the reading of a favorite romantic novel and the comfort of its old-fashioned values. Honeysuckle, for many, brings to mind the charm and old-world grandeur of the South. The possibilities are endless when the imagination and emotional memory are stirred.

Level One Action:

- While seated in their chairs, have all the students imagine themselves smelling the following objects. Call out each item in order:

  > A rose (or jasmine, magnolia, honeysuckle, plumeria, gardenia)
  > A skunk's odor
  > A freshly-cut Christmas pine tree
  > Gunpowder (after the gun has fired)
  > Old garbage
  > Chopped-up garlic
  > Freshly-perked coffee
  > A camp fire in the outdoors
  > Freshly-baked bread
  > Bleach
  > Bacon frying in a pan
  > Hot, buttered popcorn
  > The smell in the air when it's going to rain
  > Hot, salty french fries

Director's Notes: For Level One, you may want to first discuss with the students how each of the objects physically smells before they act out their responses.

Level Two Action:

- Choose two students to act out the smelling of objects that have opposite smells. Let the students decide between themselves what imaginary objects to smell.

- The rest of the class guesses from their facial expressions and movements what they are smelling and if their reactions are convincing.

Level Three Action:

- Ask the students what (if any) images, scenes, emotions, or memories come to mind when they imagine smelling each of the items. Have the students share those images and feelings with the rest of the class.

- Break up the class into two groups, one made up of boys, and the second group made up of the girls.

- Each group should create a list of their top five favorite smells, and their top five least favorite smells, and then share and compare them with the favorites and non-favorites of the other group. They should explain why they chose each object as a favorite (or non favorite), and what memories or scenes they evoked.

Goal: Increase the awareness of smell and the ability to visualize how different kinds of smells affect not just our physical senses but our emotional and spiritual memories.

Director's Notes: While there are smells that everyone likes (and dislikes), every smell will elicit widely different reactions based on the sex, unique tastes, artistic sensibilities, and personal life experiences of each person.

EXERCISE 5-5 Visualization of Touch Sense

- Students sit on the floor, allowing enough space for the director to walk among them.

- Director gives the following instructions:

Scenario One: Imagine that you have in front of you a large bowl of hot steaming water. The bowl is glass and very hot. Your goal is to wash your face. Show me how you would achieve that goal.

Scenario Two: The same situation, but this time the bowl is filled with ice water.

Goal: Increase visualization skills of the sense of touch.

Director's Notes: As you observe each student, comment out loud on the appropriate actions being taken by the actors (for example, blowing on the water, wiping the eyes from the impact of the steam, being careful not to hold onto the hot glass bowl, dipping in the finger for only a short moment to check the temperature, etc.). Also comment if the actor performs inappropriate actions, such as plunging the whole hand into the water or splashing handfuls of the steaming hot water onto the face before it cools. You may wish to have individual students try the exercise in front of the class before you have all the students attempt it.

EXERCISE 5-6 The World of Touch Sense

Level One Action:

- The students imagine touching the following items:

    Baby rabbit
    Sharp, rusty nail
    Baking flour
    Mud
    Poisonous spider
    Soft sponge
    Soap suds
    Slug
    The original Declaration of Independence document

Director's Notes: You may wish to first discuss with the students how each of the objects physically feels to the touch before acting out the sensory response.

Level Two Action:

- Choose two students to act out the touching of objects that feel different. The students decide between themselves what imaginary objects to touch.

- The rest of the class guesses what they are touching.

Level Three Action:

- Director holds up the prepared materials (the sweater and a book—either the New Testament or the Works of Shakespeare).

- The students describe the objects by physical shape, size, thickness, texture, softness, length, weight, etc. The director can pass the objects around the class.

- Ask the students to imagine themselves in each of the following situations:

  1. You are both hikers caught in a freak snowfall and the temperature is dropping rapidly. All you have is the object in your hand.

  2. You are stranded on an uncharted (or rarely visited) tropical island, with no help in sight.

- Ask the players the questions below. Complete situation 1 before you go on with a discussion of situation 2.

  a. How important is the object to you now? Has its value to you changed? Why?

  b. Which of the two objects could be fought over?

  c. Which of the two objects is the most valuable for physical survival?

  d. Which of the two objects is the most valuable for mental or spiritual survival?

  e. Which object would you prefer to have? Why?

  f. What do you do physically with this object? (Do you wear it? read it? tear it? burn it? eat it? throw it away?)

  g. How does having the object in your possession make you feel? (Does it make you feel happy, relieved, grateful, angry, impatient, hopeful, without hope?)

Goal: To help create a sensory environment through the sense of touch.

Director's Notes: Because this kind of exercise involves psychological and emotional considerations rather than just sensory reaction, be careful that the exercise does not get too complex and confusing. Remember that the goal of the exercise is to increase a richer visualization of the sense of touch.

EXERCISE 5-7 Stanislavski Says

Stanislavski urged actors to be passionate in their study of life and to carefully observe everything around them—whether people or nature—with a concentration of thought and a penetrating eye for detail. Only then can their creative work reveal what is rich, fine, and deep in life. In *An Actor Prepares,* he wrote:

> First of all, they [actors] must be taught to look at, to listen to, and to hear what is beautiful. Such habits elevate their minds and arouse feelings which will leave deep traces in their emotion memories. Nothing in life is more beautiful than nature, and it should be the object of constant observation. To begin with, take a little flower, or a petal from it, or a spider web, or a design made by frost on the window pane. Try to express in words what it is in these things that gives pleasure. Such an effort causes you to observe the object more closely, more effectively, in order to appreciate it and define its qualities.

He also urged actors to search for the beauty hidden behind all phenomena, even the darker side of nature. "What is truly beautiful," he wrote, "has nothing to fear from disfigurement. Indeed, disfigurement often emphasizes and sets off beauty in higher relief." He hoped that actors would learn to express life onstage (and in their real lives) with a noble intention, showing beauty in its true conception, rather than something "incomplete, saccharine, prettified, sentimental." When we observe beauty in nature and in man, we cultivate our aesthetic sensibilities and the power of intuition, which is the actor's greatest gift to carry out the process of "penetrating another person's soul."

- The students leave the classroom and go outdoors. Each of them finds an object growing in nature, such as a flower, a blade of grass, a leaf from a plant or tree, a tiny insect, etc.

- Each student studies his individual object with concentration for two or three minutes.

- The student then gives a detailed description of his object to the class. He should also share what he most likes about it, and why.

KEY: Getting to the heart of the issue

> The stage actor's goal is to become a finely tuned instrument, fully responsive to every real or imaginary cue.

Memorization

EXERCISE 5-8 Story Time

The actor onstage must have presence of mind. This refers not only to concentrated attention upon the intricate details of objects that make up his real or imaginary world, but the necessity to remember his lines. Proven memory skills means the actor will be able to stay "in the moment," demonstrate greater ease and spontaneity in the delivery of his lines, and feel confident that he can recall "on demand." Because most people remember words better when they can visualize a picture image, the exercises below are designed to stimulate the imagination in order to help along memorization.

- Students sit in a circle.

- Appoint a story starter. He begins a story with any opening words of his choice (for example, "Inside a tiny hole lived...," etc.).

- The director calls out "Story Time!" and the next person in line continues adding to the story. However, the next player must first repeat every word the previous player has said. Thus, each new player repeats all that has been said in the story up to that point before adding more to it.

- If a player forgets or misses part of the story, he sits out.

Goal: To have each player successfully recall all the details of an improvised story while continuing to add to it.

Director's Notes: With the little ones, it is advisable to practice a round with them or let them work in pairs. Don't let each player go on for more than a phrase or two. Keep the story very simple and short, otherwise you will discourage them.

EXERCISE 5-9 Subject, Please

- Students sit in a circle.

- Ask them to collectively choose a subject—for instance, "flowers" or "countries."

- When a category is agreed upon, each student takes a turn naming an example of the subject chosen. If "countries" is selected, for example, each player names a country. Before the next student adds his new country, however, he must repeat all the countries already named and in the order given.

You may offer a selection of categories to the students to pick from. Here are some examples of broad categories and what the students might name under each category:

Flowers—Rose, carnation, daffodil, hyacinth, crocus, lilac, periwinkle, tulip, poppy, lily, plumeria, honeysuckle

Countries—United States, England, France, Spain, Portugal, Germany, Russia, China, Israel, Turkey, Australia

Colors—Blue, red, yellow, white, orange, black, pink, purple, green, lavender, cream

Favorite Stories—The Secret Garden, Huckleberry Finn, The Little Train That Could, Jane Eyre, Little Women, A Tale of Two Cities, The Three Musketeers

Professions—Dentist, doctor, librarian, teacher, actor, engineer, lawyer, geologist, architect, plumber, electrician

Classic Composers—Mozart, Chopin, Beethoven, Grieg, Handel, Bach, Strauss, Liszt, Verdi, Wagner, Puccini

Saints—Therese of Lisieux, Bernadette Soubirous, Clare of Assisi, Francis of Assisi, Joan of Arc, Catherine of Siena, Sir Thomas More

Poets—William Shakespeare, Henry W. Longfellow, Robert Browning, Thomas Moore, John Keats, William Wordsworth, Walt Whitman, T. S. Eliot, Li Po

Classic Movie Actors—Charlie Chaplin, Greta Garbo, Gary Cooper, Bette Davis, Cary Grant, Errol Flynn, Laurence Olivier, Greer Garson, John Wayne

Modern Movie Actors—Brad Pitt, Ben Affleck, Julia Roberts, Jennifer Lopez, Angelina Jolie, Leonardo DiCaprio, Orlando Bloom, Matt Damon

Presidents—George Washington, Thomas Jefferson, Abraham Lincoln, Ronald Reagan, Franklin D. Roosevelt

Famous People in History—Jesus Christ, Ben Franklin, Florence Nightingale, Louis Pasteur, William Shakespeare, Joan of Arc, George Washington, Charlemagne, Aristotle, Mahatma Ghandi, Constantine, Confucius, Buddha

Great Movies—Chariots of Fire, Ben Hur, The Ten Commandments, Gandhi, Gone with the Wind, Dr. Zhivago, A Man For All Seasons

Great Artists—Leonardo da Vinci, Paolo Veronese, Raphael, Michelangelo, Fra Angelico, Rembrandt

Goal: Memorize all verbal cues in the correct order.

Director's Notes: If the above subjects prove too difficult for the little ones, ask them to memorize and recount the first names of everyone in the circle. The first player, for example, will state his name and the next player will state that name and then his own. The third player will repeat the first two names and then add his own, and so forth. You may do the same thing with any other characteristic, such as age, eye color, grade the students are in, or you may choose categories such as their favorite color or their favorite story book. The more familiar or personal the subject, the easier it is for the younger ones to concentrate.

KEY: Getting to the heart of the issue

An actor is a team player. The cue affects what has gone before and what will come after. Like a picture in a coloring book, the actor must color in every bit of the cue to bring the magic of his character, and thus the magic of the play, to life.

Unit

Study

Six

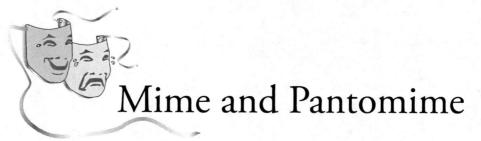

Mime and Pantomime

6

Mime and Pantomime

Class materials needed: Three medium-sized sponge balls, one a different color
A baseball hat and an historical hat (any kind)
Treasure box (to be used for the slips of paper with
mime exercises written on them)
An unbreakable cereal bowl

Repeat Theater Game 3-1: Magic Cue Ball at last level reached

Optional: Theater Game 3-2: The Roadrunner Cue

Simple Mime

Introduction

Mime is the acting out of an idea, an activity, a story, or a character using gestures, movement, and facial expression only. Mime is accomplished without saying any words or making any sounds. Simple mime involves the performance of a straightforward action like bouncing a ball or picking a flower. Though the terms mime and pantomime (or dramatic play) are used interchangeably, pantomime is more often associated with complicated scenes built on many action cues that complete a story and express more subtle and complex characterization. Pantomime, unlike some forms of mime, always represents real life.

Mime was first introduced in Greece in first century B.C., though it is believed to have existed in the cultures of the Chinese, Persians, and Egyptians long before that time. Mime reached its highest popularity as a form of theatrical entertainment in ancient Rome, where the myths of Greek tragedy were acted out by one actor (sometimes accompanied by a narrative chorus) who played all the parts using gesture and movement. Roman pantomime artists were accomplished gymnasts and dancers, known for their precision and physical grace. In the centuries that followed, pantomime continued to be associated with dance and was the precursor of classical ballet.

In the United Kingdom, pantomime includes song, dance, and buffoonery, and is traditionally performed at Christmas—the stories loosely based on children's nursery tales, such as *Dick Whittington*, *Jack and the Beanstalk*, and *Cinderella*. These performances feature stock characters in costume who sing, dance, and act out skits. Elsewhere in the world, mime is performed without dialogue or song.

Because it is the art of acting without words, pantomime teaches the young artist to rely on his facial expressions, gestures, and body language to express his meaning and emotion. A responsive and flexible body that can be precise as well as animated in its communication is essential for a stage actor, given that the body and face constitute the outward vehicle for expressing the inner life of the character.

In American silent pictures, Charlie Chaplin made his name as a great pantomime actor, while Harpo Marx was a popular mime actor in films during the 1930s and 40s. French actor Marcel Marceau is the world's most acclaimed classical mime artist. Known best for his tragicomic clown figure, *Bip*, who signifies the fragility of life, this master of "mimodrama" has performed all over the world in order to spread his "art of silence" (l'art du silence).

Classic or conventional mime, as practiced by Marcel Marceau and taught in a number of dedicated mime schools, is a specific art form and should not be confused with simple mime, which is a less complicated version of pantomime. Classic mime deals with the expression of an idea or theme, such as "Happiness" or "The Dreamer." As such, it is an abstract and highly stylized form of theater with its own makeup and costume conventions (white face, ballet shoes, etc.), training exercises (inclinations, rotations, isolations), and mime actions that are exaggerated for theatrical effect (illusory walk, the rope pull, the ladder climb). In the chapter on Pantomime and Mime in *The Stage and the School*, the authors point out that Marcel Marceau used to devote part of his one-man show to "Style Exercises," in which he showed the individual struggling with natural elements, as in "Walking Against the Wind," or making symbolic statements, as in "Youth," "Maturity," "Old Age," and "Death."

Simple mime and pantomime, on the other hand, deal only with real actions, stories, or situations of character. Though both the pantomimist and classic mime artist work with imaginary objects, the action in classic mime is exaggerated in order to highlight or draw the audience's attention to the abstract idea or theme. The classic mime artist might use parts of his body or his whole body to become an object, animate or inanimate. The opening of the hands, for example, might make a butterfly or a book. The same action in pantomime, however, would suggest a concrete action, such as accepting a gift, pleading, or offering help.

In leading Speech & Drama studios throughout England, simple mime and pantomime are a required part of the training for a classical stage technique. In American theater, they are taught as a basic form of improvisation or are used as the simplest kind of make-believe for younger children.

Outside the theater, pantomime still finds a fun and expressive outlet in the game of charades—popular at parties and family get-togethers or on camping trips. With charades, you have to act out a word or phrase without speaking. The player will break up the word into root syllables that he can act out separately, such as "foot" and "ball" for "football." Titles of movies, books, sports, or simple proverbs work best.

Preparation

In the mime and pantomime exercises that follow, the characteristics of each imaginary object must be clearly delineated and remain consistent from the beginning of the exercise to the end. It is very important that you visualize—that is, preset in your mind the exact dimensions of the object you are working with as well as your exact reactions to it. Only when you see your object as vividly as if it was really there in front of you, will the audience be able to see it, too, and believe in what you are doing. If your movements and facial expression don't get across exactly what you are doing in your pantomime, there is no other way that the audience can discover it.

The best preparation for performing a mime is to practice with the real object in the exact setting that you plan for your mime. This will help you memorize the precise position of every set piece and object that you will be using in your imaginary situation. Clearly establish in your mind the exact location of each of these objects and navigate them with definite and clear-cut intention. After you have indicated to the audience where the object is, do not break the illusion by reacting to it several inches away from where you first put it. If you shift any object during your mime, remember where you put it. Use different parts of your body to reference where different objects are—for example, whether they are at eye level, waist level, knee level, etc.

Every physical object has definite characteristics. In the same chapter that discusses pantomime in *The Stage and the School*, the authors provide a list of these distinctive characteristics, though they relate them more to characterization than to simple object mime. Many of their points, however, apply to both. When you act out an object mime, you need to reproduce the following dimensions faithfully:

Size: In conveying the size of your object to the audience, you need to take into account its height, length, width, and thickness. Small objects, such as pens, books, or jewelry, can be described by careful manipulation of fingers, wrist, and hand. Larger objects, such as chairs or tables, require the use of your whole body—for example, leaning over from your waist and using your arms to outline how long or wide the table is. Larger set pieces, such as trees or rocks, need expert adjustment of your head and eyes to make their height and width understood. If the mime object changes its size during your mime, such as a balloon losing air, make sure you follow the changes with quick and effective hand movements.

Shape: Standard shapes are round, square, rectangle, oval, and triangle. Most smaller objects, however, do not follow standard shape. You will need to use very fine adjustments of your fingers to get across the exact shape to your audience. The tension of the hand is also important in communicating the shape of an imaginary object.

Weight: A backpack full of textbooks will weigh considerably more than a backpack filled with popcorn. The way you act out the muscle tension in your hands, arms, shoulders, and back conveys an object's comparative heaviness or lightness. Practice with a real object that has the same physical weight as your imaginary one in order to figure out the muscular tension that you will need to pantomime. Practice picking up the object, putting it down, walking and turning with it, and carrying it various distances. Hardly any adjustment of the muscles is needed with a lightweight object. Tension and pressure on the muscles will increase as the weight of the object increases.

Resistance: Resistance is the solidity or force resident within an object that opposes its manipulation. The resistance of a brick when you pick it up with your hand is great compared to the resistance of a soccer ball when you grasp it. When you wrap your arms around a soccer ball, however, the resistance is markedly more than that of a down pillow when you squeeze it in your arms. Throwing a basketball requires more effort than throwing a blown up party balloon, which barely needs a tap of the finger to be airlifted. Pushing against a hurricane force wind will demand more resistance of your body than pushing against a foam mattress. The rope that makes the church bell toll will resist your pulling more than the apple that you pluck from the apple tree. The petal you pull from a rose, however, is less resistant than the apple.

Texture: Texture refers to the "feel" of your object, especially the roughness or smoothness of its surface. Quality and grain are also used interchangeably with texture. If the object is food, texture is tested by the ease with which it is swallowed or chewed. You convey texture through sensory reaction. Touching a silk cushion will create different physical and emotional sensory responses than touching a potato sack made of coarse hessian cloth.

The same general rule in building a real scene applies to simple mime or pantomime: do not think, do not feel, do not act, do nothing without a theatrical cue. In other words, every gesture, every facial expression, every movement must have a purpose. Everything you do in a pantomime needs to be clear and definite, as well as visible to the audience. Even the smallest action should be an intrinsic part of a sequence of events that finds its natural conclusion. Every motion of the body and expression of the face must be the most truthful and effective means of conveying your story.

THE SHERLOCK DEMONSTRATION

Director's Notes: In this demonstration exercise, you (the director) will perform a simple mime—preparing to thread a needle—but you will not provide all the clues at once. You will add them one by one until the students, as one body, can make a definite judgment (beyond any reasonable doubt) that (1) it is indeed a needle you are holding in your fingers and (2) that you are threading the needle.

- Without explaining what you will be doing, take your chair and sit DC facing the students.
- Following the instructions, act out the simple mime of threading a needle.
- The students guess what the action is as the clues are given.

First clue: Using your left hand, hold up the thumb and index finger pinched together. Ask the students, "What do you think I have between my fingers?" Of the many different replies, one may be a needle, but do not affirm yet what it is. Explain that it could be any of the objects suggested or it could be a piece of paper, a crumb, a stick, an ant, a flower, an earring or any one of another five thousand objects or more. Tell them that you are going to give them more *clues* to narrow the options.

Second clue: Still holding up your two pinched fingers, take the index finger of the right hand and carefully pass it directly on top of the pinched fingers, about one inch above them. Show by your expression and reaction that you pricked your finger in doing so. Ask them again what they think you are holding. Again, some will reply that it is a needle, but still do not affirm what it is. Ask for all the possibilities—a piece of glass, small knife, razor blade, rose thorn, edge of a piece of paper and other objects. Explain that perhaps the options have been reduced 50 percent and ask them to name which of the original guesses are now eliminated absolutely.

Third clue: Now pass the index finger of the right hand directly under the pinched fingers, about half an inch below. This would be the blunt end of your imaginary needle. Show a careful approach and contact with the bottom of the object as though you were aware that it could prick you. Now ask the students to describe the object in terms of its size, shape, thickness, length, weight, texture, etc. Is it something cold, hot, dangerous? Again ask them to narrow down the options. If most of them think it is a needle, play devil's advocate saying: Are you quite sure it isn't a _____? (name another object it could be, such as a small tool, knife, hypodermic syringe, a piece of glass, etc.).

Fourth clue: With the aid of the index finger and thumb of your right hand, take the imaginary needle and turn it around (as to bring the bottom of the needle to the top), then place it once again between the index finger and thumb of the left hand. Now bring the object up to eye level. With the thumb and index finger of your right hand, pick up an imaginary thread from across your (left or right) knee and proceed to thread the needle. Remember to show your concentration in your facial muscles and eyes, and keep the right hand steady as you try to thread the needle. Be unsuccessful the first couple of times, then finally thread it, pulling the thread through the needle. At this point all the students will unanimously call out that the object is a sewing needle and that the action demonstrated is threading the needle.

Simple Exercises in Mime and Pantomime

Instructions: Sometimes students have a tendency to forget exactly where they placed an imaginary object or how big they initially indicated it to be. The following exercise requires that the student interact with only one object and define it accurately to the audience through precise movements and reactions.

EXERCISE 6-1 Simple Object Mime

- Ask for a volunteer to give a series of clues using a simple object mime of his or her choice (see sample choices opposite).

- The audience guesses what the action is as the clues are given.

- Keep the action simple and do not introduce other confusing images.

- Remember the characteristics of the imaginary object. For example, if the actor works with an imaginary box, his movements should always indicate the same size, weight, shape, texture, and resistance of the box.

- Give all the students a turn.
- The other students pay attention and after the mime they critique their colleagues.

Sample action/object mimes that can be chosen for the above exercise:

1. Reading the last page of a detective story that has a surprise ending
2. Stringing beads of different sizes to make a necklace
3. Painting your nails
4. Opening the curtains of a window
5. Holding a glass box that contains a poisonous spider
6. Coloring with a coloring pencil (as distinct from a crayon)
7. Writing with a fountain pen and ink (as distinct from a pencil)
8. Drinking hot tea from a cup and saucer (as distinct from a glass)
9. Tearing up a sheet of paper into eight identical pieces
10. Removing a rusty screw from an old piece of wood

Goal: To activate the imagination, develop concentration by working with an imaginary object, free the body by encouraging a natural response to an imaginary stimulus, discipline the body to make precise and well-defined movements.

Director's Notes: Young actors need to feel comfortable receiving suggestions and advice from their fellow actors. It is a valuable experience. Encourage a friendly give-and-take between the students. The little ones will perform their mime in large brush strokes. Be patient with them and encouraging at all times. If one of them happens to show an ability to perform with greater attention to detail, tell the class how special and clever it was for that student to show such concentration and how that kind of concentration makes great actors and actresses. Your goal is to motivate them to do better, but at their own individual pace.

Homework: Each student chooses one action mime from the list above (preferably not the one he performed in class) and practices it at home. If he chooses number 4, for instance, the student should find a real curtained window in the house. He should practice opening the curtains several times, memorizing every detail, such as where his fingers go, what the curtains feel like in his hands, how much force he has to apply, and whether there is any stretching or tensing of the muscles of his face or body. Then he should repeat the action with an imaginary window. He could ask a sibling or a parent to watch what he does to see if he missed out on any detail.

KEY: Getting to the heart of the issue

Once you introduce an imaginary object, keep its imaginary dimensions consistent.

EXERCISE 6-2 Group Object Mime

The students remain seated either in their chairs or in a circle on the floor. Everyone performs the following simple object mimes at the same time and in the order given:

1. Pick up a slippery ice cube
2. Hold a baby kitten in your arms
3. Pick up a hot pan with hot oil in it
4. Break off a thorny rose
5. Pick up a furry winter caterpillar
6. Try to catch a grasshopper
7. Take a dose of bitter medicine
8. Transfer tiny grains of sand from an imaginary box into your hand

EXERCISE 6-3 Let's Imagine

- All the students sit in a circle.

- Choose a setting, such as one of the following:

  1. By the seashore
  2. In a mountain cabin in front of a warm fire
  3. In a small camping tent in a rainstorm
  4. In a flowering garden on a sunny day
  5. In a hot, sticky rainforest with large bugs nearby

- Ask the students to think about all the images associated with such a scene.

- Open a discussion prompted by key questions. For example, if you choose number 1 (by the seashore), stimulate a discussion by asking questions like these (opposite) to help the children recall specific details related to summers spent by the sea:

1. *Name the images:* sea water, salt, waves, shells, sand, sun, sky, clouds, sailing boats, rock pools, minnows, pebbles, swimsuits, sandals, beach chair, beach towels, mom and dad, sisters and brothers, spades, buckets, lifeguard, seagulls, jellyfish, crabs, snack bag, book, radio/CD player, sun glasses, suntan lotion, sun hat....

2. *Describe the physical characteristics of each image:* color of the water, texture of the sand, size of the waves, shape of the sea shells, weight of the bucket when filled with wet sand, shape of the clouds....

3. *How do you interact with each image:* you swim in the water, carry the water in your bucket, swallow the water, splash and dive in the waves, build castles with the sand, burrow your toes in it, dig with your spade, rub on lotion, lay on the towel, absorb the sun's rays, read a book, listen to a radio, eat a snack, chase after crabs, squeal if a crab nips your toe....

4. *What does each image do to you:* the sun warms you, dries you, burns you, tans you; the water cools you, gets you wet; the waves dump you, spray you; the sand sticks to you, rolls over you; the suntan lotion makes your skin slippery and sweet smelling and protects you from harmful rays; the jellyfish scares you, stings you, and leaves red marks on your skin; the towel dries you, covers you, wraps around you, warms you; the salt air invigorates you, makes you thirsty, makes your lips dry and blistery....

5. *How does each image make you feel emotionally and spiritually:* the sun relaxes and soothes you, the water refreshes and stimulates you, the sand feels like a soft blanket over your body, the waves in the ocean make you think about the power of nature behind the ocean currents and the depths of the seas, the sailing boat against the horizon makes you want to paint or draw or write, the sun makes you feel protected and surrounded by love....

Goal: To stimulate the imagination (or "eye magic") of the students so they can visualize images in many sensory dimensions.

Director's Notes: This is an open group discussion and an unstructured exercise. Encourage the students to share spontaneously what they visualize.

EXERCISE 6-4 One-Person Mime or Pantomime

Instructions: In preparation for this exercise, write one-person mime or pantomime activities, such as the following listed below, on small scraps of paper and place them in the treasure box. *(These examples are arranged in order of difficulty.)*

Ages 3 to 7

Picking furry dandelions in the woods and blowing them away
Eating a whole bag of your favorite candy
Putting your dolly to bed *(girls only)*
Walk on prickly grass without shoes
Collecting different kinds of shells and putting them in a bucket
Gathering small twigs for a fire
Bouncing a large ball
Skipping rope
Picking pine needles out of the carpet and putting them in a glass
Reading a thrilling story in a picture book
Dusting a table with a cloth or feather duster
Wiping a sticky substance off a table with a sponge
Picking up a dead spider with your bare fingers
Building a house with blocks
Washing your face with soap and water
Brushing your teeth
Combing your knotty hair
Eating a rapidly-melting ice cream cone
Unpeeling and eating a banana
Eating a piece of hot, stringy cheese pizza

Ages 8 to 12

Writing a letter and folding, sealing, stamping, and addressing it
Arranging a variety of different flowers in a vase
Raking wet leaves on the lawn with an old, splintered wooden rake
Pumping air in the tires of your bicycle
Shoveling hardened, slick ice off your driveway
Wrapping a gift for the person you like most
Peeling a big potato with a blunt peeler
Peeling a big onion with your fingers
Crossing a stream on stepping stones

Choosing the most perfect sea shells from a big batch
Watching the last few minutes of one of your favorite movies
Roasting and then eating a marshmallow

Teens and Adults

Watching the last 30 seconds of a close football, basketball or baseball
   game on television
Packing a suitcase for a trip (business or vacation, summer or winter)
Fishing with bait, hook, and casting
Typing a letter on an old-fashioned and barely working typewriter
Cleaning and moisturizing your face (*girls only*)
Putting makeup on your face from scratch (*girls only*)
Making a phone call in an old telephone booth with rotary dial
Making a cake from scratch
Cleaning a dirty mirror
Modeling in clay either a human face or an animal
Taking a gun apart
Changing a tire on a bicycle
Loading a wheelbarrow with soil, then pushing it forward

- Bring out the treasure box that has the selection of mime and pantomime activities written on small scraps of paper inside.

- Three students at a time each pick a piece of paper from the box.

- They think about their chosen activity for one minute.

- Each of the three students takes a position on the stage—one DL, one DC, and one DR—and then, at the same time, each one performs his individual activity.

- The audience watches carefully and after the players have completed their tasks, they offer their critique.

- Make sure the actor's movements accurately describe the object mimed.

Goal: To re-create in pantomime simple activities which are familiar.

Director's Notes: The selections for the older students are pantomimes rather than simple object mimes because the tasks require more complicated and well-thought-out sensory reactions in addition to accurate movements.

EXERCISE 6-5 Small Group Pantomime

Choose four to six students at a time to act out the following activities:

1. The students imagine that they are lined up in front of a toy store counter with a different toy for each of them. Before the exercise, the students decide among themselves what toy each will imagine, so there is no duplication. The audience tries to recognize each toy based on the students' facial expressions and the way they handle their respective objects.

2. The students imagine that there is a large picnic basket center stage. Before the exercise, each student decides what kind of food he wants to act out eating—chicken leg, apple, potato chips, coleslaw, or other items (a different item for each student). Onstage, the students select something from the basket and pantomime eating it. The audience guesses what kind of food they are eating.

3. The students imagine they are cleaning house. Before the exercise, they should each decide which task they want to act out—washing windows, polishing the dining room table, sweeping the kitchen floor, hanging pictures, washing dishes, or something else. The audience guesses what activities are being pantomimed.

4. The students imagine they are preparing for a family portrait photo. Before the exercise, each student decides which member of the family he or she wants to be. They then pose for the portrait and the audience guesses what member of the family each pantomimed.

5. The students work together to try and pick up something heavy. Before the exercise, they should decide what the heavy object will be. The audience tries to guess the object based on the combined actions and expressions.

Goal: To cultivate imaginary sense responses and develop precise movements of the body to match the objects mimed.

Director's Notes: These activities require little emotional interpretation or character attitude. The dramatic play has no real story plot: it may begin anywhere and stop at any time.

Mime with Character Attitude (Mood Pantomime)

Our feelings affect our posture (how we stand, walk, and move) and our facial expression. The body droops in disappointment, swells in anger, tightens with fear, and lifts up with joy. Feelings, of course, are motivated by thoughts of the same kind.

Let's imagine a little boy, Billy, waiting excitedly at the mailbox for the mailman to deliver a birthday box from his grandmother. The mailman only hands him a few letters and drives on. (Generate a discussion with the class by asking the following pertinent questions.)

What are some of the feelings Billy would experience at that moment? (Disappointment, anger, sadness, rejection)

What would he be thinking to himself? (Grandma forgot my birthday! Maybe mom told grandma about the glass vase I broke the other day! I'm not going to get that remote car she promised to send!)

How would he look as he turned back to go into his house? (Shoulders slumping, hands in his pocket, head down, eyes lowered to hide the oncoming tears, etc.)

Director's Notes: For your older students, you can substitute a more age-appropriate story. For example, you might suggest a situation of a twelfth grader who is waiting and hoping for the boy up the street to ask her to his graduation school prom. Or perhaps an eighth grader who is waiting for his report card to arrive and will only be allowed to get his new video game if he has earned at least a B+ average.

E X E R C I S E 6-6 Object and Emotion

The student is now ready to practice the dynamic of linking movement to emotion. There is no dialogue, only movement and facial expression.

A. One object can elicit many different action responses from an actor.

- Generate a discussion on all the things you could do with a *window*.
  For example, you could clean it, spray it, dust it, look through it,
  throw something at it, break it, open it, close it, hang curtains over it,

pull curtains closed and open along it, climb through it, look for your reflection in it, blow your breath on it, put your nose up against it, smudge it with your fingers or mouth.

- After the discussion, the students take turns acting out all these suggestions onstage in front of the other students.

- Make it interesting by having the students imagine windows of different shapes and sizes. One window could be one foot by one foot and a student could mime climbing through its tiny space. Another window could be very high or circular, creating a comic difficulty for cleaning or trying to reach it or look through it.

- Encourage the students to have fun with their imaginary dimensions but to make sure that everything they do looks consistent and convincing.

B. One object may also elicit many different responses based on the preconditioned emotion and circumstance of the actor. Discuss how the single object of a *window* could cause an actor to show different emotions. Have the students discuss and act out the following situations:

1. Your favorite aunt has just arrived. You look out the *window* to wave to her.

2. A prisoner has just been released from six months of solitary confinement. It is springtime and he is placed in a room with a *window* looking out to the flowering woods.

3. A crippled boy has just learned to stand by himself. He wants to take his first steps to reach the *window* in his bedroom.

4. A child who has been in bed for three weeks is finally well enough to get out of bed and open her *window*.

5. This is your first visit to the seaside. When you enter the hotel room you throw open the *window* and get your first glimpse of the ocean and smell of the fresh, salt air.

6. You pitch a baseball and watch it sail into your not-very-friendly neighbor's *window* and smash it into a hundred little pieces.

7. Your family has been living in a tiny attic to hide from communist authorities who want to arrest your father. You know that it is springtime and you are tempted to draw the curtain just a little to look out the small *window*.

8. You are a very conscientious housekeeper and are checking to see if your employer's favorite *window,* which is next to his writing desk, has been cleaned by the maids. To your horror, you discover that it has moisture and morning fog stains still on it—and your employer has just arrived home.

9. You have been kidnapped and placed in a dark, smelly, and damp room. You are gingerly feeling around and suddenly a beam of moonlight shines through the room. You look up and see a *window.*

10. After a year's absence you have returned to the lodge where you became close friends with a sick boy who lived next door to the inn. You have just been told by the landlord that the little boy died only one week earlier. You open the *window* to spy the mountain ledge where you both shared many happy hours together.

C. Repeat the previous exercise with a different spin. The students can again use one of the ten situations above or they can make up new situations, but this time each one will use a different imaginary object, such as those listed below. It is important that the student feels free to use his imagination to create storylines that give emotional relevance and meaning to his actions.

1. Book
2. Antique ring
4. Ball
5. Gold cross
6. Chair
7. Old diary
8. Knife
9. Telephone

Goal: To create responses based on preconditioned thought and emotion.

EXERCISE 6-7 Complex Sensory Response

Write out the suggested scenarios (listed below) on individual pieces of paper and place them in the treasure box.

- Divide the class into teams of two students each.

- Each team picks a scenario from the treasure box.

- Both students in the team discuss and plan out the scene, but only one student acts it out.

- Each team should be given at least ten minutes to break down the scene for performance. A sample scenario is provided below.

- Each "actor" should perform the imaginary situation he and his teammate have prepared. At the end of each performance, the audience tries to guess what it is he acted out and determine if he was convincing.

- The critique session that follows each performance should be detailed. Students, for example, should discuss the movements and facial expressions of the actor as they related to his unfolding thoughts and emotions. For instance, in the sample scenario below, what differences did the observers note in the sensory responses of the actor when he first heard the noise, and those associated with the emotions of relief and delight that he experienced once he discovered the intruder to be a baby deer? Did the audience guess what the imaginary sound was?

Sample Scenario: Scenario #11, under *Ages 8 to 12*

- A hiker stops to rest at night in the woods. What does the imaginary forest look like? How dark is the night? Is there a moon?

- As he prepares to make a fire, he suddenly hears a rustling noise nearby. It gets louder and closer by the second. From which direction does the sound come?

- What is the actor's initial reaction: fear, curiosity, excitement? Does he imagine a bear, a wolf, a rattlesnake, a skunk, a squirrel, a stranger?

- What does he do to investigate the source of the noise?

- Can the audience guess from his reactions that it is a baby deer?

Goal: To bring imaginary cues to life through physical/sensory/emotional reactions.

Director's Notes: Because the students are dealing with emotional reactions to imaginary cues, it is difficult for them not to speak or make vocal noises. Let them know that you do not expect them to act like mutes. They can spontaneously sigh or groan or make sounds that come naturally with the emotion they are feeling. There should, however, be no dialogue.

SUGGESTED SCENARIOS: (*Arranged in order of difficulty*)

Ages 3 to 7

1. In a room that is almost completely dark, you can just manage to see the outline of an object across the room but cannot tell what it is. As you slowly move closer to it, the details of the object become clearer, until you finally discover what it is. The imaginary object is a scared kitten.

2. Your mother warned you not to wear your new dress/new shirt to the picnic. You return home and reluctantly show her a big tear in it.

3. You are wearing your very best clothes and shoes as you try and cross a wet, muddy field on stepping stones. Do you slip and fall or do you get across safely?

4. You have just lost the valuable necklace your grandmother gave you for your birthday. Search in the high grass for it. Do you find it?

5. Close your eyes and put out your hand. Someone puts an object in it. By your reaction, can the audience guess what the object is? A spider? A pretty gemstone? An ice cube? A feather that tickles? A clump of mud?

6. You arrive home from school with a note from your teacher. You are very curious to know what the note says. You very carefully take it out of its envelope and read it. Can the audience guess if you are happy or sad?

Ages 8 to 12

1. The day for the school picnic has arrived and you, the star athlete, expect to win all the races. You wake up, go to the window, push aside the curtain, only to see the rain beating against the window pane.

2. In the dark, you see a strange flit of light going across parts of the room. What are your different reactions to this? After investigation, what does it turn out to be?

3. You have been waiting on a lonely street corner for half an hour for your mother to pick you up. It is growing darker by the minute. You see a car approaching slowly along the curb? Do you recognize it?

4. You reluctantly open up your report card and read, one subject at a time, the grade for each. How do you react to each subject's grade? Any failing grades?

5. You have to meet someone in 10 minutes. You go to your bedroom to get your makeup bag, only to find that your little brother has emptied out its entire contents, removed the lids of every jar and tube, and scattered the items all over the carpet. You start to tidy up and put them away.

6. You have just finished painting your nails and go to pick up the bottle of nail polish remover when it tips over and the contents spill onto your mother's new mahogany dining table. It is a chemical that immediately starts to eat away at the shiny wood. Do you clean it off in time?

7. You try for the sixth time to get the answer to a difficult math problem.

8. You open and read a letter containing unexpected news. Is it good? Is it bad? Are you angry, relieved, disappointed, excited?

9. You transfer your mother's valuable crystal vase from one table to another. In the process, it slips from your hand and crashes to the floor.

10. You are taking a deeply embedded splinter out of your finger.

11. A hiker stops to rest at night in the woods and suddenly hears a rustling in the bushes nearby. He discovers it to be a baby deer.

12. Try on some of your great grandmother's or great grandfather's old-fashioned hats. Can the audience guess what they look like?

13. You walk into your bedroom to find your prized model airplane in broken pieces all over the floor.

Teens or Adults

1. An exotic flower has a strong and alluring fragrance, but its pollen is poisonous if inhaled. You try and smell it without getting close enough to stir up the pollen.

2. Imagine a footbath containing warm to hot soothing liquid and the essence of lavender. Your feet are sore from a long march, so sore that you can immerse them only very gingerly. Once immersed, they respond to treatment as your feet and body become less and less tense.

3. You enter your bedroom in a happy mood to fetch the 1,000 piece puzzle you just finished putting together and wish to show a friend. To your shock, you discover the tiny pieces scattered all over the floor. What could have happened? Who could have done this?

4. Listen to birds singing on a beautiful morning in early spring. Can you identify what birds they are and where they are perched?

5. Walk past a pastry shop at baking time before you have eaten lunch. What do you see in the window? Can you resist going in?

6. You are preparing to go to your first school dance. You cannot decide how to wear your hair. *(For girls only)*

7. You have just received a letter from someone who you hoped would ask you to the school prom. Did he ask you? *(For girls only)*

8. After an unexpected delay, you finally arrive at the ticket counter of a movie theater. You check the time on the board, then your watch. Yes, you're in time. You open your purse to get some money, but the money isn't there. You search again, look down at the floor and all around in a panic. Again you search the purse, turning it inside out. You are resigned to the fact that you have lost the money. As you walk away, you suddenly remember something. You reach into your pocket and there it is!

9. You have been struggling for an hour over a math problem. No matter how many ways you try to solve it, you can't get the right answer. You look at your watch. It's late and you're tired. You feel like giving up but decide to give it one more go. Suddenly, as you are adding a column of figures for the fifth time, you find your mistake. At last you can go to bed!

10. As a result of a rare operation, you may be able to see for the first time. The bandages are being removed slowly. Can you see? *(This exercise should be done in pairs—one student acts as the patient, and one the nurse or doctor.)*

Director's Notes: Before performing the pantomimes, the older students may need more time to talk out and plan their scenes. For example, in scenario 10 above, they should ask the following questions: How long and thick is the bandage? How many layers have to be unwound before the patient begins to see light? Does he see everything clearly at first? What kind of emotional adjustment would it be to see people and objects for the very first time? Would he feel frightened, overwhelmed, overjoyed? What would he look at first—the room, the furniture, the other people, his hands, his clothes? Would he immediately want a mirror to see what he himself looks like? What would be the sensation of walking for the first time without being blind? Would he be familiar with the room?

The more advanced pantomimes listed above for the teens and adults require not just one mood but a change in mood. The actor starts with one expectation and has to move through several emotions to arrive at another mood as his expectations are either fulfilled or denied. This introduces the first elements of drama.

EXERCISE 6-8 Changes of Mood

Ages 8 to 12

1. You are in the adjoining room to the kitchen doing your homework and watching your mother as she ices a chocolate cake. She has almost completed her task when the phone rings. She leaves the kitchen. The chocolate icing is a great temptation. You walk over to it. You see the last creamy chunk of it on the knife. Mmmm, that looks good. All you have to do is spread some of the icing that is already on the cake just a little more thinly and it would cover the remaining portion. Then you could eat what's on the knife. You pick up the knife, ready to put it in your mouth, when you get a sudden pang of conscience. Even though it's just a little bit of icing, eating it without your mother's permission would be dishonest. You stare at the knife and, with fortitude and determination, put it down, breathe a big sigh of yearning for the icing, then go back into the family room.

2. You are happily playing in the sand (or simply reading a book) by the seaside. The sun is shining and there is a lovely breeze. You hear in the distance a rumble of thunder, but it hardly gets your attention. After a few moments, you notice little raindrops spitting down. You are not too concerned and just brush them off or absent-mindedly try to catch them in your hand. Several moments later, the thunder breaks so loud that it makes you jump. Suddenly, huge raindrops begin to fall. In a panic, you gather up your things and run off hurriedly to find shelter.

3. You joyfully walk into your bedroom with a prize 1,000 piece puzzle you have finally completed. You inspect it proudly and carefully place it on your shelf. You stand back and again eye it with great satisfaction and content. You make just one more minor adjustment to the placement of the puzzle, take a big breath of happy delight, and turn to leave. After just two or three steps, you hear a crashing sound. You turn and see your puzzle on the floor, collapsed into hundreds of pieces—the pieces you so painstakingly put together with such loving care.

4. You joyfully wake up and stretch with a great yawn. This is the day of the big school picnic by the shore. It means a day of no school work, just games, swimming, cooking hot dogs, and roasting marshmallows over the open fire. Nothing but fun! A droning sound invades your daydream. You get up, walk to the window, and lift the shade (or push aside the curtain). To your utter dismay, you see a steady downpour of rain. Yet, there still may be hope! You look up at the sky. It is dark with gloomy, threatening clouds as far as your eyes can see. There is no hope the skies will clear any time soon. The teacher told the class that if it rains, the picnic would be automatically canceled. What a huge disappointment after all these weeks of happy planning! Despondently you go back to bed and pull the covers over you.

5. Pretend that you are Cinderella, poor, ragged, and sorrowful. You have just watched your stepsisters go off to the ball that you so longed to attend. Miserably unhappy and exhausted from your unending household chores, you sit down by the fire to warm yourself and rest. You fall into a kind of dream sleep. A far-off sound of tinkling bells wakes you again to the present. You open your eyes and are amazed at the change all around you. The room is transformed and seems alive with a magical beauty. You stand up, then look down at yourself. You are dressed in a shimmering white gown and you are wearing the most delicate glass slippers. Can it be true or are you imagining it all? You touch the satin and fine lace of the dress. You look into the wall mirror and see the reflection of a pretty face with soft, shining hair set off with a diamond tiara. Yes, it's real. It's you. You look outside the window and see a grand carriage waiting for you. With great joy, you leave the room to go to the prince's ball.

Teens or Adults

1. You have been asked by your great-aunt to house-sit her old home while she is out of town. Ever since you were a child, you heard stories about it being haunted but, of course, you never really believed them. This is your first night. You have unpacked your suitcase and you sit down to read a bit before bed as you always do. When did that wind come up? It's rattling the window pane. And you hadn't noticed before that it was raining outside. Is that thunder in the distance? You shiver with cold and try to go back to reading. But you can't concentrate on the book. You keep telling yourself that you are letting your imagination get the best of you, especially on a stormy night. You're a big grown-up person, after all.

Wait...what was that? That's not the wind. It sounds like someone scratching. Where is it coming from? The attic? No. You listen intently. Every scary movie you ever saw seems to come to mind. The scratching is insistent and then...oh, what was that strange noise? It sounded like a child's cry. Trembling with fear, you move across the room, listen at the door, and cautiously turn the door knob. You peek out and see, there, on the threshold, a pathetically soaked, shivering puppy (or kitten), looking up at you with pleading eyes. Relieved and grateful, you pick it up and cuddle it protectingly in your arms.

2. The day has finally arrived—the day of reckoning for you and the other 23 students who are sitting for this special examination to qualify for the college freshman scholarship in English. Well, you can't be anxious. What will be, will be. Besides, you think, as you look around at the other candidates, they are just as nervous as you are. You studied hard and prepared as well as you could. Yet, what if they give you James Joyce instead of Jane Austen in the novel section or T. S. Eliot instead of Longfellow for the interpretive essay on an American poet? Modern authors were just never your cup of tea. You're a classics lover. Admit it. It's all you really like to write about. Well, you can only hope for the best.

There's the auditor handing out the papers. The exam is in front of you. Whoops, nearly opened it. You're supposed to wait until she gives the signal. She's talking now. Okay, it's time to open it up. Big breath! Here goes my future! You turn the first page. You scan the novel section and then the poetry section. Wow! Austen and Longfellow! You can do it now. You *will* do it!

3. You have just finished a five-mile run in the country. Out of breath, you collapse into a chair and wipe the sweat off your face with your hand towel. You feel satisfied, elated with your effort, and very happy. This is the best time you have made in weeks as you prepare for the big cross-country run. You reach around your neck for the heirloom stopwatch your grandfather gave you over a year ago when you won the county finals. The cord is still around your neck but not the stop watch! You frantically start to search. You look around the floor, get on your knees and check under the table and sofa, but you know it is hopeless. You desperately try to recall where it might have fallen. It doesn't take much to conclude that the watch is lying somewhere along that five-mile country stretch and heaven knows where it could be!

How can you tell grandfather? The old fashioned time clock, as he used to refer to it, was given to him by his father when he qualified at the age of 17 for the Olympic trials. How could you have been so careless, especially when he asked you so many times not to wear it while training. But you insisted that it was a lucky piece. Now what will you do? You could go over the whole country stretch, foot by foot. But what if it fell under a stone or inside a bush as you were racing by.

You sit down with your head in your hands. How could you have been so thoughtless, so reckless? And how disappointed grandfather will be. That's what hurts the most. He made you promise to take extra special care of it. What do you do now? You decide you might as well at least try and find it, hopeless as the task seems. Maybe some angel will leave it out on the path for you. Feeling a little more encouraged, you put your hands in your pockets and set about to give it your best effort. But a few steps later, you stop. Deep down in your right pocket, your fingers touch something cold and round. For a moment you hold your breath. Could it be? You pull it out. It's the stopwatch! You breathe a deep sigh of relief and hold it up and kiss it. Taking it tightly in your hand, you walk out, immensely relieved and a lot wiser.

4. Your father has been caught inside a building that collapsed due to an earthquake. Along with family members of other trapped workers, you have been waiting for over 12 hours to hear word about your dad and other possible survivors. It's after dark now and getting cold. The emergency workers have only been bringing out about two people every hour and you are losing hope. You begin to think of all the wonderful things about your dad. You remember when he was the coach on your little league team (or girl's soccer team), and the cub scout master for the cadet group when you hiked nearly three days over the Rocky (or Yosemite or Appalachian) Mountains. You never thought you would make it, but *he* kept saying you could—and you did! What about all the times he sat with you and helped you with those algebra problems.

What if he's blinded or crippled...or doesn't come out alive at all! How will your mom deal with the four of you without dad? It has been 45 minutes now since the rescue team brought out the last survivor. You've got to be brave, for mom's sake. Just look at her standing over there. You've never seen her so drawn and pale. You know she is thinking the worst and there is nothing that you can say or do that will make her feel better. If only there was something you could do to help your father! You can pray—that's what you can do. "Dear Lord, please, please let them find my dad. He's a good man. Mom needs him and we need him so much. Please don't take him from us, not now, not yet."

The crowd is surging forward. What is it? You can't see. Suddenly, a great yell erupts from those closest to the shaft. The rescue party must be coming out with someone. You can't see because of all the people in front of you. You look over to your mom. She is laughing and crying hysterically as she pushes through the crowd. You follow her and then you see, with your own eyes, that the man the rescue workers are helping out is your father! And he's alive! You joyfully run forward to meet him, with a prayer of thanks in your heart and on your lips.

Goal: To increase the student's ability to analyze the ebb and flow of thoughts in an imaginary situation involving complex changes in mood and then conveying them to an audience.

THEATER GAME 6-1   I Spy!

Description: This game can be played by all age groups.

- The students sit in a circle on the floor or in their chairs.
- The director hands an object to someone in the circle, naming that object. Use objects that are not made of glass or anything breakable.
- The person who has received the object thinks of something else it could be. For example, if the object were a pencil, the director would hand it to the first player in the circle and say, "I spy a pencil." The first player would reply, "I spy a stick of uncooked spaghetti."
- The first player then passes the object to the next player in the circle, repeating his assertion, "I spy a stick of uncooked spaghetti."
- The second player receives it and replies in turn, "I spy a _____" (names the object he imagines it to be).
- The action continues until everyone in the circle has had a turn.
- The last player hands it to the director, who affirms its original identity as a pencil.

Level One Action:

- For the first round, use an unbreakable cereal bowl.

- Give the bowl to the first player in the circle, saying, "I spy a bowl." You will be surprised at what children can imagine a bowl to be, including a hat, a sea shell, a fairy boat, a bird bath, an ear muff, a clay pigeon, a mushroom top, a cone, a wheel, an art artifact, a fossilized bone, a piece of rubber, a flying saucer, a knee cap, half a coconut, a puddle of oil, or a decorative doily.

- For the second round, use a hat of any kind as long as it is modern—for example, a baseball cap.

Level Two Action:

- Use a hat again, but this time make it a period hat—that is, a hat worn in an earlier period of time—for example, a man's hat from the 1940s, a turn-of-the-century boater, a musketeer hat, a prairie bonnet, a World War II helmet, a newsboy hat, or an old-fashioned top hat.

Level Three Action:

- Hide any object of your choice in a paper bag or a bag made of cloth material. It can be anything at all, such as a piece of wood, a pack of chewing gum or a tube of lipstick.

- Students use all their senses except their sight to guess what the object could be.

Goal: To improve the student's ability to "think on his feet"—that is, to come up with an appropriate and creative answer immediately, without time for preparation. An actor on the stage is always in a state of action, even when he is not saying or doing anything. Once the action starts in a scene or a play, the actor must be able to keep it going until its logical completion. This ability to react on the spur of the moment to an unknown or unexpected cue introduces the concept of improvisation.

KEY: Getting to the heart of the issue

An actor must learn to respond to an imaginary situation with precise movements and true feelings if his character onstage is to be believed.

Unit Study Seven

Improvisation

7

Improvisation

Class materials needed: Three medium-sized sponge balls,
                                        one a different color

Repeat Theater Game 3-1: Magic Cue Ball at last level reached

Simple Improvisation

As much as we may hope and plan otherwise, life consists of a sequence of unknown situations in which we, as individuals, are called to act with only a minimum of foresight and preparation. Armed with proper instincts, we can make the best of every challenge that confronts us and have it return dividends. The more opportunity we have to exercise independent judgment, the greater those dividends can be. Leadership is based on quick and insightful thinking—or the application of the inner genie within us to troubleshoot and find solutions. In drama, the actor must also learn to act with a minimum of preparation and must defer to his trained instincts to sustain a credible stage presence, especially when confronted with situations of missed cues or extraneous interferences.

Improvisations require the actor to respond spontaneously and appropriately to a given cue or initiate a cue on his own without direction. He has no time to think or plan what to do or say, as is often the case in life. He must invent his way in and always out of any imaginary situation. Unlike a scripted scene, the actor must rely on the power of his imagination to create the appropriate reactions. His mental imagery, in turn, derives from heightened awareness of his senses of hearing, sight, smell, taste, and touch, and his ability to vividly recall previous sensory experiences.

Improvisation compels the actor to think quickly and with mental purpose before he moves or speaks onstage. He has to trust his best instincts and try things he has never done before. In this way, he can discover within himself new words, new voices, and new expressions of personality in a controlled theatrical environment. Improvisation places each student under the constant obligation to invent, and thus develops his ability to adapt with confidence to meet any dramatic emergency. If prearranged cues break down, improvisation helps the student create a bridge or lynch pin to keep the magic going.

One of the most important attributes of a good actor is his ability to live in the present moment of his stage action so that everything his character does or says appears spontaneous and natural. Improvisation is a tried and true means of teaching the young actor how to know and create the moment and thus fill it in with purpose.

Above all, improvisation stimulates and expands the creative imagination. The creative imagination can be compared to Adventureland at Disney World, where everything we experience is fun and full of wonderful interest. Walt Disney was a man who had one of the most colorful imaginations the world has known. With a rare genius and a hard-working team of experts, he was able to bring all his exciting and sometimes fantastic images to life so that the rest of us could experience their wonder and joy and be inspired to live our lives with courage and goodness. Not everyone who makes movies and television shows has the same kind of imagination as Walt Disney. Many people in Hollywood produce stories that are filled with images that do not promote joy, virtue or goodness. Even in junior literature, many tales of science fiction and dark fantasy contain images of violence and horror. Though the darker aspects of life are legitimate subjects for drama, it is better in the early training of an actor to work with situations that are positive and upbeat, especially for the little children.

Imagination can be defined as the nation or land where we make magic. As children—and even adults—we love to imagine beautiful things and thus experience the dreams that we are meant to fulfill. This is the kind of "creative imagination" we will be developing in this drama course, for it takes our "eye magic" into places of light, not darkness. Improvisation is a wonderful way to stimulate our imaginations to spontaneously create in a carefully prepared environment that is both safe and fun.

Director's Notes: Discourage the younger children from imagining things of a frightening nature. It is just as easy and far more beneficial to coax beautiful, heavenly images out of a child than those that come from a netherworld of fear, darkness, and psychic invention.

EXERCISE 7-1 Single Word or Phrase Cue

Improvisation can be difficult for some students, so do not be discouraged if you, at first, do not succeed. Good improvisational techniques take time and patience to develop. Stanislavski wrote that "the greatest obstacle in the artistic development of an actor is haste—the forcing of his immature powers." Actors who are brilliant at improvisation always bring vitality and immediacy to their character roles. On the other hand, there are many accomplished actors who have never been able to improvise well. Remember that the skill is a means to an end, not an end in itself.

- Ask two students to volunteer to act as a pair without any preparation. The only knowledge they share is the word or phrase that will be spoken, one of seven chosen from the list below. Each actor must "cue" off what the other actor gives him, reacting to how the first actor says the word or phrase. Each cue should be spontaneous.

- The first student is preset on the stage, sitting in a chair.

- A second actor enters and the first actor responds with one of the single words or phrases listed below that they have agreed upon.

- The same pair of actors should repeat the situation at least three more times, expressing different interpretive meanings of the same word.

- For example, in the first round, the first actor may confidently look up and say, "No."—conveying a flat denial (I've made up my mind once and for all and you're not going to change it). The second time, he may gingerly look up, then away saying, "No..." with a pained, cowardly expression—conveying that he doesn't want to face the situation (I can't do it! I can't go out there and tell them what I did). In the third round, he may jump up when the second actor enters and hysterically go to the other side of the room, calling out a "No!" that means he wants to escape a situation that threatens him (You won't get me to do it! I won't tell you). Or his "No" may be spoken as a stern rebuke, forbidding reply (I am not going to do what you want, so get out).

- Each time, the second actor should react appropriately to the first actor, even though he doesn't say anything and doesn't know ahead of time how the first actor will deliver his word or phrase.

- After each round, the audience analyzes what the motivation of the first actor might be in saying his words the way he did. Did the second actor react convincingly?

- Repeat the same exercise, but switch the pairs so that both actors have the chance to speak the verbal cue.

- Choose other pairs of students to work together using the same or other simple words or phrases from the list below:

    1. No
    2. Yes
    3. Come in
    4. It's you
    5. It's over
    6. Did she tell you?
    7. Are they here yet?
    8. Do you know?
    9. Is it time?

- The students discuss the work that is performed, so that everyone has the chance to comment on his own or his fellow students' efforts.

Goal: To develop confidence in your instincts and trust in your fellow player to help sustain plausible cues.

> *Director's Notes:* Because some children find improvising difficult or embarrassing, make sure you set an atmosphere in the drama studio that is friendly and fun. Ask for volunteers rather than assign students to participate in these exercises. Each student will let you know when he is ready to try the next step.

EXERCISE 7-2 Building Word Cues

This exercise expands on what you did in the previous exercise. You can build more dialogue from the initial cues. Make sure that what you add is appropriate and helps to create a storyline. Some of you will be more interpretive and dramatic in expressing your character's thoughts. Others will not be so eloquent and may struggle at the start with just monosyllables. The important thing is to be truthful in your response even if that response is short. Silence is better than an artificial or untruthful response.

- Use the same words or phrases listed above as starter cues for the actors to improvise further dialogue.

- There is no preparation beforehand between the two actors.

- The actor who first speaks decides upon his mood and keeps it a secret from his partner until he speaks. Once that mood is set, however, both actors must build upon it for the remainder of the scene.

- The second actor reacts to the first actor's utterance and responds with his own improvised words.

- The first actor should continue with another response and so forth as a storyline begins to develop. For example, after the first actor's initial "No," the second actor may respond with: "You have to come and tell mom and dad what you did. It was your fault and I'm not going to take the blame." The first actor may then reply, "But they'll ground me if they find out." Then the second actor may continue with: "That's just what you deserve for being so thoughtless," and so on.

Goal: To initiate the students in stage dialogue and healthy codependence onstage.

KEY: Getting to the heart of the issue

> **A word or line of dialogue that is improvised must grow out of the cue that went before it if you wish to build a stage action that is convincing and real to the audience.**

EXERCISE 7-3A Two-People Improvisations *(6 to 12 years)*

As the pantomime exercises 6-7 and 6-8 in Unit Study 6 demonstrated, a dramatic situation involves the ebb and flow of a character's thoughts and feelings before he opens his mouth to express those thoughts and feelings in words of dialogue. If you are not convincing when performing without words, you will not be convincing when you perform with spoken lines.

Before you attempt the following scenes with preliminary dialogue, think through the situation and in your imagination try out different possibilities of dialogue. Remember, though, that you are not to plan out any prearranged dialogue with the other actor who will share the scene with you. The challenge of the scene will be to respond to the unknown, spontaneous word cues of the other character. Try to make meaningful, connected statements to each other, even if they are only one or two lines of dialogue. The scene is meant to be short and not continue beyond a minute or two. Try and choose an appropriate time to end the dialogue and the scene.

Suggested Scenes:

1. *Setting:* An empty classroom before the teacher arrives. Two children are sitting for a special scholarship test. Only one can win. Actor #1 is seated. Actor #2 enters.

   A. Both know each other and like each other very much.

   B. Both dislike each other intensely.

   C. They are best friends but archrivals and there can be only one prize winner.

   D. One child is confident and excited. The other is shy and nervous about the test.

2. *Setting:* Outside the principal's office. Two children are seated together.

   A. Neither have any idea why they have been called to the office.

   B. One child knows, the other doesn't. The child who knows will not tell.

   C. One child is guilty and the other one is innocent and doesn't know that the other is guilty. The guilty child tries to make the innocent one feel guilty.

   D. Both are guilty and are very nervous. Will they both lie or both tell the truth?

3. *Optional Settings:* In a library, on the beach, at McDonald's, in the dentist's waiting room, locked in the ladies or men's locker room, at a football game, standing in line at the movies, on a merry-go-round, in a crowded restaurant.

Director's Notes: These improvised scenes are meant to stimulate appropriate verbal responses to verbal cues. If the dialogue between the two actors goes on too long or begins to lose its connectedness, you can end the scene. Make sure you provide encouraging comments on what was performed, even if it was not the best effort. Do not let a scene continue to the point where the actors are uncomfortable onstage or can no longer sustain concentration.

EXERCISE 7-3B Two-People Improvisations *(Teens and Adults)*

1. You are sitting alone in the living room, reading. There is a knock at the door. You look at your watch. It is late. You rise, try to peep out through the window but can't see. There is a second knock—this time more urgent. You carefully open the door. Show by your reactions and words who it is. Is it a friend? A stranger? The little girl down the street with a deep gash in her bleeding knee? Do whatever the situation you imagine calls for and say at least two lines of dialogue.

2. A new student has arrived. This student is from a foreign country and speaks absolutely no English. You have been assigned to sit down and talk with him or her and find out as much information as possible so that you can introduce the student to your class.

3. You are preparing to go to the annual school dance. You are adding the finishing touches to your makeup and hair when your brother comes in to tell you that your date just called to say that he has the mumps. Can you convince your older brother to take you?

4. You have just been dropped off at your female cousin's birthday party and have no way to get home until the party is over. When you walk into the room you notice, to your horror, that you are the only boy amongst at least 30 girls. One of the girls approaches you.

5. It's April 1 and your birthday. Your older brother (or sister) gives you a beautifully wrapped box. You can't believe he could be so thoughtful. You excitedly unwrap the present and find...nothing! The box is empty! Your brother bursts out laughing and says: "April Fool's Day, sis!" Are you disappointed? Angry? Disgusted? Amused? Just as you are about to leave the room, he calls you back and hands you a tiny box. You unwrap it and find a beautiful pocketbook that you have been wanting.

6. You have spent six months knitting a special sweater for your younger sister who is starting high school next year. You have used every spare moment of your time to make it. You have wrapped it, made a personalized card, and now your sister has arrived home. You have been waiting for a special moment to give it to her. She unwraps it carelessly, doesn't even look at the card, holds up the sweater and then tosses it back in the box with a "Thanks, Jennie!" Then she tells you she has to get ready to go out with some of her friends and hurries off.

7. You have just found out from your mother that the new boy up the street is dropping by to meet you in 5 minutes. She left for errands before you could find out any more information about him. You are dressed in a stained t-shirt and jeans, and your hair is dirty. You decide to wash and dry your hair in the few minutes before he arrives. You quickly wet your hair under the kitchen tap and reach for the detergent, forgetting that it's not shampoo. You cannot get the suds out of your eyes and reach for a towel, but there is none. Then...there is a knock at the door. What do you say when you greet him? What does he say when he meets you for the first time with bedraggled wet hair and squinting eyes?

Goal: To build dialogue around spontaneous verbal cues from another actor.

Director's Notes: Don't be concerned so much with the depth of characterization or the cleverness of the dialogue. Encourage the actors to create simple, appropriate action and build convincing lines of dialogue both from imaginary cues and from the spontaneous statements of the other actor in the scene. This early in acting training, do not expect great fluency or range of dialogue construction. Characterization skills need to be developed before dialogue will prove adequate to the dramatic incident and to complex mood changes.

KEY: Getting to the heart of the issue

Improvisation helps you to stay in the present moment and build each real or imaginary cue out of the intrinsic action.

There is something I consider more important than brains, education, energy, and that is knowing the moment: the moment to act, or not to act; the moment to speak, or keep silent. On the stage, as every actor knows, timing is the all-important factor. I believe it is the key to life, too. If you master the art of knowing the moment, in your work, your relationship with others, you won't have to pursue happiness and success. They'll walk right in through your front door!

—Charles Coburn (American actor)

Advanced Improvisation

Previous pantomime exercises were designed to stimulate your imagination, focus the five senses to respond to imaginary cues, and encourage you to think and feel not as yourself but as someone else. Simple improvisations introduced the beginnings of speech with another character on the stage. All the exercises that follow involve advanced improvisation—that is, the impromptu making up of an imaginary scene with lines to speak that unfold a definite storyline and character development—all this without any rehearsal or preparation. Using only limited information about the character and the dramatic situation, you will use what you have learned in class about posture, stage movement, and blocking to convey both the physical and emotional traits of your character.

Performing improvisations with dialogue promotes spontaneity, adaptability, and inventiveness in building your imaginary character. It also teaches you natural timing in the execution of your lines and actions. When you do not know what lines are next and you have to build your character and your scene moment by moment, you will discover the dynamism of interacting with another player on the stage, and depending upon him or her to make a scene meaningful, as well as dramatic.

If you learn to love the experience of creating on the spot and making every action and reaction count in conveying your character's thoughts and feelings, your scripted performances in a play will never lack freshness and immediacy. You will always feel confident about filling in a missed cue. As an actor, you become more skilled at creating characterizations with interest and depth when you use improvisation. Improvisation helps you feel the role and sense the enormous possibilities of where you can go with it. Many scripted scenes and plays are the finished products of classroom improvisations. You literally can become a playwright on your feet.

Expressiveness is largely determined by the emotional attitude or motivation of the character. The exercises below start with the matching of simple phrases and dialogue lines to different character attitudes, and evolve to advanced scenes that require more complex characterization involving change and development.

E X E R C I S E 7-4A Character Attitudes

Level One Action:

- Have each of the students choose one of the following ten lines and speak it with at least five different character attitudes chosen from the list below.

- Remember to adapt the voice to suit the character attitude, taking note of elements of vocal expression, such as emphasis, inflection, pitch level, etc.

- The student suggests a reason (or motivation) for each of his five different character attitudes. For example, in #10, the motivation of the "happy" character speaking these lines may be that he or she has been hoping to go skiing all winter and finally the snowstorm that is forecast for the next day will make it possible. Or with #4, the "angry" character may be fed up with the disorder of toys, candy wrappings, and books scattered over the floor and impatiently tells the person responsible to pick it up.

- Have the class tell you why the reading of the lines sounded different with each character attitude. How did the voice show the changing emotional moods? Was it higher with some emotions, or louder with others, softer or sweeter? Was the inflection a rising or falling one? Was the voice high or low in pitch? Did one word get more emphasis than the other?

Suggested Lines:

1. I'd like to be an actor on the stage.
2. Do you think, sir, that I was right, after all?
3. What a great day!
4. Would you please pick up the mess?
5. I got seven A's and three B's on my report card.
6. I will *never* go there again!
7. Thank you very much. You are so kind!
8. The car went around the corner and didn't come back.
9. Please don't tell me that again.
10. A snowstorm is forecast tomorrow.

Suggested Character Attitudes:

Shy	Angry	Proud
Polite	Suspicious	Surprised
Happy	Mysterious	Grateful
Embarrassed	Fearful	Deceitful
Jealous	Joyful	Intrigued
Aggravated	Upset	Sulking

Level Two Action:

- Have each of the students choose any two of the character attitudes—for example, shy and polite, happy and surprised, or jealous and suspicious.

- Each student reads his line again, combining both adjectives to create a more complex character attitude in the reading of the line—for example, happily surprised or jealously suspicious.
- The students can combine two opposites, such as fearfully happy or joyfully upset, etc.

Level Three Action:

- Have each student make up his own dialogue line and decide upon his own character attitude using one or two adjectives on the list, or his own.
- The student keeps it a secret until his turn comes to speak.
- Let the rest of the class guess the meaning of the interpretation, including a motive for the speaker's words.

E X E R C I S E 7-4B Character Attitudes for Little Children

Level One Action:

- Assign each of the younger students one of the following words or phrases from the "Suggested Words" list below. Also assign to each of them a character attitude from the "Character Attitudes" list. Explain that they are to imagine being that kind of character when they say their line.
- Little children like to have everything explained to them very clearly. If you need to show them how to perform the exercise, do not choose a character attitude from the list. Make up one of your own. Otherwise, they will imitate exactly what you did when it is their turn.
- Have the children take turns acting out their word or phrase according to the character attitude assigned.

Suggested Words:

1. Come in
2. Is it me?
3. Hello
4. Goodbye
5. Maybe tomorrow
6. All right
7. Don't go
8. What is it?

Character Attitudes:

> Angry
> Bored
> Sad
> Happy
> Very afraid
> Stubborn
> Disappointed
> Excited
> Shy

Director's Notes: Make sure the little ones understand the meaning of all the words describing their characters.

Level Two Action:

- Have each child now repeat the same words but let him decide upon his own mood or character attitude (he can choose from the list or make up his own).

- The student should keep it a secret until his turn comes to speak.

- Have the other children guess what his character attitude is.

Level Three Action:

- Have each child read the same words but as one of the following character types:

  1. A king or queen of old
  2. A scheming villain
  3. A good fairy
  4. A mischievous elf
  5. A very important statesman
  6. A kind and beautiful lady or a brave knight
  7. A soldier
  8. A clown
  9. A movie star
  10. The President of the United States

THEATER GAME 7-1 Family Portraits

(Adapted from the 1970s television game show *Family Feud,* and from a similar exercise in *On Stage* by Lisa Bany-Winters)

Description: Divide the students into groups of four or five. Assign each group a family number (Family #1, Family #2, etc.). Each group represents the members of a family unit. Those members may decide amongst themselves who they wish to represent— that is, father, mother, sister, brother, etc. Each family group takes turns on the playing area, pretending that they are posing for a professional studio portrait. The director acts as the photographer and calls out the Family Character or *kind* of family it must be—for example, The Cowboy Family. (See suggested list below.) The family group has thirty seconds to demonstrate the "character attitude" of that family by appropriate posture, gestures, facial expressions, and body language that best and most colorfully represent the stereotyped characterization of such a family. They "energize" that character attitude until the photographer is satisfied enough to call *Freeze.*

Level One Action:

- Call out Family Group #1 and assign it a character name.
- The players now have 30 seconds to take on their roles in their family character attitude.
- The photographer (director) calls *Freeze* when time limit is reached.
- Have the rest of the class judge if it was a successful portrait.

Level Two Action:

- The players are told in secret who they are.
- A student is assigned the role of photographer.
- The players have 30 seconds to characterize their family attitude.
- The photographer calls *Freeze* after time limit.
- The rest of the class guesses their identity.

Level Three Action:

- Set up a bench or two chairs (or stools) center stage.
- A student is assigned the role of photographer.
- Another student acts as an assistant to help the family players.

- This time, the players need to pose using the chairs.
- The photographer allows up to 60 seconds for characterization.
- The photographer calls *Freeze* when time limit is up.
- The rest of the class guesses what kind of family it is.

Level Four Action:

- The players may add family pets to their characterization—that is, one or more of the players can take on the character of a dog or a cat, and adopt the same character attitude as the rest of the members of the family.

Level Five Action:

- The players may add dialogue to their characterization. They may also wish to try dialects—for example, The Cowboy Family may choose a Texan accent, or The Strictly Formal Family may adopt a British accent, and so forth. Each group should be inventive and imaginative. Assign a longer preparation time for this level before calling *Freeze*.

Suggested Family Characters:

The Cowboy Family	The Stuffy Nose Family
The Happy Family	The Hypochondriac Family
The Suspicious Family	The Perfectly Polite Family
The Silly Laughing Family	The Very Old Family
The Highly Inspired Family	The Robot Family
The Military Family	The Baby Bunch Family
The Strictly Formal Family	The Sleepy Family
The Grim Family	The Nearly Blind Family
The Fearfully Shy Family	The Big Smiley Family
The Paranoid Family	The Physically Fit Family
The Very Nervous Family	The Cave Man Family
The Spy Family	The Proud Family
The Irritable Family	The Bored Family
The Ballerina Family	The Cold Family
The Musical Family	The Hot Family
The Constantly Busy Family	The Slow Family
The Sneering Family	The Speedy Family

Goal: To develop quick thinking and teamwork in group improvisation.

Director's Notes: Each individual portrait must be complete and convincing in itself so that it contributes to the total "family" character portrait. Each member must not only assume his own individual character but also blend in as part of the overall group effect.

THEATER GAME 7-2 I Am Happy

Description: This is a game for all ages. Have the children sit in a circle on the floor or in their chairs. Assign them, as a group, a character attitude. Then have each player, in his turn, say why (or when) he feels that way.

Level One Action:

- Start with the character attitude of "happy." Examples of possible reasons why or when someone is happy are listed below:

  I am happy because I was born a girl.
  I am happy because I got an A in Algebra.
  I am happy because the sun is shining and I love sunny days.
  I am happy because God loves me.
  I am happy because I am an American.
  I am happy when I eat chocolate ice cream.
  I feel happy when I am swimming in the ocean.
  I am happy when my brother doesn't talk to me.
  I am happy whenever my homework is done.
  My happiest time is when grandma comes to visit.
  Happiness is sitting all by myself reading a book.
  I am happy when I know my parents are pleased with me.
  I am happiest when mom gives me a hug.
  Happiness is wrestling with dad on the family room floor.
  My happiest time is when my sister isn't talking on the phone.
  I am happiest when I get a new Boy Scout badge.

Level Two Action:

- Reverse the character attitude—that is, I am *un*happy...

Level Three Action:

- After each player makes his statement, ask for an expanded explanation. For example, if someone has answered that he is happy when he receives a new Boy Scout badge, his expanded explanation may be that he feels proud knowing that he helped out someone in the community.

Level Four Action:

- Have each of the children choose from the list of character attitudes below and repeat Level Three above:

I am hopeful	I am excited
I am loving	I am bursting with energy
I am angry	I am prayerful
I am sad	I am smart
I am enthusiastic	I am upset
I am serious	I am irritable
I am quiet	I am "cool"
I am inspired	I am confident
I am suspicious	I am depressed
I am joyful	I am helpful
I am worried	I am determined

Goal: To begin the association of dialogue with different character attitudes.

EXERCISE 7-5A Change-of-Mood Scenes for One Character *(8-12 years)*

Instructions: The goal of this exercise is to expand simple one-character scenes in order to develop your skills at building a character. We will start with some of the complex sensory response and change-of-mood pantomime exercises in Unit 6. It's always fun to return to characters that are old friends and settings that are familiar. With original analysis and discussion of these exercises already completed in earlier classes, you can concentrate on creating your characters.

Level One Action:

- For a demonstration exercise, let us start with #13 in the 8-12 years category of *Suggested Scenarios* which follows Exercise 6-7.

(Introduce it in this manner:)

Remember the scene about the boy who runs happily into his bedroom and finds his model airplane scattered in pieces all over the floor? Let's expand this into a scene with emphasis on building a character with some dialogue. First, let's give a name to the young boy.

(Choose a name from the ones suggested by the students, say Johnny.)

What would Johnny say as he looks at the model airplane lying in broken pieces on the floor?

(Suggested dialogue: "Wow, look at my airplane! It's all busted!...All those pieces broken. My airplane is ruined!")

As he sadly goes over to pick up the broken pieces, realizing he will have to begin all over again, what do you think he might be feeling and what might he say?

(Suggested dialogue: "I wish I didn't have a creep like my little brother taking my things and breaking them. When I find him, I'm going to beat him up.")

He would be feeling very upset with his little brother for taking his model airplane in the first place and playing with it like a toy. He'd probably also say he wished he could get his hands on him so he could punish him for his mischief. You have just told me what you *think* Johnny would say. Now I want you to imagine that you *are* Johnny and I want you to think and speak his thoughts. Don't say that Johnny would think this or say that...just speak the words yourself as Johnny would think and speak them, and don't be afraid to put some real emotion into the words. Think of the expression on Johnny's face as he looks at what his little brother did; how he would hold his fists clenched tight, and perhaps even shake with anger.

(Have the students act out some of the dialogue suggested, for example: "Just wait 'til I get my hands on Jeffrey. I'll teach him not to touch my things again. I'll beat him up. I don't care if he is only two. Why can't he stay out of my room? I've told him lots of times not to play with my model airplane.)

Johnny's words would certainly reflect his anger, unless, of course, he is so heartbroken that he is more sad than angry—so sad that all he can think about is his much-loved model airplane. In this case, what do you think Johnny would say?

(Suggested dialogue: "My favorite model airplane! After all the work I did to make it look perfect. Dad was so proud of me putting the wings together all by myself. Now, it's all in pieces. I might never be able to get it back the way it was again. It's just not fair.")

We can even make Johnny angry at first but then, as he remembers how small his little brother is, he might be more willing to forgive him. Or perhaps Johnny may accept the responsibility himself for not putting it in a place out of little Jeffrey's reach. What would he say if he thinks this way?

(Suggested dialogue: "Little brothers are pests. Why do they have to be such brats? Well, maybe it wasn't his fault. He really is just a baby. I shouldn't have left it on my bed this morning when I went to school. Little kids always think everything's a toy. I guess I should have put it up on my top shelf where he couldn't reach it. Mom told me to, but I forgot to move it. Next time I'll know better.")

As actors, we don't let our feelings get carried away as we imagine a situation where the character is angry or upset like Johnny. We never use swear words in rehearsal or onstage. And we don't use bad grammar, no matter how angry we might feel, unless the character naturally talks like that, such as Huck Finn. We do not touch or strike another character unless the director blocks it as a necessary part of the action or expression of the character. Any physical contact between actors must be choreographed with theatrical control.

Director's Notes: With a change in the kind of object broken, the character can be a girl instead of a boy.

Level Two Action:

- Have each of the children take turns acting out the scene, using the dialogue suggested by the class, or making up their own.
- Each player enters from the same playing area, such as UR.
- Encourage students to add their own original dialogue and extra action.

Director's Notes: Boys tend to be more independent thinkers so don't be surprised if they entirely ignore the lines of dialogue suggested by the class and invent their own. They might also take the action of the scene and change its direction, which is fine. Just make sure that the players understand the flow of the character's thoughts and can express those thoughts with appropriate dialogue. Speaking in front of others, let alone making up things to say on the spot, can be a big chore for some students. Don't be concerned if some only say a word or two in their initial attempts at verbal improvisation. Fluency and confidence will come in time with practice and observation of others in their class.

E X E R C I S E 7-5B Change-of-Mood Scenes for One Character *(Teens)*

Instructions: These exercises teach you to create dialogue around a character's thoughts and feelings in a given situation. When you first start doing improvisations, it is expected that you will use your own thoughts and feelings when making up lines for your character. Even though your own thoughts and feelings might be identical to the character's, always remember that acting is all about playing somebody else and not yourself. It will become easier to separate the two when you have a character assigned to you that has a different personality to yours.

You will be acting out one-character scenes. This allows you to concentrate on lines that flow out of your own character's mood rather than having to respond to the spontaneous cues of other characters in the scene. The dialogue should express the transition from one mood to another, each mood making up one acting unit.

Director's Notes: The actors should not use slang or swear words. The discipline that a "character" enforces on a young actor's way of thinking and feeling can be compelling. Thinking and feeling how another person would speak and act requires more than just imagining; it requires an ability to reason objectively and dispassionately, and takes the student not only out of his own lazy habits of expressing himself, but also out of his own self-conscious awareness. That is why improvisational drama has been used successfully to change and even rehabilitate poorly adjusted or troublesome children.

Level One Action:

- Have the students as a group choose one of the four pantomime scenes in Exercise 6-8 Changes of Mood–Teens.

- Discuss each mood change in the character's feelings and state of mind, and the motivation behind that change.

- Have the students suggest lines of dialogue to match the flow of the character's thoughts as described. (Be aware that these particular scenes can be expansive. More dialogue is required of the teens than the few lines expected of the younger children in their simple scenes. If you do not think that your teens are up to the challenge of creating dialogue for Exercise 6-8, then start off with choices from Exercise 6-7.)

Level Two Action:

- Once the character has been discussed and dialogue suggested, invite each of the students to perform the improvisation.

- Have the rest of the class critique each performance and offer positive suggestions.

Level Three Action:

- Have the students divide up into pairs and work out dialogue for the remaining scene choices in Exercise 6-8 (or 6-7) Teens.

- Invite each student to perform the scene.

- Have the rest of the class critique each performance and offer positive suggestions.

EXERCISE 7-6 Change-of-Mood Scenes for Two Characters

(Use the Unit 7 Exercises 7-3A and 7-3B: One and Two People Improvisations.)

Instructions: It is time to flesh out the characters in the preliminary improvisations introduced earlier in this unit. Interactive dialogue is far more challenging than monologue because it involves more than one thought and feeling pattern for the character that you play. Each time there is a change in mood for your character, you create a new acting unit. This exercise will require you to create several acting units that are meant to blend together into one unbroken sequence. Your goal is to dramatize, by your actions and spoken statements, the thoughts and feelings of the two characters you are playing in the scene. Each new reaction needs to be thoughtful and directly related to the action or words that immediately precede it. All dialogue should progress meaningfully to advance the storyline.

To develop your characters, you will need to exercise your imagination. You have to concentrate hard if you hope to convey to your audience the real life drama of the situation and its impact on your characters. Except for the basic information given in each exercise, you have no time to think or plan what to say once the scene starts, or how to react to the other character, given that the other character will be making it up as he or she goes, too. You will be moving through a story of your own spontaneous invention, connecting each link moment by moment with new words, new expressions, and new actions.

Project your voice so that every word can be heard. In preparation, do some breathing and relaxation warm-ups. The physical and emotional states of a character directly affect the quality and energy of the voice. Every effort to adapt your voice to the character will make your performance that much more theatrically convincing.

Level One Action:

- Divide the class up into partners and assign a scene to each pair. Each actor should think through and analyze his character's motives, thoughts, and feelings and all the possible things he could say and do.

- The two actors who will be sharing a scene should not plan together what they will say or how they might react. This is still a format of improvisation, not scripted scene or play structure.

- After the players conclude their improvisation, have the rest of the class critique their effort. Did the dialogue flow naturally between them? Did the dialogue progress the storyline? Was it clear what each character was thinking and feeling? Were there changes in mood with each character? Can you identify what these changes were? Could each of the players have used his voice better to play his part?

- Have each pair of actors who played the scene discuss what they found easiest to do and what they found the most difficult.

Level Two Action:

- Have the same students repeat the identical scene, but this time incorporate the suggestions made by the rest of the class.

- Have the other students do a critique on this second effort. Were there significant improvements in building more convincing characters?

- How did the pair of actors feel about their scene the second time around?

Director's Notes: Even though the students have not yet studied voice in class, do not let them get away with careless or sloppy speech. They should not mumble, use slang, look down at the floor or turn upstage when speaking their lines. They should speak loud enough to be heard and clear enough so that every word can be understood. You should also encourage them to think in terms of giving their voice, and not just their thoughts and feelings, a character attitude.

EXERCISE 7-7 More Dramatic Incidents for Improvised Dialogue

Instructions: Dramatize the following scenes, following the process used in previous exercises. These scenes have been adapted to suit different age groups. Use them as models to analyze other scenes of your own invention. When alone on the stage, the player should verbalize all the changing thoughts and feelings of his character, as if the character was speaking to himself out loud.

5-10 year olds

1. A young girl is sitting on a bench on a lovely summer's day. She is alone. She shuffles her feet back and forth and looks and acts very bored. Suddenly she hears a squeaky little "meow" and looks around to discover the source of the sound. There, just a few feet from her, is a tiny newborn kitten. She makes a cry of delight and gets up to go to it, but as soon as she moves, the kitten scurries away several more feet. She is disappointed but realizes at once that she must be still and quiet if she doesn't want to scare the kitten away again. She sits down very slowly and remains still, hoping the kitten will come closer. She speaks very quietly to it and very sweetly in soft, warm tones so as to coax it nearer. After a few moments her smile shows that the kitten is approaching her. Very slowly she slips down off the bench and onto her ankles, being careful not to move abruptly. Cautiously, she extends her open palm to the kitten and tells it gently not to be afraid. Within a few seconds the kitten licks her hand. Very slowly she puts out her other hand and lifts the little kitten close up against her chest. Resting her head against its soft fur, she walks away in a state of utter enchantment, with the purring kitten securely wrapped and thoroughly content in its new owner's arms.

11-18 years

2. A young teenage boy is sitting reading a book. He can't focus his attention for more than a few seconds at a time, but keeps checking his watch and looking over to the right as though he is expecting someone. Another boy, coming from the opposite direction, greets him and asks him if he's ready to go to the football game. He reluctantly tells his friend that he can't because he has to baby-sit his little sister until his mom gets back from running an errand. The other boy reminds him that this is the finals and that they'll miss the kick-off. He tries to convince him that his sister will be fine and to just leave a note for his mom. The boy is tempted. The friend even offers him a pen. The boy takes it and starts to scratch out a note on a piece of paper he finds nearby. He puts the note on top of the book and gets up to leave. Just before exiting he hesitates, looks back guiltily at the note, turns back and sits down again. The friend questions him and he explains why he can't go.

15-18 years

3. You have just arrived home from school. You throw down your backpack and notice your beautiful prom dress laid out carefully on the arm of the sofa. Your mom must have finished the hem for you. You lift it up and look at it admiringly. Then you place it up against your body and look at yourself through the living room mirror. Perfect! And so flattering to your figure. It is then that you see a written note with your name on it by the telephone. You pick it up and read it. It is a telephone message left for you from your date, who was supposed to take you to the school prom that night. The note says that he can't take you because he has the mumps. You can't believe that a boy of sixteen could get the mumps! And the boy who just happens to be your date! It's just too embarrassing for words. The whole school will know about it and make you the subject of jokes for the rest of the school year! You just want to hide away from everyone forever.

You cross to the sofa and place your dress carefully, even lovingly on the sofa back and flop down on the sofa, tears brimming in your eyes. You start to think of all the hours you spent helping your mom make it. You sigh with disappointment as you touch its silky softness.

You'll never wear it, ever, because you couldn't face going to another dance after this humiliation.

In the midst of your unhappiness you hear someone come into the room. You don't turn around to see who it is. You certainly don't want your parents or your brother to see how upset you are. And you are hardly in a mood to talk. You just want to be left alone. Then you recognize your brother's voice. He starts off the conversation by asking if you got the telephone message. You nod your head. He tells you how sorry he is about Howard getting the mumps the day of the prom. You can hear genuine sympathy in his voice. He tells you that he's been thinking about the situation and that maybe it's a blessing Howard got the mumps since everyone knows what a lousy dancer he is, and that now you won't be stuck with him all night on the dance floor.

He says all this in a lighthearted way and you know that he's just trying to cheer you up, but his comments don't make you feel any better and you tell him that. He then reminds you that he's one of the best dancers in the school as well as being pretty popular with the girls. He walks closer to you but you still have your head turned away from him. Then he tells you that, although he's a senior, and seniors don't normally attend the 10th grade proms, he's willing to be your date if that would make you happy.

You turn to face him for the first time and are taken aback to see that he is fully dressed in his tuxedo. You never saw him look so handsome. There is a big smile on his face. You begin to see that he planned it all out before he came into the room. You are overwhelmed at how sweet and thoughtful he is to want to help you like this. It suddenly occurs to you that he is doing all this to help you save face and escape the gossip, and because he knows how much time and care you put into making your dress.

Gratefully, you get up, wipe the tears away, pick up the dress, and tell him to order the carriage in half an hour. Just before passing out of the room, you turn and smile at him and say, Thank you!

Older Teens and Adults

4. (Developed from Improv #7 in Exercise 7-3B in this unit.) You are sitting at the kitchen table, doing some homework. On her way out the door, your mother calls out that the new boy up the street

will be stopping by to introduce himself in 10 minutes or so. You are stunned! Before you can get any more information from her, you hear the front door slam. This is the boy you saw from a distance the other day and who looked so nice! You look down at your dingy jeans and old t-shirt. No, that won't do for a first impression. You'll have to change clothes. But no. You suddenly remember that your hair is dirty. Oh, how you wish you'd have washed it last night! Forget changing clothes. Since your mom just picked up your purple silk sweater from the cleaners and it's hanging right there over the chair, you'll put that over your t-shirt. You put it on hurriedly, zip it up, and jump up and down trying to see your reflection in the kitchen window. Oh, well, you already know it looks pretty on you.

Making your hair look nice is the priority now. You just couldn't face him with greasy hair! Oh, why didn't your mom give you some warning! Well, better get busy and make it look acceptable. You stand in front of the kitchen window and try styling it in different ways, but nothing helps. An idea occurs to you. You check your watch. Seven minutes! You have seven minutes...or so. The "or so" probably means that he'll be late. Yes, you can do it. You can wash and dry your hair in that time. You impulsively throw your hair under the kitchen sink tap and get it wet. Suddenly you realize that this is not your bathroom sink, and that you don't have your bottle of shampoo handy. You spy the dish detergent and figure that it's got to be better than nothing. You take the detergent bottle, squeeze some on your hair, and start washing it. Then you rinse. But you can see through the reflection of the kitchen window that there are still suds all over your hair, and you smell like the kitchen sink. You rinse again. Still not good enough. You rinse one more time, then blindly reach for a towel. The towel!

You forgot to go get a bath towel! Well, maybe the dishtowel will work. Where is it? You can barely open your eyes and when you do, some of the detergent suds get into them and your eyes start stinging. Now, you're almost totally blind. Oh, where is the towel? Maybe it dropped off the oven rack onto the floor. Still trying to hold your hair up from dripping, you search blindly on your knees all around the floor, but still no towel. Suddenly, you hear a door knock! It couldn't be him! He's too early. But what if it *is* him? You get up off your knees, and wring out your hair the best you can.

Another knock. Maybe you can just ignore it and he'll think no one is home. No, your mom told him you were home. Frantically, you look everywhere for a towel—anything to dry your hair with! But, half blinded, you can't find a thing. Again, another knock—this time louder and more insistent. Finally, you face the fact that there is no way out. You take a big breath, twist your hair up on top of your head, hold it in place with your left hand, and blindly feel your way to the door with your right hand, still trying to rub the soap suds from your eyes.

Reluctantly, you open the door and, with soap still stinging your eyes, cheerily say, "Hi!" Though you are not sure exactly where he is, you extend your hand forward for him to shake, with accompanying words, such as: "I'm Janice. Won't you come in?" In fact, you are at least two feet in the wrong direction with your hand. He reorients your hand and shakes it. You explain in the most nonchalant way (as thought it is perfectly natural) that you have detergent suds in your eyes. He walks in and gallantly takes out a large white handkerchief from his pocket and hands it to you. You gratefully try and wipe the stinging suds from your eyes. You see his face more clearly now and he really is as good looking as you thought. You notice that he has a surprised and bemused look on his face. You observe between your squinting eyes that he is looking down at your jeans. You look down and for the first time you notice that the water from your hair has dripped onto your new purple sweater and caused the dye to bleed onto your pants, creating a polka dot effect. You are utterly humiliated.

Suddenly, he bursts out laughing. You are stunned and don't know whether to cry or run away. Then with a cheery, good humored voice, he says something like: "Wow, I'm so glad you're real. I saw you from a distance the other day and couldn't get up enough courage to come and say hello. You looked so together. But you're not a bit like what I thought. It's great to meet you, Janice. I'm Paul." You are relieved beyond words but still self-conscious and stumbling in your attempt to explain why you were so unprepared. Still amused by the situation, he tells you that he'll leave and come back in an hour, and maybe the two of you can go see a movie. Before you know it, he has gone. You stand at the door and wave to him abstractly, still squinting, as he disappears from view.

THEATER GAME 7-3 Costume Day—Let's Dress Up

Preparation: Visit your local Good Will store or any second hand clothing shops to search out clothes that could be used or adapted for period costume items. Sometimes parents and grandparents have all sorts of odds and ends in the attic that their children or grandchildren use for dress up that they would be willing to donate or loan to you. Get everyone you know to help look for costumes.

It is a good idea at the beginning of the school year to let parents know about the Costume Day and have them start on their search early. Every drama group should develop a costume shop and a costume fund. Monies from intermission refreshments during recitals and play presentations can be used just for this purpose. If you are a non-profit organization or working under the umbrella of one, you can freely ask fabric stores to donate material to you. For formal recitals and full-length plays, you may need to rent specific period costumes and accessories, such as bonnets, canes, collars, swords, parasols, etc., from a professional theatrical shop.

Look through the recital scenes that you are planning to perform and identify the kinds of costumes that will be needed. Even though you won't be casting the scenes until half way through the second quarter, make a list of all the characters in the scenes, and the time in which each character lived. Add any special notes. For example, if the character is the child Jane Eyre, the historical period would be around the 1820s or 30s. Additionally, her costume would vary depending upon the scene setting. In the Gateshead Hall scene she would be dressed fashionably, though not as finely as her cousins. At Lowood Institution, she and Helen Burns would wear the plain brown calico pinafores and Quaker-type bonnets that all the orphans were required to wear. Send a letter out to parents well ahead of time to start researching the styles of the costuming you will be dealing with. Line up parents who can sew.

Because the students come in all sizes and shapes, not all the girls will fit into the costumes you have. Have at least one long skirt with an adjustable waistband for the chubbier girl. Use fabric duck tape to make temporary hems to adjust to the different heights of the girls. The same applies to the boys. Make sure at least one pair of trousers or knickers has an elastic waistband.

Organize the costumes according to historical period—that is, separate the slim, Victorian turn-of-the-century skirts from the Civil War hoop skirts. Keep costume accessories in a plastic bag on the same hanger as the costume it goes with. Put a couple of the teenage girls and at least one parent in charge of organizing the costumes, and dressing and undressing the younger female students. Have one or two of the teenage boys help the young boys. It is important to keep the costumes hung up and not left where they can be soiled and torn.

Description: Have a session where the students try on period costumes and explore how to walk, sit, stand, move, speak lines, and even dance in them. The children should also learn how to use costume accessories, such as theatrical swords, knives, fans, eye-glass pieces, feather pens, turn-of-the-century telephones, scrolls, canes, top-hats, etc. Watching movies set in earlier times teaches a lot about proper manners and theatrical movements in costume.

Level One Action:

- Have each of the children choose one costume.
- Establish a common pattern of things to do onstage.
- Girls: a) walk to center stage and sit down; b) stand up; c) curtsy; d) hold hand out to be kissed; e) fan yourself; f) move to waltz or minuet music; g) speak a line of poetry; h) exit
  Boys: a) walk to center stage and sit down; b) stand up; c) make a bow to a lady; d) stand like a soldier or a courtly gentleman; e) take a lady's hand and kiss it; f) walk quickly onstage and flex your sword as though getting ready for a duel; g) waltz with a lady; h) exit boldly

Level Two Action:

- Choose a class day and dedicate it to a particular historical time. Have the students decide what period in history they want to dress up in.
- The director and the students must dress in the costume of that time, and act according to the mode of that period, even while performing exercises.

Director's Notes: Try and find someone who has practical knowledge of and works professionally with historical costumes. You might contact a regional theater company or the drama department of a local college and invite the costume mistress to come and talk with the students. You could also contact a local costume theatrical shop and have the owner or manager of the shop bring some of his costumes to the class and discuss how he makes them, cleans them, repairs them, etc. Some of these people have expert knowledge and experience in the field. This enthusiasm can easily transfer to your students.

Unit

Study

Eight

Drama Is Conflict

8

Drama Is Conflict

Class materials needed:

Two medium-sized sponge balls of different color
Handout #8-1, *Drama Is Conflict*

THEATER GAME 3-1 Magic Cue Ball

Level Four Action:

- Appoint a captain (preferably one of the best throwers and catchers).

- He stands in the middle of the circle and throws the ball to anyone he likes in the circle of players and they throw it back to him.

- The captain should throw accurately and rhythmically but randomly so that the players cannot detect a predictable pattern.

- If a student drops the ball, he sits out.

- When the number of players is reduced to less than six, the remaining students start walking in a circle.

- The captain throws the ball to the remaining students more quickly now and each player must catch the ball while he is in motion. Again, if a student drops the ball, he sits out.

- Make sure there are no big gaps anywhere in the circle and that the students keep moving steadily.

- The winner becomes the next captain.
- Repeat the exercise at least three times.

Level Five Action:

- Same as above except this time appoint two captains (usually the two who were the victors in the previous rounds), who will each have a ball to throw, distinguished only by color.
- Both captains throw the cue balls to the circle of players, but do not throw their individual balls at the same time to the same student.

Goal: To increase concentration skills and physical and mental coordination as well as strengthen the ability to focus on the immediate dramatic action.

> *Director's Notes:* Use the same spongy balls every week. Throwing a soft, lightweight ball is like trying to project in a barn with poor acoustics. The actor has to learn to exert and extend effort to achieve his goal.

The Drama of Life

Theater is life itself heightened and held captive inside a make-believe frame that is outside time and space. The movement of life inside that frame, whether proscenium stage or celluloid film, is dynamic. It is made real, energizing, and forceful by the living imagination of the actors and the audience. When we watch a play or movie, what we see and feel is larger than life—more vibrant and often more persuasive in its intensity than real life. This is so because within that magical frame the essence of life has been concentrated.

If that "concentrated essence" is portrayed to be of noble and pure substance, and the director, playwright, and actor comprehend the "drama" of life to be a journey of growing and overcoming, then the actor has an enormous power to influence his audience for the good. If the essence portrayed is of dark substance, and the drama of life is conceived to be a journey of self-indulgence in every base passion, then the actor has an equally enormous power to influence his audience negatively.

Theater that upholds the elements of good drama invites the audience to enter the proscenium door and vicariously live that essence without running any personal risk. We can witness the joys and triumphs of accomplishing a hero's dreams without having to fire a single shot or endure the loss of life or limb. At the same time, we can experience the moving thoughts and feelings of an evil person without having to incur the consequences of performing his bad deeds or taking in the poison of evil ourselves. With our soul's wings, we can touch the purest expression of love or travel to the darkest pits of degradation and shame through the magic milieu of theater. In short, we can enter this glorious frame of virtual reality and exit enriched, illumined, and ennobled.

EXERCISE 8-1 A Routine Day

Level One Action:

- A student outlines a typical day in his life, describing everything he does from the moment he wakes up to when he goes to sleep.

- After he relates the events, ask the rest of the students if they think his story would make a good movie script and hold the audience's attention from beginning to end.

- Unless that student's daily activities entailed a lot of unusual excitement and adventure, the students will unanimously reject his account as "boring stuff."

Level Two Action:

- A student walks across the stage from UL to UR.

- Ask the other students to comment if they thought the action offered any interest.

- The same student repeats the same walk, but this time a second student tries to stop him from getting to the other side. The second student can use any means to do this except physical contact.

- Ask the students: Did you find that action any more interesting than the first time the student walked by himself across the stage? Why?

In the first action, the actor performed a simple act: walking. In the second action, we witnessed a *conflict*—a struggle between the two actors on the stage. Actor #1 had a *goal* to get to the other side. Actor #2 was the *obstacle* in the way of actor #1 achieving his goal. When we create an *obstacle* to a *goal* onstage, we have *conflict*. Conflict creates dramatic interest because the audience wants to know how the story will end.

EXERCISE 8-2 Simple Conflict

- The students stage the following simple conflict actions, some of which will require verbal exchanges.

- After each action, the students identify the goal, obstacle, and nature of the conflict.

A. Conflict actions with imaginary cues (for one actor)

1. The actor walks across the stage. A few feet from the other side, a snake appears in his path. How does he get across?

2. The actor is halfway across the stage when he hears a voice behind him crying out in distress. Should he continue on and ignore the voice or retrace his steps and find out where it leads?

3. The actor sits down to read an absorbing letter. She is interrupted by the baby's screams in the next room. Does she finish the letter or does she go to the baby?

4. The actor walks into a room and smells freshly-baked cookies. He spots them. He knows he is not allowed to take one without permission. Does he take one anyway?

5. The actor angrily walks across the stage from DL to DR. Just as he reaches DR, he hesitates and turns back. Should he leave the other person in anger or go back and resolve the problem?

B. Conflict action with another actor (requires dialogue between actors)

1. Actor #1 is seated on a chair. She opens a letter she's been dying to read. Actor #2 enters and insists on telling her about some unrelated and inconsequential event. Will actor #1 finish reading her letter?

2. Actor #1 is seated by himself and is practicing asking a girl to go to the school prom. Actor #2 enters, overhears him, and tries to talk him out of asking the girl he wants to ask.

3. Actor #1 needs to memorize information that's written on a piece of paper in her purse, without attracting attention. Actor #2 stands suspiciously close by. Actor #1 is afraid that actor #2 will discover her secret.

Life does not always make enthralling drama because much of life is made up of mundane activity that has little audience appeal. Drama takes the long gray line of life experience and compresses it so that all the static, ordinary downtime is eliminated and only the high points of character testing, decision, and overcoming in times of conflict and crisis are brought into sharp focus. This process of extracting drama out of everyday life and presenting it in a theatrically exciting and aesthetically pleasing way is accomplished through obedience to the elements of good drama.

The Elements of Good Drama

The traditions that define the elements of a well-written play or movie script find their source in ancient Greek tragedy and in the principles set forth by the Greek philosopher Aristotle (384–322 B.C.) in his treatise *Poetics*. These principles were later adapted by French and Italian neoclassicists of the sixteenth century and refined by French nineteenth-century playwright Eugene Scribe into what has been referred to as "the well-made play." Aristotle, who composed his treatise fifty years after the death of Sophocles—the greatest of Greek tragedians, considered *Oedipus the King* the perfect drama. The most beloved plays of the ages embody Aristotle's principles, which is why they have endured and still dominate the theatrical scene. It is also why his *Poetics* are our first reference when studying the elements of good drama.

1. S T R U C T U R E (Also referred to as the *charting* of the play)

Drama is the most intimate and compelling of the disciplines of the arts because it touches upon the deepest parts of man's soul in a very personal and human way. The characters portrayed are infused by the actors with a living spirit that can transmute the burdens of the heart and move the audience to a rare pity and understanding. How that spirit of the actor makes contact with the spirit of the audience and brings about various levels of catharsis and healing is largely dependent upon how the play's action unfolds—that is, how the events that make up the plot (or storyline) reach a convincing dramatic climax and find their logical conclusion.

During the twentieth century, playwrights broke away from traditional laws of play structure. Many modern authors ignore the division of their plays into the customary three, four, or five acts, and write them in two acts with an intermission or as a mere succession of scenes with no intermission. Rules of structure are sometimes adapted to fit the kind of theater in which the play will be mounted, especially if it is an open stage, where audience intimacy replaces the aesthetic distance, or proscenium separation of audience and actor.

Many playwrights also adapt their writing to accommodate the growing use of improvisation—popular among modern method actors—in place of written dialogue and directed blocking. Throughout his career, for example, Swedish movie director Ingmar Bergman would write just the ideas for his existential stage and film scripts and let his actors improvise their own dialogue along the general direction of his storyline. Like many modern directors and playwrights, Bergman viewed the cinematic arts as a deeply personal form of expression that justified his rebellion against traditional structure.

Our understanding of structure, however, needs to be modeled upon traditional principles rather than current trends, which reflect changing tastes and may not deal with the great issues of life that inspire and uplift the soul. Dramas such as the Greek tragedies and Shakespearean plays survive the ages because their structure rests on principles of unity and aesthetic beauty that can rise above even the most inadequate (and sometimes outrageous) staging and acting conditions. It is the traditional play structure that exemplifies the true elements of drama and the art of theater.

When Aristotle discussed the principles of great tragedy in his *Poetics*, he identified plot (or the unfolding of the human action) as the "first principle" and thus the most important feature of play structure. He defined plot not as the storyline itself but as "the arrangement of the incidents" as presented to the audience. He stressed the importance of a tightly constructed cause-and-effect chain of actions that must be complete in itself, with a beginning (initial action), middle (climax), and end (resolution). The incidents must unfold logically and reach a plausible conclusion.

Analysis of Handout, *Drama Is Conflict*

Director's Notes: Distribute Handout #8-1, *Drama Is Conflict*

Beginning Action (Exposition) or Establishing Shot: A play or film begins with the exposition, or establishing shot, which introduces the main character and beginning action of the story as well as the time, mood, and locale—in other words, the *who, when, where, and why*. In Picture No. 1 of the handout, a man is walking with a great deal of energy and determination along a stretch of rocky terrain. The mere action of walking, however, is not very exciting. We need to find out where the man is going and why, if the action is to keep our interest.

Development and Conflict: In Picture No. 2, the man is no longer simply walking; there is a new *development* (a factor leading to a change in the character's behavior).

He has come to a steep, rugged mountain. Barehanded, without any equipment, he embarks on the dangerous task of climbing it. His first steps show us clearly that he has set himself a *goal:* to scale the mountain. We judge easily that this mountain poses a great *obstacle* to his goal. The man is pitting his raw strength and determination against the impossibly steep gradient and jaggedness of the cliff. Between these two opposing forces—man and mountain—a struggle will ensue. The action in the story has drawn our interest. Why? Because *conflict* has been introduced. Action alone cannot create a story. *Conflict* (a struggle between opposing forces) *must* be present. With action and conflict, we have the beginnings of a *plot* (main storyline).

Action Plus Conflict: In Picture No. 3, the man is fighting his way up the mountain. His struggle has given our story some action and conflict, but we still do not have a storyline. Why has this man set himself such a difficult, life-threatening task? What could possibly motivate him to scale such a treacherous, unyielding mass of rock? Of course, we could construct a *plot* centered solely on the man's struggle to conquer the mountain by thinking of all the possible incidents that could occur during his climb. These events, growing out of the hardships offered by the mountain itself or of Nature, would provide a workable plot, for plot consists of the series of overcoming situations that confront the main character during the course of the story. (*Ask the students to suggest situations that would intensify the hero's struggle.*) A fierce wind might catch him, for example, and nearly force him off the ledge. Or he might step on some loose gravel and lose his footing. Yet somehow he manages to hold on and continue his ascent... until a sudden storm breaks out and violent flashes of lightning threaten to strike him, but on he climbs...until he hears a strange rattle by his hand. As he looks over, a snake is poised to strike. In that frozen moment, the fear of death and the failure of his mission pass before him, but some falling rock frightens the snake away. Our hero continues on with bleeding hands, cut knees, and bruised, aching arms.

Halfway up, the man speaks these desperate words: "I must reach him in time! I must reach him before it's too late!" The plot takes on a higher intensity of interest. The goal of the main character is not just to climb the mountain but to reach another person in time, before some possible peril befalls him—if it isn't already too late. Our mountain climber is now the key player in an important struggle. Another person's life may depend on the success of his actions.

More Conflict: Picture No. 4 shows that he has reached the top of the mountain. A child is lying there, apparently injured or dead. Now the story has taken on some *pathos* (the quality or power of evoking pity or compassion). Has he arrived in time? Is the child his son? The outer conflict of seeing his child unconscious leads to inner conflict. Can I save my child? Is he dead? If alive, how badly injured is he? Will I be able to get him back down the mountain? Then a new dynamic is introduced, providing *more conflict*. Another person comes into view hiding behind the rock. Why is this third person hiding? We immediately identify him as the villain. Will the hero see the villain? The plot is now more complicated, the dramatic tension increased, and the audience wants to know what will happen. No time for intermission.

Crisis: In Picture No. 5, the hero is approaching the child. The hero is nearing his goal. Victory seems within reach, only a few more feet away. But, no, the villain creeps from his hiding place as if ready to spring an attack. Will the hero see him in time? The plot has begun to create *suspense* (mental uncertainty accompanied by anxiety or excitement). Events will soon reach a *crisis*. The term *crisis* refers to an incident or situation that could change the events to follow, for good or for ill. This is like reaching the end of the trail or being caught in a canyon cul-de-sac surrounded by a group of enemies, forcing some final action. Goal and obstacle are pitted in the closest possible proximity. Will the third person be successful in his attack on the hero, thwarting the fulfillment of his goal? Or will the hero triumph and overcome this new obstacle?

Climax and Resolution: Picture No. 6 indicates the answer. The villain loses his footing—another new incident—and hurtles below to his death. This new incident may have been accomplished in many ways. *(Ask the students to suggest ways the hero may have overcome the attack of the villain. Did the villain just lose his balance or was there a fight?)* This final incident provides the story with a *climax*—the highest point of dramatic tension, and the most decisive and crucial moment in the development of the dramatic plot. The *climax* is the turning point that decides the way the story is to end. This final action brings the plot to its *resolution* (ultimate outcome). The defeat of the villain and the overcoming victory for the hero in rescuing his child is the happy resolution (or conclusion) of the story. Then again, we may need an epilogue to find out just how he got his son down the mountain safely!

Summary

The plot, therefore, is the arrangement of a story's incidents from beginning action, action and conflict, further conflict leading to crisis, climax, and resolution. The resolution—a happy or tragic ending—always flows out of the consequences of the climax, which in turn has grown out of the unfolding dramatic action. The term *denouement* is sometimes used interchangeably with *resolution* but it refers more specifically to the final part of the plot in which the cause-and-effect chain of action has unravelled, and everything is made clear. The audience knows what is going to happen to the protagonist (or the antagonist if he is not killed). The denouement explains the outcome.

If the plot of a play possesses this continuous, unbroken flow of incidents, with each action leading inevitably to the next—beginning action with further incidents that intensify conflict and suspense, rising steadily to a crisis, climax, and resolution—then it is complete and has, what Aristotle termed, "unity of action." Proper structure ensures the dramatic possibilities of a story by promoting action that moves quickly and holds the audience's interest.

Aristotle also believed that the plot must be "of a certain magnitude," by which he meant it should present a complexity of incidents that bring into focus a theme of "universal significance," which contributes to the play's rich, artistic value. The more spiritually illuminating and comprehensive the action in the working out of its theme, the more the playwright can hold fast the emotions of the audience and influence them toward catharsis and the inevitable purging and upliftment of the spirit.

> *Director's Notes:* For the little ones you may wish to use the story of little Billy at the mailbox from Unit Study 6 to illustrate the different aspects of structure.

E X E R C I S E 8-3 Billy's Birthday Gift: A Study in Structure

- The *establishing* scene is Billy waiting at the mailbox for the mailman to bring his present. The next incident catches our sympathy and stirs our interest: the mailman does not deliver a birthday box from Grandma. This is the element of *conflict*.

- We feel sorry for Billy because he did not get what he was waiting for, and we all know how that can feel. We follow a sad and disappointed Billy into the house and are eager to see whether something will happen to assure him (and us) that he will get his present.

- His mother greets him with a reassuring smile, telling him that his Uncle Frank will be arriving for a visit. Perhaps he will bring Grandma's present with him. Billy feels a burst of eager expectation.

- With this new element of *suspense*, the pivotal character of Uncle Frank arrives on the scene. Billy looks out the window and sees him approaching the house. There is no package under his arm—nothing!

- This is the moment of *crisis*. Billy feels like running into his bedroom and crying out his disappointment, but he knows that wouldn't be polite. He also doesn't want to act like a baby. Uncle Frank gives Billy a hug and tells him that there's a large package in the car that he'd like Billy to go and get.

- With an expression of joy on his face, Billy runs to the car, where he sees a big box wrapped in brightly covered paper with his name on it in Grandma's handwriting.

- The *climax* approaches. He wildly unwraps the present and, behold, his first remote car!

- Billy achieves his *goal* and we are all satisfied with a happy ending.

KEY: Getting to the heart of the issue

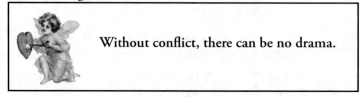

Without conflict, there can be no drama.

Homework: Ask the students to watch one or more of the movies listed below. You may substitute other movie titles or even use the Veggie Tales or Odyssey series of videos, especially for the little ones. The three sample movies are perfectly suited for children aged 8 years and older. They beautifully show the development and unfolding of the story according to the structure required of good drama.

Lassie Come Home—an MGM movie production (1943) based on the novel by Eric Knight and starring Roddy McDowell and Elizabeth Taylor. This is an enthralling adventure story about the loyalty of a dog, Lassie, to her young master, Joe. Because of difficult financial times, Joe's father has to sell Lassie to a wealthy lord. Lassie makes several attempts to escape and return to Joe. The dog is finally transported to her new owner's estate in the north of Scotland, over 1,000 miles away. Determined to get back to Joe, Lassie again runs away. With a great and faithful heart, this dog overcomes every obstacle, including injuries and near starvation, to make the long and arduous journey to find the master she loves.

Iron Will—a Walt Disney movie (1994) starring Mackenzie Astin and Kevin Spacey. Set during World War I, the movie tells the true-life story of a courageous young man and his team of dogs who enter a perilous 522-mile cross-country dog-sled race that begins in Winnipeg, Canada, and ends in St. Paul, Minnesota. When Will Stoneman's father dies suddenly and their family's farm must be sold, Will sets himself the goal of winning the $10,000 grand prize money to save the farm for his mother. Competing with the most hardened and accomplished sledders in the world, he faces impossible odds and treacherous obstacles that arise not only from the frozen wilderness itself, but from men who are willing to cheat and kill for the prize. Inspired by the intrepid determination of the young hero, a journalist coins the name Iron Will. The whole country gets behind "Iron Will" with a thrilling patriotism and faith. It is a story of high courage and triumph in the face of overwhelming adversity.

Durango—a Hallmark Hall of Fame movie for television (1999) starring Brenda Fricker, Matt Keeslar, and Patrick Bergin. Set against the verdant Irish countryside on the eve of the Second World War, this is a wonderful tale about searching within to find the strength to overcome insurmountable obstacles. A young farmer is in love with the pretty daughter of a very belligerent and protective father, Fergus Mullaney, who has threatened to destroy any young man who wants to come courting his one and only daughter. Before confronting Fergus, Mark, the young hero, feels he must prove himself a worthy suitor. Applying himself to the task of breaking up the local cattle buyer's corrupt monopoly, Mark organizes a never-before-attempted undertaking—an Irish cattle drive. With the help of his canny aunt and a motley group of small farmers and their small herds, he sets out for another town, where they hope to get higher prices for their cattle. In the course of the journey, they must deal with physical dangers and villains sent to stop them. With the help of some lively country folk, Mark finds the resolve to overcome every difficulty. He not only breaks the monopoly, but also wins the consent and respect of the father of his bride-to-be.

Director's Notes: You can buy any of these movies by searching eBay or Google. I recommend that you arrange a special showing of the movie (or movies) rather than take up time in class. Use this movie event as an opportunity to bring the families together. At the next class, the students should discuss the structure of the storyline.

2. GOAL and OBSTACLE

Goal refers to the purpose, objective, or victory towards which your effort is directed. *Obstacle* refers to what stands in the way to achieving your goal. Goal + Obstacle = Conflict. The character has a goal. The character acts to pursue that goal. All his actions are directed to obtain that goal. For his actions in pursuing the goal to be dramatic and therefore worthy of interest, the goal must be difficult to achieve.

The nearer the character is to his goal, the more perilous is his task of overcoming. The greater the challenge of overcoming, the more profound and far-reaching the consequences of failure or victory. When the goal requires that the hero risk his life for the sake of others, the goal is considered noble and the dramatic action heroic.

Example One: To take a breath is an unconscious, everyday action. However, when we place an obstacle before that goal, the simple action may be transformed into a challenge of life-threatening proportions. Ask the students to suggest possible obstacles to the simple action of taking a breath (some examples would be swimming underwater, being in a room with smoke or poison gas, having a pillow placed over the face, swallowing a bone that gets caught in the throat).

Taking the example of being underwater, we can compound the obstacle by having the character get his foot caught in coral. This immediately intensifies the struggle between goal and obstacle. Not only is the water itself an obstacle to breathing, but having his foot stuck in the rock coral sharply reduces his chances of getting to the surface in time. Now let us add another incident to build dramatic suspense— a shark suddenly appears, cruising above the swimmer. Even if the character gets his foot free, the odds of the shark finding him are not in the character's favor. If we add to this yet another incident, such as the man's foot starting to bleed from the sharp coral and the scent of his blood attracting the shark, we raise the stakes to impossible odds against the hero's survival.

Example Two: To walk across a log is an action. To walk across a log to reach a child is an action with a goal. To walk across a log three feet above treacherous whitewater is an action made dramatic because of an obstacle in the way—life-threatening currents. To walk across a log three feet above treacherous whitewater to save a child in peril is strong conflict with elements of suspense (the struggle to overcome the obstacle) and pathos (a child's life is dependent on your victory). To walk across a log three feet above treacherous whitewater to save a child in peril, with the water rising six inches a minute, is *high drama*. High drama must have a noble goal and impossible obstacles in the way of the character's overcoming. High drama tests the mettle of the spirit and fulfills Aristotle's requirements for a plot being "of a certain magnitude," and of universal significance.

EXERCISE 8-4 Reaching for a Goal

- All the students stand and reach up as far as they can, first with the left arm and then with the right arm. By itself, this is a calisthenic exercise.

- Ask each student to imagine an object they desire very much, such as a diamond ring, an autographed baseball bat or a million dollars.

- Have the students repeat the stretching exercise, but this time as if reaching for the object they really desire.

Now the action has a purpose, a goal, and you are committed with all your strength to achieve that goal. You reach more vigorously, more intensely. You may reach so hard that you lose your balance and have to try again.

> *Director's Notes:* In reaching, we are working *against* an obstacle—our own physical limitations. This exercise shows how a goal that is greatly desired and can benefit us personally makes the action of overcoming an obstacle more dramatic and dynamic.

EXERCISE 8-5 Overcoming the Obstacle

By creating more conflict, we intensify the struggle between goal and obstacle.

- Students discuss the dramatic situation described below or act it out.
- *Optional:* Students imagine other situations presenting dramatic conflict where an obstacle must be overcome or they give examples from movies, television shows, or novels that show the overcoming of an obstacle.

Dramatic Situation: Imagine that you are a volunteer Christian social worker who has been kidnapped by an Al-Qaida terrorist group and is held in a terrorist camp somewhere on the Syrian border. On the way into the camp, you noticed a large underground tunnel that was being packed with ammunition. You have learned from some of the other prisoners that American troops have patrols in a village less than 5 miles away. You know that the only way to prevent being beheaded is to reject your Christian faith and convert to Islam, as other prisoners have done. You also know, with equal certainty, that you will never deny your faith, not even for the sake of practical expediency. Your only chance of staying alive, therefore, is to escape your cell while the terrorists are engaged in a raid away from the camp. You also want to get the information about the hidden ammunition depot to the coalition forces.

The main core of terrorists left nearly two hours ago. You have spent that time working your hands out of their bindings and prying open the door of your room—a room without windows or fresh air. You have heard no noise during that time. You are not sure, however, if there are guards outside the half bombed-out building that houses the prisoners. You are hoping they all went on the raid.

Your wrists are bloody and tender. You are weak, sick, and afraid. Time is precious. You could escape out the back of the building and have a good chance of making it alone. You are familiar with the northern villages of Iraq and can navigate your way to safety. The sooner the US forces know about the ammunition dump, the sooner it can be destroyed. But you also feel compelled to help free the others, whose lives are as expendable to the terrorists as yours. You have no knife to cut them free. Can you still free them in time, before the terrorists return? What do you do?

The *goal* in this situation is escape. The *obstacle* is not only the physical prison and its constraints, but the threat of discovery by either the guards or the returning terrorists once the escape is initiated. Both inner and outer conflict intensify the dramatic action. The *outer conflict* is the struggle to escape the room and the prison building without being seen. The *inner conflict* is whether the leading character should save himself and get back with the strategic information, or risk everything to save the others. The act of escape has a much greater dramatic intensity. The overcoming of the obstacle to reach the goal has profound consequences: victory will result in the release and possible escape of all the prisoners. Failure will result in the hero's death and the possible death of many others who will be the victims of the stored arsenal. This one action of escape is a moment of great decision and overcoming for the character. Every part of his being must focus to achieve what has now become a noble goal.

KEY: Getting to the heart of the issue

 Drama is conflict—the confrontation between an obstacle and the leading character's pursuit of a goal. The leading character plays toward a goal and against an obstacle. The greater the conflict, the more dramatic the action.

3. PROTAGONIST and ANTAGONIST

We learned that a good play sets up the events of the plot in a logical sequence, which finds its plausible conclusion. After plot, Aristotle believed character to be the next most important dramatic element. The plot is made up of the unfolding actions of the play. Wrapped around them are the characters who react to these events. According to Aristotle, the main character needs to be of "fine" stuff—a person of noble stature and greatness. If his fall is to arouse in us the emotions of pity and fear, it must be a fall from a great height. Therefore, he must be a man of his word, of personal honor, true-hearted in his motivations, and possessing moral beauty. Much like Shakespeare's Hamlet, Aristotle's archetype is "true to life and yet more beautiful." His presence ennobles the plot and sets forth the ideal of what man can be.

This ideal character should also suffer, not because he succumbs to a vice or moral weakness, but because of a "tragic flaw" which brings about a dramatic change in

The Vigil

After the ceremony of knighthood, the young knight is conducted to the chapel, where he spends the night in keeping holy vigil.

Sir Lancelot

The role model of the knight still enthralls the imagination of children and adults. The knight embodies chivalric virtue and the quest for moral beauty.

Sir Galahad, the purest knight of the Round Table, on his quest for the Holy Grail

fortune, and his ultimate downfall. This flaw does not lessen his nobility because it is not a moral flaw but one that derives from his lack of knowledge about himself. The catharsis that he goes through because of his suffering teaches him (and us, through our solemn pity for him) the essential self-knowledge to which he was previously blind. His soul is purged through this gain in self-awareness, which Aristotle calls "discovery," and we are left with a profound sense of healing and hope.

The *protagonist* (from the Greek, meaning "first actor") is the hero or leading character who moves the dramatic action of the plot to its final resolution. He is also the conscience or moral center of the play or movie. In olden times, we might have visualized the ideal protagonist as a white knight in shining armor who fights terrible dragons and braves murky swamps and gnarled forests to reach the fair princess locked in the high chamber of the castle tower. Although we no longer describe our heroes in such allegorical terms, the symbology still applies when talking about good drama.

The knights and ladies are the embodiment of chivalric virtues, such as courage, purity, honor, righteousness, faith, decisiveness, selflessness, tenacity, and fearlessness before the foe. Their loyalty and adherence to principle is unquestioned. They strive for an ideal and serve that ideal. The outer symbols of giants, dragons, black knights, and evil dwarfs are but the physical manifestation of the unseen obstacles that assail our truest self and self-expression, those we love, and the high principles and values we stand for and seek to embody.

The *antagonist* is the character who struggles against the hero and tries to thwart the hero's pursuit of his noble goal. He is generally associated with the villain or someone who does not have good intentions towards the hero. When the protagonist sets in motion actions to achieve his goal, it is the antagonist who counteracts those actions by interference. This interference may be brought about by such actions as deception, lies, or physical violence. The motives of the antagonist are rarely lofty and his behavior is the meanest. The antagonist may not necessarily be an evil person, but his decision to obstruct the hero must be a deliberate one, made with full awareness that he is preventing the highest course of action. Someone is not considered an antagonist if he has good intentions and believes that he is serving the highest good by obstructing the hero. This might happen in the case of a hero's family member trying to prevent the hero from making the right decision. Such a person would be considered a "foil," not a true antagonist. A "foil" means well but does not understand the highest action called for. The true antagonist fully comprehends the highest action but chooses to obstruct it.

In many of today's dramas, the differences between the protagonist and antagonist are blurred. Good and evil are not clearly delineated. In fact, many of our modern movies that follow Aristotle's formula for unfolding an uplifting message with heroes who grow in self-discovery, are mocked. Traditional protagonists are often viewed as "fleeting do-gooders" carrying out "standard issue heroics," as one reviewer of the 2006 movie *The Guardian* wrote. It is hard to believe that even a jaded Hollywood journalist could describe the selfless actions of the elite Coast Guard rescue swimmers, who daily lay down their lives "so others may live," as standard issue. It's no longer a moral or artistic imperative to make the protagonist a person of virtue or even of relative goodness. In the 1994 film *The Professional,* protagonist and antagonist are juxtaposed. A hit man (someone who murders for money) is the protagonist. An innocent child who loves him unconditionally is meant to persuade us to be nonjudgmental of his "profession." He is depicted as the hero, despite the unapologetic characterization of him as a pathological killer with an unrepentant heart. The police, on the other hand, along with assorted Mafia figures, are portrayed as corrupt.

In perusing the local cinema fare, we increasingly find negative portrayals of those who represent the law (human or divine) and positive portrayals of those who defy, outsmart, or willfully act against those laws, as in the popular television show *Hustle.* In the tradition of *The Sting* and *Ocean's Eleven,* this slick drama, featuring "bad" guys you can't help but love, glamorizes the conman and his deliberate choice of the low moral road. Yet the ability to make the highest moral choice is the mark of a true protagonist. We do not expect our hero to be perfect, but we want him to honestly strive for the highest action, accept accountability for any errors he makes, and take action to change his behavior. Only then is he a hero worthy of a good drama.

David Copperfield, after a life of hardship and overcoming, described the true protagonist in words that describe the true man in all of us: "Anything, Steerforth, you could have done, anything—reached the stars! Waste, waste. Waste, all waste. Life asks more of us: demands it. It is not enough to be talented, Steerforth, or beautiful, Dora, or even simply loving: yes Mother, or even simply loving. We must be strong or else the gifts that God sends us into the world with will just fade and wither in the first cold wind that blows on us....The best steel...must go through the fire." As in fiction, so in life. Those whose imaginations soar above their fears, who dare to "face reverses boldly and never suffer them to frighten us," and thus follow their individual star, prove the truth that each of us can be a hero in our own life drama if we have the courage to strive toward the highest course of action with the highest moral good.

The great dramatists and novelists of the ages have created protagonists who embody this kind of courage and vision, even amidst their imperfections. In fact, those imperfections only make them more endearing to our hearts. When they strive to overcome their weaknesses, we project our hopes and fears and strive with them. The through line of great characterizations is their true-heartedness. Reading about, watching, or portraying honorable characters inspires us to seek beyond our ordinary expectations and choose the highest path of action in our lives. It is the reason the Shakespearean plays are so beloved. Shakespeare's characters clearly show the difference between the protagonist and the antagonist and clearly identify the great issues of life that are at stake. There is no compromising middle ground. We come away with a certain vision of who is noble and good, and who is cowardly and evil. No truer words have been spoken of Shakespeare's plays than those of E.T. Roe, who edited E. Nesbit's *Beautiful Stories From Shakespeare* a hundred years ago:

> Shakespeare's plays alone contain more actual wisdom than the whole body of English learning. He is the teacher of all good—pity, generosity, true courage, love. His bright wit is cut out "into little stars." He ever kept the highroad of human life. He did not pick out by-paths of feeling and sentiment. In his creations we have no moral highwaymen, sentimental thieves, interesting villains, or amiable, elegant adventuresses—no delicate entanglements of situation, in which the grossest of images are presented to the mind disguised under the superficial attraction of style and emotion. He flattered no bad passion, disguised no vice in the garb of virtue, trifled with no just and generous principle. While causing us to laugh at folly, and shudder at crime, he still preserves our love for our fellow-beings, and our reverence for ourselves. There is scarcely a corner of the world today which he does not illuminate, or a cottage which he does not enrich. As his friend, Ben Jonson, wrote of him, "He was not of an age but for all time."

The Bard's characterizations are unforgettable because their humanity is framed by a divine understanding. No matter the injustice or suffering, nothing of nobility is ever lost, nothing that is pure and true is ever destroyed because life is set against the eternal order. His characters are brightly etched as if we know them already and have always known them. Like the great Bible personalities, they are with us and yet live outside of the human life experience. They are filled with the essence (not the wasteland) of life and we take them to our hearts—even in their tragic humanness. And this defines the genius of Shakespeare. He created characters that were both human *and* transcendent because they possessed the quality of pathos—the power to draw from our heart true sympathy. Actors love playing Shakespearean roles because of the concentration of this pathos in the spoken word and its power to move an audience. Shakespeare was able to capture and render this dramatic pathos with a skill near divine.

The fine ideas and codes of conduct of the Shakespearean characters make for great protagonists in drama because they reinforce the eternal values that go straight to the heart. They also teach us about the proven qualities that help us be successful in life in ways that really matter. Like other great characters in life and fiction, such as Ivanhoe, Parsifal, Sir Galahad, The Cid, Hypatia of Alexandria, Empress Wu Ze Tian of ancient China, or later figures, such as Joan of Arc, Florence Nightingale, Madame Marie Curie, Nurse Edith Cavell, and Frederick Douglass, the hero in all of us possesses a high sense of honor and a love of truth and justice. To be truly noble, as those great lives remind us, our conduct towards our companions-in-arms as well as our enemies must be impeccable, and our love and compassion for all must rise above the petty concerns of the cliques and clowns that come across our life's stage. Edith Cavell's last words before she was executed by the Germans in 1915 as a spy, eloquently embody this quality of moral beauty: "Standing as I do, in view of God and Eternity, I realize that patriotism is not enough; I must have no hatred or bitterness toward anyone." This same message is also the theme that is beautifully worked out in *Jet Li's Fearless*.

Stories that uphold principled action, where the hero plays for high stakes with grave consequences, provide the most vigorous outlet for young actors. Scenes adapted from real-life tales of American adventurers, pioneers, frontiersmen, military leaders, and the great achievers throughout our history, are perfectly suited to the idealism of the age 8-13 group. Older students enjoy dramatic selections that have substance and depth, and deal with the trials of real flesh-and-blood men and women.

EXERCISE 8-6 The Greatest Story Ever Told
_____

Level One Action:

- The students break down the life of Jesus or any great spiritual leader or famous historical figure according to all the elements of good drama.

- What was the storyline of his life and mission?

- If Jesus (or famous figure) is the protagonist, who were his allies in helping to achieve his goal and who were his antagonists?

- What was his goal?

- Who or what was the obstacle to his goal?

- Can a person who has a high and noble goal still be victorious even if he is defeated or killed?

- Is the story of Jesus (or famous figure) worthy of high drama? If so, why?

Stories that make the greatest dramas set the highest good against the darkest evil and include a protagonist that represents not just a person but also a principle or ideal. The noblest goals are rooted in principle. As good drama shows, even when human justice fails, there is a heavenly justice that waits to right that earthly injustice, and crown a noble (though seemingly failed) effort with immortal glory. Those who sin against divine law may be victorious for a time, even prime time, but history teaches us that they will ultimately be held accountable for their actions. Shakespeare made this point very plainly in many of his plays.

"I am glad to end a day that can never come back, gladder to end a night when I've given my all, gladder will I be to end my life when for God my service is complete."

—Florence Nightingale

And slow, as in a dream of bliss,
The speechless sufferer turns to kiss
Her shadow, as it falls
Upon the darkening walls.

A Lady with a Lamp shall stand
In the great history of the land,
A noble type of good,
Heroic womanhood.

—*Santa Filomena* by Henry Wadsworth Longfellow

Hypatia

"The beautiful can never die. If the Gods have deserted their oracles, they have not deserted the souls who aspired to them. If they have ceased to guide nations, they have not ceased to speak to their elect. If they have cast off the vulgar herd, they have not cast off Hypatia!" (Charles Kingsley)

Joan of Arc listens to her celestial voices, who command her to lead France to victory. She remains an inspirational figure in life and in dramatic fiction.

Frederick Douglass

"You have seen how a man was made a slave, you shall see how a slave was made a man....One and God make a majority."

Heaven is above all yet: there sits a Judge
That no king can corrupt.
                    —King Henry VIII, Act 3, Sc. 1

Cowards die many times before their deaths;
The valiant never taste of death but once.
                    —Julius Caesar, Act 2, Sc. 2

Tis not the many oaths that make the truth,
But the plain single vow that is vow'd true.
                    —All's Well That Ends Well, Act 4, Sc. 2

The devil can cite Scripture for his purpose.
An evil soul producing holy witness
Is like a villain with a smiling cheek,
A goodly apple rotten at the heart.
O, what a goodly outside falsehood hath!
                    —Merchant of Venice, Act 1, Sc. 3

O, but man, proud man!
Drest in a little brief authority
Most ignorant of what he's most assured,
His glassy essence, like an angry ape,
Plays such fantastic tricks before high heaven,
As make the angels weep.
                    —Measure for Measure, Act 2, Sc. 2

Every inordinate cup is unblessed, and the ingredient is a devil.
                    —Othello, Act 2, Sc. 3

One may smile, and smile, and be a villain.
                    —Hamlet, Act 1, Sc. 5

What stronger breastplate than a heart untainted!
Thrice is he armed that hath his quarrel just;
And he but naked, though locked up in steel,
Whose conscience with injustice is corrupted.
                    —Henry VI, Part 2, Act 3, Sc. 2

I charge thee, fling away ambition:
By that sin fell the angels. How can man then,
The image of his Maker, hope to win by it?
Love thyself last; cherish those hearts that hate thee;
Corruption wins not more than honesty.
...Be just, and fear not;
Let all the ends thou aim'st at be thy country's,
Thy God's, and truth's; then, if thou fall'st,
Thou fall'st a blessed martyr!
                              —King Henry VIII, Act 3, Sc. 2

Foul deeds will rise,
Though all the earth o'erwhelm them to men's eyes.
                              —Hamlet, Act l, Sc. 2

If these men have defeated the law, and outrun native
punishment, though they can outstrip men, they have no
wings to fly from God.
                              —Henry V, Act 4, Sc. 1

Though those that are betrayed
Do feel the treason sharply, yet the traitor
Stands in worse case of woe.
                              —Cymbeline, Act 3, Sc. 4

Level Two Action:

- Divide the students up into four groups.

- Have each of the groups choose one of the Shakespearean play quotes above and think of a literary, historical, or modern-day figure who embodies the truth of the quote. The students can choose a hero (protagonist) or a villain (antagonist).

- After fifteen minutes or more, have all the groups come together and share their choices. Each group should explain why they chose that person and how his or her actions embody or prove the meaning of the quote. Every statement must be backed up by fact and not merely express an opinion or personal angst, as in the discussion of a politician or his policies.

KEY: Getting to the heart of the issue

 In good drama, the protagonist, though he may not be perfect, clearly seeks the highest action. The antagonist, though he may not be entirely evil, makes a willful choice to obstruct what he knows to be the greater good.

4. NOBLE THEME

The theme, or what Aristotle speaks of as "thought"—his third element of good drama—is the specific idea or inspiration that gives unity and purpose to the action of the play. Theme is the dramatic *through line* of the play. Through line is a term that was first used by Stanislavski as a simplified approach to interpreting a character. He believed the actor should not only understand what his character's objective was in any given scene—that is, what the character was doing and why he was doing it—but he should also strive to understand the through line that linked these individual objectives together and thus moved the character forward through the drama. The through line, then, is like the spine of the play around which the character's actions are wound. The through line gives meaning to those actions. This applies to all the characters in a play but especially to the main character, or protagonist.

The theme, or through line, of a drama also describes the playwright's reason for writing the play. It represents the message he wants to convey to his audience. All of the objectives of the main character should together unfold the play's theme, which Stanislavski also referred to as the *superobjective* of the play. He characterizes the superobjective of *The Brothers Karamazov,* for example, as "the author's search for God and Devil in the soul of man." With Anton Chekhov's *The Three Sisters*, it is "the aspiration for a better life." With Leo Tolstoy's works, it is "the search for self-perfection." In other words, the theme represents the essential meaning of the play—its profound content, spiritual insight, or vital force. Sometimes the dramatist will let his protagonist state the theme in his own words, or prove it by his actions during the course of the play. For example, in *The Man of La Mancha*, author Miguel de Cervantes expresses his theme when Don Quixote says, "Too much sanity may be madness, but the maddest of all is to see life as it is and not as it should be."

Great dramatists employ noble themes that deal with permanent, enduring values that live as fiery coals in the heart and give meaning to life. For a theme to be noble, it must be placed in a moral or eternal setting. In most modern plays and movies, the themes are mundane and never lift beyond some commonplace statement about human nature, with no reference whatsoever to morality or any higher spiritual authority. We define the goal of the protagonist by the theme of the play. If the theme stays solely within human parameters, such as "diamonds are a girl's best friend," or "life is short so let's eat, drink, and be merry," the protagonist's goal is limited to justifying that theme. If, however, the theme is a noble one, framed by some eternal principle of moral beauty, the protagonist's goal will likewise soar heavenward (and so can the actor's art). A movie that masterfully demonstrates the intricate working out of theme and character is *Chariots of Fire*, produced in 1980.

The movie tells the true-life story of Harold Abrahams and Eric Liddell, two champion runners who successfully competed for Great Britain in the 1924 Olympics. Essentially, we have two protagonists. The playwright provides dual and competing themes with dual and competing character goals, both of which are clearly juxtaposed early in the movie. The first theme is stated when Harold Abrahams arrives at Cambridge as a freshman. The master of Caius Hall welcomes the new class—the first one to follow those who died in World War I—and urges them, on behalf of the honored dead, "to examine yourselves, assess your true potential, seek to discover where your true chance of greatness lies." Shortly after, following a student societies fair, Harold takes up the challenge of running around the Trinity Court perimeter in 46 seconds—a feat that has not been accomplished in 700 years. His goal is set: train as a runner for the upcoming Paris Olympics and win the gold.

Immediately the scene changes to the Scottish Highlands, where a local athletics competition is taking place. Eric Liddell, a famous Scots rugby player and son of an Evangelical missionary, wins the 200-yard dash. Following the race, his father states the second theme: "You can praise the Lord by peeling a spud if you peel it to perfection. Run in His name and let the world stand back in wonder."

Both Harold and Eric go on to justify these mutually inclusive but personalized themes. After Harold loses to Eric in a national meet, he agrees to be trained by a professional sprinting coach so he can get the edge on Eric. The board at his college hear of it and denounce his lack of team spirit and what they view as a ruthless pursuit of individual glory. Harold, however, is determined to gain any advantage he can. He rebukes their "archaic values" and sets forth how he will achieve his goal: "You know, gentlemen, you yearn for victory just as I do, but achieved with the apparent effortlessness of Gods...I believe in the relentless pursuit of excellence and I'll carry the future with me!" Harold's "relentless" ambition is further fueled by the desire to use his running as a weapon against anti-Semitism—a desire he confides to his actress girlfriend, Sybil, when they first date.

Meanwhile, Eric tells his brother and sister that though he plans to be a missionary in the Far East, his goal right now is to dedicate all his time to training for the Olympics. He further refines the theme, clarifying his goal as he does so: "I believe God made me for a purpose. But he also made me fast, and when I run I feel his pleasure. To win is to honor him." Everything he does from now on fully represents the pursuit of this goal. On the boat to Paris, Eric learns that the qualifying heats for the 100-meter race, for which he is the favorite, will be held on a Sunday. He informs the Olympic Committee that he will not run on the Sabbath. When the Prince of Wales reminds Eric of his obligation to king and country, Eric simply tells him that his first allegiance is to God. Not until one of his teammates, who has already won a medal in the hurdles, unselfishly gives up his spot in the 400-meter race, does Eric get the chance to run.

Harold takes on the Americans in the 100-meter race and wins gold. That night, he and his coach, Sam, celebrate together, though something is achingly missing in Harold's soul. On the last day of competition, Eric runs in the 400 meter. As he is warming up, the American runner Jackson Scholtz hands him a note. It reads: "In the Old Book it says 'He that honors me, I will honor.' Good luck." Not only do the words turn out to be prophetic when Eric wins the race, but they fulfill the theme of the movie.

Both Harold Abrahams and Eric Liddell win Olympic gold and glory for themselves and their country, but only one—Liddell—chooses the higher road to victory. His true-heartedness, demonstrated by his willingness to surrender what was most important to him, made him the real hero of the Olympics and lent to the 1924 British team of competitors a legendary greatness. Abrahams' win also contributed to the historic greatness of his team, but in his heart and soul he knew that the victory was not hallowed by personal honor, noble intention, or moral beauty.

Both characters pursued their goals and achieved them. Both justified the themes that underwrote their actions. Both themes were good, even great, but only one was noble. Beyond the film's success in authentically dealing with such issues as the challenges of athletic competition, the nature of winning and losing, and the question of ethics in amateur sports, what contributes most of all to the film's aesthetic glory is its noble theme.

Homework: Assign each of the students the task of watching *Chariots of Fire*. You can arrange it as a family event.

KEY: Getting to the heart of the issue

The theme is the central, unifying idea that gives purpose to everything that happens in the play. The more noble the theme, the richer the play's aesthetic value.

5. DIALOGUE

Dialogue, or "diction," as Aristotle referred to this fourth element of good drama, is the medium by which the author dramatizes the action, sets forth his theme, portrays the life of his characters, and expresses the spirit of his play. Great plays, like great movies, are first and foremost great stories with great characters, and it is dialogue that unfolds the story and the characters. Aristotle called this element "the expression of the meaning in words." Dialogue is the language that brings the essence of the play poignantly alive to the audience. In great plays, that essence is of noble substance.

Great drama can always be identified by its great dialogue. Though different kinds of dialogue are created to suit the genre of the play, the dramatic works that endure are known for dialogue that has any combination of beauty, clarity, economy, imagery (especially the use of metaphor and simile), cleverness, and naturalness of speech— that is, as it is fitted to the individual character, his class, his education, and the time in which he lives. Aristotle wrote that "the greatest thing by far is to have a command of metaphor...it is the mark of genius, for to make good metaphors implies an eye for resemblances." Both the Greek tragedies and the Shakespearean plays, which abound in brilliant metaphor, prove his point.

Through skillful dialogue we see not only the unfolding of the cause-effect chain of events in which the characters are engaged, but we learn what the characters are thinking and feeling and how they view the other characters and the world around them. Even more than action, dialogue paints the true portraiture of the characters, especially the protagonist, who often speaks in soliloquy in moments of conflict and heartfelt introspection. Just as in real life, speaking is the way the character processes what is going on in his mind and heart. The more eloquent, evocative, precise, and immediate the dialogue, the clearer the lens for the audience to look through and discover the real man or woman—his desires, aspirations, fears, joys—and thereby unite with his spirit. It is dialogue, then, that keys the spectators into the inner action—the real life—of the characters, and thus the play.

Dialogue represents, above all, the personal vision of the playwright. In *Creating a Role,* Stanislavski wrote, "The verbal text of a play, especially one by a genius, is the manifestation of the clarity, the subtlety, the concrete power to express invisible thoughts and feelings of the author himself. Inside each and every word there is an emotion, a thought, that produced the word and justifies its being there."

As we come to know the characters through the words the author gives them to speak, we also come to know the author himself. The dialogue, more than anything else in the play, embodies the distinctive soul and spirit of the playwright as it is projected into his work. We know, for example, from his plays and sonnets, that Shakespeare had a scholarly and erudite mind, an intellect that was keen and just, and a piercing understanding of the interior life of the soul. With the compassion of a divine psychiatrist, he plumbed the depths (and heights) of God's purpose for man, expressing hope amidst man's tragical errors. With the exception of the Bible, his plays are quoted more often than any literary work in our western civilization. His dialogue breathes with an idealism and dramatic pathos as he paints the moral struggle of humanity against the backdrop of eternal principles. His dialogue possesses an eloquence and glory where prose is poetry, and each word and phrase an illumination—heaven sent. His superior spirit affords us infinite joy.

One could randomly choose a hundred different verses from the Plays and discover each thought to be a concentrated pearl of light—a seed ideal that long afterwards grows and flourishes in the soul's understanding, bringing that soul closer to the spirit. His dialogue is intrinsic to each and every character, from Hamlet to Falstaff, from Othello to Malvolio, from Lady Macbeth to Juliet's Nurse, so that everything the character says enthralls the spectator with interest and excitement. If a playwright becomes so attached to his characters' dialogue being "organic" and "true to nature," as is the case in much of our modern drama, beauty and erudition suffer and the very realism of the dialogue can kill the spiritual life of the characters. To paraphrase British Nobel laureate John Galsworthy, their characters' words become "ashes to our mouths." Stanislavski says, "Empty words are like nutshells without meat, concepts without content; they are no use, indeed they are harmful. They weigh down a role, blur its design; they must be thrown out like so much trash."

Shakespeare set the standard for true dramatic dialogue. He gave life to Aristotle's injunction that "it is not enough to know what to say—one must know how to say it." In every one of his plays, his dialogue is, to quote Galsworthy again, "hand-made, like good lace; clear, of fine texture, furthering with each thread the harmony and strength of a design to which all must be subordinated." Good dialogue must also search out the spiritual action of the play—that is, those events that are significant to the making of the inner drama. Shakespeare never appeals to the corruptible aspects of human nature; he appeals to man's higher spirit, which is why his dialogue is timeless. His plays fulfill the craving of man's spirit for something nobler and purer. His immortal words grow in our souls. They are a part of us forever.

When one begins to quote the great character-revealing passages, the list becomes an infinite wonder. There is Portia's "The quality of mercy is not strained," and Othello's "Speak of me as I am," and the divinely apt testimony by Katherine, "Thy husband is thy lord, thy life, thy keeper." We recall Caesar's prescient wisdom, "There is a tide in the affairs of men, which, taken at the flood, leads on to fortune; omitted, all the voyage of their life is bound in shallows, and in miseries," and Macbeth's haunting cry at the death of Lady Macbeth:

> To-morrow, and to-morrow, and to-morrow,
> Creeps in this petty pace from day to day,
> To the last syllable of recorded time;
> And all our yesterdays have lighted fools
> The way to dusty death. Out, out, brief candle!
> Life's but a walking shadow, a poor player
> That struts and frets his hour upon the stage
> And then is heard no more; it is a tale
> Told by an idiot, full of sound and fury,
> Signifying nothing.

Hamlet is probably the most played figure on the world's stage—at once noble, complex, and true. Great tragic art conveys a sense of profound respect or sympathy for the hero, and that is exactly what we feel when Hamlet speaks or is spoken about. Hamlet paints his own portrait theatrically with thoughts of beauty and depth that are unequalled in all our language. His first soliloquy, beginning with the line, "O, that this too too solid flesh would melt, thaw, and resolve itself into a dew!" conveys the betrayal wrought upon his mind and soul by the marriage of his mother to his uncle so soon after his father's death. When his father's ghost reveals that he was foully murdered and demands revenge, Hamlet plunges into even more concentrated anguish: "O all you host of heaven! O earth! What else? And shall I couple hell? O, fie! Hold, hold, my heart." Our own hearts are drawn to this tender and nobly descended prince, so "courteous from the heart," with a profound sense of right and a love of all that is good and beautiful. Such a summons to commit evil overwhelms his sorrowful heart, for his soul is unequal to the performance of it, and thus he begins to walk the line of sanity and madness as he tries to come to terms with fulfilling this bitter duty of punishing the usurper. Goethe explains the dilemma: "A beautiful, pure, and most moral nature...sinks beneath a burden which it can neither bear nor throw off; every duty is holy to him—this too hard." Incapable of killing his uncle in cold blood, he masterminds how "the play's the thing wherein I'll catch the conscience of the King."

No soliloquy is endowed with more tragic pathos than Hamlet's "To be or not to be, that is the question." In this speech he deliberates whether to suffer the "slings and arrows of outrageous fortune" that have rent and harrowed his soul or simply end them all through death. Here more than anywhere else we can feel ourselves in intimate communion with the young prince, who is utterly sincere. At the same time, he speaks for all of us. In the course of this most perfect confessional, he uses the pronouns "we" and "us" and the indefinite "who." He uses the impersonal infinitive and speaks of what "flesh" is heir to and of what "we" suffer at the hands of "time" and "fortune." His personal struggle is Everyman's struggle. As he experiences the dark night of the soul, it is Everyman's spiritual struggle.

Each character in *Hamlet* is fully revealed by the verbal text. The dialogue is a rich study that contributes to the overall tragic exposition of the protagonist. Think of the King's words, "O, my offense is rank, it smells to Heaven; It hath the primal eldest curse upon it..."—how they theatrically belong not only to the character speaking but to Hamlet and others in dramatic impact with the King. In Ophelia's moving soliloquy, we grieve Hamlet's madness (or quixotic sanity) as much as we grieve the woman bound in love to him, who will soon become even more poignantly mad:

> O, what a noble mind is here o'erthrown!
> The courtier's soldier's, scholar's, eye, tongue, sword:
> The expectancy and rose of the fair state,
> The glass of fashion and the mould of form,
> The observed of all observers, quite, quite down!
> And I, of ladies most deject and wretched,
> That sucked the honey of his music vows,
> Now see that noble and most sovereign reason,
> Like sweet bells jangled, out of tune and harsh;
> The unmatch'd form and feature of blown youth
> Blasted with ecstasy: O, woe is me,
> To have seen what I have seen, see what I see!

And how could we ever forget Horatio's parting words to Hamlet after he dies—two of the most heart-wrenching lines in dramatic literature:

> Now cracks a noble heart. Good night, sweet prince,
> And flights of angels sing thee to thy rest!

Each of Shakespeare's works is a chalice. His words, so true, so inspiring, so full of delight, so soul provoking, remain imprisoned within each chalice "to which we may put our lips and continually drink," to quote Galsworthy. Because of their exquisite dialogue, Shakespeare's plays are art in which heaven finds its perfect expression.

If dialogue in a play or in a movie does not bring nearer to us the beauty of life, and so the vision of what God dreams for us, what is the purpose of the drama?

KEY: Getting to the heart of the issue

When dialogue can penetrate to the heart of life, and the actor can bring that experience to the audience, the playwright achieves true magic.

The Magic of Great Drama

The Greek tragedies and the Shakespearean plays combine all the elements that make for good drama. They excel in play structure that compels intense interest and suspense, unforgettable protagonists who grow to heroic heights in our imagination, language that is unsurpassed in beauty and solemnity, and noble themes. These components, however, do not fully explain why these works are great. The secret to their majesty is their ability to bring us in touch with the highest and best in ourselves —or, as Sheldon Cheney writes, "close to the gods." As the highest form of drama, they purge human life of all that is shallow and corrupt, and inundate the spectator with an exaltation and noble pity that lifts our souls heavenward.

Take, for instance, Sophocles' *Oedipus*. The play treats the subject of murder, incest, and suicide. The poetry carries us through the darkest and most immoral depths of the human condition as it is revealed to Oedipus and his wife that they are really mother and son and that Oedipus has unknowingly killed his own father. Oedipus suffers the consequences of his own evil actions, though that evil had not been intended. As the Messenger tells of the Queen's terrible despair and immediate demise, of Oedipus' wrenching sorrow and subsequent self-blinding, we are shaken. This tragic man reaches deep into his broken soul, even as the Chorus turns away to escape the sight of his abject misery. As Cheney describes it: "He [Oedipus] gropes his way forward, calling on the gods, glorying that he has made himself a dungeon, 'dark, without sound...self-prisoned from a world of pain,' cursing the shepherd who saved him as a babe."

As Creon brings to Oedipus his two little daughters, he clings to them, but only for a moment, as we see them dragged from him forever. No god could exact a more poignant justice, and Oedipus accepts it nobly. To quote Cheney, his soul seems to "stand up and take the light, naked and glorious." And somehow we are cleansed as well. There is a glow of beauty in our souls and a healing that is deep and sure. We have not shuddered at Sophocles' telling; our suffering and grief, like that of the players in the drama, has been kept on some loftier plane where our spirits become one with God's spirit and his healing love. This is, as Cheney reminds us, "nobly proportioned theater." It is art that in its ultimate simplicity and obedience to eternal laws, achieves spiritual completeness.

In a world that has forgotten the things of the divine, this revealing moment of immersion in the spirit —both for the actor and the audience—is magical, and sums up the true art of theater. As Cheney writes, "This [moment] is as near as we are likely to come to the divine and the spiritual. It is the Dionysian experience, our ecstatic participation in the divine life. Unless you have known that moment, you have not really penetrated into the theater."

Shakespeare's
HEROES
AND HEROINES

Lady Macbeth: Look like the innocent flower,
But be the serpent under it.
    —*Macbeth*, Act 1, Scene 5

Touchstone: Ay, now am I in Arden;
the more fool I.
    —*As You Like It*, Act 2, Scene 4

Titania: Set your heart at rest.
The fairy land buys not the child of me.
    —*A Midsummer Night's Dream*, Act 3, Scene 1

Juliet: O, think'st thou we shall ever meet again?
—*Romeo and Juliet:* Act 3, Scene 5

Arthur: Good ground, be pitiful and hurt me not.
—*King John,* Act 4, Scene 3

Prince: For never was a story of more woe
Than this of Juliet and her Romeo.
—*Romeo and Juliet,* Act 5, Scene 3

Isabella: O faithless coward! O dishonest wretch!
Wilt thou be made a man out of my vice?

—*Measure for Measure,* Act 3, Scene 1

Constance: O if thou teach me to believe this sorrow,
Teach thou this sorrow how to make me die.

—*King John,* Act 3, Scene 1

Malvolio: Jove knows I love
But who?

—*Twelfth Night,* Act 2, Scene 5

Posthumus: For my sake wear this:
It is a manacle of love. I'll place it
Upon this fairest prisoner.
—*Cymbeline*, Act 1, Scene 2

Hamlet: Give me that man
That is not passion's slave, and I will wear him
In my heart's core, ay, in my heart of heart
As I do thee.
—*Hamlet*, Act 3, Scene 2

Ophelia: Take these again: for to the noble mind
Rich gifts wax poor when givers prove unkind.
There, my lord.
—*Hamlet*, Act 3, Scene 1

King Henry: Once more unto the breach, dear friends, once more!

—*King Henry V,* Act 3, Scene 1

Richard: But shall I live in hope?
Anne: All men, I hope, live so.

—*Richard III,* Act 1, Scene 2

King Henry: For he, today, that sheds his blood with me, shall be my brother.

—*King Henry V,* Act 4, Scene 3

Prospero: I have done nothing but in care of thee—
Of thee, my dear one! thee, my daughter

—*The Tempest,* Act 1, Scene 2

Leon: Let no man mock me
For I will kiss her.
—*The Winter's Tale,* Act 4, Scene 3

Cressida: And is it true that I must go from Troy?
—*Troilus and Cressida,* Act 4, Scene 4

Katherine: Spirits of peace, where are ye?
Are ye all gone,
—*King Henry VIII,* Act 4, Scene 2

Joan: Look on thy country, look on fertile France,
And see the cities and the towns defaced
By wasting ruin of the cruel foe!
—*King Henry VI,* Part 1, Act 3, Scene 3

Cordelia: Then poor Cordelia!
And yet not so; since, I am sure, my love's
More richer than my tongue.
—*King Lear,* Act 1, Scene 1

Proteus: O, how this spring of love resembleth
The uncertain glory of an April day.
—*Two Gentlemen of Verona,* Act 1, Scene 3

He was met even now
As mad as the vexed sea; singing aloud;
Crowned with rank fumitor and furrow weeds,
With burdocks, hemlock, nettles, cuckoo flowers,
Darnel, and all the idle weeds that grow
In our sustaining corn.
—*King Lear,* Act 4, Scene 4

Falstaff: I would make thee my lady.
Mrs. Ford: I your lady, Sir John! alas, I should be a pitiful lady!
—*Merry Wives of Windsor*, Act 3, Scene 3

Portia: But mercy is above this sceptered sway;
It is enthroned in the hearts of kings;
It is an attribute to God himself;
And earthly power doth then show likest God's,
When mercy seasons justice.
—*The Merchant of Venice*, Act 4, Scene 1

Othello: Why, what art thou?
Desdemona: Your wife, my lord,
your true and loyal wife.
—*Othello*, Act 4, Scene 2

Plays

of

&

William Shakespeare

THE Globe Theatre · 1613

All the world's a stage,
And all the men and women merely players:
They have their exits and their entrances;
And one man in his time plays many parts.
　　　　—As You Like It, Act 2, Scene 7

Unit

Study

Nine

The Spoken Word

9

The Spoken Word

Class materials needed: Three medium-sized sponge balls,
                            one of different color

Repeat Theater Game 3-1: Magic Cue Ball, Level Four Action

Oral Tradition In Literature

The spoken word has a rich and glorious tradition as the recorder of our history. The poets (or bards) of past societies and civilizations were the original motion picture producers; their poems, centuries later, bring to life not only the character of an ancient people—their religion, politics, and social manners—but the spirit that guided them in their progress toward self-knowledge. Through exciting narrative, imagery, allegory, rhyme, and meter, they tell the story of the soul's struggle and overcoming in a way that excites the imagination and is welcomed in our hearts.

We begin with Homer (about 1000 B.C.), one of the greatest of our epic poets and traveling minstrels, who was also blind. The *Iliad* and the *Odyssey* constitute in themselves an encyclopedia of the vibrant and expansive life of the early Greek civilization (as distinct from the later Greece of Sophocles) known as the Achaians (also spelled Achaeans), to whom Homer's poems gave immortal fame. *Iliad* is the story of the siege of Troy. *Odyssey* is the tragic tale of the wanderings of Odysseus, a great man, who spends 20 years of his life trying to make his way back to his homeland after sacking the holy citadel of Troy. What these poems present cannot be captured from mere knowledge collected by historians and anthropologists, for though they are part fact and part fiction, they convey the action and living spirit of the times—that spirit being the presence of God as His wisdom and divine guidance are revealed in a noble people who lived one thousand years before the birth of Christ.

The wonder of Homer's poems is that they were not written down but passed on through the spoken word to the accompaniment of a lyre-like stringed instrument. This oral process was made possible by the high position accorded poets in Greece (more properly, Achaia, and afterward Hellas). Homer did not actually sing his poems; he would use his musical instrument to mark rhythm or to play an interlude that provided a kind of dramatic pause or phrase or that simply gave him time to invent the next verse (if he was improvising). He might also use the lyre to create mood (such as playing a major chord to introduce or sustain an action, a minor chord to heighten suspense or pathos, and resolving into a major after some climactic action). Musical accompaniment was indispensable to Homer and his contemporaries.

Schools were formed in Achaia to teach the art of oratory, dramatic recitation, and song for the express purpose of passing on these particular poems in the original spirit and precise form that inspired them. As Charles Horne tells us in *Great Men and Famous Women,* students were trained in memory skills so that the story songs could be rendered accurately. Errors were corrected by holding public competition, which tested the word-for-word accuracy of the recitation (and not merely its entertainment value). It is important for modern students to understand that the Homeric epics were never intended to be read, which partly explains why many college students find them boring or just too alien from our modern culture. Their intrinsic power and virtue can only be transferred by listening to them being recited by trained artists.

The great institution of the Games also facilitated the public's love for and appreciation of the spoken word. By the time Homer roamed the country reciting his verses, public recitations were a popular and revered part of Achaian life. Those selected to be the orators at the schools of Achaia were eminently endowed with the literary faculty and with a sense of the sacredness of their art. They knew the importance of handing down faithfully a record which was the chief authority touching the national life—the religion, history, political divisions, and manners—of their country.

The Greeks called the poet *poietes,* or "maker." Homer fulfilled that high office. His work was preeminently the making of a language, a religion, and a national patriotism. That was the purpose, of course, to be wrought by any poet of the times. But Homer succeeded magnificently. His poems make the national life of an ancient Greece come vividly alive, despite the difference of three thousand years. The Achaian civilization with its Phoenician influence in architecture, ship building, navigation, and natural knowledge, can be felt with a freshness, power, and even sacredness. Though war, with its death, conquest, and bondage, was part of the fierce passion of this ancient people, we learn from Homer that religion was a moral spring of great force, while liberty had a very real place (if informal) in the public institutions. Moreover, personal manners embodied a high level of civility and refinement. Though not a perfect society, it was, according to Charles Horne, "a wonderful and noble nursery of manhood."

It would not be until the fifth century B.C. that something akin to the high social and moral ideas of the Achaians and their Olympian religion would emerge, though never reaching the former civilization's moral splendor. One only has to read the remarkable prayer of Achilles to Zeus in Book XVI of the *Iliad*, when he sends forth Patroclus, to have a window into the spiritual life of this people. The prayer represents the moral principle that binds the whole action of the poem. Homer was able to harmonize the diverse spiritual elements in the thearchy (a hierarchy of rule by gods) that his work of art presents, much like the people of this ancient time were able to combine and absorb the best of each other's religious traditions, with an end goal of moral beauty in mind. In the *Iliad*, the gods themselves are not given equality. Homer portrays the sensual Aphrodite with contempt. On the other hand, he conveys a deep reverence for Apollo, whose cardinal virtue is obedience to Zeus, and for Athene, who represents a profound and practical wisdom that never fails of its altruistic purpose.

Homer's Olympian assembly is largely human in its passions and appetites, but in the government of the world, it works for justice and for the special care of the humble suppliant and the stranger. Accordingly, we find that the cause, which is to triumph in the Trojan war, is the just cause. In the *Odyssey*, the hero is led through suffering to self-knowledge and peace. When he inflicts his terrible retribution, we believe it to be well deserved, and justice restored according to divine plan.

Without Homer's poems, recorded by those who cherished the spoken word, little would be known, let alone spiritually felt, of this classical period of Greek civilization, in which the great chieftains, Achilles, Ajax, Diomed, Menelaos, and Patroclus, appear to exhibit the Achaian ideal of humanity. Even in the house of Odysseus we find upheld one of the noblest characteristics of a moral society—the sanctity and perpetuity of marriage. Indeed, the purity and trueness of Penelope are, like the humility and penitence of Helen of Troy, unmatched in our ancient history.

The *Iliad* and the *Odyssey* demonstrate the value of Homer as a recorder of antiquity long before later historians of Assyria and Egypt could verify it in fact. Much like Shakespeare, his work reveals the simplicity and practical idealism of the structure of his mind. Charles Horne splendidly sums up Homer's place:

> With an incomparable eye for the world around him in all things, great and small, he is abhorrent of everything speculative and abstract....He is of all poets the most simple and direct. He is also the most free and genial in the movement of his verse....In the high office of drawing human character in its multitude of forms and colors he seems to have no serious rival except

Shakespeare. We call him an epic poet, but he is instinct from beginning to end with the spirit of the drama, while we find in him the seeds and rudiments even of its form. His function as a reciting minstrel greatly aided him herein. Again, he had in his language an instrument unrivalled for its facility, suppleness, and versatility, for the large range of what would in music be called its register, so that it embraced every form and degree of human thought, feeling, and emotion, and clothed them all, from the lowest to the loftiest, from the slightest to the most intense and concentrated, in the dress of exactly appropriate style and language. His meter also is a perfect vehicle of the language....So long as the lamp of civilization shall not have ceased to burn, the *Iliad* and the *Odyssey* must hold their forward place among the brightest treasures of our race.

Second to Homer as poet and dramatic minstrel is Virgil (70–19 B.C.), the greatest of the Roman poets, who lived at the time of Marc Antony and the first of the Roman emperors, Octavius (later known as Augustus) Caesar. Constantine, the first Christian emperor, professed to have been converted to Christianity by reading one of Virgil's *Eclogues.* Dante would later claim Virgil as his master, guide, and model. Virgil's most famous work, other than his *Eclogues* and the *Aeneid,* is his *Georgics.* This perfect poem, with its beautiful and tenderly plaintive episode of Orpheus and Eurydice, is a tribute to the mystic nature of man's relationship with God, the key to which is the right use of man's *amor,* or inner energy, as he strives toward harmony and order, and thus reconciliation with his destiny. The *Aeneid* has similar themes. Those who cannot master the sacred fire of their inordinate desires, as Dido could not in her passion for Aeneas, are destroyed by those desires.

We learn from the poet Sextus Propertius (50–16 B.C.) that Virgil's fame was not alone what he wrote, but how he recited his poems, both while he was composing them and after they were completed. Propertius wrote of the remarkable beauty and charm of the poet's rendering of his own words and its powerful effect upon his listeners. The first century Roman historian Suetonius agreed. He wrote: "He [Virgil] read at once with sweetness and with a wonderful fascination." Roman statesman and dramatist Seneca (3 B.C.–65 A.D.) recounted a story about the poet Julius Montanus, who professed that he himself would only attempt to steal something from Virgil if he could first steal his voice, his elocution, and his dramatic power in reading, since the very same lines had the power to move the audience profoundly when the author himself read them, but were empty and dumb without him.

It would appear that only Virgil could bring alive the true spirit of his verse and hold power over his audience. Only he could capture with his voice the melancholy of man's longing for a return to a relationship of harmony with God (or the gods). It is a lesson that has practical application. Only if the actor is rightly attuned to the deep current of feeling in the verse he interprets, only if his soul can respond to the great truths which the poem or drama teaches can that verse or drama come fully alive in all its original beauty and high purpose. Without true responsiveness, the actor cannot weave the genius of the author into his own deepest feelings and highest aspirations, which are essential to his interpretive art.

The Roman world in which Virgil lived lacked the presence and the light of God, though all still yearned for it. Rome was a pagoda of evil, deliberately chosen, in which the soul descended through lower and lower stages of self-will until he sank into such self-corruption that he was utterly emptied of God, and filled only with the loathsome emptiness of self.

Only the true poet, as the true actor, can render the tragic pathos of man when he is out of tune with the universe and with his divine self, and thereby prove how essential God is to man's happiness and wholeness. Only the true poet, as the true actor, can make his verse live with the kind of divine romance that makes his work magical and prophetic, as was the case with Virgil.

Virgil read to Augustus Caesar the whole of his *Georgics,* and on another occasion three books of the *Aeneid* to Caesar's wife, Octavia. His dramatic rendering had such a powerful effect on her that when he recited the touching lines about her own son and his premature death, which begin, "Tu Marcellus eris," it is said that she fell into a dead faint and was recovered only with great difficulty.

The genius of the poet-actor would not be revived until the troubadour of a courtly medieval Europe appeared on the world stage between the eleventh and thirteenth centuries. The troubadours were gallant men, usually knights, who embodied the romantic maxim of the true poet: "What has been made known to the eyes, has also been made welcomed to the heart." As poet-musicians, chiefly in the south of France and northern Italy, they were messengers of the life and legends of courtly love.

As the original tale master, the troubadour strolled through the land with only his minstrelsy to win him a way. To paraphrase author Annie Fellows Johnston, in every baron's hall and cotter's hut he found a ready welcome. And while the boar's head sputtered on the spit and the ale sparkled in the shining tankards, he told such tales of joust and valor, and feats of brave knight errantry that even the kitchen maids left their tasks to listen. Such was the enchantment of the minstrel of old.

The minstrel brought to his art a romantic sentiment that appealed to a knightly age that cherished deeds imbued with a personal honor and holy valor. Women especially were held in something akin to a reverent awe. The love for a woman was of the unselfish, adoring, chivalrous type, and a man was content to worship in silence. His love was not the kind that attained to a lofty level of spiritual purification as much as it was a purely romantic love. By the thirteenth century, when Catholic Christendom was dominant, great respect and devotion was accorded to the Virgin Mary and other female saints. Mary was the role model of purity, piety, and motherhood, representing the beauty of maidenly form and grace. It was no unusual thing for a knight or a troubadour to select a certain lady, celebrate her virtues in his songs, call on her name in the hour of danger, and wear her color in battle. That the adored or the adorer might be married made no difference. As Charles Horne tells us, the tender litany of devotion would sometimes run on for years, long after the idol's hair was silvered and her form less than graceful, as in Petrarch's verses to Laura, which immortalized her youth even when she was old and plump. It was the fashion of the day to proclaim by the spoken word in song or recitation the beauties and graces of her who first awoke within the troubadour or knight his ideal of romance. They wove out of woman an ideal being, who was then woven into his own deep feelings and most aerial fancies.

Though the divine poetry of Dante (1265–1321) and Petrarch (1304–1374) would trail clouds of glory in the history of our dramatic literature—embodying the eternal elements of the life of the soul—the oral tradition of the spoken word had, by the early fourteenth century, lost much of its splendor. There was, however, a rainbow moment with the courtly appearance of Chaucer and his *Canterbury Tales*.

Much of the deep love and reverence that is still shown to Geoffrey Chaucer (1328–1400) finds its origin in his role as a tale master of remarkable grace and invention. His work had the "golden touch"—a manly understanding of the merry, vigorous heart of the common people, which he was able to convey in his readings. Though he was a scholar in the classics and the sciences, it was Chaucer's winning grace and joviality as a reader of his own verse that quickly brought him into favor at court. His varied professions as law student, soldier, prisoner-of-war, court valet, political ambassador, and head of customs under Edward III provided him with a panorama of colorful men and women who would fill his *Canterbury Tales*. Before Chaucer, there was no standard English. By naturalizing and then popularizing many French words, he created the foundation for our English language as we know it. It would take the bold innovations of Shakespeare to imbue the spoken and written word with the great richness, vigor, and flexibility that would lift it out of its medieval roots.

The Renaissance, which brought with it a revivifying of the beauties of language, had its highest expression in England in the art of the drama. Owing almost exclusively to the matchless genius of Shakespeare, the spoken word was the summit of theatric art in Elizabethan times, as it was in the Greece of both Homer and later Sophocles. There were no trappings, no scenery or sets to distract from its dramatic force. From Shakespeare, the audience learned a passion and appetite for words that only he could quench and which set the immortal standard for all ages to come. With the exception of the Romantic period, which gave to us the highest traditions of the spoken and written word, there has been a steady decline over the last century in both the literary and aesthetic content of literature and, thus, in the dramatic experience itself.

We live and work in a technology-driven world of audio and visual saturation, where the spoken word, much like the art of handwriting, has been replaced by state-of-the-art communications. Never before have the nations and peoples of this earth been so connected and information made available to so many in so short a time. If we can't find the necessary data on a topical subject at our local Borders or Barnes & Noble, we can certainly track it down in a thousand newspaper editorials across the country. We can hear a selection of experts analyze the issue on television news programs and on talk radio, or express our own opinion by calling in or emailing our thoughts to the host. We can explore any number of worldwide websites, and interactively discuss the issue of our choice in chat rooms, on blogs, and at online town hall meetings. We can also expect to see the most riveting of these subjects in a made-for-television movie within months of its emergence on the national scene.

Cyber-space highways of global communications have expanded man's freedom of speech and his ability to connect with humanity anywhere on the planet with unprecedented speed. At the same time, this remarkable freedom and diversity of self-expression has been gained too often at the expense of our time-honored standards of literacy, aesthetic beauty, and truth. If the spoken word in past ages was used to tell a noble story, it is used less so today, as the state of our artistic life and our political discourse demonstrates. The recitation of the minstrels of old fostered patriotism and chivalry. They told of heroic deeds and spoke of the purity and ennobling influence of women, and of the sacredness of a man's trust in her virtue. In Chaucer's tales, we met the merriest of characters who played out their roles on the stage of life. Today's arts are no longer focused on such images of divinity or even the simple principles of moral goodness. Nor are aesthetic ideals, for their own sake, aspired to in many cases.

Professions such as journalism, writing, publishing, law, politics, ministry, teaching, broadcasting, corporate management, and sales all require accomplishment in the spoken and written word but not necessarily aesthetic skills. This is not the case when we work in the theater because the task of the actor is to not only make an audience believe something is real when it really isn't, but to do so in an artistically persuasive way—transferring something of beauty and worth, it is hoped, in the process.

We have ventured far from the schools of Achaia, and even from the pure, though primitive, aesthetics of Shakespeare's plays as they were first performed at London's Globe Theater. Sadly, the spoken word and the actor's rendering of it has been fatally degraded on our modern stages and cinema screens. Yet a free society can only be enlightened by the best thoughts and imagination of its people. Here is where the art of the spoken word can and should rise to its highest perfection. It is therefore incumbent upon our acting schools and our educational institutions at large to return to those oral traditions that brought the greatest literary minds to the fore of society and provided the key to searching out man's finer nature and nobler aspirations.

Homer reciting his *Iliad*

Octavia overcome as Virgil reads his verses from the *Aeneid*

The Golden Age of the Troubadour

Kept at the court of a great lord, or wandering from castle to castle, these minstrels of song and recitation kept alive the age of chivalry. In May, 1324, troubadours from all over the world gathered at Toulouse, France, to recite their tales of romance and knightly heroism. The chief prize, a golden violet, was awarded to a French competitor.

Chaucer at the Court of Edward III
Reading his *Canterbury Tales*

A Weapon of Defense and Attack

The spoken word is both a science and a mystery, and therein lies its great power. While we can break down the voice into physical elements and master those elements for stage acting, we also have to recognize that the voice can take on powers that transcend its mere physical use as a tool to express and communicate thoughts and emotions. When imbued with loving intent and the desire to inspire or teach others, the voice may be an instrument of a higher purpose.

The spoken word plays an important part in many of the world's spiritual traditions. Whether the devotional chants of Hindus, the mantras of Buddhist monks, the fiery rebukes of the Jewish prophets of old, or the prayers and songs of Christian devotees, the spoken word can be a dynamic expression of love and an instrument for transformation. The voice itself as well as the words charged by that voice can penetrate the most hidden and defended recesses of someone's heart and transmute the very cause and core of despair into hope.

Because of its great power, the spoken word has been used as a weapon of defense and attack throughout the ages. In the many martial art forms, it is used as an advance warning to break the mental concentration of the opponent through a combination of vowel tones that are vocalized a split second before the actual physical attack. The sound is intended to shatter the "Tao," or center of focus, of the opponent. Likewise, the barbaric Moors during their centuries-long crusade against the Christian "infidels" sent out their Islamic monks known as "howling dervishes" just before battle to perform whirling, frenzied dances accompanied by shrieking chants to Allah to inspire terror in their Christian foes.

On October 7, 1571, Don Juan of Austria, commander of the naval forces of the Holy League, won the decisive Battle at Lepanto in the eastern Mediterranean by the power of the spoken word. To achieve the sea victory, he used a shrewd tactic that the Turkish janizaries themselves had successfully applied against the crusaders—a line of attack that involved a devastating use of the spoken word. It was a strategy that had largely contributed to the mythical belief in the invincibility of the Turks. As recorded history tells us, the critical battle occurred on board the Muslim flagship Sultana. After Don Juan's men boarded the ship, fifty of his select soldiers, dressed in the garments of the Turkish "howling dervishes," mounted the masthead. Performing their own version of the Turkish flying dances, they shouted the battle cry "Christ and the King! Christ and the King!" to their fierce enemy below, confounding them entirely. Don Juan completed the intimidation by personally climbing to the poop deck, seizing the sacred flag of the prophet, and propelling it down into the hands of his Spanish harquebusiers. He then hoisted the flag of the Holy League, which caused a last surge of rage from the never-before-beaten Turks as they capitulated in defeat.

Perhaps one of the greatest historical uses of the spoken word as a righteous weapon of attack was when the children of Israel, led by Joshua, brought down the walls of Jericho by a great rhythmic shout. God directed Joshua to have his people steadily build upon a repetitious chant commonly used in Jewish ritual until it reached such a consummate power of divine energy that the walls would come tumbling down. Because of his impeccable obedience, Joshua won the battle of Jericho.

In the mid-1800s, the French Basque people, like other European emigrants, traveled in wagon trains from New York across the virgin American continent to California. From their homeland in the French Pyrenees, the Basque brought grapevines that were carefully and lovingly preserved so they could plant them in the fertile Californian soil. It was their masterful use of the spoken word as a powerful instrument of defense that enabled their safe journey across Indian infested territory.

The young Basque men convinced their wagon train bosses to send them forward as scouts, positioning themselves in mountain canyons and valley ridges at regular distances 20 or 30 miles out from the wagon train. Whenever a scout spotted Indians or an approaching war party, he would transmit a vocal message in the form of a modulated, encrypted call that sounded like a musical scale that rose in pitch by microtones and incrementally increased in volume to a crescendo. Because the variant microtone pitches that made up the sound represented particular letters, the Basque battle cry acted like a Morse code that relayed pertinent messages to the next scout further down the line all the way back to the wagon train, thus supplying advanced reconnaissance data that helped the wagon train prepare more effectively for a possible Indian attack.

The speaker executed this unique sound by means of highly developed resonating chambers within his vocal apparatus. The Basque scout had learned to utilize his voice as its own recording studio with built-in amplifiers and resonators. The resonating cavities (the chest, soft palate, pharynx, nasal cavity, throat, ears, mouth and head cavities) were used as internal acoustic chambers to broaden and enhance the original tone, just as we create powerful resonance electronically in a real recording studio. The physical environment—the mountain canyons—acted as echo chambers to further augment the sound so that it could be projected and heard for miles and thus be passed on by the next scout in a continuous transmission.

In their own country in the Pyrenees mountains, situated between Spain and France, the Basque had mastered their distinctive cry as the primary means of fast and reliable communication between villages across miles of mountainous terrain. They were able to adapt this skill in their new circumstances in America as an unprecedented means of defense. Moreover, many accounts tell of how large numbers of Indians were routed by the sound itself. The incredible strangeness of the Basque cry, as it resounded through the mountain passes and canyons, gave it an almost supernatural magic that the Indians grew to fear. The 1959 Paramount picture *Thunder in the Sun*, starring Jeff Chandler, Susan Hayward, and Jacques Bergerac, immortalizes the Basque cry.

Another example in our history of the remarkable use of the voice as a weapon of defense and attack is the accomplishment of a group of Navajo Indians who were enlisted in the United States Marine Corps during the Second World War and trained as an elite force of "code talkers," officially called "Windtalkers." The security of a nation, especially in times of war, relies heavily on masking the communication of sensitive intelligence information. If the enemy should pick up the messages, especially if those messages contain orders to initiate a tactical action on the battlefield, the consequences could be costly. The threat of enemy interception during World War II spurred the development of codes and ciphers, which were techniques to disguise a message so that only the intended recipient could read it.

Using their Native American language, the Windtalkers developed a wartime radio cipher, called the Navajo Code, which transmitted secret messages about important logistics, intelligence, and mission strategy in the Pacific war zone. The Japanese were never able to decipher the code. It was an ingenious weapon to protect and defend our forces and achieve our military objectives in the vital Pacific battles. The 2002 movie *Windtalkers* paid tribute to the brave Navajo codetalkers and their critical role in achieving victory in the Pacific.

In recent history, one of the most powerful ways of using the spoken word as a weapon of defense and attack was through the Hollywood film industry of the 1940s, considered by many to be the golden age of movies. The far-reaching impact of the film media at that time is no better illustrated than in Winston Churchill's response to the poignant wartime drama *Mrs. Miniver*, produced by MGM during Hitler's blitz of Britain. The film was directed by William Wyler and starred Walter Pigeon and Greer Garson. It told the story of a middle-class English family struggling to meet the challenges and heartache of life during the Battle of Britain, when England was fighting for her very survival. The movie paid homage to the qualities in ordinary men and women that make them rise above extraordinary circumstances with a simple faith in what is right and a deep trust in God to defend that right.

Churchill predicted that the film's contribution to defeating the Axis powers would be more powerful than a fleet of battleships. He urged President Roosevelt to press for the movie's immediate worldwide release, especially in England. Louis B. Mayer, the head of MGM—an idealist and patriot himself—happily agreed, and *Mrs. Miniver* premiered June 4, 1942, coinciding with the second anniversary of Churchill's famous "We shall never surrender" address to the English people. It was an exalting tribute to the British. The film was nominated for twelve Academy Awards and won six. Because of its urgency and humanity, the support for American involvement in the European war rose dramatically.

The most poignant scene in the movie is the closing scene. The setting is the village church, which has been partially bombed. The lovely young bride of Mrs. Miniver's son has been killed in a bombing raid. The old station master, who had just won his first flower contest with his homegrown hybrid rose, "the Mrs. Miniver," is also a casualty. The vicar, standing in the pulpit, addresses a congregation that he knows is struggling with the grief of these and other wartime tragedies. His words and the way he delivered them sum up the pathos of indomitable resolve in the face of war.

> This is not only a war of soldiers in uniform; it is a war of the people, of all the people. And it must be fought, not only on the battlefield, but in the cities and in the villages, in the factories and on the farms, in the home and in the heart of every man, woman, and child who loves freedom. We have buried our dead, but we shall not forget them. Instead they will inspire us with an unbreakable determination to free ourselves and those who come after us from the tyranny and terror that threaten to strike us down. This is the people's war. It is our war. We are the fighters. Fight it then. Fight it with all that is in us. And may God defend the right.

The film was a huge box-office hit, the biggest of the decade after *Gone With the Wind.* Three of its Academy Awards included Best Picture, Best Director, and Best Actress for Greer Garson. Meanwhile, President Roosevelt had pamphlets of the rector's stirring speech airdropped over Europe. To complete the spirit of patriotism that this film embodied for a world besieged by Nazism, on the night his Oscar was awarded in absentia, director William Wyler was flying a bombing mission over Germany.

Director's Notes: Try to get a copy of the movie *Thunder in the Sun.* The students will enjoy a demonstration of the Basque cry, and may imitate it themselves. *Windtalkers* can be purchased or rented, but it does have an R rating due to its many violent battle scenes. *Mrs. Miniver* has been released on DVD.

EXERCISE 9-1 Voice in Our Lives

- Students discuss any personal experiences where the spoken word played a significant or life-changing role. For example, one child might relate how his father saved him from getting run over by a car when he yelled out to him to stop.

- Invite a local martial arts teacher to talk about and demonstrate to the class how the voice is used as a weapon of defense and attack.

- Older students discuss films (old or new) that have proven effective in influencing people or transforming a situation (political or otherwise).
- Make a list of spoken words that have become part of the lexicon of our country's history—for example, Patrick Henry's "Give me liberty or give me death!" and Paul Revere's "The British are coming!"

Goal: To get students to think about all the dynamic and important ways the spoken word can influence us and sometimes even save our lives.

Author's Story: During my childhood, I spent all of my school vacations with my grandparents on their sheep and cattle station (ranch) in the northern part of New South Wales in Australia. One of these vacations coincided with the shearing of the sheep. Every morning after I had helped my grandmother with the chores, I walked through the long grass from the house to the shearing shed to watch the shearers remove the wool from the sheep. I was about eight years old at the time and I had heard my grandfather say on many occasions that there was money in wool, so I was highly motivated to search through the shorn-off wool at the end of each shearing session to see if I might find that money first. This provided my grandfather and the shearers with some hearty entertainment, though I was much older before I understood why! The distance from the house to the shed was about 300 yards. On this particular warm and sunny morning, I left my grandmother on the porch steps as I trudged my way to the shed. I had walked about 100 yards when I heard my grandmother shout out, "Snake! Snake!" With a beating heart, I stopped in my tracks and looked around. Not three feet to my right was a large, black, and very venomous snake making its way through the grass. In the time it takes to blink, I turned and raced back to the house. In the meantime, my grandmother, who stood barely five feet in her boots, and weighed no more than 100 pounds, had grabbed the long stock whip hanging on the porch and passed me as I collapsed, more out of fear than exhaustion, onto the steps. I soon heard two cracks of the whip, followed by my grandmother's swift return to a shaking and trembling "city" girl. The snake was dead, but I was alive, thanks to the piercing cry of alarm from my dearest "Ma!"

E X E R C I S E 9-2 Voice Characterizations

- In an open class discussion, the students describe the different voice characterizations an actor would use to convey the following emotions:

  1. Speaking to someone for whom you feel only contempt
  2. Speaking to someone with the intention to intimidate or scare him
  3. Correcting a small child who has been naughty
  4. Facing down a bully
  5. Comforting a close friend or relative who is very sick
  6. Putting a baby (or a doll) to sleep
  7. Responding to an unjust accusation with amazement or shock
  8. Being so angry that you can barely control yourself
  9. Inspiring hope and courage in a seemingly hopeless situation

Director's Notes: The students should describe the different voices in their own words. You are not looking for technical answers. For example, in situation 8, the voice would be higher and louder than normal and perhaps raspy or squeaky in tone. The words might be broken up due to shorter, quicker breaths. In situation 5, the voice would be calm, soothing, and lower in pitch, conveying warmth and deep caring, and reflecting steady and quiet breathing. These suggestions are not meant to promote external cliches of voice, but merely to offer guidelines.

Level Two Action:

- Students work in pairs and choose one of the situations listed above.

- They decide on an imaginary buildup or setting for the situation, then act it out onstage before the class as a short scene using a minimum of words. Only one of the students in the pair speaks.

- Each student in the pair takes a turn in being the actor who speaks.

Director's Notes: Keep each scene short and simple. The goal is to have the student learn to suit his voice to a specific emotion. This is not meant to be an exercise in improvisation and scene building. Though he doesn't speak, the silent partner, to whom the other actor addresses his words, should still take on a character.

The Misuse of Voice and the Spoken Word

Director's Notes: This section is suitable for older students and is intended to illustrate various examples of the misuse of the spoken word both in our history and present society. Please feel free to incorporate into your instruction only those portions you deem appropriate for your class. The purpose of these examples is not to promote a particular political viewpoint but to point out the destructive consequences that can result to societies and nations from the misuse of the spoken word.

The highest purpose of the dramatist is to express himself with clearness and simplicity, and to carry to the hearts of his listeners a truthful eloquence that will not only provide understanding but inspire them to live their lives a little more beautifully. Throughout the history of the world, however, the spoken word has been employed to serve selfish and corrupt ends. Rasputin, personal companion and spiritual advisor to Tzar Nicholas of Russia, was known to exercise extraordinary powers over the royal family and particularly over the women of that household. His voice could literally hypnotize people into total trances and persuade them to do his will, a will that many believed was given over to the practice of black magic.

Many Islamic terrorist organizations, including Al-Qaida, Hamas, and Hezbollah, train their followers in the misuse of the power of the word. They chant words in rhythmic unison, such as "Death to America," that are charged with personal and group hatred. When misused, the spoken word can become a compelling negative force in people's lives, fueling a frenzy of mob hatred and spurring them on to murder.

The most notorious misuse of the power of the spoken word in this century was the mental programming of the German people by Adolf Hitler. Through relentless, manic affirmation of the superiority of the Aryan race, accompanied by the institutionalization of atheism as the state religion with Adolf Hitler as a national god, a whole nation was programmed to believe and obey one psychopathic tyrant's perception of reality. Lenin and Stalin, though not as charismatic in their oratory as Hitler, were also masters at using words to persuade a nation of profoundly religious people to overturn their ancient spiritual and cultural identity and follow them.

As a consequence of the surrender of the soul and conscience of the German people to Hitler, fifty million lives were destroyed during World War II. Eleven million people were murdered by the most gruesome means, including starvation, execution, gassing, torture, electrocution, medical experimentation, and disease. Six million of them were

Jews from countries all over Europe. The other five million were simply members of other ethnic groups and individuals, like gypsies and Slavs, who had been branded as enemies of the Nazi state. Germany, one of the most civilized and technologically advanced countries of the world, became one of the most heinous in modern history. Such is the power of the spoken word when used for evil.

Poisonous words, like any virus, infect in degrees. When words that arouse hateful emotions are used frequently enough by a portion of a population, they can become institutionalized as acceptable behavior. The large-scale use of the word "nigger" as a racial slur in the American South in the first half of the twentieth century is such an example. Any words that appeal to man's basest instincts can exert a mesmerizing power over even intelligent people. Where reason and civility should prevail, a mindless kind of fanaticism can take over, as in the blatant anti-Semitic statements by Iran's president Mahmoud Ahmadinejad, or the anti-American vitriol of Venezuelan dictator Hugo Chavez. Words that are spoken to incite hatred or undermine truth by sowing doubt, discouragement, and confusion always create division, not unity, and are the "bad seed" that fester and grow into the future holocausts of a nation and a world.

Freedom goes hand in hand with the power to influence, and therefore with freedom comes the great responsibility to use it wisely and well, especially in a world where communication is both instantaneous and global in its outreach. Sadly, even in our charmed Republic, we can see many examples of prejudice and bias, spin-doctoring (selling a version of events that you want others to believe rather than the version you know to be true), and distortion of facts that can confound and confuse those who are not fully informed about the issues. How indeed can there be anything but cognitive dissonance in our citizenry when a lopsided percentage of the press use their voice to excite envy and distrust and to flagrantly undermine our nation's security? Where once our journalists acted with a boldness to search out truth and separate the ideological wheat from the chaff; where once they were patriots and believers in the greatness of our country, today's press are largely co-conspirators with liberal demagogues in the furtherance of a worldview that attacks all that is right and good about America. In their propaganda of progressive "righthink," the media are creating dangerous fault lines in our society. Words that are used to mislead pander to the lowest intellectual and moral standard, relying on fear-based emotion rather than substantive fact to persuade. History has taught us, with a shining clarity, that such deliberate and unconscionable misuse of the spoken word can only lead to a nation's demise.

If we would master the instrument of our voice effectively as performing artists in our theatrical life, we need to fully comprehend the power of voice and the spoken word to influence our own personal lives—the way we think and feel and view the world at large. Acting provides an awesome opportunity and a unique public platform from which to inform, inspire, and benefit humanity for generations to come.

EXERCISE 9-3 The Power of Voice

- Students work in small groups and choose a situation from the media, politics, or from the world of celebrity (past or present)—including any films or television shows—where the spoken word has been misused and has caused injury to our nation, or to some individual or segment of society.

- Each group shares their example with the rest of the class. They should discuss the nature of the abuse and the negative results produced.

- Students discuss as a class examples of individuals from the media, politics, or the world celebrity who have made a positive difference in using their high profile to advance a positive cause or to speak out against some injustice. Discuss the nature of those positive results.

KEY: Getting to the heart of the issue

 Our goal as actors on the theatrical stage, and actors on the stage of life, is to seek the highest truth and highest good in all we do. The spoken word is the most powerful and effective means to accomplish this goal.

The great goal of our art [is] to create the life of a human spirit in a role or a play. Your ability to make the most of your speech possibilities will depend on your experience, knowledge, taste, sensitiveness and talent. The actors who have a real feeling for words, for their native tongues, will raise their methods of coordination, of creating planes and perspectives in their speech to a point of virtuosity. Those who are less talented will have to be more conscientious in acquiring great knowledge, studying their own language; they will have to work harder to achieve experience, practice and art. The greater the means and the possibilities at the disposal of an actor the more lively, powerful, expressive and irresistible will be his speech.

—Constantin Stanislavski, *Building a Character*

Unit

Study

Ten

Voice for the Stage

10

Voice for the Stage

Class materials needed:

Four medium-sized sponge balls
One dozen small, thin rubber bands
One dozen long, thick rubber bands
Handout, *Sample Recitation Pieces*
Box of kitchen safety matches
Voice Handouts

Voice Is Dynamic

In his book *The Voice of the Mind*, E. Herbert Caesari states that of all art, singing is the nearest to expressing divinity, and that voice itself is the truest vehicle for expressing the soul of music, and the soul of man. The seventeenth-century composer and master of Baroque chorals Claudio Monteverdi described music as "speech in song." We can take these words and apply them to the art of voice for the stage.

EXERCISE 10-1 Your Voice

Level One Action:

- Each student describes his own voice, commenting not only on the physical qualities of his voice (loud, soft, nasal, throaty, deep, high, etc.), but also on how he relates his perceived personality (shy, humorous, serious, outgoing, sensitive, artistic, etc.) to the character of his voice.

- The students discuss the voices of familiar movie or television stars and relate the actors' voices to the characters they portray on the screen. For example, the deep, raspy baritone voice of Humphrey Bogart was just right for gangster or tough-guy roles. John Wayne, on the other hand, had a great nasal twang that suited western cowboy characters. Students may optionally contrast the actors they chose above with theater-trained artists such as Laurence Olivier or Timothy Dalton and discuss the classical roles for which both these actors are well-known, such as Olivier's Academy Award winning role of Hamlet in the movie *Hamlet*, or Dalton's distinguished portrayal of Mr. Rochester in the 1983 BBC production of *Jane Eyre*. Could the students imagine Humphrey Bogart or John Wayne playing Hamlet, or Laurence Olivier playing an American cowboy?

Level Two Action:

- Assign each student the homework task of choosing a famous line of dialogue from an old movie, such as Bogart's "Here's looking at you, kid" from *Casablanca* or Sean Connery saying, "Bond. James Bond."

- At the next class, place the suggested lines in the treasure box and have each student pick a line from the box and say the line using a character voice. He can imitate the original actor or make up his own rendition.

Goal: To make each student aware of the sound of his own voice and how its special qualities can be used to portray different character roles.

Voice is dynamic—that is, energetic, vigorous, and ever-changing. Voice is not a static part of the self, like the color of the eyes or the shape of the nose. Nor is the voice a mechanical instrument, like a can opener, that we employ to accomplish a specific task. Voice is the most intimate and revealing expression of who we are—our energy, our intelligence, our will, our originality, our psychological health, our spiritual well-being, our personal vision. It is a moving barometer of our emotions and our spirit at any given point of the day. As such, our voice is one of the most accurate recordings of our identity and our evolving soul.

From the moment of our first squeal as a newborn baby in our mother's arms, we have grown up hearing our own voice and using it unconsciously. We have become so familiar with it, however, that we take it for granted. Even when our voice is suffering from chronic abuse with symptoms of voice breaks, laryngitis, or hoarseness, we tend to adopt an attitude of complacency and acceptance. Only when we perform as public speakers, singers, or actors, do we begin to view our voice with the respect we automatically give a grand piano or a Stradivarius violin.

Voice is a powerful instrument, both lyrical and dramatic in its ability to convey intent. One of the most important ways of appreciating language is to experience it and make it come alive with our own voices. This is even more critical in the singing, acting, and storytelling arts, where the rich emotion and spiritual content of the language can only be rendered by clear, beautiful, and vivid speech—in other words, through proper schooling in vocal artistry. Nothing is more satisfying than to hear Shakespearean verse spoken with full deference to its inherent iambic pentameter or the plays of Sophocles performed with fidelity to their glorious poetic cadence.

E X E R C I S E 10-2 Speak and Listen

- Hand out the sheets of paper titled "Sample Recitation Pieces." Sample pieces for the younger children are provided on a separate handout. (The recitation samples are included with the rest of the handouts at the back of the book.)

- Each student chooses his own piece from the handout and reads it out loud with expression to the best of his ability.

- Afterwards, the students critique each other. Since no one has received any formal instruction in voice yet, students should look for positive qualities in each performance—that is, what the speaker did to make it interesting to listen to.

Goal: To encourage the children to consciously listen to their voices when speaking or reciting.

Director's Notes: Encourage each child to have a turn but do not make this exercise mandatory. Ask the students to volunteer and let them choose their own selections. For the little ones, you may first have to read the selections aloud to give them an idea of the content and difficulty level of each piece.

Like a musical instrument, voice can render more than just the textual meaning (or "melody line") of the spoken message. Voice can also convey to a listener the speaker's true motives—motives that his words are sometimes intended to belie or mask. This is accomplished by *subtext*—the unexpressed meaning that can be identified from the tone of voice that overlays the spoken words. Sometimes subtext refers to what we "read between the lines." If the listener is discerning and pays careful attention, he may learn much about the speaker's real character, state of mind, insinuating bias, and force of will even when the words indicate something directly opposite. A good actor must learn to "play" the character with subtext if he wants his performance to have subtlety and depth.

Voice is a potentially divine instrument. As such, it can be an accurate index of the spiritual energy that can move through the consciousness of an inspired speaker. It is this dimension of voice that makes it so dynamic and revelatory, even mystical. Just as the spoken word, in its highest conception, should be the expression of the noblest and purest thoughts of God, so we can prepare the voice as a chalice to convey the finest nuances and subtlest expressions of the Spirit that moves through us all. No matter what you do in life or who you are, your voice can be an instrument of true love and illumination. The *mechanics* of the voice that you develop will become the *dynamics* that release this authentic power through you to the hearts of your listeners.

In Chapter Seven of his book *Building a Character*, Stanislavski writes of the power of beautiful speech. He says:

> Speech is music. The text of a part or a play is a melody, an opera, or a symphony. Pronunciation on the stage is as difficult an art as singing, it requires training and a technique bordering on virtuosity. When an actor with a well trained voice and masterly vocal technique speaks the words of his part I am quite carried away by his supreme art. If he is rhythmic I am involuntarily caught up in the rhythm and tone of his speech, I am stirred by it. If he himself pierces to the soul of the words in his part he takes me with him into the secret places of the playwright's composition as well as into those of his own soul. When an actor adds the vivid ornament of sound to that living content of the words, he causes me to glimpse with an inner vision the images he has fashioned out of his own creative imagination....
>
> Think how much can be packed into a word or a phrase, how rich language is. It is powerful, not in itself but inasmuch as it conveys the human soul, the human mind....
>
> Just as atoms go to make up a whole universe, individual sounds convey words, words phrases, phrases thoughts, and out of thoughts there are formed whole scenes, acts and the content of a great play which embraces the tragic life of a human soul—of Hamlet, Othello, Hedda Gabler, Mme. Ranevskaya. These sounds form a whole symphony!

Much is demanded of the actor's voice. He simply cannot use his normal voice to accomplish theatrical goals. A normal voice will not hold up under the intense requirements of the stage. Unless the voice has been trained in the proper elements of vocal production—breathing, phonation, resonance, articulation, and expression, it will fall victim to misuse and abuse, sometimes with irrevocable results. A voice fitted for the stage must have efficiency (power and control) and artistry (tonal beauty, cadence, diction, and lyrical expressiveness). Even performers whose regular speaking voices are capable in radio, television, and movies find their voices unable to meet the challenges of the stage. The theater is a taxing master, and only the stage voice that is competently trained will fulfill all the demands placed upon it.

As our society has become more mechanized, there has been less and less reliance on the trained perfection of the voice to render expressive meaning in performance. During the last 40 years, the theater and music recording arts have seen degraded standards of vocal technique and reliance upon electronic devices to compensate for essentially poor or badly produced voices. Nowhere is this more apparent than in the popular culture of rap and heavy metal, where vocal violence is rampant and former musical values are often carelessly discarded. Many of the groups of this genre are rogue performers whose very claim to fame is their "in your face" defiance of true vocal art and the long-held standards for cultivated artistry.

At times, Broadway performers are taught to adapt their voices to torturously bleed out intense feelings with every lyric line, playwrights are directed to adapt once-bookmarked classics to be politically correct, and actors are advised to speak their words with exaggerated and condescending emphasis, as though the public were unable to interpret life's realities for themselves.

There is a clear trend in the theater arts across the disciplines of dance, drama, and the musical to use the excuse of "creative expression" to justify the staging of disrespectful and sometimes offensive subject matter, sexually explicit choreography, and coarsened vocal technique—all of which degrade and mock traditional aesthetic values. It is important that the new student not get caught up with these trends but instead strive to master techniques of performance that are intended to preserve the highest and most beautiful elements of their art form.

EXERCISE 10-3 Using Drama to Inspire

- Students discuss how artists or actors they admire are making a positive contribution to society through their art form.

- Students discuss how drama can be used to promote family values and enduring ideals that inspire and uplift people.

Suggestions: In the first part of the exercise, encourage the students to talk about actors or performing artists whom they admire not just for their talent but for the use of their talent to contribute something relevant to our society like making an important film, recording a meaningful song, or raising awareness about a topical issue, such as drugs or violence in schools. An example of an actor using his celebrity to help young people is Martin Kove, who played the ruthless "ultimate bully" karate instructor in the popular 1985 movie *The Karate Kid*. In the movie he trains his students to punish their opponents without remorse since "mercy is for the weak." Kove now uses his role to promote a campaign called BullySafe International. His program's goal is "to change the culture of a school so that bullying and school violence are no longer accepted or tolerated."

Darryl Worley is a popular recording artist who has used his art and high profile as a country music star to contribute his patriotic support of our military. Not only has he traveled with the USO (United Service Organizations) to Afghanistan to entertain the troops there, but he wrote and recorded a song/ode called "Have You Forgotten" that looks back to the terrible day of September 11, 2001. The song is a patriotic call to battle that poignantly evokes the falling New York Twin Towers, the ruined Pentagon, and the heroes in the Pennsylvania field. The song stormed to the top of the country music singles charts in only five weeks and became a rallying cry to Americans to never forget that infamous day. The singer continues to remind Americans to honor all those who have ever served this nation in uniform, especially those who have given their lives doing so. Worley attends fundraisers and gives concerts to solicit money for the military families of the fallen.

The second part of the exercise is meant to stimulate discussion about how the students, themselves, would like to see the arts used to make a difference in the world. Encourage them to think about what they would do to contribute to the great social and moral issues of the day if they achieved celebrity in the arts.

Freeing the Voice

We all meet people who have naturally gifted voices—voices that express their owner's intent with animation and lyrical sensibility and are able to enthrall the listener for hours, as did the troubadour of old. There are many such talented artists who have never had one formal lesson in their craft and yet are thoroughly convincing and engaging before a crowd of spectators. Indeed, one of the goals of a successful actor is to make his audience feel at home with the character he is portraying. That implies that his vocal delivery needs to sound relaxed and natural, and altogether realistic, so that he can draw his audience into the life he is creating onstage or on the screen.

To paraphrase John Quincy Adams in his *Lectures on Rhetoric and Oratory*, although learning the principles of good speech doesn't guarantee mastery of the art, people who understand the principles upon which good speech is based, have a much better chance of speaking in a masterful way. Those who have a naturally winning voice will be even more effective with training, just as a diamond in the rough displays its true value and real quality when carefully polished and placed in a beautiful setting. However, the reverse is not always true; those who have little raw material to begin with will rarely transcend their mediocrity despite the most carefully designed and advantageous setting.

Only through the art of speech can the actor effectively convey with subtlety and beauty all the intricate shadings of thought and feeling intended by the playwright. The actor, therefore, needs to have a voice that is freed from the limitations of his own personality and capable of sustaining a convincing characterization until the final curtain. While it has become acceptable for television and film actors to be typecast in roles that fit their personalities and vocal identities, this does not apply to the stage actor. Indeed, the measure of the stage actor's skill is how successfully he can execute a role that is in striking contrast to his own personality. That is why a sound vocal technique is essential to the achievement of "artistic freedom."

Stanislavski believed that the greatest possession of a stage actor is "a beautiful, vibrant, expressive and powerful voice"—one capable of conveying all the complexities of the inner pattern of a role. When an actor can achieve such a voice, he has achieved true artistic freedom. We hear of a prima donna being 'in good voice,' but we rarely apply that to a dramatic artist. Yet an actor must have the power to direct his sounds, command their obedience, and know that they will vividly and profoundly convey every modulation and subtle shading of his creative inspiration, whether it be, as Stanislavski says, "the exalted feelings in the tragic style or the simple, intimate, gracious speech of drama and comedy."

Today the concept of "freeing" the artist does not reflect the high aesthetic standards originally set forth by Stanislavski, especially as those standards apply to voice training. Too many acting teachers do not comprehend the value of teaching a complete vocal technique—like the ones conceived, developed, and applied in the tradition of the classical English Schools of Speech and Dramatic Art. Instead, they teach acting not as an artistic discipline, but as a purely subjective exploration of the inner workings of the character. The voice is viewed not as the main instrument of characterization but merely as one of the colors or textures to be blended into the role.

The student is encouraged to focus on himself, to merge his psyche with that of the character he plays—shaping his thoughts and emotions to reflect powerful dramatic intensities without learning how to control and channel those intensities by means of a finished vocal technique. This is common among many modern method schools, which have moved away from the original work and aesthetic purity of Stanislavski's concepts. As is often the case in so many traditions, these teachers have altered Stanislavski's original intent generations later to suit their personal agendas. The result has been a devastating decline in the performance technique of the American actor, especially in the training of his voice.

In the great tradition of legitimate theater, actors have relied on vocal technique to give them dignity, strength, and a "larger than life" presence on the playing stage. The training of English actors has long emphasized elocution and technical eminence. British actors still train this way. Before the advent of movies an aspiring actor applied himself to a stagecraft of skilled beauty. Live theater was the measure of an actor's art; "fame" was won by earning the critical applause of the playgoers. To the stage then the actor fixed his star.

Many of the truly skilled actors of the nineteenth century, such as Sarah Bernhardt, Joseph Jefferson, Henry Irving, and Tomasso Salvini, left behind accounts of their struggles to master a vocal technique that gave them the freedom to transmit each genuine thought and emotion of their character clearly, and in such a way that even the audiences in the upper balconies could be moved. They were drilled in the components of pitch, vibrato, and modulation as integral elements of performance—elements that are largely a lost art today because of the realism required by directors who encourage "actual" speech that is intimate and real rather than theatrical. To paraphrase Dave Menefee, an expert on the stage actors of an earlier era, the modern actor crosses over from television and film to stage with little change in his vocal delivery or deportment since he has not learned how to execute the shading of tonality, the use of vibrato, or creative pitch—components that were thoroughly mastered by actors who did not have microphones to amplify them.

As the trend towards naturalism made itself felt at the end of the nineteenth century, critics looked for even more subtlety in the actor's interpretive art. Press reviews of Italian actress Eleanora Duse in 1897, when she made her debut appearance in Paris, described her "meditative silences, by the words coming now rapidly, now slowly, by signs no more emphatic than a tremor of lips or the faintest movement of a hand. In the place of...string-plucking and tear-jerking, came something more profound, a stirring of soul which makes one question what so far had passed for the finest art."

The celluloid magic of the screen changed this emphasis on technique. The camera and not the actor projected the moving drama. Action, reaction, and interaction could be artificially created through camera angles, lighting, and editing, with the final product distilled through the consciousness of the director. Actors who looked good in screen tests were signed; studios appointed personal hairdressers, make-up artists, and voice coaches to transform flesh into sensuous image; scripts were commissioned to further enhance the 'starry essence,' and the golden age of glamour, type casting, and big studio profits was ushered in. Though Hollywood borrowed its best talent from the English stage, thus ensuring a higher integrity of performance and technical skill from its leading studio players, the abandonment of the 'old school of the stage' had become a fact. The public now scurried to the cinema box office to see their favorite movie star.

In the classical disciplines—ballet, opera, musical instrument—technique is the mandatory requirement. To it the performer brings his own interpretive inspiration and spiritual light. Together, they form his individual artistry or genius. Technique, wedded to the inner light of his spirit, is the description of an artist's greatness. It has nothing to do with his personality appeal or his sympathetic oneness with the great swamp of humanity's feelings. Great artists are recognized because of their unique ability to blend a beauty of interpretation with impeccable technical execution.

The training of a classical artist does not tamper with the components of his personality because it is technique or craft-oriented. His art is an expression of his technical craft to which his mind and heart are naturally united. But his psyche—his spiritual life—remains separate and impersonal from that expression, even as it forms the principal source of his inspiration. Indeed, the very physical demands of technical excellence when pursuing a career as a ballet dancer or a concert pianist forbid immersion into the murky luminescent world of "becoming his art."

Teachers and directors in the classical disciplines do not feel the need to liberate a performer from his natural inhibitions or deeply held religious constraints in the name of 'freeing' him as an artist. They do not feel compelled to tamper with his soul and inner spirit. They trust to technique and the artist's innate interpretive flame to form the perfect "genie" of his artistry. This is largely no longer the case in the professional acting world.

Since the 1960s "realism" has become the golden calf to which the aspiring actor must give his unquestioned allegiance, even if it means sacrificing his very conscience at its altar. Realism, as Hollywood has defined it, is the micro-study of man and his society without reference to any divine standard. Realism is therefore the executioner of idealism—and thus, moral beauty. Like a dark curtain closing off a beautiful sunrise, it blocks out the light of all that is a revelation of the ideal images in which divinity clothes itself. Realism more often reflects an unhappy, if not joyless world view.

Hollywood method schools have manipulated Stanislavski's genius to endorse and give authority to their own cult of realism in direct contrast to Stanislavski's exalted idealism. Surrogates of this cult have reinterpreted and reinvented the founder's concepts, so that these later revisions have become, in most of the theater schools of America, the accepted Bible of acting training. The young actor is the sacrificial lamb. All inhibitions must be stripped from him so that he can fully comprehend and engage the labyrinthian depths of his character's emotions. Only through personally experiencing those emotions, or at least accommodating their reality within his own psyche, can he express them truthfully to his audience, or so he is told. This kind of approach to preparing the actor nurtures a perverse kind of exhibitionism and self-absorption that works against the higher aesthetic purposes of his art.

The training of actors should always be altruistic, so that the actor learns to leave "self" in the wings, while he works to bring his character to life on the stage. There must be a separation between the artist and his art. Instead of developing in the actor a joyous freedom from himself through reliance upon a complete stage technique, many modern actors have become blind or at least indifferent to their own deficiencies, no more so than in the training of their voices. Acquiring a theatrically proven technique is the only way to attain a *true* condition of artistic freedom—one that serves the aesthetic end, while preserving the integrity and wholeness of the actor.

The spoken word defined the dramatic arts in Elizabethan times, as it did in ancient Greece. The love of the beautiful and true trumped the "anything goes" philosophy that characterizes our modern theater. If the best of our theatrical heritage is to survive, acting schools must get back on track.

We cannot ignore the compelling evidence of a century or more of classic trained English and American actors who have graced the stages of the world with their impeccable vocal technique and skilled presence. Vocal artistry alone enables the student to achieve the rich abandonment, the transport of emotions, the inventive genius, and the truthful representation of the sentiments of the character being portrayed. A complete vocal technique goes a long way to ensure that the actor can consistently, effortlessly, and compellingly convey the intent of the playwright and the artistic vision of the director.

What is a complete vocal technique? A complete vocal technique is one that resides in nature, in the simplicity of the natural processes of the vocal apparatus. If the actor is to produce a voice that has a clear and beautifully balanced tone with carrying power and expressiveness matching the demands of the dramatic situation, then he must have a working knowledge of the physiological and acoustical laws that govern his vocal mechanism, and the ability to apply them effectively. Additionally, the five dynamics that form the basis of true vocal production—breathing, phonation, resonance, articulation, and expression—have to be mastered until they become second nature to the actor. Proper vocal schooling is the true definition of a "free" voice, and a free voice is what a *theatrical* or *stage* voice should be.

KEY: Getting to the heart of the issue

> **You speak in the shadow of yourself until you free your voice. Only in the freedom of complete vocal schooling can you realize the full life of your character.**

A Theatrical or Stage Voice

A *theatrical* or *stage* voice is the actor's working voice, as distinct from his normal speaking voice. A theatrical voice is not phony, contrived, or "put on." It is simply *enhanced normal voice*. We tend to think of an artistically cultivated voice as affected and insincere because of past stereotypes of actors delivering their lines with exaggerated emphasis and intensity. The stage voice, in fact, is an Olympic-trained voice—that is, one that can hold up and produce under the most exacting circumstances. It does not tire or develop symptoms of abuse, and retains its power, durability, and resonance with either brief or extended usage. A stage voice ensures that the true and full meaning of the words is expressed without excessive emotion or artificiality. A complete vocal schooling, like military basic training or professional athlete training, allows our voice to be all it can be. Only a well-produced theatrical voice can fully define and bring to life a theatrical character, which is the purpose of acting.

We achieve a stage voice when we build upon and strengthen the natural patterns of the voice that are obedient to existing physiological and acoustical laws. The stage voice uses its own internal means of amplification and resonance, much like the voice of the Basque scouts. The stage voice blends and perfects all the required vocal elements—power, tonal beauty, control, cadence, diction, and expressiveness—to fulfill the twin mandate of artistry and efficiency.

An actor's goal is to acquire the best speech habits possible so that he can represent the truth of the sentiments he expresses and do so with an effortless restraint and self-control. With the exception of the discipline of mime, an actor's voice is his most important instrument of expression and interpretation. Without it, he cannot come out on the stage and convey to the audience the inner spirit of his character in those "clear, pregnant, deeply felt, intelligible, and eloquent terms" that Stanislavski himself described as the mark of a true dramatic artist. When an actor strives for technical excellence in voice, he is, in fact, striving for perfection in the art of characterization. This is accomplished only when the voice is perfectly tuned and flexibly responsive to every artistic call of style, mood, and emotion.

KEY: Getting to the heart of the issue

"A first class musician should never play on an instrument out of tune." (Constantin Stanislavski)

Elements of Vocal Artistry

Technique, from a Greek word, means skill or mode of artistic execution acquired by study and practice. Every artist should have a tried and true technique. A *true* vocal technique is both scientific and artistic in its application. It is always faithful to what is natural and beautiful. In *The Alchemy of Voice*, E. Herbert-Caesari reminds us that tonal quality is the golden key. We can all identify the gliding tones created by a fine violinist, where the melodic line flows persuasively and convincingly, winging its way through the theater house. A theatrical voice also strives to give wings to its tones. It weds technical perfection to dramatic interpretation of the word and is achieved by mastering the six elements of vocal artistry that make up true vocal technique.

1. **Power:** the strength of the voice or its ability to project over long distances and large spaces with tone and diction intact. Power also refers to a voice that provides a maximum amount of vibrant sound with a minimum amount of effort. This is achieved by proper breathing, tone focus, and vowel expansion. Power should not be confused with volume, which means loudness.

2. **Tonal Beauty:** the quality of tone that is clean, bright, and bell-ringing, has great carrying power, and is highly expressive. Tonal beauty is brought about by proper phonation (production of vocal tone) and resonance (the amplification of sound).

3. **Control:** the ability to sustain strength and quality of tone while ensuring the clarity of the words. Control is achieved by proper breathing, tone placement, and resonance.

4. **Cadence:** the musical quality of the voice that contributes to the beauty, subtlety, and rhythm of the sound. Cadence is achieved by resonance and effective use of intonation patterns.

5. **Diction:** the clarity and completeness of each spoken word. Diction is achieved by vowel expansion and strong, precise articulation of all consonants in speech.

6. **Expressiveness:** the subjective and imaginative interpretation of the words or lyrics. Expressiveness refers to a speaker expressing his heart and emotions through the words. It is achieved partly by proper use of emphasis, inflection, pitch, pausing, and phrasing—all of which add color, music, and beauty to the voice. Expressiveness is also dependent on the artist's intuitive temperament, which can translate subtleties of feeling and thought.

A theatrical voice ensures that an actor is:

1. Immediately heard and understood in any theater.

2. Fully effective in conveying the dramatic interpretation of the word while sharing with his audience the full complexities of the inner and outer life of his character.

3. Credible and convincing in portraying his character no matter what accent, dialect, or character quirk is demanded for the role.

4. Effortless in sustaining power, control, and flexibility of the vocal processes.

5. Sensitive and responsive to the intuitive subtleties of each word spoken or each lyric line sung.

The Five Dynamics of Vocal Production

The following five dynamics of voice are the foundational building blocks of the elements of vocal artistry:

1. **Breathing**

2. **Phonation**

3. **Resonance**

4. **Articulation**

5. **Expression**

1. Breathing

Like speaking with our voices, breathing is a natural, unconscious process that we do all the time, starting from the moment of birth. We tend to take breathing for granted and are not concerned about the way we breathe unless our breathing is suddenly interfered with or stopped, as in the case of a throat blockage or some kind of a paralyzing heart stroke. The majority of people do not breathe properly, naturally, or completely, and do not know *how* to do so.

The respiratory membrane covers an area of around 150 square yards. This may seem to be a large number, but not when we realize there are some three million alveoli (tiny air sacs) in each lung through which oxygen exchange takes place. We can imagine the volume of air necessary for aerating, cleansing, and maintaining this great army of cells. Every single one needs a continual supply of oxygen, but they rarely get it unless the person has a habit of regularly taking big breaths, a practice that is usually only common for opera singers, athletes, or those who daily practice yoga.

The Correct Way to Breathe

Breathing is the most important thing we do. The object of breathing is to bring oxygen into our bodies and especially into our blood. We cannot live without oxygen. The word that describes the act of breathing is *respiration*. Respiration consists of two actions, *inspiration* (or breathing in) and *expiration* (or breathing out).

When we inhale or breathe in, the air passes through the nose or mouth and down the windpipe, a tube about six inches long that leads from the back of the mouth to the lungs. We have two lungs, which are situated in our chest. They take up nearly all the room in the chest, leaving a very small space for the heart and blood vessels. You can think of them as two pear-shaped sponges, the narrow part being at the top of the chest and the wider part at the bottom of the chest. The lungs contain millions of tiny tubes and cells that hold air. The two lungs are connected by branches of the windpipe called the bronchi. The lung tissue is very elastic, like a balloon, and can easily expand.

There are two kinds of muscles we use when we breathe, the diaphragm (pronounced "Die-uh-fram") and the intercostals. Both muscles are equally important and can't work without each other. The diaphragm is a large, powerful muscle that divides the chest from the abdomen (or the belly). The diaphragm forms the floor of the chest and the roof of the abdomen. In a state of rest—that is, when we have no air in our lungs, the diaphragm has the shape of a rounded bowl turned upside down and it arches up into the chest. When we breathe in, the diaphragm flattens, making room for the lower part of the lungs to fill with air.

The intercostals are the muscles that wind in and around the lower ribs on both sides of the chest. They interlace the ribs. At the same time that the diaphragm flattens, the intercostal muscles push the ribs outwards or sideways. This action of the ribs also makes more room for the lower part of the chest to hold more air. The two movements—the diaphragm moving downwards and the rib muscles pushing across— take place in one steady, smooth action in women. In men, it is a one-two action: only when the lowering of the diaphragm is complete do the ribs expand sideways, making two distinctly separate though continuous actions—down and out.

Since the lungs are shaped like a cone or a pear, it is important for the breathing muscles to get out of the way so that the chest can fill up its tank from the bottom to the top. When we breathe out, the diaphragm returns to its original dome-shape at the foot of the chest and the ribs relax, allowing the chest to return to its normal size.

E X E R C I S E 10-4 The Little House of the Diaphragm

Director's Notes: The exercise is presented in simple terms so that students of all ages will understand.

- While in a relaxed sitting position, spread the palms of both hands across the lower part of your chest, just above your waist. Find your ribs. Your hands should be covering the lower ribs on both sides of your chest. If you go any lower, your hands will be over your abdomen (or tummy), and your fingers will be under, instead of over, your lower rib cage.
- Now let the fingers of your hands slide into the center so that the fingertips of your left hand touch the fingertips of your right hand. The palms of your hands should now be flat against the area between the chest and the abdomen, fingertips touching.
- Now push your fingertips up while turning the palms of your hands out so that the thumbs rest against your chest and your hands make an arch like a roof on a house (or you can imagine your hands resting on top of a globe). This rounded vertical position of the hands is just how the diaphragm looks after you have breathed out.
- Breathe in through your nose to a count of four. As you do, let your fingers flatten out again keeping the palms open and facing down rather than flat against your body. Now your little house is flat, not arched. Think of the breath you draw in as a big wind that pushes your little house down, with the walls collapsing to each side.
- When we breathe the air out, the house magically comes back together again, roof and sides and all.

You will notice that when you make the arch, your hands are pointing upward toward your heart, but when you flatten out the arch of your little house, your hands push down and out. This is exactly what happens when we breathe. The diaphragm looks like the roof of your house when it is resting. Actually, it looks a little rounder, like a bowl turned upside down. When we take in a breath, this muscle flattens out, pushing against the ribs on both sides of the chest, and making them stretch out just as your fingers did. When we breathe the air out, the ribs and diaphragm come back again to their holding (or resting) position.

We know that speech is impossible without breath. Good speech requires correct breathing. By correct breathing, we mean the coordinated use of the diaphragm and the rib muscles to create the space at the bottom of the lungs so that the lungs can fill with air. Only then can we have a strong and continuous flow of air, which is necessary if we want to be able to continue talking and to use our voice effectively.

We can also have *control* of our breath, and thus control of our voice, when we breathe correctly. The bottom of each lung (which looks like the bottom of the pear) fills out like a balloon. You know that if you do not control the air in a balloon but instead allow it to escape, the balloon will move about wildly and uncontrollably through space until all of its air is expired. In breathing, *control* is the most important factor. In normal breathing, we simply let the air escape in much the same way as it escapes from a little penny balloon. However, in speaking and singing, our job is to conserve a regular and continuous supply of breath for all the vocal sounds we wish to make.

Once again, the diaphragm comes to our rescue. It supports the base of each lung, it allows the chest wall to expand, and it helps to hold the upper chest in position. Only when the upper chest is held in position are we able to control the supply of breath. The diaphragm is the controller of the breath. It helps to create space for the air and it lets that air be used very economically.

EXERCISE 10-5 How to Breathe Correctly

- The students lie down on their backs, place the palms of their hands on the lower chest, as described earlier, breathe evenly and naturally through the nose, and concentrate carefully on what movements are made as they breathe in and out.

- Director can walk around to check if the students are breathing deeply enough to allow adequate rib expansion and to correct any bad habits such as tensing the muscles or raising the shoulders too much when breathing in.

- Students stand up and breathe in the same way. The director can check individual students to make sure that old habits are not recurring.

Some points to remember:

1. *Don't raise the shoulders.* If you do, (a) the chest wall will not expand, (b) only the tops of the lungs will be filled, (c) the throat muscles will be restricted and feel tight, and (d) you will lose control of your breath supply.

2. *Avoid puffing out the breath or rushing.* Breathe smoothly with a regular, rhythmic flow.

3. *Breathing through the nose is best* for ordinary purposes because the air is filtered and warmed as it passes to the lungs. When we act or sing onstage, we cannot always nose breathe, so practice breathing in quietly with the mouth slightly open. Avoid noisy intakes of air at any time.

4. *Try to keep your ribs slightly stretched in place* after you have taken your breath. You can accomplish this by holding a straight (but not rigid) deportment and keeping your chest upraised. This will help the lower chest muscles and the diaphragm control the flow of breath. Avoid any slumping of the shoulders or back when you breathe in.

5. *Avoid straining the throat muscles.* It's very important not to tighten up the throat muscles or hold the mouth and neck stiffly. Keep all muscles relaxed and natural.

KEY: Getting to the heart of the issue

> **Correct breathing, and the control it brings,
> is the foundation of good singing and speaking.**

How Breathing Out Affects Vocal Tone

It is not the quantity of air breathed in that determines the desired vocal tone but the *economical expenditure of the air* as we breathe out.

Expiration, or breathing out, refers to the synchronized return of ribs and diaphragm to their normal state of rest. This return should occur smoothly because the way we control the outbreath of air dramatically affects the way the sound will come out.

ILLUSTRATION 10-1 How We Exhale
_____

To illustrate the synchronized movement of breathing out, lay a single sheet of notepaper lengthwise. Place the middle finger of each hand firmly on both ends. Press and move the fingers slowly inward until the paper is nicely arched. The inward movement of the ends represents the return of the ribs, and the arching of the sheet represents the return of the diaphragm as it presses up against the base of the lungs. If we reverse the movement, going from the arched position to the flat position, we have an illustration of the down-and-out movement of breathing in.

When we are breathing out, the return of the diaphragm and ribs to their initial states of rest must be smooth. Our goal is to carefully manage the outgoing breath to permit just the right amount of air to compress underneath the vocal cords, thereby forcing the vocal cords to vibrate and make the proper tone. This will be discussed further in the next section under the heading of Phonation. The miracle of voice is that the vocal cords, on their own, will take up the exact quantity of breath for the correct production of a particular tone at a particular pitch. They do their own instinctive calculation of the minimum breath needed. We have to cooperate by making sure that they get exactly what they need in order to perform their specialized work.

KEY: Getting to the heart of the issue

 By controlling the way we breathe out, we help the vocal cords do their job of converting air into the desired sound or tone.

A Common and Incorrect Way to Breathe

A common but unnatural way many people breathe is chest (or clavicular) breathing. The clavicle, also called the collarbone, is the long, curved bone that connects the upper breastbone with each of our shoulder blades. Chest breathing happens when, in the act of breathing in, we raise our shoulders as if forcing the air upward into the narrow, upper part of the lungs. Because there is little lowering of the diaphragm or expansion of the ribs when we breathe this way, the holding tank at the base of the lungs does not fill with air. The breathing space at the upper part of the chest is very limited with minimum muscular control there anyway. Ultimately, this kind of breathing diminishes the capacity of the lungs and upsets the smooth and gradual release of the air as it passes out through the throat for careful adjustment by the vocal cords.

Chest breathing also results in cramming or overfilling the upper portion of the lungs, which we could liken to the narrow end of a T-bone steak. Obviously, this upper section of the lungs is not meant to be the main holding tank, and therefore chest breathing is not only very tiring for all the muscles involved, but it also makes controlling the breath difficult, not to mention unnatural. The feeling created by an overfilling of air instinctively impels the speaker or singer to get rid of the load as rapidly as possible, to the detriment of smooth vocal tone.

A Stage Voice Requires Adequate In-Breath and Measured Out-Breath

Our goal in breathing, then, is to make sure that we are breathing naturally to ensure adequate breath capacity and assured control over the out-breath. That support and control must be effortless and unconscious or it will interfere with the desired vocal quality. An accurate definition of an effective stage voice, as it applies to this element of breathing, is one that utilizes only the amount of breath that is necessary for the production of the desired tone. An ineffective voice is one where the equation of breath and tone is no longer in perfect balance—when either too much breath is being pumped through the vocal cords in a desperate effort to make the voice physically audible, or not enough breath is compressed under the cords to force the cords to resist the air, and thus create the desired vocal sound.

KEY: Getting to the heart of the issue

He who knows how to breathe knows how to speak. And he who speaks well breathes well.

EXERCISE 10-6 Breathing Correctly

This is not an exercise to develop the diaphragm, as it is not necessary to do so. It is designed to reeducate the diaphragm muscle, while strengthening the action of the rib muscles in those who are breathing incorrectly.

Level One Action:

- All students lie down with their backs on the floor, placing the palms of their hands just below the chest but above the abdomen.

- The hands should press lightly across this area of the diaphragm and lower ribs, with fingers stretching toward each other.

- Breathe in through the nose to the count of four, hold the breath for 4 seconds, and breathe out to the measured count of four. (Director can count out loud for the class.)

- Do this uninterruptedly for five minutes.

- With the intake of breath, students will be able to feel some expansion of the lower ribs sideways. Though the downward movement of the diaphragm cannot be seen or felt, it should give a freer sensation of the lungs having more room to fill with air. The ribs gradually expand as the diaphragm descends.

- Students should perform this exercise at least once a day for no less than a five-minute period at home. They should maintain this daily five-minute regimen from the very first time they do it in class, which is usually about two or three weeks into the course. After two weeks of doing the exercise to the count of four, two additional seconds should be added per week. Thus the schedule would look like this:

  Second and Third Weeks: 4 seconds in, 4 seconds hold, 4 seconds out

  Fourth Week: 6 seconds in, 6 seconds hold, 6 seconds out

  Fifth Week: 8 seconds in, 8 seconds hold, 8 seconds out

  Sixth through Tenth Weeks: 10 seconds in, 10 seconds hold, 10 seconds out

After ten weeks, students can stop doing the exercise. If it is performed regularly and conscientiously at least once a day as directed, the exercise should bring about a normalization of the breathing muscles both for inspiration and expiration. At the end of this period, the breathing mechanism should be largely automatic. Students who suffer from asthma or related respiratory problems may benefit from continuing their practice of the exercise.

Level Two Action:

- Once students develop ease and regularity in performing this exercise, at about the third week, they should perform the exercise sitting upright in their chairs, still keeping their hands across the diaphragm and ribs.

Level Three Action:

- At about the sixth week, students perform the exercise standing, hands in place across the diaphragm and ribs.

Director's Notes: Whenever possible, students should inhale through the nose, where the air is warmed, moistened, and cleansed before reaching the lungs. A four-second count is a very little time to begin with, but this is necessary for the slow reeducation of the muscles concerned. No conscious attention needs be given to the breathing muscles during performance, whether singing or speaking. A ten-second count is a comfortable average for most children after regular practice, although some may work up to a more robust count.

How Breath Is Controlled in the Making of Voice

No one knows the exact quantity of air required for a particular note at a particular pitch because mathematically it is an unknown quantity. Our body performs an instinctive calculation based 1) on the adjustments of the vocal cords, and 2) on the resonating chambers of the pharynx (or back area of the throat). When the vocal cords adjust the breath and turn it into sound, that action has an inhibiting effect on the movement of both ribs and diaphragm, preventing their rapid return to a state of rest. In this way, there is a check on the breathing muscles and all excess breath pressure is prevented. When the speaker, breathing correctly, has learned to sustain his breath during the act of speaking or singing, no strain whatsoever is placed on the vocal cords through this staying action on the muscles.

EXERCISE 10-7 Whistling

- The students try to whistle.
- Director separates the students into two groups—those who can whistle and those who cannot, explaining that dividing the class into two groups is just for the purposes of learning about correct breathing.

You will notice that those who can whistle use only a minimum of breath. The breath, and thus the breathing muscles, are governed or controlled when we whistle. You will also notice that no matter how much the children in the second group try to force the breath out through their lips, they will find it impossible to whistle properly. The action of whistling requires a minimum of breath.

Frequently Asked Questions

Question 1: Is it helpful to practice a series of forced inhalations and exhalations of breath like athletes do?

Answer: Yes it is. Sometimes before doing the regular breathing exercise, as in Exercise 10-4, it is a good idea to clean out the lungs, as athletes do, by performing a series of quick, forced in-breaths and out-breaths. But this should not be employed for normal breathing or for use onstage.

Question 2: Can a good voice tone be produced just by the action of the diaphragm without the rib muscles?

Answer: A well-produced voice is not possible without the combined action of the rib muscles and the diaphragm. The chest cannot fill with the needed quantity of air if the ribs do not expand sideways. Nor is there enough room in the base of the chest if the diaphragm does not flatten out. Both the diaphragm and rib muscles work together.

Question 3: Why is rib expansion so important?

Answer: Rib expansion is not only important, it is essential for completing the action of breathing in. When the ribs expand, the chest cavity can fill with air. Additionally, the ribs control the action of the diaphragm during exhalation as the diaphragm returns to its former arched position. When the ribs are extended, they provide a dependable platform for adequate breath support and control, which translates into giving the actor or singer a "braced" feeling of confidence and assurance.

Question 4: Should we be consciously aware of the movements of the diaphragm and ribs when we are breathing in and out?

Answer: The only time we should be consciously aware of what the muscles are doing during the process of breathing in or breathing out is when we practice our exercises. If our intent is to strengthen the rib muscles, we need to know if we are successful. In performance, during speaking or singing, the movements of the breathing muscles, as they make room for air to come into the lungs and then squeeze the air out of the lungs and return to their original positions, should be unconscious and smooth.

Question 5: Are everyone's diaphragm and rib muscles naturally strong?

Answer: In most people, the diaphragm is naturally strong and does not need any "developing" exercises. In some individuals, there may be a locking or partial locking of the diaphragm in its arched position and this directly impacts the breathing process, causing shortness of breath or an inability to get full breaths. This, in turn, prevents the speaker from sustaining a continuous and strong tone. The rib muscles, on the other hand, can always be strengthened. Most people have developed some form of chest breathing, so that the ribs are not strong enough to support the diaphragm during the expenditure of breath for speaking and singing. That is why exercises that increase the strength and force of the rib muscles are always advisable, especially for singers, who rely on the lower ribs returning very slowly and smoothly to their original state when singing is in progress.

Question 6: Do men and women breathe the same?

Answer: Men and women breathe out the same way, but they do not breathe in the same way. When a man inhales, the diaphragm moves first as it flattens out. Only when the lowering of the diaphragm is complete do the ribs expand sideways, making two distinctly separate though continuous actions: down and out. When a woman starts to breathe in, there is a dual, synchronized action of both the lowering of the diaphragm and the sideways expansion of the ribs. There is no one-two action as in men, but just a smooth one step.

KEY: Getting to the heart of the issue

> **When you control the breath, you control the vocal tone. When you control the vocal tone, you are on your way to developing a true technique of vocal artistry.**

2. Phonation

Instructions: When presenting the following material to the younger students, make sure that you are not going over their heads. I have provided an optional simplified explanation at the end of this section for the little ones. If you don't wish to go into any depth on this subject, the simplified version will be more than adequate for all your students. Additionally, most speech books refer to the entire larynx as the Adam's apple, while medical explanations are more exact, describing the Adam's apple as the thyroid cartilage or shield, which is the most obvious part (in terms of physical visibility) of the larynx. In other words, the larynx is more than just the Adam's apple, but for convenience and expediency, I have used the terms interchangeably.

Overview: The Making of Sound

Phonation refers to the production of sound by the vocal cords. When we inhale (breathe in) the air passes through the nose or mouth and down through the windpipe (or trachea). The windpipe is a tube about six inches long through which the air is carried into and out of the lungs. The voice box (or larynx) is situated on top of the windpipe. It does not have a fixed position and may be pushed from side to side in the throat. It is here, in the voice box, that sound for speech is born.

Inside the voice box and attached to its sides are the vocal cords—also referred to as vocal folds. They are two highly sensitive bands of tissue. In the normal adult, the vocal cords are about three-quarters of an inch to one inch in length. The cords are shorter and thinner in women and children, which largely explains why the voices of women and children are higher-pitched.

The cords are stretched across your larynx like two rubber bands. When you prepare to speak, and the neurons from the brain alert the muscles directly surrounding the vocal cords that breath is coming up from the lungs, the muscles press against your vocal cords. This causes them to draw close together with maximum tension, thus providing resistance to the oncoming air. The breath passes up through the windpipe, and is forced between the tightly drawn vocal cords, causing them to vibrate. This vibration of the vocal cords is what makes sound.

The original sound that is produced (also called primal or fundamental tone) passes from the vocal cords in a torpedo-like sound column to the back of the throat, called the pharynx, where vowel tone is shaped and made fuller and louder. The sound can also be directed to other echo chambers, such as the nose, mouth, and head cavities, where it receives further strengthening and reinforcement.

The throat, the mouth, and the cavities of the skull act as loud speakers, increasing and amplifying the original tone—re-sounding it to be the character you intend it to be. These echo chambers are called resonators, while the action they perform is called resonance. (Further information about this process is provided in the section under the heading Resonance.)

You can think of the vocal cords as the mother and father of the original sound, giving it birth and opportunity to live a full, rich life. Because the echo chambers exert such a vital influence on the primal sound, they can be considered character builders. The sound goes through final modification as it passes through our nose or mouth where recognizable speech sounds are produced through contacts of the voiced breath with the tongue, teeth, hard and soft palates, and the lips. This final stage of the formation of individual speech sounds will be discussed in the section under the heading of Articulation.

EXERCISE 10-8 How Breath Makes Voice

- Students gently place their fingers on the little bump in their throat directly under the chin.

- They take a regular breath, make the sound AH, and feel the sound vibrations of their vocal cords.

- Students take another breath and say out aloud, "May I speak now?" Or they may make up their own sentence that contains several different vowel sounds.

The Larynx and the Vocal Cords

The voice box (or larynx) is a hollow tube about two inches high in the normal adult and is made out of tough cartilage. It is located at the top of the trachea (or windpipe) and extends up to the pharynx (in the back of the throat). The larynx can be felt at the front of the neck, under the chin, as demonstrated in the previous exercise. The most visible feature of the larynx is the protrusion known as the thyroid shield, more commonly called the Adam's apple. It is inside this "shield" that the vocal cords are situated. The larynx therefore acts like a fort that is designed to protect the highly sensitive vocal cords, as well as the delicate muscles supporting them, from coming into contact with anything that might enter the larynx to harm them.

The Adam's apple is more prominent on a man's throat. That is because the underlying cartilage is thicker and longer in a man to accommodate his thicker and longer vocal cords. As mentioned earlier, the shorter and thinner vocal cords in women explain why they have higher voices than men. Another reason why it's not so easy to see the Adam's apple in a woman's throat is that women have more body fat than men do. This fat hides the larynx and gives the neck a smoother appearance. There are many explanations as to why the larynx is called the Adam's apple. The most picturesque story is that when Adam bit into the forbidden apple in the Garden of Eden, a piece of it got stuck in his throat and, from that time onwards, the bump became known as Adam's apple!

The vocal cords are made of muscular tissue that is elastic and pliable. They are covered with a delicate membrane and are packed with nerve cells, or touch centers. You experience their extreme sensitivity when a crumb or some liquid goes down your windpipe instead of your esophagus (which is your food passage). When this happens, the vocal cords violently evict the unwelcome guest from their house. Much like rubber bands, the cords are stretched horizontally across the larynx in a V shape. The top or front ends of the cords are solidly attached to the front middle part of the thyroid shield and cannot move, while the two rear or back ends are maneuverable and stretch down to the corners of the left and right arytenoid cartilages respectively at the bottom of the cords. The cords therefore divide their little fort into two levels. The lower floor houses more than sixty muscles that are attached to the arytenoid cartilage. These muscles directly enable the vocal cords to do their important work. The upper floor houses a thicker pair of bands, which remain in an open, relaxed state. These are called false vocal cords because they are not involved in voice production.

When we are breathing normally and not speaking, the vocal cords remain relaxed and stretched wide apart—the breath flowing in and out through the wide gap between them. The vocal cords are very sensitive to our thoughts. When we desire or will to speak, the nerve cells (or neurons) transmit this message from the brain along the central nervous system to the muscles immediately surrounding the cords. In this way, the neurons act like Central Intelligence agents passing on vital information. The nerves innervate the muscles—that is, they give them the go-ahead to prepare the cords for action. The vocal cords act like the chief executive or prime mover in the production of our voice, much like the president of the United States acts as the chief executive or prime mover in the governing of our country.

The vocal cords are so important that they are surrounded by sixty muscles that act like specially trained security guards. The job of these muscles is to make sure that nothing interferes with the vocal cords doing their singular work of making sound for speech. These muscles urgently press against the cords, forcing them to get as close together as possible with only the narrowest gap between them. At this highest point of tension, the cords are said to be adducted. The outbreath from the lungs now bears upwards against the adducted cords. Though the vocal cords strenuously resist the oncoming barrage of air, they cannot hold out and are forced apart, quivering and vibrating as they do so. As soon as they are forced apart, however, they immediately close up again. This lightning quick action of opening and closing is one cycle of vibration. A single cycle of vibration for the vocal cords normally takes between 2 and 5 milliseconds. A series of these cycles of vibrations of the vocal cords is what we identify as vocal sound.

Whether the pitch of the sound is higher or lower is determined by the number of vibrations per second of the vocal cords (the vibrator). That number will depend on the tension or degree of resistance of the cords. What we call pitch is the frequency of audible vibrations of the voice when we are speaking. Our pitch is altered by tightening or slackening the tension of the vocal cords. The tighter the vocal cords are stretched, the higher the pitch of the note.

The process of phonation is largely automatic; we are not conscious of any effort on our part. However, to help the process along to its completion, it is important to provide an adequate supply of breath that can overcome the resistance of the closed vocal cords. This is one of the key reasons why breathing exercises are so important.

EXERCISE 10-9 How Pitch Is Determined

Level One Action:

- Students each take a standard-sized elastic band and stretch it as tightly as they can—that is, they increase the tension of the band.
- Without breaking the band, students pluck it with their fingernail (or a guitar pick).
- Students listen to the high-pitched twang it gives.
- Students slacken the tension of the elastic band, pluck it again, and listen to the pitch of the tone. Is it lower or higher than before?

Level Two Action:

- Half the students take a small, thin rubber band, stretch it as tight as they can, and pluck it.
- The other half of the students take a longer, thicker rubber band, stretch it, and pluck it.
- The two groups compare the pitch of the twang.

The exercise above demonstrates that when you decrease the tension of the elastic band, and pluck it, the pitch will be lower. The vocal cords act in the same way: the greater the tension of the cords, the higher the note (or pitch) and vice versa. When we pluck a shorter, thinner rubber band, we hear the high-pitched twang it makes when it's stretched. The longer and thicker rubber band makes a deeper, lower-pitched twang. This exercise also demonstrates why the female voice, with its shorter, thinner cords, has a higher pitch range than the male voice.

Before a boy reaches puberty, his vocal cords are smaller and thinner, which explains why his voice is higher. As he goes through puberty, the larynx gets bigger and the vocal cords lengthen and thicken, making his voice deeper. The cracking and breaking of his voice are part of the process of the larynx finishing its growing.

The Science of Pitch

As we learned, the pitch of each sound is determined by the number of vibrations per second of the vocal cords. The lower the pitch, the less vibrations per second. On ascending the scale, the frequency per second of the vibrations increases rapidly from note to note. The Encyclopaedia Britannica approximates the individual ranges of the singing voice to extend from about 80 cycles per second in the low bass to about 1,050 cycles per second in the high C of the soprano. The lowest recorded musical singing note is a low B-flat with 58 cycles per second. This is found in bars 473, 475, 477, and 632 of the bass voice of the chorus in the fifth movement of Gustav Mahler's *Symphony No. 2* (Resurrection). The highest note is a high F above high C, with almost 1,400 cycles per second sung by the Queen of the Night in Mozart's *Magic Flute*.

Bel canto teachers believe that pitch is fixed in terms of these vibrations per second. Their estimates are therefore even more exact: If middle C is spoken or sung, the singer's cords will open and close, or vibrate, exactly 261 times in one second. When C an octave above middle C is sung, the cords vibrate at 522 cycles per second. On ascending yet another octave to high C, the frequency will have reached 1,044 cycles per second. In other words, the vocal cords open and close 1,044 times when a singer holds the note of high C for one second.

You can see how hard the vocal cords work for a performer, especially a singer. Should a soprano hold her high C for five seconds, her cords will open and close no less than 5,220 times, creating the same number of vibrations, or vortices, of sound—quite a vocal feat!

The average actor or singer has to deal with considerable heights and depths of pitch. If we are to ensure an effective and enduring stage voice, we must try to understand and be obedient to clearly defined natural laws. The process of phonation and pitch adjustment is more or less automatic, but there are exercises the voice student can perform to create good habits. These exercises will help guarantee that the breath is used efficiently and economically in speaking and singing and that the vocal cords remain healthy and functional.

As a note of interest, all sound is created by air vibrating at a frequency that can be detected by the human ear, which is normally sensitive to vibrations between the frequencies of 20 to 20,000 cycles per second. Vibrations above or below that are usually unnoticed by us although animals, notably dogs and birds, can hear vibrations outside this range. Whales communicate by means of high-frequency vibrations.

KEY: Getting to the heart of the issue

> **Pitch is controlled by varying the tension on the vocal cords. The less tension, the lower the number of vibrations per second and the lower the pitch. As we increase the tension, the frequency of vibrations increases rapidly, with resulting higher pitch.**

Step-by-Step Summary of Phonation

1. You take a breath. The breath is driven from the lungs by the compressing action of the ribs and diaphragm.

2. This breath passes up the two bronchi tubes to the windpipe, which leads to the larynx (or voice box).

3. Inside the voice box are the vocal cords. The edges of the vocal cords are placed across the interior of the voice box. In a state of rest or silence, the back ends of the vocal cords remain open so that the air passes easily between them.

4. If you will to speak, that message is carried from the brain along the nervous system to the muscles immediately surrounding the cords.

5. In their state of alertness, the muscles urgently press against the cords, forcing the cords to get as close as possible to each other without actually touching. When the cords are brought so close together that they leave just a razor's edge slit between them, they are said to be adducted. This is their highest point of tension and resistance to the oncoming breath.

6. A split second after the cords come together, there is a suspension of the breath as it accumulates and is compressed underneath the adducted cords. Because the resistance of the adducted cords is always slightly less than the air pressure applied, the outgoing breath forces them apart. The cords always give way, open out, then close again immediately. The cords keep this alternating opening-closing movement going until the breath runs out.

7. One complete opening and closing of the cords is called a vibration. A series of cycles of vibration is called a vibratory action. This vibratory action is what we identify as vocal sound. It continues as long as the outgoing breath lasts.

8. The vibratory action might also be thought of as a series of whirlpools or vortices of sound. When a flowing stream encounters an obstacle, such as a large rock, a whirlpool is formed as a result of the resistance to the flow. In much the same manner, when moving air encounters

an obstacle of resistance (the vocal cords), a vortex or whirlpool of sound is formed and shot upwards into the throat.

9. The number of vibrations of the vocal cords per second will determine the pitch (or note) of the sound that is produced. The tighter the tension of the cords, the higher the pitch.

10. After the initial vibration or primal sound produced by the vocal cords, the muscles continue to act upon the cords—tightening, shortening, and thinning them vertically in depth if the pitch scale ascends from a lower to a higher note. If the scale descends in pitch from a higher to a lower note, these same muscles relax and release the cords degree by degree—lengthening, vertically thickening, and reducing tension on them. The front ends of the cords, solidly attached to the larynx, cannot move, while the back ends float, being attached to maneuverable bones and muscles so that they can adjust the breath to certain levels of pitch during the process of phonation.

11. The initial sound that is produced is weak. These vortices of sound are shot into the throat, the mouth-pharynx cavity, and the head cavities, shaking up the air in these cavities and setting up vibrations back and forth and all around that amplify or resonate the original sound. As this vibrating air swirls within the mouth-pharynx cavity that is appropriately shaped for a vowel, we get a vowel sound of AH, AW, EE or whatever vowel the speaker or singer intends to produce. A vowel, therefore, is shaped vibration. (This is discussed in more detail under the heading Resonance.)

12. Vowels are only some of the sounds that make up speech. After the original sound is amplified in the pharynx, it passes out through the mouth and nose. The organs of speech, such as the lips, teeth, tongue, hard palate, and soft palate can take over and create other speech sounds we call consonants. (This is discussed in more detail under the heading Articulation.)

13. No sound will come forth from the voice box if the cords don't come together to provide the necessary resistance to the outgoing breath. Without the muscles pushing the cords to resist, there can be no vibration and thus no sound. When we have no desire to speak and the muscles around the cords are relaxed so that the cords themselves

are open, the breath passes noiselessly through the open cords, and we have a state of silence. When the neurons tell the muscles to press the cords together and resist the oncoming breath, that resistance creates vibration. We recognize the vibration of the vocal cords as sound.

KEY: Getting to the heart of the issue

Without the resistance of the vocal cords to the oncoming air, there can be no vibration. Without vibration, there can be no sound or voice.

Common Problems with the Larynx

Though the action of the vocal cords is essentially automatic, the vocal cords themselves do not always do their assigned work perfectly. Some of the common problems that speakers or singers experience with their vocal cords include the following:

1. *Laryngitis*, or the inflammation of the vocal cords. This inflammation can be caused by such irritants as smoke, stomach acid, or continued overuse or misuse of the voice, which can in turn lead to hoarseness or huskiness. Chronic laryngitis can progress to malignant growths on the vocal folds, and to cancer.

2. *Paralysis* of the vocal cords (also called paralytic dysphonia). In this condition, the nerve cells do not innervate the muscles correctly and therefore the muscles cannot effectively push the vocal cords close together. The result is either breathy voice, or, if the nerve control of the muscles proves too erratic, a choking sensation. Many voice doctors and therapists recommend vocal retraining in these cases, regardless of the prognosis.

3. *Scar tissue* on the muscles supporting the cords. This causes breathiness and can be life-threatening if swallowing is impaired.

4. *Abnormal growths* on one or both of the vocal cords, such as polyps, nodules, or cysts. These can cause hoarseness, pain, and possibly lead to cancer of the larynx.

Simplified Explanation of Phonation for Little Children

The Magic of Making Our Voice

Place your fingers gently on the little bump in your throat directly under your chin. This is your Adam's apple. As the boys get older, their Adam's apple will grow bigger, and that will explain why their voices grow deeper. The Adam's apple is a very special part of your throat. Does anyone know why? *(Some students will normally guess correctly.)* It is special because that is where we make sound. We also call this bumpy place in our throats the larynx or voice box. Larynx is a hard name to remember, so it is okay to call it by its simple name, the voice box. If some of you want to remember the more difficult name, it might help to give it a play name, such as Larry the Larynx.

The voice box is the house that the vocal cords live in. The vocal cords are the sound makers that come together when we want to speak. They are very sensitive bands of tissue and we cannot do without them. That is why they need a house so that crumbs of food and other harmful material don't accidentally go down the windpipe and upset them. The vocal cords are so extremely sensitive that they have sixty muscles surrounding them at all times, just like security guards, to protect them and warn them when they need to be on alert.

These vocal cords perform one of the most important jobs in our life. They produce our voice. We know that when someone is a businessman, he has a lot of responsibility. In a big company, he is called an executive. The executives in a company are the people who make all the critical decisions. The president of the United States is called the chief executive because his job is to make the most critical decisions for our country. The vocal cords are the chief executive in producing our voice. That is why they are surrounded by so many muscles that act just like the Secret Service agents who guard our President. The job of these muscles is to protect the vocal cords and make sure that nothing interferes with them doing their special work of making sound for speech.

Now, exactly how do these vocal cords make sound? Well, it's a magical process and it happens all by itself, without us even trying to make it happen. When we are just breathing in and out and not speaking, the vocal cords are lazily stretched out across the inside of the voice box with an opening between them that allows the breath to easily flow in and out. The vocal cords are very sensitive to our thoughts. When we decide that we are going to speak, and take in a deep breath, the brain sends an electrical message, express mail, through the nerves to tell the special muscles that protect the vocal cords to wake up and get ready to go to work. The muscles push vigorously against the vocal cords, forcing them to get as close to each other as they can in order to stop the air that is determined to pass through. The cords are pressed so tightly together by the muscles that the opening between them is quite narrow.

The cords try to resist the air as hard as they can, but the air is just too strong. Like a big hurricane wind, it storms its way through the narrow opening, causing the highly strung and sensitive cords to vibrate. To vibrate means to create a rapid, quivering motion. The continual resistance of the vocal cords to the powerful air as it forces its way between them is what makes the delicate strings of the vocal cords vibrate. That continual vibration of the vocal cords is what we hear as sound, or voice.

If you left a musical instrument like a harp out in a windy storm, you would hear the wind rush through the strings of the harp and make those strings vibrate with musical sounds. The same kind of thing happens with our vocal cords, except that they offer a much greater resistance to the wind than the strings stretched across the harp do. When the air passes through the cords, it is like plucking a tightly stretched elastic band. We hear that noise or vibration as the sound of our voice in our throats. The tighter the vocal cords and the more fiercely they resist the air, the more rapidly the vocal cords vibrate, making higher sounds. This is what causes human voices to have different pitches. The pitch of our voice can start very low, like the sound of a bass drum, or go very high, like the songbird notes of a nightingale. Now let us try some experiments just to see how these vibrations, called sound, are produced.

Director's Notes: At this point, guide the children through Exercises 10-8 and 10-9 above.

KEY: Getting to the heart of the issue

 The resistance of the vocal cords to the air as it forces its way between them is what makes the delicate strings of the cords vibrate. That continual vibration of the vocal cords is what we hear as sound, or voice.

E X E R C I S E 10-10 Creating Sound with the Vocal Cords

Guide students through this exercise with the following instructions:

Level One Action:

- Think of and will in your mind to produce the rounded vowel sound of O as in the word *pot.*

- Take your breath, and intone this vowel sound on a comfortable pitch and as four separate staccato (or quick) sounds: O-O-O-O.

- As you do, listen to the rounded note and then feel how your throat has shaped itself without any direct effort on your part.

- Then ask yourself: "What did I do to make this particular tone?" The answer will be "nothing"—nothing, that is, except the thinking and willing in your mind beforehand of the sound and pitch you wanted and the required slight breath pressure.

Level Two Action:

- Students repeat the exercise, but this time, after thinking and willing the O-O-O-O staccato sounds, they try to deliberately produce the sound by performing any of the following: forcing the breath more, stretching the soft palate, opening the mouth wider, or adjusting the lips and tongue and jaw to create the shape of the vowel.

When you try to deliberately produce the sound, you end up with distorted and unbalanced tone. You cannot superimpose a conscious physical adjustment-shaping on top of the automatic one that the vocal cords and the adjustable parts of the throat perform. Their work is specialized and exact, and any conscious controlling on our part is unwelcome interference. All vowel shaping should happen automatically as the result of thinking and willing the desired sound, which then finds immediate response within the vocal apparatus.

KEY: Getting to the heart of the issue

"Kiss your cords with your mind" is an accurate command that the bel canto masters gave their students.

How to Spoil a Stage Voice

Vocal Image: Despite the vocal cords working automatically to produce the kind of voice we want, sometimes we can and do interfere with their work. One of the ways an actor hinders the natural unfolding of his stage voice is by trying to change his voice to be something that it is not. Author, lecturer, and speech therapist, Dr. Morton Cooper, describes an unnatural voice pattern as a vocal image. In his book *Modern*

Techniques of Vocal Rehabilitation, he talks about the most common vocal image sought and cultivated by many actors: a rich, low-pitched voice. Theater teachers tend to encourage a lower-pitched placement because they believe it promotes a more appealing image both on the stage and on the screen. Up until the 1970s, many teachers even recommended smoking as a way to create deeper, froggier tones that were deemed to be more "alluring." For a male, a low-pitched voice was supposed to suggest power, masculinity, and savoir faire, much like the iconic James Bond voice of Sean Connery. For the female, the image of control, sophistication, and sexiness was believed to be enhanced by lowered tones.

Unfortunately, when a low-pitched voice is unnatural to the speaker and has to be forced, long-term problems can develop. Dr. Cooper calls such problems "vocal neurosis." It refers to the state of anxiety that characterizes a voice that has been made to act in a way unlike itself.

Most actors who cultivate a low-pitched speaking voice are forcing their voice into an unnatural pitch level and range. Every voice has its own optimal pitch range. If we wish to realize our truest vocal technique as performers, we should stay within that range. While it may satisfy an actor's ego to adopt a voice that makes him more interesting and glamorous, forcing a lower pitch to create synthetic tone means that the voice will eventually lose its natural richness. Over time, the "new" voice will be characterized by breathy, woolly, expressionless tones with no carrying power. This also inevitably develops symptoms of hoarseness, throat clearing, coughing, throat pain, periodic loss of voice, and even growths on the vocal cords, such as nodules and polyps—all of which hasten the destruction of the *true* voice and can result in what Dr. Cooper has identified over thousands of case studies to be vocal suicide.

Color Label: Another way an actor can prevent the development of a complete and competent stage voice is to color label every line he speaks. Just as you only need to think and will a particular tone or note to enable the vocal cords and resonating cavities of the throat to characterize that tone perfectly, so you only need to think and will a certain emotion to enable the *sound* of your voice to carry that mood, whether you are whispering, shouting, or simply speaking. You do not have to wring out the feeling in all of its raw and living intensity, as many Broadway artists do, or to saturate the words with intruding personal emotion to make sure the audience "gets it," as we observe with many sitcom actors. The distinguishing timbre (the quality or color of tone) of the actor's voice will adequately convey the implied feeling without conscious effort or highlighting on his part.

A well-schooled actor, like a good singer, lets the words or lyrics speak for themselves. Just by thinking the emotion, we subconsciously inject into our speech the character of that emotion. As our mood or emotion changes, so the timbre changes too, giving a distinctive nuance to the tone of the words expressed. This nuance is easily identified by the listener. For example, in speech, even the slightest tinge of sarcasm is readily discerned, though it may be veiled by an engaging smile. A natural color is already attached to every human mood as it is expressed in speech and we do not have to paint over or *label* that existing color with a highlighter just to make it perfectly clear to the audience what we want them to think and feel.

Sometimes dialogue that is intended to persuade an audience to a particular way of thinking and feeling makes actors believe that the added "highlighter" is necessary. Yet good acting, like good writing, stands on its own and doesn't require extra force or coloration to be convincing to an audience. Excessive emphasis is overkill. The only time it is legitimate for actors to use excessive emphasis is in the genre of melodrama and farce, where the physical action and the characters performing that action are depicted with extravagant theatricality for comedic purposes. The words of a good play or movie script have their own authentic life. The actor's challenge is to develop his theatrical voice to the point that it can render that world of meaning intended by the playwright and inherent in the dialogue itself with the perfect balance of naturalness, expressiveness, and control.

Our modern theatrical arts, particularly film and television, promote the exploitation and exhibition of every raw pain and pleasure before the world's eyes. This pattern is also reflected in the way acting is taught in most of the professional method schools. They dwell far too much on analyzing and constructing emotions for the stage, with the result that some acting classes turn into self-stroking, ego massaging therapy sessions that lose sight of the supremacy of technique. Indeed, a possible reason for this obsession with the emotive process is the lack of emphasis on vocal technique. A beautifully controlled and expressive voice, wedded to imagination and intuition, can produce all that an actor desires, and all that an audience will delight in, as the classic trained actors of the past proved to us. Like them, we need to cultivate a vocal technique that is perfectly fitted to fulfill the artistic demands placed upon it, and to do so with naturalness and true beauty.

EXERCISE 10-11 Discovering Tone

- Students act out the following simple scenes using the same dialogue:

    1. You accidentally bump into a stranger you are passing in the street and immediately say, "I'm so sorry."

    2. You are standing in line to buy tickets for a show and inadvertently step on the foot of the person behind you. You immediately say, "I'm so sorry."

3. You are sitting in a cinema next to a stranger. You stand up and inadvertently spill your large soda on the stranger's lap. You immediately say, "I'm so sorry."

4. You are studying. Your brother comes up and tells you that he failed to win a scholarship to the college he really wanted to attend, which is also the one you are presently attending. You say, "I'm so sorry."

5. You are walking with your best friend who has just found out that a loved one in his immediate family has died. You say, "I'm so sorry."

- After the improvisations are performed, students comment on the distinguishing timbre of voice in each of the five situations. Elements for discussion could include the following: What were the differences between number 1 and number 5? What was the actor thinking and feeling when he said his words in each of these circumstances? Did you notice, as we moved from the first to the last situation, that the voice changed from a matter-of-fact tone to something rounder, warmer, and charged with true sympathetic feeling?

Director's Notes: The changes in vocal tone for the five different scenarios should be noticeable. In the first scene, the actor would be no more than polite and sincere. Unless he caused injury to the stranger, the apology would be matter-of-fact. In the second scene, the actor might show more concern because the stranger is sitting next to him and would react to the pain of having his foot stepped on. In the third scene, the actor's words would be charged with a sense of his own wrongdoing and embarrassment, simply because he sees the terrible mess he has made. With scene 4, his tone would be imbued with a sense of commiseration and regret for his brother's disappointment, and his own. In scene 5, the actor's words would be heartfelt and intimate, expressing true sorrow for the tragic nature of his best friend's loss.

What Is a Natural Voice?

When we say that someone has a natural voice, most people under mean that the person has an untrained voice—that is, a voice no fulfill an artistic goal. Ask a friend who has never had a voice les Shakespeare and you will be convinced that naturalness does not in self-expression. Similarly, when we speak of a young actor as a "i that he appears to possess the aptitude (or potential) to be a professional—meaning an actor who is fit to competently portray his character onstage. In both instances, the word *natural* implies *untrained*. There is, in fact, a truer meaning for the word *natural*.

Everyone's voice is "natural," but a *truly* natural voice is one that perfectly fulfills physiological and acoustical laws—in other words, laws provided by nature. Only when following natural laws is a voice capable of producing consistently beautiful tone with flawless control—an accomplishment that takes many years of study and practice. Nature holds the blueprint of perfection for all, but that blueprint remains just a potential unless it is fully developed. Even though we want naturalness of expression on the stage, we cannot rely on the untrained voice to convey the desired warm-blooded feeling, imaginative expressiveness, and refined delivery that each word being spoken or sung requires. With the average voice, we will hear exactly the same tonal product for a dozen different phrases. Untrained voices, trying to be artistic, tend to be loud, unmusical, and unvarying because they lack the intuitive refinement, imaginative probing, and vowel expansion that only proper vocal schooling can give.

Ear training helps the aspiring actor or singer to develop vocal skill. He can benefit by listening to the fine timbre of bel canto trained voices like Caruso, Luisa Tetrazzini, Madame Melba, Joan Sutherland, Gigli, Mario Lanza, Ezio Pinza, and John McCormack—all of whom can now be heard on newly released CD's and DVD tapes. It also behooves the young artist to listen to the classically trained Shakespearean actors like Dame Edith Evans, Sir John Gielgud, Dame Sybil Thorndike, Sir Ralph Richardson, Sir Laurence Olivier, Dame Gladys Cooper, and Paul Scofield—many of whose performances are also available on VHS or DVD.

These renowned artists demonstrated vocal truth and vocal beauty because they realized the highest point of vocal fitness in perfectly expressing their art. E. Herbert-Caesari defines a truthful and beautiful voice as one whose outward form or technique perfectly fulfills its artistic function. When we hear such a voice, we sense and touch beauty. Rarely do singers or actors today sing or speak the full value of each voweled tone as these original greats did. The voices of these masters glided melodically into the next tone, "like a dewdrop melting into another drop." The cuts of the consonants they pronounced were almost imperceptible. The vocal cords were allowed to sing and "purr" freely to release beautiful timbre of all tonal colors and textures. They also conveyed in their artistry the joy of striving after beauty of vocal expression. That joy is imparted to us when we hear or see them perform. Their joy in producing a voice of intrinsic beauty and form is ever-present no matter what role they played or song they sang. Of popular actors, few approximate that same excellence. Anthony Hopkins, Christopher Plummer, Patrick Stewart, Ian McKellen, Sean Bean, Judi Dench, and Timothy Dalton—in the tradition of Laurence Olivier—embody the exception.

Unfortunately, audiences today tend to be unenlightened tonally and aesthetically because they are unaccustomed to hearing really first-rate acting and singing and therefore will uncritically accept and loudly applaud vocal performances that lack meaning or artistic value. With the exception of esteemed opera artists who perform in the major opera houses, or dedicated Shakespearean-trained repertory actors, tonal beauty plays little or no part in much of modern American theater. Too many actors rely mainly on natural gifts of voice with a few lessons thrown in to carry them to the professional arena.

Actors in training need to master all the elements that make up vocal technique. No element, however, is more essential than the ability to create beautiful vowel tone. It is the golden key to true vocal artistry.

3. Resonance

Director's Notes: For the little ones, I have provided an optional simplified explanation at the end of this section.

What is *resonance* and what is a *resonator?* The term resonance is derived from the Latin *resonare*, which is made up of the prefix *re* (meaning "back" or "again") and *sono* (meaning "sound"). It is a re-sounding, or reinforcement, of a relatively weak primal tone. Strike a tuning fork and place its stem on the lid of a piano or against a wood door and you'll hear how additional vibrations are set up in the wood and how the original weak sound of the fork is greatly increased. So through resonating—or re-sounding—we make the tone bigger and enrich its quality.

A resonator is a cavity (or enclosed space) that will reinforce the weak primal tone. Other words that are used interchangeably with cavity are *cave* and *chamber.* It is the resonators that give form, character, body, and carrying power to the vowel tone.

The main resonators are:

> The *chest.* Place your hand on your own chest and feel the vibration when you speak.

> The *larynx,* which is the voice box. The voice box, containing the vocal cords, is where the original sound is produced.

> The *pharynx,* the space between the back wall of the throat and the back of the tongue.

The *mouth*, whose roof contains:

> a) the *hard palate*—the hard, bony, fixed sounding board
>
> b) the *soft palate*—the pliable, elastic area in the back roof of the mouth. At the end of the soft palate is a small, hanging pendant called the uvula. The raising or lowering of the uvula signifies the raising or lowering of the soft palate itself. It is raised to allow the sound (or voiced breath) to escape through the mouth; it is lowered so that the sound can escape through the nose (as in the production of nasal consonants like *m*, *n*, and *ng (*as in the word *sing).*

Although I listed the hard palate, the soft palate, and the pharynx as individual resonators, they really form continuous parts of one big resonating cavity called the mouth-pharynx cavity. Moreover, since the soft palate forms the adjustable roof of the pharynx, it is more accurate to consider it as part of the pharynx cavity itself, especially when talking about its function as a resonator.

In addition to the resonators I just described, there are cavities of the nose and forehead, ear canal and skull that also act as resonators.

All resonators have two ways that they increase sound: the wall of the resonator itself that picks up the initial vibrations, plus the mass of air inside the resonator that swirls around and amplifies the sound. The nineteenth-century German physicist, Dr. Hermann Helmholtz, established conclusively that the sphere-shaped resonator was the most efficient. He proved the natural effectiveness of a domed hard palate and a domed pharynx, with its flexible roof of a soft palate that expands upwards, like a parachute opening, as the pitch rises. Dr. Helmholtz's experiments showed that the spherical shape of a resonating cavity assists the rapid, smooth flow of the vibrations with a minimum of friction as they pour into and out of the cavity. Few singers (or actors) know how well-equipped they are in this sense.

Which part of this all-encompassing mouth-pharynx cavity do you think has the greater space? Is it the bony, fixed arc of the hard palate at the top of the mouth, or the pharynx that leads down into the back of the throat? *(Let the students answer.)* The pharynx, with its adjustable soft palate, has more space. It expands and opens out like a miniature umbrella, thus providing a gradually increasing space for the rising tonal stream as the pitch scale ascends higher and higher. This spacious area of the pharynx is considered by bel canto teachers to be the real mouth of the singer and the antechamber to the head resonating cavities. In summary, the whole of the mouth-pharynx cavity comes into play as we begin to sing or speak. The front, bony section of the hard palate, however, is the less important part.

Every resonating cavity has its own special "note." This note refers to the frequency (number of vibrations per second of the sound) that is natural to it—a frequency to which it responds harmoniously when invaded by a tonal stream of equal frequency. Unfortunately, when an alien frequency enters it, the invader is given asylum, but under duress, and the resonator protests by producing an inharmonious, unmusical note of poor quality. This is to be expected since, from the point of view of physics, resonance happens when two systems are vibrating within the same frequency range. When resonant waves meet, they create order. In contrast, when two waves vibrating at different frequencies meet, they create chaos or dissonance.

The front, bony section of the mouth not only has fixed physical dimensions, which are unalterable, but it also has a fixed frequency that is intrinsic to it. For all practical purposes, this cavity frequency is the lowest of all the cavities the singer or speaker possesses. You can prove this convincingly to yourself by tapping your forehead with the tips of your middle three fingers. You'll hear a fairly high-pitched sound when you do this. Keep on tapping while gradually moving your fingertips down to just above the bridge of your nose. You'll note how the sound has dropped in pitch already. Keep on tapping your fingers down the bridge of the nose until you are finally tapping against your upper lip. Note again how the sound has dropped considerably to reach its lowest pitch. This is because at the back of the lip lies the fixed, bony part of the mouth. To enable proper resonance of a higher-pitched primal note, the upsoaring stream must be lodged in a resonating cavity that matches its frequency, not a cavity with a lower frequency like the front of the mouth.

If the frequency note of the resonator matches that of the primal note, we get a perfect vibratory "marriage" that is compatible with the desired pitch and the willed intensity of the singer. The result will be a beautifully reinforced and balanced vocal tone. It is unfortunate that not all singing teachers or voice coaches understand this concept. Many still teach a method called forward mask production or "dans la masque," in which the singer or actor tries to force, by willed effort, a higher tone into the mask or front part of the mouth and nose—which are resonating cavities meant for lower tones. In other words, they take a *high*-pitched note (a high-frequency primal note) into a *low*-pitched resonating cavity, such as the mouth cavity. The result is an intrinsically bad sound, though the singer or speaker himself may not be aware of it, having been taught that it is the right vocal tone to "produce." Under no circumstances can such a sound be balanced because the two different frequencies (the low mouth cavity and the high primal note) are not matched—are not "in tune" with each other. How can high and low possibly agree? How can these opposing frequencies dovetail into one another to form a perfect whole? They cannot, and the resulting friction is heard in the product, which is inevitably compromised in its integrity.

The Italian bel canto masters of a former era understood this completely. It is both physiologically and acoustically wrong to force all vowel tones, irrespective of high or low pitch, into the fixed and limited (both in space and in frequency) resonating section of the hard palate. All vowels, no matter what language, are formed entirely in the back part of the mouth with its soft palate rising and descending as required together with the tongue assisting in that adjustable raising and lowering. The front part of the mouth, with its hard, bony arc, has no part in the actual vowel-shaping.

Far too much importance is assigned to the lips and tongue for creating the tonal shape of a vowel, such as an AH, an EE, etc. In fact, the character of every vowel is fully shaped in the pharynx before it reaches the mouth. The lips and tongue merely respond to and work in conjunction with the resonating chamber of the pharynx, which is the primary shaper. We might call the lips and tongue junior partners in the production of vowel sounds. They help focus the forward projection of the vowel after it has received its primary shaping and resonance, and they more clearly define its individual character when it is combined with consonants to form words.

Although the mouth-pharynx is the main resonator and character shaper, other resonating cavities, including the front part of the mouth, the nasal passages, and the cavities of the skull assist in enhancing the original tone.

E X E R C I S E 10-12 Finding the Tone

The lips and tongue are *not* intrinsically responsible for the original shaping of the vowel. You can demonstrate this by performing the following exercise:

- The students hold their mouths in a relaxed, barely open position with the tongue low in the mouth and either speak or sing the five vowel tones—AH AY EE OH OO—on any low note.

- The students intone eight staccato notes with the open AH vowel on any low note. (A staccato tone is sharp and neatly detached.)

- Follow these staccato notes with a legato (that is, smooth and continuous) intoning of the five vowels—AH AY EE OH OO—repeated twice. Just think and will these vowels. It should be executed like this:

  AH AH AH AH AH AH AH AH (staccato)
  AH AY EE OH OO (legato)
  AH AY EE OH OO (legato)

You will find that the shape of the vowel is clearly recognizable and remains fully intact with little or no contrived movement of either the lips or tongue.

Summary

All vowel sounds are made inside the mouth-pharynx cavity. The most important part of this cavity is the back area of the soft palate where it is pliable and fully adjustable. All parts of the tongue are used to form consonants, while the back of the tongue is what mainly assists in the formation of vowels. The higher the pitch, the more the back of the mouth expands in order to provide more space to accommodate the greater frequency of sound vibrations being beamed up from the vocal cords. The front part of the mouth—the hard palate, the lips, the teeth, the tip of the tongue, and the lower jaw—while essential for consonant formation, has nothing whatsoever to do with actual vowel formation. Their different positions vis-a-vis different vowels are more of an after-fact. They assist in focusing the tone and emphasizing the shape of the particular vowels when they are spoken or sung in words.

The work of a good ventriloquist illustrates this point. If you watch a ventriloquist, you will see little or no lip movement, whether he is speaking or singing, yet we hear every word clearly. He can do this because he creates all his vowels in the back part of the mouth and throat—that is, in the pharynx. The front part of his mouth is used only to help resonance and articulation. For example, to make the labial (or lip) consonants—which are sounds such as *p, b,* and *m*—the ventriloquist will press the tip of his tongue against the hard palate, where he can substitute dental sounds for labial, such as *n* for *m, d* for *b,* or *t* for *p.* Sometimes, he might engage the back of the tongue to produce a nasal *ng* sound to substitute for the labial *m.* Simulation of the consonants, however, is not enough. It is the expansion of the back of the tongue and the soft palate that allows for the kind of vowel enlargement needed to form his words perfectly, as well as help mask any consonant substitution. Of course, his speed of delivery and the "funny" voice and antics of his puppet further sustain the illusion.

Resonance, or vowel expansion, is the key to effective speech on the stage, which is why the pharynx is the most important cavity. The organs of speech, including all parts of the mouth, are needed to produce crispy consonants and to guide the vowel tone forward for greater projection, especially since the mouth acts as a resonator.

The Musical M's and N's

Director's Notes: Distribute Handout Voice #1, *Making Music*

One of the best ways to feel the largeness of the back area of your throat is to yawn. You will notice that the soft palate stretches up in a domelike shape, giving lots of room for the sound beamed up from the vocal cords to be reinforced with echo.

Many artists in the last fifty years have been trained to speak and sing through the front part of their mouth and nose cavities. As explained earlier, this technique of forward mask projection is both incorrect and harmful. Since many of us have been used to speaking and singing this way, we have to reeducate our muscles to direct the sound column toward the back of the throat into the adjustable area of the pharynx, especially if we want to create a musical quality in our voice.

The terms *resonance, tone focus,* and *placing your voice* are interchangeable. The most effective way to guide the sound column so it is "placed" correctly is to:

1. *Think* the sound as far back as possible, then visualize it being lifted up into the imaginary parachute.
2. *Do not force* the sound once it is high up in the back of your throat. Inside that domelike area, the perfect tone quality is always produced. Only the resonator of the pharynx can produce clear, bright, and bell-ringing tone, using the least amount of breath. That is nature's purpose for it.

EXERCISE 10-13 Making Music

Level One Action:

The *m, n,* and *ng* sounds are the music makers, and the most resonant.

- Students intone the first two lines on the handout, starting with HUM.
- Repeat HUM nine times. HUM is a robust sound combination that trains the voice to stay in the back of the throat to find its optimal resonance (reinforcement and enlargement).
- Follow with the second line, HUM TRAM (pronounced Trum).

The best produced sound is always the one that uses the least amount of breath. The more breath in the voice, the less resonant and musical the sound will be, and therefore the less carrying power it will have.

Director's Notes: Some of the children may intone the HUM almost exclusively in the nasal cavity with a lot of air escaping through the nose. This usually occurs with those who have poor breathing habits. Work patiently with these students. Supervise their breathing exercises closely so you can help them develop better habits. Suggest to them that they practice the HUM exercise as often as they can at home, and enthusiastically praise even the smallest improvement.

Level Two Action:

The *m* and *n* consonants, when sandwiched in the middle of words, have a tendency to be run over when speaking. Unless these sounds are pronounced with emphatic distinctness onstage, they will be completely lost to the audience. We can improve our articulation of these sounds by strengthening the contacts of the speech organs (lips, teeth, tongue, etc.) every time we practice.

- The students read together the first four sets of verses, ending with the four-line stanza that begins "Merry are the bells...."

- Alternatively, half the class does the first two sets of verses and the second half does the remaining two.

- If the class is willing, they can continue on with the rest of the verses on the page, or set them aside for another week.

- The students underline all the *m* and *n* sounds sandwiched in the middle of words. For example, *u*n*der, se*n*d, e*m*broider, rou*n*delay, mo*n*th, a*n*d, o*n*ly.*

- The students say each of these words out loud. They hold onto the middle *m* or *n* sound until the director gives them a signal (like bringing thumb and forefinger together) to complete the closure of the whole word.

Level Three Action:

- The students circle all the words on the handout that end in *ng*, such as *humming, coming, murmuring, ring, sing, morning, evening.*

- The children say these words out loud, making sure that the *ng* sound is given extra emphasis. Students should *not* pronounce the final *g* with a hard *g* as in *go.*

The three musical sounds cannot be produced without breath escaping through the nose. That is why they are called *nasal* sounds. When an actor has a cold and congestion blocks his nasal passages, there will be little or no resonance, only nasality.

Director's Notes: Babies have the most resonant voices of all because they are close to nature in their vocal development and have not had time to develop bad habits. A young child's voice is naturally pure and piercing in its clarity and can be sustained effortlessly for a long time—as many parents find to their dismay! When intoning the HUM sound, the students should strive to produce a childlike tone, even if the higher pitch that may result sounds strange.

Simplified Explanation of Resonance for Little Children

Director's Notes: Distribute Handout Child's Voice #1, *The Music Makers*

The human voice is just like a musical instrument consisting of three parts:

1. A Motor
2. A Vibrator
3. A Resonator

In previous classes, we talked about how to breathe correctly and how we make sound with our vocal cords. The motor power of the voice is the breath, the stream of air driven upwards from the lungs when we breathe out. The lungs provide this motor power. They are just like the bellows that blow the air into the pipes of an organ. When we exhale, the air passes back up the windpipe to the voice box on top. As we learned earlier, the voice box is the house that the vocal cords live in. The vocal cords are the vibrator part of the human voice—or the sound makers.

When the vocal cords are lazily stretched out, the breath passes right through them. But when we decide to speak, the sixty muscles that guard the vocal cords push against them, forcing them together. Who remembers what the vocal cords do when the air comes up? *(Wait for answer.)* They put up a brave fight to resist the oncoming air. But the air is too strong and it forces the vocal cords apart, making them quiver or vibrate. That vibration is the sound we hear—the sound we call voice.

Now we come to the last part of the human voice—the resonators. The word *resonance* means "to sound again," like when we make an echo with our voice. That's what resonators do. They are echo makers. The *resonators* are special caves in our throat and head that create echoes of the sound passing through. If you stand inside a real cave and call out, you will notice that your voice bounces all around you, creating continuing echoes, making that sound bigger and louder than normal. That is what happens inside the back of the throat and mouth and inside the nasal passages and skull. They are special domelike caves *(make the shape of a dome with your hands)* that make the sound coming up from your vocal cords bigger, richer, and fuller.

Right at the back of the throat is the soft palate. It's the fleshy part of the roof of the mouth near where we swallow. That's the place where the doctor looks to see if you have a sore throat. If he presses the little stick too far down, you will gag. So don't go putting your finger back there to try and feel it!

When you yawn, the soft palate stretches up high and looks like a parachute. The same thing happens when the breath comes up the windpipe and pushes its way through the closed vocal cords and becomes sound. That sound is beamed up, as if on a very fast elevator, and becomes much fuller inside the resonating caves. Resonance makes sound bigger, rounder, and more beautiful.

Do any of you play the violin or have you ever attended a concert where you have seen musicians play the violin? We can also compare the resonating caves to the sound box in a violin. The sound box is what resonates the music vibrating off the strings, making it more beautiful, just like the fairy godmother changed Cinderella from a poorly dressed servant girl into a gorgeously arrayed princess. That's just the kind of magic the resonators perform on the very plain sound that comes up from the vibrating vocal cords. Only when those tones are sent ringing through the echo caves, can they sound like music. The boys' voices will sound rich, strong, and melodious and the girls' voices will sound clear and silvery soft like a queen.

EXERCISE 10-14 Musical Sounds (For Little Children)

The *m*, *n*, and *ng* sounds are the most resonant in our language because they are the music makers. What are three words beginning with the *m* sound? *(The children volunteer answers.)* Let's say these words together. *(Lead the children in saying the words they suggested.)* What are three words starting with the *n* sound? *(Repeat the same process.)* What are three words ending with the *ng* sound? *(Repeat the same process.)*

These sounds cannot be produced without breath escaping through the nose. That is why the musical sounds are also called *nasal* sounds. It's not very good when an actor has a cold because his nose gets blocked up, so that the breath can't escape through the nose and make the musical sounds. When your nose is all stuffed up, your voice has very little resonance, only nasality, which doesn't sound very nice at all.

a) Say the words *singing* and *ringing,* holding onto the sound as it passes through the echo caves in the back of the mouth and nose. Then pinch the nose with a make-believe clothespin of your thumb and forefinger. *(Demonstrate which fingers you mean and lead them in the exercise.)* What happens to the sound? Does it stop? Why?

b) Place your hand on top of your head and feel for vibration there when you say the words *mommy* and *tummy.*

c) Imagine that you are looking at a bird flying higher and higher in the sky as you say, "The bird flew up, up, up, and far away." Did you hear your voice rise in pitch, going higher and higher like the bird? Now, imagine yourself throwing a stone down into a deep well, as you say, "The stone dropped down, down, down, to the bottom of the well." Could you hear your voice go down, down, down in pitch, like the stone?

EXERCISE 10-15 The Music Makers (For Little Children)

- Students intone the first two lines on the handout, starting with HUM.
- Repeat HUM six times. HUM is a special sound that let's us feel the voice vibrating way back in our throats.
- Follow with the second line, HUM TRAM (pronounced Trum).
- Students speak the rest of the verses out loud, making sure that all the musical sounds are given extra emphasis. Students should *not* pronounce the final *g* with a hard *g* as in *go*.

4. Articulation

Director's Notes: Distribute Handouts Voice #2A and 2B, *Making Consonants*. A simplified description of the making of vowels and consonants has been provided at the end of this section for the younger children.

Articulation refers to the distinct pronouncing of syllables (combinations of speech sounds) to effectively convey the meaning of words. The English language is composed of two kinds of speech sounds: vowels and consonants. There are five vowel letters and twenty-one consonant letters. Together, they make up twenty-six letters of our alphabet. From these twenty-six letters we make our words.

Sometimes, after we mix around the consonants and vowels, we end up with a lot more combinations of sounds. In other words, one letter may stand for several different sounds. For example, take the single vowel letter *a* and see how it sounds different in these four words: *man, car, mate, mecca*. It can even sound different when used twice within the same word: *again, matador, radar*. So these twenty-six letters do not accurately represent all the sounds of our language. Both singly and in combination, they actually make up some twenty-five possible vowel sounds and twenty-five consonant sounds. To keep track of them all, speech authorities have assigned special phonetic symbols to them. Because there are many different variations of these phonetic symbols, especially between English-speaking countries like England, Australia, and America, we will not represent the sounds by these symbols, but rely on simple description to identify them.

As we learned earlier, breath from the lungs forces its way through the closed vocal cords and makes them vibrate. This vibration is sound. This sound is then shot up into the resonating cavities, where it is given definite shape and fullness. Each shaped sound is what we identify as the different vowels. All our vowel sounds receive their individual character in the resonating cavities. The lips and the tongue, which are organs of speech, cooperate by taking certain positions to help the vowel sound pass out through the mouth unhindered or to further refine its shape when it is used in combination with consonants to make different words.

Consonants are produced when the outgoing breath—whether voiced or not—is obstructed by the organs of speech: the lips, tongue, teeth, hard palate, soft palate, and, in the case of the *h* sound, the vocal cords. The kind of obstruction that takes place, whether by the lips or teeth or some other organ of speech, will determine the kind of consonant the sound will become, whether a *b*, *k*, or *t*, etc.

If you look at the handout showing the sectional diagram of the mouth and nose, you can see where the organs of speech are located. These are the organs of speech:

Lips: The lips play a key role in forming our speech sounds. They must take the correct shape to help the vowel sounds follow their proper projection course. They are also used vigorously to articulate consonants.

Tongue: This is the busiest and most flexible of all the speech organs. The position of the tongue plays a major role in the formation of our speech sounds, but especially the consonants. We can identify three parts of the tongue that are used in articulation: the tip or blade; the middle or body; and the back of the tongue. The tongue normally rests on the floor of the mouth with the tip behind the bottom teeth, but in some of us, the tongue gets bunched up high in the mouth, and we end up talking with a nasal sound. Depending upon where we grow up, we will develop an accent that influences the position of the tongue in forming our words.

Hard palate: The hard palate is the solid, bony part of the roof of the mouth. It extends backward from the top front teeth. The area of the hard palate closest to the teeth is called the alveolar or tooth ridge.

Soft palate: The soft palate is the soft, fleshy portion of the roof of the mouth. It is the flexible continuation of the hard palate as it descends backwards into the throat as far as the uvula (the small pendant that hangs from the soft palate). If we were to put our finger too far back into the throat, and cause ourselves to gag, that is where the soft palate is. The soft palate normally takes one of two positions—either it is raised up to close off the entrance to the nasal cavity, so that the sound escapes through the mouth, or it is lowered to open the entrance to the nasal cavity and at the same time block the mouth exit by means of contact between the soft palate and the back of the tongue.

Vocal cords: As we learned earlier, these are the sound makers. When they are lazy and spread apart, the breath passes through them. When the cords are drawn tightly together to resist the oncoming air, they vibrate and cause voice. When we produce the voiceless *h* consonant, the cords act as an organ of speech—the only time they do.

Articulation is carried out by these organs of speech. Distinct speech is best achieved by firmly controlled activity and accurately coordinated contacts of these organs. Other terms used interchangeably with articulation are diction and enunciation. All three refer to the clarity and distinctness of pronouncing words in speech or singing—in such a way that each word is clearly heard and the meaning understood. This implies more than just clipped and distinctly enunciated consonants. In fact, good diction involves properly expanded and well-shaped vowels along with appropriately formed and released consonants.

The vowel in a word determines the rhythm of the word. Since the vowel tone moves in cycles or sine waves, it must be allowed to expand fully so that the rhythm of the word can fulfill its cycle. If the vowel tone is cut short, it won't really matter how perfectly enunciated the consonants are because the rhythm of the word will already be aborted. Both consonants and vowels work together and require equal attention to form perfect speech. Consonants need to be light, crisp, compact, and efficiently released to clear the road for the soaring vowel tone. If the movements of the speech organs are lazy, the words will lack clearness. If the movements are exaggerated, the consonants will be overly magnified and impair the quality and power of the vowels. Stanislavski reminded us in *Building a Character* that "vowels are a river and consonants are the banks," and it is therefore necessary "to reinforce the latter lest there be floods!"

Each word is a complete picture unit. We could also say that vowels are like a painting and consonants are the frame around the painting. Both are required to achieve picture perfect speech for the stage. Words are not mechanical units of syllables; words are images made from the thoughts that our mind and heart conceive and that our spirit can energize—whether for good or evil. Words are, therefore, living sounds—each letter an essential component of the blueprint of that creative thought. It behooves us, then, to respect and give deference to every syllable in a word if we want to release the full life of that word according to its proper matrix.

As we have seen, sounds can impact life in a dramatic way, depending on the intention behind our use of those words. The vowel gives words their fire power, or to quote Stanislavski, their "spiritual content." You can also think of the vowel as the soul of the word, and so we must make every effort to ensure that the vowel is allowed its full expansion and rhythmic completion.

KEY: Getting to the heart of the issue

 "To an actor a word is not just a sound, it is the evocation of images." (Constantin Stanislavski)

ILLUSTRATION 10-2 The Matchstick

Director's Notes: Take a common box of kitchen safety matches, remove a match from the box, and explain the following to the students:

- This small wooden matchstick represents a word you wish to speak. The red match head is the consonant, which usually, though not always, begins a word. The vowel is the flame that is ignited once we strike the match head against the striking surface or plate on the side of the box. The striking plate represents the organs of speech, which provide stoppage or friction of the outgoing breath in order to create individual consonants, and thus make words.

- I am going to take this match and strike it against the plate. *(Take match and strike it lamely against the plate so that the head does not ignite a spark, or if so, only a flicker of one at best. Then ask the students:)* Why didn't the match ignite? *(They will answer that you didn't strike it hard enough.)* If you don't strike the match head hard enough against the plate, you will not create enough friction to produce a big enough spark that can ignite the match and explode it into flame.

- Let's make a second attempt. *(This time, press the match hard and firm against the striking plate so that a bright flame lights up.)* Notice what a bright, strong flame was ignited after I pressed the match head hard and firm against the striking plate.

- The flame is the vowel tone of a word that can only come to full life if the match head (which represents the consonants) presses firmly against the plate, ushering in the life of the flame (the vowel).

An interesting note: The first match, invented in 1827 by English chemist John Walker, was called a friction match. The matches were later patented by a man called Samuel Jones and were sold under the name *lucifers*—so named, the story goes, because of all the problems they created. The flame was unsteady and the initial reaction of the head striking the rough surface was alarmingly volatile. Additionally, the odor produced by the burning match was anything but heavenly. Fortunately, by the mid 1840s, safety matches, which separated the combustible chemicals between the match head and a special striking surface, replaced the more wildly flammable and unstable lucifers. Efficient and carefully controlled contact between the head and the striking surface was the underlying principle for producing the safety match. The same principle applies if we wish to produce perfectly articulated speech.

The Making of Consonants

Consonants are created when the speech organs partially or completely obstruct the outgoing breath, whether that breath is voiced or not. If the stoppage is complete, the consonant produced will have an explosive quality, caused by the sudden and rapid release of the air. If the stoppage is partial, the consonant will have a continuous or sustained quality, caused by the gradual release or escape of the air. Consonants are further subdivided into voiced (with vibration of the vocal cords) or unvoiced (breathed or without vibration of the vocal cords). While the making of vowels is an automatic process of the vocal cords and resonating cavities, we do need to take a conscious and active role in the making of consonants.

Look at the sectional diagram of the face in your handout and observe the various points of contact for the articulation of the different consonants. In the formation of English consonants, the obstructions of the voice or breath are caused by contacts at several distinct points, which may be clearly identified. These contact points are described by the organs of speech involved and are listed on the handout—for example, the consonants *t* and *d* are formed by the contact of the tip of the tongue against the hard palate. Below is a more detailed description of all the consonant sounds.

Description of Consonant Sounds

Instructions: You can discuss all of the consonants in the list below in front of the entire class or break the class up into several smaller groups and assign each group the job of studying among themselves four to six consonants that you choose for them from the list. Using their handouts to guide them, they can practice making the sounds and figuring out the specific organs of speech involved in making them. Beforehand, you can type out or copy the information (provided below) on the consonants that you will assign to each group. You can go round the class and check on each group, making sure they understand what they have to do and the terms involved. After all the groups have had enough time to thoroughly discuss their sounds, bring them back together again as one group and begin Exercise 10-16.

In his book *Speech Training and Dramatic Art*, John Miles-Brown provides an excellent description of the consonant sounds and how they are formed by the different articulatory organs. The following list summarizes his main points. The first sixteen consonants are arranged in pairs. The two consonants making up each pair are formed with the same organs of speech in the same position, but the first sound is unvoiced (breathed) and the second is voiced. All the consonants in the list are categorized as either explosive (complete obstruction of air) or continuous (partial obstruction of air). Some teachers use the term "stop" instead of "explosive."

> *P b:* explosive—complete obstruction by the lips. The outgoing breath builds up behind the closed lips. When the lips part quickly, the air explodes with a popping or bursting sound (unvoiced in the case of the *p* sound and voiced in the case of the *b* sound).
>
> *T d:* explosive—complete obstruction by the tip of the tongue and hard palate. The breath builds up behind the tip of the tongue, which makes a firm contact with the hard palate (tooth ridge area). The quick lowering of the tongue creates a clear, crisp sound (unvoiced in the case of the *t* and voiced in the case of the *d*).
>
> *K g:* explosive—complete obstruction by the back of the tongue and soft palate. The breath pressure builds up behind the back of the tongue, which rises to make a firm contact with the lowered soft palate (or velum), releasing a sound with a vigorous guttural intensity (unvoiced in the case of *k* and voiced in the case of *g*).
>
> *Ch j (ch* as in *choice, j* as in *joke):* explosive—complete obstruction by the front of the tongue and hard palate. These are compound consonants. The unvoiced *ch* comprises *t* plus *sh*. The voiced *j* is made up of *d* plus *zh (*as in *azure).* The front of the tongue presses up against the hard palate and stops the breath. The first part of the sound is heard as the tip of the tongue lowers enough to give the *t* or *d* sound. The flat front of the tongue does not fall but stays close enough to the hard palate to produce the *sh* or *zh* sound as the air rushes out to escape through the narrow gap.

Th th (same spelling for two different sounds—th as in thick and th as in the): continuous—partial obstruction by tongue tip and top teeth. This sound is made by placing the tip of the tongue between the teeth, with the restriction on the outgoing breath occurring between the top front teeth and the tongue tip. The bottom teeth contact the underside of the tongue to regulate the pressure of the tongue tip on the top front teeth. These consonants can be sustained because of the continuous escaping breath (unvoiced in the case of the first sound and voiced in the case of the second). Both these sounds are also *fricatives*, so named because the incomplete contact of the tongue tip and top teeth allows some of the breath to escape, thus causing the sound by friction.

S z: continuous—partial obstruction by the tongue, hard palate, and teeth. Both of these sounds are made by the air rushing between the tongue tip and hard palate and escaping out through the teeth. The *s* consonant is called a *sibilant* because of its hissing sound, while the *z* sound is classified as a *fricative* because of the incomplete contact of the tongue tip, hard palate and teeth, and the resultant friction.

Sh zh (sh as in shirt, zh as in azure or pleasure): continuous—partial obstruction by the tongue, hard palate, and lips. These sounds are similar to the *s* and *z* but also include the rounding and pushing forward of the lips. The restriction of the air is caused more by the body of the tongue raised near the hard palate than the tip of the tongue, as in the *s* and *z*. *Sh* is also classified as a sibilant and *zh* as a fricative sibilant.

F v: continuous—partial obstruction caused by the bottom lip and the top front teeth as they come together to restrict the outward passage of air. These two sounds are also fricatives, the first unvoiced, the second voiced.

L: voiced and continuous—partial obstruction caused by the tip of the tongue in firm contact with the hard palate just behind the (alveolar) tooth ridge. In the making of this sound, the air moves around the sides of the tongue, which is why the sound is referred to as a *lateral* consonant. Some elocutionists make a distinction between a light (or clear) *l* and a dark *l.* The light *l* has a higher resonance and a cleaner, more forward quality, and is heard at the beginning of words and before vowels, as in the words *light, letter, line, look, flute, delight.* The dark *l* has a deeper resonance and does not appear to be produced so forward in the mouth. Though the tongue tip retains the same position as in the light *l,* the body of the tongue is lowered a bit so that the mouth cavity behind the tongue becomes larger, thus amplifying the sound more and giving it a deeper resonance. The dark *l* can be heard in words *kill, peril, rule, peal, silk, bells.* You can hear both *l* sounds in words such as *label, legal,* and *liberal.*

R: voiced and continuous—partial obstruction caused by the tongue tip curling up towards the hard palate, the air passing between them. There are two kinds of *r's:* the short tapped (or flapped) *r,* made when the tongue darts up to the hard plate and touches it lightly, and the trilled (or rolled) *r,* made when the tongue produces a succession of rapid taps against the hard palate (alveolar ridge), vibrating against it. The trilled *r's* can be heard in the northern English dialects and in the Scottish language.

M: voiced and continuous. Though there is complete obstruction of the outgoing breath by the closed lips, the soft palate lowers to permit the breath to escape through the nose, giving the sound a distinct nasal resonance.

N: voiced and continuous. The mouth is open, but with the air exit blocked by the tongue, which is raised up against the hard palate. The soft palate is lowered to permit the air to come out through the nose as for the *m* sound.

Ng (as in sing): voiced and continuous. The mouth is open, but the air exit is blocked by the back of the tongue rising to meet the lowered soft palate so that the air is directed out through the nose as in *m* and *n.* Because of their nasal resonance and forced exhalation of air out through the nose, all three sounds, *m, n,* and *ng,* have their own special category as *nasal* consonants. They are sometimes referred to as the musical consonants.

H: voiceless and continuous. This sound is made by the breath brushing through the vocal cords and then up against the sides of the open throat and mouth as it rushes out. It is the softest and breathiest consonant. Though classified as continuous, it cannot be sustained for long because so much breath is used to make the sound.

W: voiced and continuous. In forming this consonant, there are two simultaneous obstructions: a front obstruction caused by the rounding of the lips in the shape of a tight circle and a back obstruction between the soft palate and the back of the tongue. Once the lips are opened, the voiced breath flows out freely.

Hw (written as *wh*, as in *what*): breathed and continuous. Similar in formation to the voiced *w*, but prefixed by an *h* sound made by air rushing out through the rounded and almost closed lips. For the little children, I call this consonant the magic dust letter, because in order to make the sound, we have to blow a large volume of air (magic dust) through it.

Y: voiced and continuous. The sound is made by the front of the tongue rising up towards the hard palate, which acts to partially restrict the outgoing breath. Some speech teachers consider the *y* sound a semi-vowel because the tongue is very near the position for the formation of the *ee* vowel. You only have to raise the tongue a tiny bit more against the hard palate and the *ee* becomes a *y*.

Note: The x consonant is generally not phonetically represented because it consists of the combination of *k* and *s*. As such, it can be classified as a continuous, unvoiced fricative.

As you can see, there are twice as many voiced consonants than unvoiced ones in our alphabet. The voiced consonants carry better and are more musical in quality. When we deliver our lines onstage, it is important to articulate the unvoiced consonants with an extra force of effort so that the audience can hear every letter of every word we speak—especially those that contain the soft, breathy consonants.

EXERCISE 10-16 Making Consonants

- As a group, students read out loud the word listed in the left column of the handout, followed by the consonant sound in the right column that matches the first letter of that word. The consonant should be said as it is phonetically sounded—that is, as it is actually spoken—rather than how we pronounce it in its letter form. For example, the students read out loud the word *bat* and then sound out the consonant *b,* rather than say the letter *"bee."* Consciously feel the specific organs of speech coming together to produce each different consonant.

- Alternatively, the director can have each student say one word in the list, starting at the top and following down the list in order.

- After every student has had a turn sounding out loud at least one word and its corresponding consonant, the director can ask the students to explain how each of the consonant sounds is made, beginning with the first one at the top of the list. Normally, those students who studied that particular consonant in their small group will know the answer.

Classifying Vowel Sounds

In our English speech, twenty-one vowel sounds have been officially recognized and four extras considered possible vowels. Though there are as many classifications of vowels as there are speech authorities, a common classification is as follows:

Monothongs (also called simple vowels) are vowels with one sound only. There are twelve monothongs, which are subdivided into short or long.

Short monothongs are: *a* (as in *bat*), *e* (as in *bet*), *i* (as in *bit*), *o* (as in *dot*), *u* (as in *cut*), and the neutral vowel *e* (pronounced *uh* as in *about*), which is the shortened form of the longer *ur* sound (as in *hurt*).

Long monothongs are: *oo* (as in *hoot*), *oo* (as in *book*), *aw* (as in *awe*), *ah* (as in *lark*), *ur* (as in *hurt*), and *ee* (as in *he*).

The phonetic symbol for the neutral vowel is an *e* written backwards. (If the students have trouble describing the difference between the shortened neutral *uh* and the longer *ur* sound, they can simply refer to the neutral vowel as the "backward e" sound.) The neutral vowel can be placed anywhere in words, at the beginning (such as *a*board), in the middle (such as met*a*phor), or at the end (such as th*e* or butt*er*). Since British-speaking people do not pronounce the *r* sound when it is placed in the middle of words following a vowel (such as hea*r*t), or at the end of words (such as butte*r*), it is easier to hear the neutral vowel when spoken by an Englishman. Because Americans pronounce the *r* sound, the neutral vowel often ends up sounding like the longer *ur* sound. A sentence that helps you remember all the twelve monothongs is:

Do put thought on the mark. Thus can men learn with zeal.

Director's Notes: Students should always pronounce the word "the" with the short neutral monothong vowel *uh*. Only when it is immediately followed by a vowel, as in "the end" do we pronounce it with the longer *ee* vowel sound, as in *thee*.

Diphthongs (also called compound vowels) are made up of two simple vowels that blend into one sound. The diphthongs are: *oh* (as in go: o + u), *ow* (as in cow: a + oo), *ay* (as in bay: e + i), *oy* (as in boy: or/aw + i), *ie* (as in idle: u + i), *oor* (as in tour: oo + er), *air* (as in bear: e + ur), *ear* (as in fear: i + ur).

Note: In the British dialects, the second vowel in *bear* or *fear* is pronounced as the neutral *uh* instead of the long *ur*, as in America.

Triphthongs are vowels that contain three simple vowels that blend into one sound. There are two triphthongs: *our* (as in tower: ah + oo + ur) and *ire* (as in fire: u + i + ur).

Homework: Students make up their own sentence containing all twelve monothongs.

Vowel Expansion

Director's Notes: Distribute Handout Voice #3, *Vowel Expansion*. Read the guidelines below to the students, which are also printed on the handout, before you lead them in Exercise 10-17: Vowel Expansion.

Guidelines for teaching Exercise 10-17:

- Preset each consonant. Visualize the particular organs of speech coming together to stop the breath, then execute the contact vigorously. For example, if preparing the *Hah dah*, firmly press the tip of the tongue against the hard palate before releasing the breath to make *dah*. A strongly articulated *d* consonant is the springboard for a fully projected *ah* vowel.

- Follow the vowel through its course. Imagine you are standing on one side of a mountain gorge and you want to send the sound across to the other side in a high circular arc. It is the consonant that launches each vowel. Visualize the vowel traveling with the same trajectory as a rocket. Keep the mouth open and stretched so the vowel tone is fully expanded. The sound should be placed in the back of the throat, where it receives maximum resonance and can be launched effortlessly with no strain on the vocal cords. Apply the same practice to all the different vowels listed on the handout.

- Words are living sounds. Respect each letter in a word for each letter contributes to the full life of that word. Every word that is spoken is a cup of meaning, and sometimes a chalice of light and illumination. The release of that creative flame within each word depends upon the bold, controlled action of the lips, teeth, tongue, hard palate, and soft palate, as well as the breathing muscles.

EXERCISE 10-17 Vowel Expansion

Director's Notes: All the voice exercises can be performed sitting in chairs.

- Director leads students in the vowel expansion exercises beginning with the AH vowel. (Say, "Hah hah," and then direct the children to repeat it after you.)

- Director goes on to the next one, "Hah lah" with the students repeating.

- The class completes the list of six sounds before the director goes on to speak the adjacent sentences, followed by the students. (Take one sentence at a time with the students repeating each sentence. If you do not hear clearly enunciated consonants, correct them before you go on to the next group. Ask the students to circle every consonant on their handout. This will help them remember to articulate each consonant with strength.)

Common observations:

- Beginner students are not used to consciously working their speech organs. To help compensate for lazy habits, tell them to exaggerate the pressing together of the tongue and hard palate, or whatever organs of speech are involved in making the particular consonant sounds that go before the vowels in this exercise. The contact needs to be strong in order to push the vowel sound forward.

- The *f* and *v* consonants are weak because of the force required to push the air through the narrow opening. To compensate, the student needs to make the contact of the bottom lip and top front teeth extra firm.

- Make sure two words are not slurred together, as in saying *wanto* instead of *want to.*

- Make sure the students clearly articulate the *m, n,* and *ng* sounds that are sandwiched in the middle of words—for example, *and, angry, wind, pageant, brings, country.* Any *ng* sounds at the end of words, like *singing* and *ringing,* need to be held longer than other consonants. Make sure *ng* sounds do not end with a hard *g.*

- Don't forget to articulate the *d* and *t* consonants at the end of words—for example, *and, cried, that.*

- Remember to articulate the *l* sound at the end of words, such as in *ball, fall, wall*. This lateral consonant tends to fade away into nothingness.
- Any words that begin with *wh* need to be aspirated, as though blowing air through the sound.

EXERCISE 10-18 More Vowel Expansion

Director's Notes: Distribute Handout Voice #4, *More Vowel Expansion*. These drills and sentences are demanding and should not be attempted unless the students have achieved some degree of competence with the previous exercise.

EXERCISE 10-19 Crispy Consonants

Director's Notes: Distribute Handout Voice #5, *Crispy Consonants*. The students should separate each of the words cleanly and not merge the ending consonant of one word with the beginning consonant of the next word. For example, the *d* at the end of *dad* must be separate from the beginning *d* of the next *dad*.

EXERCISE 10-20 The Double Do's

Director's Notes: Distribute Handout Voice #6, *Double Do Consonants*.

A "double do" means that the same consonant ends one word and begins the next one. Go around the class and have each of the students repeat one of the double do word pairs. Make sure the double do consonant is cleanly separated.

EXERCISE 10-21 Tongue Twisters

Director's Notes: Distribute Handout Voice #7, *Tongue Twisters*. Do a few tongue twisters each week. Don't cover them all in one session.

Level One Action:

- Students separate into two sections—boys on one side of the room and girls on the other.

- Both groups together read aloud the same tongue twister from the handout. Then each group reads it separately.

- Without looking at the handout, each group, separately, repeats the tongue twister by memory.

- Director decides which group did the best job.

Level Two Action:

- Students form small groups and compose their own tongue twisters.

- Director gives a small prize for the best tongue twister and incorporates it as part of the weekly tongue twister exercises.

- Director may also assign this exercise as homework and have the students read aloud to the class the following week the tongue twister they made up at home. Once again, a prize can be given to the best one.

Stanislavski believed that vowels are carried out from us on "vocal waves." They should soar joyously as though rising from the actor "like a rocket." He decried the "insidious" vowel "which whirls out to drill its way into the person who hears it," and the "ponderous" vowel "which, like an iron weight sinks in to the bottom of one's wellsprings." He wanted his actors to acquire an "unbroken line of sound" that we normally associate with good singers. Without this "there can be no true art of the word." He spoke of this unbroken line lending a quality of beauty and music not only to common conversational speech but also and especially to the elevated poetry that is so much a part of great drama.

In his chapter titled Diction and Singing in *Building a Character,* he wrote:

> This unbroken line emerges only when the vowels and consonants ring of their own accord the way they do in singing. If only the vowel sounds are sustained, and the consonants merely bang along after them, all one gets is a chasm, a break, a vacuum; instead of an unbroken line one has sound shreds. I soon realized that not only the stop consonants but the others too—the sibilant, the whistling, the tinkling, the hushing and hawking, the raucous consonants must also participate in and contribute their reverberations and sounds to the creation of the unbroken line....

An actor, when he appears on the stage, should be fully armed and his voice is an important item in his creative implementation. Moreover, when you become professional actors a false self-esteem may prevent you from working like a pupil who is learning his alphabet....If you do not carry out this training now you will not do so in the future, and at all points in your creative career on the stage the lack of it will act as a brake on your work.

Every true artist has realized the same essential truth: you can best appreciate the beauty of language by experiencing it with a well-trained and well-executed voice.

KEY: Getting to the heart of the issue

> You cannot sing a song or play a sonata well and artistically if you do not first master your scales. Voice exercises are the basic scales in tuning and refining the musical instrument of your voice.

Simplified Explanation of Articulation for Little Children

Director's Notes: Prepare a sheet of paper for each of the children with all the letters of the alphabet written on it in large font. Pass this out to them before you start the class. Make sure the vowels are either typed in a different color or have something that distinguishes them from the consonants. The material provided below can be taught over several weeks, depending on your class time and the interest level of your littlest students. Remember that very young children learn by doing more than by listening to someone lecturing to them.

Today we are going to learn about articulation. Articulation is a big word, but it simply means that we speak all our words very clearly and loud enough so other people can hear and understand us.

Who knows how many letters there are in our English alphabet? *(Usually some child in your class will volunteer the correct answer.)* There are twenty-six letters. How many of you can say the alphabet all the way through? *(Usually at least half the class will raise their hands.)* Let's recite it together. *(You can also sing it.)* If you don't know it by memory, you can read the letters on the sheet of paper I handed out to you. If you can't read yet and don't know the alphabet by heart, you can just listen to the rest of us. *(Director leads the class in saying or singing the alphabet out loud.)*

These twenty-six letters make up two different kinds of speech sounds. Can anyone tell me the names of these two kinds of sounds? *(Though many children will know once you remind them, very few will know the names up front.)* The two speech sounds that make up the alphabet are vowels and consonants. There are five vowels *(read as letters)*: a, e, i, o, u. These are the letters that are colored in *(name color you chose to print the vowels in on the handout)* on your handout.

Now, if there are twenty-six letters in the alphabet, and five of those are vowels, who can tell me how many consonants there are? To find out the answer, you will have to do some math in your head, because you will have to subtract (or take away) five from twenty-six. Or, if you are good at adding up, you can look at your handout sheet and count up all the consonants. *(Usually at least one child will be able to work out the answer.)* There are twenty-one consonants.

Let's say out loud together the five vowels in the alphabet. This time, let's sound them out as we hear them spoken in words. For example, instead of saying the vowel letter A, we are going to sound it out as we hear it spoken in the word "bat." *(Lead the class in sounding out the five vowels: a (as in bat), e (as in bet), i (as in bit), o (as in dot), and u (as in cut).)* These are called short vowels. We can use the same vowel letters to make them into long vowels, such as *ah* (as in car), *ee* (as in bee), *oo* (as in moo), and *ur* (as in hurt). They are called long sounds because we can hold onto the sound for a long time, until we run out of breath. So you see that we can make lots of different vowel sounds out of the five original vowel letters of the alphabet.

Now let's say all the consonants in the alphabet, starting with the first one, which is *b*. We don't want to say the letter "bee," because that is not how a *b* consonant really sounds when we speak it in words. Let's recite all the consonants as we would speak them. If you choose, you can read them on your handout. *(Lead the class in reciting all the consonants phonetically: b, c, d, f, g, h, l, m, etc., to the end.)*

As you can see from reciting all the alphabet letters, the vowel sounds are very different from the consonants. That's because they are made differently inside our throat and mouth. There are certain parts of our mouth, like our lips, our teeth, and our tongue, that we could not do without—not just because we would look funny without them, but because they are needed to produce our speech sounds. They have a special name. They are called organs of speech.

The organs of speech are the lips, the tongue, the teeth, the hard palate, and the soft palate. They work closely together to help give the right shapes to the vowels and to create all the different consonant sounds. Because they are so important in forming our speech sounds, I want to make sure everyone knows where these organs of speech can be found inside the mouth and throat. *(Using some of the notes from above, point out where each organ of speech is located. Make sure the children don't try and stick their finger down their throats to feel the soft palate.)*

A vowel is a sound that passes out through our mouth without anything stopping it. It's as though the sound has a green light. *(Demonstrate by sounding an* AH *vowel.)* As you could see, the *ah* sound came up from the back of my throat and continued straight out through my open mouth. Nothing got in its way or made it stop. Did you also notice that my tongue was relaxed and low in the mouth? This was so it wouldn't get in the way. My lips were relaxed and normal, but my jaw was dropped. The lips and tongue will change their position a bit for each of the vowel sounds.

Who can tell me which vowel is sounded when we spread the lips wide like this *(demonstrate by spreading your lips as if saying the vowel* ee. *Normally one or two of the children will answer correctly).* You can see that the tongue and the lips help us to recognize the shape of the different vowel sounds, all of which have their own personality when they come up from the back of the throat. Let's say the five short vowel sounds again and see if we can describe what the lips are doing. *(Slowly say out loud each of the short vowel sounds phonetically.)*

A consonant is produced when the breath coming up from the throat is stopped by at least two organs of speech coming into contact with each other. In other words, the organs of speech act like a red light, stopping the breath right at the contact point where the organs of speech meet. Sometimes the breath is stopped completely, and other times some of the breath escapes. A consonant formed by the lips coming together and stopping the breath is *b*. Let's make that sound together *(lead students in doing so)*. Can everyone see how the lips press firmly together and stop the breath? Then, when we open the lips quickly, the air explodes with a bursting sound.

Can you think of another consonant that is formed the same way, with the lips closed tight? *(Usually several of the children will discover the* p *sound.)* That's right. The consonant *p* is another sound produced by the lips. But when the lips part, the sound is more popping than bursting. That's because the *p* is a quieter sound than *b*.

Let's make some other kinds of consonants. Let's make a *t* sound. Everyone take in a breath and press the tip of their tongue very hard against the area just behind the top teeth, so that the breath is stopped. When you suddenly lower the tongue, you create a crisp, clean *t* sound, like this *(demonstrate)*. We can use the same organs of speech to make the *d* sound, except that the *d* sound will be noisier than the *t*. Let's all make these two consonant sounds together. *(Lead them in forming both sounds—t and d.)*

The last consonant we will make today is the *m* sound. The *m* sound is special because it is one of the three musical consonants. The other two are *n,* as in the name Nancy (or use one of the children's names), and *ng,* as in the word *sing*. Who would like to try and make a *m* sound for me? *(You should get lots of volunteers.)* Now who can tell what organs of speech are involved in forming the *m* sound? *(Let the children answer.)* That's right, the two lips again. Though the closed lips stop the breath, the soft palate—that soft fleshy part of the roof of the mouth way in the back of your throat—drops down to allow the sound coming up from the vocal cords to escape.

Can anyone tell me where the voice escapes to? *(Again, there is normally one child who guesses correctly.)* That's correct. The sound (or voiced air) escapes through the nose. That is why the *m* sound, along with the *n* and *ng* sounds, are called nasal sounds. When the nose is blocked up, it is impossible to say *m, n,* and *ng* properly. You get the same effect if you hold your nose. Let's try saying the sentence, "I am speaking with a cold in my nose" while holding our nose with our thumb and forefinger acting like a clothespin: *(Lead the class in holding your nose and saying the sentence. It should sound something like* "I ab speakig with a cold id by doze.")

The *m* sound is different from the others we covered today because the sound can keep going. For that reason, it is called a continuous consonant. When you make the *m* sound, you can continue it until you run out of breath. Perhaps, when you go home, you can find other consonants on your list that are continuous. With continuous consonants, the breath escapes with the sound.

We don't have time in class to talk about all the consonants on your list (and some, like the *ng* sound, that are not on your list). Take the sheet home with you, and practice making different sounds in the mirror.

Director's Notes: You can choose other consonants from the complete list and either substitute them for the ones above or talk about a few different ones each week before the children do their voice exercises.

EXERCISE 10-22 Vowels and Consonants (For Little Children)

Director's Notes: Distribute Handouts Child's Voice #2, *Vowels and Consonants* and Child's Voice #4, *Magic Dust Letters* to children who are 3 to 7 years old.

- Lead the little ones in speaking the verses, exaggerating all the vowel sounds. Some of the lines, such as *Bow, wow, wow* and *Caw, caw, caw* should take on the voice character of the animals that make those sounds.

- Demonstrate to the class how to say the magic dust letters. Then have all the children speak the words and sentences with you. Remind them to speak the lines with expression. Have the children make up their own sentences containing the magic dust letters and use them in future classes.

E X E R C I S E 10-23 Tongue Twisters for Little Children

> *Director's Notes:* Distribute Handout Child's Voice #3, *Tongue Twisters (For Little Children).*

- Do a few tongue twisters each week. Don't cover them all in one session. If you have a sufficient number of children, you can divide the class up into two groups and have them compete with each other saying the tongue twisters. You can also invite them to make up their own tongue twister either in class or at home, and give a prize for the best one.

5. Expression

> *Director's Notes:* Any of the poetry or prose samples listed in this section that you want your students to read out loud in class should be typed out on a sheet of paper and given to the students before you include them in the lesson.

A good stage voice is preeminently natural. To achieve naturalness takes long, hard study and work. A natural voice is one that proves itself perfectly fit to do its job. This can only be achieved through proper schooling in breathing habits, phonation, resonance, and articulation. However, there is one other attribute that a voice must possess to qualify as artistically fit: expressiveness in interpretation and rendition.

The term *elocution* is a term that is used in English speech and drama schools to describe expressiveness. It refers to the imaginative use of all the interpretive elements of speech by which an actor draws out the drama and pathos and conveys it to his audience. It is said that no one can act or speak well who is not an elocutionist.

The interpretive elements of vocal expression are phrases and pauses, rhythm, rhyme, emphasis, inflection, pitch, intonation, atmosphere, modulation, speed, and climax. All these different components are utilized by the actor to bring meaning and vitality to his performance and to achieve his desired artistic rendering. Knowledge of these elements is as essential to a dramatist as an understanding of color and perspective is to a painter, or rhythm and harmony to a composer. Though it is not considered an element of expression, an understanding of dramatic genre can also be an important interpretive tool for the actor.

When used imaginatively and with skill, these elements can draw out the spirit of the piece, while producing a powerful emotional and spiritual effect on the listener.

Phrases and Pauses

A short passage of music that forms part of a longer piece is called a *phrase*—or group of musical sounds. The same grouping applies in speech. Quite naturally, words fall into groups or phrases irrespective of the punctuation (or stop) marks. A *phrase* is a group of words that communicates a unit of sense. The first rule in conveying meaning is to make it coherent. That is why when we speak, we naturally break up what we want to say into small, bite-size units that are more easily understood by an audience. Remember that a live audience does not know what we are going to say nor can they put us on instant rewind if they miss something.

We phrase our words in order to make what we are saying clear. That can only be accomplished by the careful use of the *pause* in prose, poetry, and drama as well as in ordinary conversation. The *Oxford Dictionary* defines pause as "an interval of inaction or silence." This definition does not mean that the pause is a wait; rather it is a purposeful, if not eloquent, silence. There are several types of pause:

a) *Breath pause* is a short stop in speech that allows a quick intake of breath. Good breath control reduces the number of breath pauses.

b) *Grammatical pause* is indicated by the punctuation marks (or stops). The structure of a sentence demands certain pauses, which provide both an opportunity for breath and the means for deciding the relationship of the words to one another.

c) *Rhetorical or phrase pause* is a natural pause, unmarked by punctuation, and introduced into the reading of a line by its phrasing or syntax. Rhetorical pauses are most often used in carefully prepared speechmaking or dramatic performance. The words are delivered in well-defined groups that constitute clear units of meaning. A rhetorical pause is usually short, but definite in its effect. An oft-used example is:

> I tell you / there are many people / who fail miserably / because they think
> it easier to find fault / than to do the work / which lies before them.

These *phrase pauses* are sometimes in conflict with the punctuation of the written word. Don't be led by punctuation in phrasing your delivery, because punctuation is generally intended to aid those who are reading silently and is not placed with the intention to explain or communicate the meaning to a listening audience. Punctuation in the written word is a sufficient guide for the reader, not the performer. As a speaker and as a dramatist of the written word, the actor will usually need to add more pauses than those indicated by the period, comma, and other grammatical marks.

E X E R C I S E 10-24 The Phrase Pause For Dramatic Speaking

- One or two of the students read the following excerpt from Joseph Addison's *Spectator, No. 112* following the grammatical punctuation guides indicated.

  > I am always very well pleased with a country Sunday; and think, if keeping holy the seventh day were only a human institution, it would be the best method that could have been thought of for the polishing and civilizing of mankind.

- Another one or two students read the same passage but with the following additional phrase marks applied. In actual performance, these phrases are more mental than physical and would not be spoken to sound like train stops. The slashes indicate where the pauses are to be observed by the speaker:

  > I am always very well pleased with a country Sunday; / and think, / if keeping holy the seventh day / were only a human institution, / it would be the best method / that could have been thought of / for the polishing / and civilizing / of mankind. //

One line of dialogue generally contains several phrase pauses. The audience needs more time than a reader does to assimilate not only the story content, but also something about the character who is speaking those lines. The actor needs to phrase his words in expressive units of meaning or he will lose his listener's interest. This is especially so if an actor has to dramatize dry and didactic prose like the excerpt above!

d) *Caesura or sense pause.* This is a natural pause or break in a line of poetry, which may or may not be determined by punctuation. The sense pause is similar to the phrase pause used in prose. Its use depends on meaning and on the interpretation of the reader. Examples of this kind of pause are:

   > How do I love thee? / Let me count the ways.
   > —*Sonnet 43 From the Portuguese* (Elizabeth Barrett Browning)

   > Offend her / and she knows not to forgive.
   > Oblige her / and she'll hate you while you live.
   > —*To a Lady* (Alexander Pope)

e) *Emphatic or dramatic pause*. In order to impress a particular word more forcibly on the listener, we may pause either *before* or right *after* the word or both. This kind of pause is subjectively determined. Dramatic speeches are deeply meaningful to the speaker and to the person addressed. Therefore, emphatic pausing is used to draw from the spoken lines their intended power, poignancy, and climax. Some common examples are:

> O, pardon me, thou bleeding piece of earth,
> That I am meek and gentle with these / *butchers!*
> —*Julius Caesar*, Act 3, Scene 1

> And Nathan said to David, / *Thou* / art the man.
> —*2 Samuel*, xii, 7

Emphatic pauses are dictated by the rhythm of the speech in dramatic verse, as in the example from *Julius Caesar*. Rhythm is the smooth barge upon which the individual sense units in speech are conveyed. A pause must contribute to and not distract from the coherence of a speech. An actor's pause must be a temporary stop while allowing mental and emotional continuity so that the dramatic atmosphere is sustained.

Rhythm

We talk of dance bands keeping rhythm or we refer to the rhythmical lilt of an express train traveling at full speed. What do we mean? In the dance band, a drum or guitar beats out a regular time. The wheels of the express train beat upon the gaps in the rails, and because the gaps occur at regular intervals, the beats are also regular.

Rhythm is present in nearly everything we do in our daily lives. When we walk, we walk to a rhythm, unconsciously. When we sing or dance, we do so to a set rhythm. We hear and recognize rhythm in music by the speed of the metronome as it measures the tempo or regularity of the beat from andante to presto. Based on such regularity, a whole symphony of sound in perfect order can be created. This is not the case with the voice, because voice is dynamic—its rhythm constantly changing in response to emotional nuance. While the musician relies primarily on the set rhythm to convey the imaginative mood of his work, the actor's use of rhythm is infinitely more subtle. It is incumbent upon him therefore to study every aspect of this element of expression so that he can apply it skillfully in creating the right tempo and proper atmosphere for his character, and thus hold the audience's attention.

Regularity is the key to rhythm. In poetic verse we have a beat that recurs regularly. That is the rhythm. Rhythm refers to the ordered and regular recurrence of strong and weak beats in the natural flow of speech.

The word *rhythm* is derived from a Greek word meaning *beat* or *stroke*. When we recite verse, we find heavy and light stresses, which make up the rhythm. These stresses are the basis of meter. Meter is derived from the Greek word meaning *measure*. We can measure lines of poetry into what are called "feet" after first marking heavy and light stresses. There are four main rhythmic feet in English verse:

IAMBUS (Iambic): Each foot contains a non stress (short) syllable followed by a stress (long) syllable. A two-syllable pattern (of a non stress followed by a stress) is called an *iamb*. There are five iambs in the first two examples below and four iambs in the line from Marlowe's poem:

> If mú/sic bé/the fóod/of lóve,/play ón./
> —*Twelfth Night* (Shakespeare)

> That tíme/of yéar/thou máyst/in mé/behóld,/
> —*Sonnet 73* (Shakespeare)

> Come líve/with mé,/and bé/my lóve./
> —*The Passionate Shepherd to His Love* (Christopher Marlowe)

TROCHEE (Trochaic): Each foot contains a (long) stress syllable followed by a (short) non stress:

> Thén the/líttle/Hía/wátha/
> Léarned of/évery/bírd its/lánguage./
> —*The Song of Hiawatha* (Henry W. Longfellow)

Iambic and trochaic verse seem to roll 'trippingly off the tongue,' giving us a sense of ease, familiarity, and uplift as we are carried along by the internal momentum of the rolling beat. These two metric patterns also have a gentling effect, which is probably why most devotional hymns and poems are written in these two rhythms. The first two examples below are strictly iambic. The last two examples are trochaic, with variations in the final feet:

> Should áuld/acquáin/tance bé/forgót,/
> And né/ver bróught/to mínd?/
> Should áuld/acquáin/tance bé/forgót,/
> And dáys/of áuld/lang sýne.//
>
> —*Auld Lang Syne* (Robert Burns)

Be yóu/to óth/ers kínd/and trúe,/
As yóu'd/have óth/ers bé/to yóu./
—*Our Saviour's Golden Rule* (Dr. Isaac Watts)

Hé is/méek, and/Hé is/míld,/
Hé be/cáme a/líttle/chíld./
—*The Lamb* (William Blake)

Húsh, my/déar! lie/stíll, and/slúmber,/
Hóly/ángels/gúard thy/béd!/
—Hymn: *The Cradle Hymn* (Dr. Isaac Watts)

Poets do not normally write in one strict rhythm pattern for a whole poem, though Longfellow's *Song of Hiawatha* is striking for its trochaic consistency throughout.

DACTYL (Dactylic): Each foot contains a (long) stress syllable followed by two (short) non stresses. In rhythmic terms, the two short syllables are equivalent in tempo to the long syllable, just as in music two eighth notes equal one quarter note. This rhythm matches the waltz beat in dancing, and is used by poets to create a sense of flowing grandeur and space, and of high aspiration. Three examples of this rhythm are:

Wé that had/lóved him so,/fóllowed him,/hónoured him,/
—*The Lost Reader* (Robert Browning)

Thís is the/fórest pri/méval. The/múrmuring/pínes and the/hémlocks,/
—*Evangeline* (Henry W. Longfellow)

Práy but one/práyer for me/twíxt thy closed/líps,/
Thínk but one/thóught of me/úp in the/stárs./
— Sonnet: *Summer Dawn* (William Morris)

In the last example, the poet has a stressed syllable left over at the end of each line, which contributes a lyrical continuity of his loving thought. In the example from *Evangeline*, the first five feet of the line are dactyls, and the sixth is a trochee, though it can be spoken as a spondee (see below) with two equally stressed syllables on the word "hémlócks" for more dramatic effect. Similarly, the last foot of the *Auld Lang Syne* verse (quoted under the heading of Trochee) can also end with a spondee, with two equal stresses on the words, "láng sýne."

ANAPEST/ANAPAEST (Anapestic): Each foot contains two non stresses followed by a stress:

> And the shéen/of their spéars/was like stárs/on the séa,/
> When the blúe/wave rolls níght/ly on déep/Galilée./
> —*The Destruction of the Sennacherib* (Lord Byron)

> Twas the níght/before Chríst/mas, when áll/through the hóuse/
> Not a créa/ture was stír/ring, not é/ven a móuse./
> —*Twas the Night Before Christmas* (Clement Clarke Moore)

> Oh! yóung/Lochinvár/is come óut/of the wést,/
> Through áll/the wide Bór/der his stéed/was the bést;/
> And sáve/his good bróad/sword he wéa/pons had nóne,/
> He róde/all unármed/and he róde/all alóne./
> So fáith/ful in lóve/and so dáunt/less in wár,/
> There né/ver was kníght/like the yóung/Lochinvár.
> —*Lochinvar*, Canto V of *Marmion* (Sir Walter Scott)

In *Marmion,* we see a pattern of one iambic foot that opens every line of verse, followed by three anapest feet.

In addition to the four main *feet* described above, there are two other less frequently used feet, *spondee* and *pyrrhic*. The spondee is a two-syllable foot with two equally stressed accents—for example, rólls-róyce, bréad bóx, páncáke. An example found in poetry is:

> Whíte fóunts/ fálling/ in the cóurts/ of the sún/
> —*Lepanto* (G. K. Chesterton)

In the example above, the poem is mainly written in anapest rhythm. The first foot in the line replaces the anapest with a spondee (Whíte fóunts) while the second foot replaces the anapest with a trochee (fálling). The third and fourth feet are anapest. As we notice with this and earlier examples, using two or more stressed syllables in a row (spondaic meter) breaks the rhythm of the verse and requires the speaker to slow down. This forced pause adds an emotional emphasis, even profundity to the phrase.

A *pyrrhic* foot consists of two syllables, both unaccented. In the following example, a pyrrhic foot is followed by a spondee. This is also referred to as a "double iamb" consisting of two unstressed syllables followed by two stressed syllables—that is, a pyrrhic foot followed by a spondee.

> in the/rólls-róyce
> as he/lóved Gód

While one poetical foot generally contains two to three syllables, a line of poetry may contain from one to eight feet. These are respectively termed:

> monometer (one foot)
> dimeter (two feet)
> trimeter (three feet)
> tetrameter (four feet)
> pentameter (five feet)
> hexameter (six feet)
> heptameter (seven feet)
> octometer (eight feet)

Shakespeare wrote his plays mostly in iambic pentameter (five iambs per line)—for example:

> And hé/that thróws/not úp/his cáp/for jóy/
> Shall fór/the fáult/make fór/feit óf/his héad./
> —*Henry VI*

> The qúa/li/tý/of mér/cy ís/not stráin'd./
> It dró/ppeth ás/a gén/tle ráin/from héaven/
> —*The Merchant of Venice*

> But sóft!/What líght/through yón/der wín/dow bréaks?/
> —*Romeo and Juliet*

> A hórse!/A hórse!/My kíng/dom fór/a hórse!//
> —*Richard III*

Iambic pentameter is the most common meter in English poetry. In addition to the Shakespearean plays, we also find it in Milton's *Paradise Lost,* Spencer's *Faerie Queen,* Tennyson's *The Idylls of the King,* as well as in most of the longer poems of Pope, Keats, Shelley, Wordsworth, and Browning. Sonnets are made up of iambic pentameter lines, with some variations. The stately dactylic hexameter (four feet containing three syllables each) is the common meter for the Greek and Latin epics such as Homer's *Iliad* and the *Odyssey.* Longfellow wrote *Evangeline* in dactylic hexameter. Of course, we do not beat out the metric rhythm like a metronome marking every stressed syllable; we simply blend it in with the other elements of expression.

Rhyme

Rhyme goes hand in hand with rhythm. There are three principal kinds of rhyme:

Head rhyme (or *alliteration*) is the repetition of the same consonant at the beginning of each stressed word in a line of verse. The most common examples are tongue twisters, such as:

*R*ound the *r*ugged *r*ock the *r*agged *r*ascal *r*an. (Repetition of *r*)

Shakespeare parodies alliteration in Peter Quince's Prologue to the Pyramus and Thisbe play in *A Midsummer Night's Dream:*

Whereat, with *b*lade, with *b*loody *b*lameful *b*lade,
He *b*ravely *b*reach'd his *b*oiling *b*loody *b*reast. (Repetition of *b*)

An example of a poem that uses head rhyme is *Pied Beauty* by Gerard Manley Hopkins. Its use helps to express the poet's joyful love for God's creation:

*G*lory be to *G*od for dappled things—
For skies of *c*ouple-*c*olour as a brinded *c*ow;

Middle rhyme: The word in the center of the line rhymes with the word at the end of the line. Coleridge's *The Rime of the Ancient Mariner* provides a splendid example:

The fair breeze *blew*, the white foam *flew*
The furrow stream'd off free
We were the *first* that ever *burst*
Into that silent sea.

End rhyme is the repetition of the same vowel sound at the end of mainly successive or alternating lines of poetry. The last word at the end of each verse is the word that rhymes—for example:

Rhyme, the rack of finest *wits,*
That expresseth but by *fits.*
                    —*A Fit of Rhyme Against Rhyme* (Ben Jonson)

Of all the waltzes the great Strauss *wrote,*
Mad with melody, rhythm—***rife***
From the very first to the final *note,*
Give me his "Artist's ***Life!***"
                    —*Artist's Life* (Ella Wheeler Wilcox)

EXERCISE 10-25 Rhythm and Rhyme in Poetry

- Ask one or two students to speak the following verses out loud from the poem *Paul Revere's Ride* by Henry Wadsworth Longfellow:

> A hurry of hoofs in a village street,
> A shape in the moonlight, a bulk in the dark,
> And beneath, from the pebbles, in passing, a spark
> Struck out by a steed flying fearless and fleet;
> That was all! And yet, through the gloom and the light,
> The fate of a nation was riding that night.
>
> So through the night rode Paul Revere;
> And so through the night went his cry of alarm
> To every Middlesex village and farm,—
> A cry of defiance, and not of fear,
> A voice in the darkness, a knock at the door,
> And a word that shall echo for evermore!

- Ask the rest of the children to describe the rhyme and rhythm that they experienced while listening to the recitation. (The tempo is vigorous and rollicking, fitting the action of Paul Revere riding at a break-neck pace on his horse to spread the alarm that "the British are coming." The end rhyme helps to convey the emotional excitement and determination of the Americans to stop the British.)

- Ask the same student/s to speak the verse again, but with the following changes:

> A hurry of hoofs in a village street,
> A shape in the moonlight, a bulk in the dark,
> And beneath, in passing, a spark from the pebbles,
> Struck out by a steed flying fearless and fleet;
> That was all! And yet, through the light and the gloom,
> The fate of a nation was riding that night.
>
> So through the night rode Paul Revere;
> And so went his cry of alarm through the night,
> To every Middlesex village and farm,—
> A cry of fear, and not of defiance,
> A knock at the door, a voice in the darkness,
> And a word that for evermore shall echo!

- Ask the other children if they experienced something different this second time. (The students can see that the changing of the order of the words changes the rhyme, and thus completely destroys the rollicking tempo and the steady building of the emotional excitement and high purpose of the midnight ride.)
- Ask one of the students to read the following verses from Alfred Lord Tennyson's famous poem *The Charge of the Light Brigade:*

> Forward the Light Brigade!
> Was there a man dismayed?
> Not though the soldier knew
> Someone had blundered:
> Theirs not to make reply,
> Theirs not to reason why,
> Theirs but to do and die:
> Into the valley of Death
> Rode the six hundred.

- Ask the other students to describe the rhythm and the feeling conveyed by it. (The ordered tempo of the soldier trotting on his horse into the face of certain death becomes apparent by the steady, deliberate rhythm of the dactylic dimeter—two feet of one long stress followed by two short stresses. The variation of this meter in the last foot of the final two lines conveys the solemnity of sacrifice of these noble six hundred.
- Have one of the younger children speak out loud the following verse taken from Charles Wesley's sacred hymn/poem, *Gentle Jesus, Meek and Mild.* (The director may wish to recite each line first and have the child imitate her if the child cannot read.)

> Gentle Jesus, meek and mild,
> Look upon a little child;
> Pity my simplicity,
> Suffer me to come to thee.
>
> Loving Jesus, gentle Lamb,
> In thy gracious hands I am;
> Make me, Savior, what thou art,
> Live thyself within my heart.

Director's Notes: This is a perfect devotional piece for the little ones to read or speak out loud. The sweet and ordered flow of the trochaic tetrameter (with each fourth foot a variation of a stressed syllable) combines with the pure and exquisite simplicity of the images to create very moving and inspiring verse.

Emphasis

Emphasis is the added measure of stress or prominence given to a certain word or words in order to obtain a special effect. Emphasis also refers to the added stress or prominence given to individual syllables in order to give a particular meaning or pronunciation. Emphasis comes from the Greek word *emphaino*, meaning "I make clear." There are two kinds of emphasis: sense emphasis and emotional emphasis. Emphasis used to convey a particular meaning is known as *sense* emphasis. Consider the following sentences. According to the meaning intended, we may place our emphasis on any one of the words in the sentence and convey a different meaning:

Sentence: Shall we walk through this forest?

Interpretation	*Implied Meaning*
Shall we walk through this forest?	(Do you think we should?)
Shall *we* walk through this forest?	(Rather than someone else)
Shall we *walk* through this forest?	(Walk, not run or crawl)
Shall we walk *through* this forest?	(Rather than around it)
Shall we walk through *this* forest?	(Not the one with the waterfall)
Shall we walk through this *forest?*	(And risk running into a bear!)

In normal speech, we adjust the stress in our sentences without any conscious effort, since the meaning and intent is usually understood. However, in its artistic application, emphasis is greatly governed by the emotional state of the speaker as well as by the dramatic events of the story. We call this *emotional* or *dramatic emphasis*.

> What a *terrible* accident!
> How could I *know* what he'd do!
> Will he ever *forgive* me?
> Help *finally!*

As the speaker, therefore, you need to be responsive not only to the obvious meaning of the words being spoken, but also to the full range of emotions (and their powerful or subtle intensities) that the author wants you to convey. The following passage from Sir Walter Scott's *Marmion* is an excellent example:

The war, that for a space did fail,
Now trebly thundering swell'd the gale,
And *Stanley!* was the cry–
A light on Marmion's visage spread,
And fired his glazing eye:
With dying hand above his head,
He shook the fragment of his blade,
And shouted *"Victory!*
Charge, Chester, *Charge! On*, Stanley, *on!"*
Were the last words of Marmion.
                    —*Marmion*, Canto VI (Sir Walter Scott)

We can see from the excerpt above as well as in the examples given earlier under the heading of *Emphatic pause* that it is not merely the emphasis placed on a particular word that creates the dramatic appeal, but its combined use with the emphatic pause. By isolating the critical word, the emphatic pause increases the meaningfulness of those words and amplifies the speaker's inner feelings. In normal conversation, our speech is brightened considerably when we use emphasis (if only unconsciously). On the stage, the actor needs to apply it consciously and with artistic skill, in combination with the other elements of expression, if he wants his dialogue to carry with bold, dramatic relief.

In choosing ways to achieve emphasis, the actor's own instincts and interpretive sense are his best guide. Just as a good singer tries to render the song as the composer wrote it, a good actor tries to deliver his lines as he thinks the writer "felt" the line. In his book *The Art of Speech*, H. W. Traynor makes the point that truly great writers build their emphasis into the poetic life of the verse itself, and thus leave it to you, the actor, to easily interpret their intentions—for example:

Sweet Portia,
If you did know to whom I gave the ring,
If you did know for whom I gave the ring,
And would conceive for what I gave the ring,
And how unwillingly I left the ring,
When nought would be accepted but the ring,
You would abate the strength of your displeasure.
                    —*Merchant of Venice* (Shakespeare)

When I was a child, I spake as a child, I understood as a child, I thought as a child: but when I became a man, I put away childish things. And now abideth faith, hope, charity, these three: but the greatest of these is charity.
                    —*I Corinthians 13*

Inflection

Inflection refers to the rise and fall of the pitch of the voice over a word or syllable. Inflection may be either simple (that is, with a single upward or downward glide of the voice) or it may be compound (with one or more upward and downward glides on a single word or syllable). Simple inflections imply straightforward utterance, the rising inflection indicating lack of conclusion and the falling inflection indicating finality. For example, a genuine question always ends with a rising inflection, while the reply is spoken on a falling inflection, indicating resolution, as in the first line:

"Are you leaving now?"........."Yes."

"Are you leaving now?"........."Yes."

A compound inflection is employed to express a more subtle meaning. It can convey indecision, irony, sarcasm, or scorn. In the second line above, the "yes" has a compound inflection—that is, a combination of a falling, followed by a rising inflection on the vowel *e*, in which case the speaker would mean to say, "Yes, but I'm really not sure if it's a good idea." We apply a compound inflection as one continuous intonation of the voice, much like a swimmer dives down into a pool and rises back up to the surface—all in one uninterrupted motion. The effective use of inflection in public speaking and acting lifts the voice out of prosaic flatness and imbues it with a musical quality and lyricism. A voice is not flexible and pleasing to listen to if it cannot demonstrate some level of control in the rising and falling of the tones.

E X E R C I S E 10-26 Change the Inflection, Change the Meaning

- Speak the word "mother" using different inflections in response to the situations described below, so that the students practice different interpretations of the meaning of the word.

  a) Your mother has just arrived home unexpectedly.
  b) Your mother has just told you that you are grounded for a week.
  c) Your mother has just arrived home when it was thought that she was stranded in a dangerous snowstorm.
  d) Your mother has just caught you in an embarrassing situation that is hard for you to explain.
  e) Your mother has just accomplished something extraordinary.
  f) Your mother's arrival has just meant your deliverance.
  g) Your mother has just embarrassed you in front of your new friend.

E X E R C I S E 10-27 Inflection Drills

Director's Notes: Distribute Handout Voice #8, *Inflection Exercises.* Some students do not have an innate sense of the rise and fall of their voices. In other words, they have no ear when it comes to hearing the musical pattern of their own speech. Repetition is the key to faithfully reproducing proper inflection. This exercise promotes ear-training, which is necessary to detect the many variations of speech tunes—that is, the intonation of a language.

- Individual students read through one or two of the inflection drills, each student having a turn.

Pitch and Intonation

Pitch is the level of the voice as it rises and falls. Though defined by the frequency of vibrations of the vocal cords, pitch is determined by the content of what is being spoken and the feeling of the speaker. In ordinary conversation, we all tend to talk in about the middle of our vocal range. We respond to pitch unconsciously. When we become excited or angry, the pitch rises, while any sad or solemn emotion is associated with a lower pitch. It is essential, however, that the actor be in full command of his stage voice and not allow his emotions to carry his speech either above or below his optimal pitch range. An actor may also have to modify his pitch based on the acoustic conditions of the theater or auditorium in which he is performing. The pitch he adjusts to must have carrying power.

Intonation refers to the musical rising and falling of the pitch of the voice during speech. We might call intonation the melody of speech. Each language and dialect has its own intonation. One of the great challenges of being an actor is to speak different dialects or foreign accents. The best way to master another language, so that we sound authentic when trying to speak it, is to faithfully reproduce its speech tunes. It helps to have a good ear in order to detect the various combinations of rising and falling intonations on individual syllables.

The English language has several basic speech tunes:

> a) a rising intonation when the pitch rises,
> b) a falling intonation when the pitch falls,
> c) a level intonation when the pitch does not change.

These can be combined to create many variations, depending on the meaning or emotion of the speaker. A change of tune will often bring a change of meaning.

Take the following sentence:

What is the time?

When I speak these words, ending with a rising intonation, my listeners recognize from my speech tune that I have asked a simple question. If, however, I change my tune to a falling intonation, there is now an underlying tension suggested.

What is the time?

In the example above, an imminent threat can be implied, as though time is running out, and there will soon be trouble.

The intonation pattern concentrates on the rise or fall required for the word, which gives the key to the meaning. Intonation is used in conjunction with emphasis. There is always a pitch rise or fall on a word that you decide will convey your meaning best. The meanings of words are always compounded by sensitive and subtle intonation.

For an actor to take on a comedic role and a foreign accent as part of that role, is a major undertaking. Few artists are capable of sustaining the intricate speech tunes of their character's nationality as well as render the comic intent of the lines with perfect timing. Peter Sellers and Alec Guinness are two of these rare masters.

Atmosphere

Atmosphere is of supreme importance to interpretation. It begins with a knowledge of the context of the scene, a full understanding of the storyline of the play, followed by a sensitive perception of the mood and emotions of the character speaking.

E X E R C I S E 10-28 Atmosphere and Mood

- Three children read the sample text that follows, each in one of these three different ways:

    1. Imagine that the lady is on her way to the church to be married.

    2. Imagine that she is leaving her family and home for the first time to do volunteer medical or missionary work for an indeterminate time in a third world country that is in severe social and political turmoil.

    3. Imagine that she is on her way to prison.

Sample Text:

> The road was familiar to her, but she had never expected to travel it under the circumstances in which she now found herself. Her wildest dreams had failed to picture anything like what was happening to her now. The man by her side seemed to be unmoved by such external circumstances, being intent only on escorting her to her destination. Question after question surged through her mind: Was she ready to embrace what was before her? What would the future be? How could she face it away from all she loved, or all who had loved her? When would she see home again? But, suddenly, all questioning ceased. The car slowed to a standstill; the door opened. With every nerve quivering, she stepped out and walked up the concrete steps, through the open gateway...and into a new world!

Still other elements that influence expressiveness come into play during performance. These include speed (or pace of delivery), change in volume, tone color (whether warm, tender, hard, cold, brittle, etc.), modulation, and the use of climax—or the progressive build-up of dramatic intensity. The purpose of all these elements of expression is to search out and render the inner content of the dialogue being spoken. Together they can create a montage of color, lyricism, and dramatic power in the voice. They are all governed by understanding and feeling rather than by objective laws of physiology, as in the case of breathing, phonation, resonance, and articulation.

Sometimes it takes but the merest change of an inflection, a pause, or subtle emphasis in a word to arouse one or all of the five senses in the audience—resurrecting the aural and visual images, tastes, smells, or tactile sensations suggested by that single word. As Stanislavski wrote, "There should never be any soulless or feelingless words used on the stage....On the stage it is the part [function] of the word to arouse all sorts of feelings, desires, thoughts, inner images, visual, auditory and other sensations in the actor, in those playing opposite him and through them together in the audience." Such is the power and magic of the spoken word when rendered expressively and with accomplished technique.

A play text can be made vivid and meaningful by the imagination of a reader, but it cannot take on a life of its own until the actor infuses it with his own dramatic expressiveness. The essence of a script cannot be felt in all its cathartic power without the artistic execution of the actor. The same can be said of a musical score. It is not a living work of art until it is played by the musicians who make up the orchestra. As soon as the actor, singer, or musician breathes the life of his own artistry into the performance piece, its spiritual well-spring is released into the hearts of his audience. That is the alchemy that awaits the true artist—the opportunity to use all the resources of his craft to make magic.

Stanislavski wrote in *Building a Character*:

> It is only on the stage that a drama can be revealed in all its fullness and significance. Only in a performance can we feel the true spirit which animates a play and its subtext—this is recreated, and conveyed by the actors every time the play is given.
>
> It is up to the actor to compose the music of his feelings to the text of his part and learn how to sing those feelings in words. When we hear the melody of a living soul we then, and only then, can come to a full appreciation of the worth and beauty of the lines and of all that they hold concealed.

No one element of vocal expression is used in isolation. The trained actor blends them as his intuition directs to best convey the meaning he intends. Vitality, penetration, subtlety, charm, and conviction are the direct benefits of expressiveness.

KEY: Getting to the heart of the issue

 The different elements of expression are like the colors on a painter's palette. The actor can mix and match them to create exactly what he wants his audience to see and feel.

Understanding the Genre

Though not considered one of the elements of expressiveness, understanding the genre of the play you are performing helps you to comprehend how the playwright imagined his work to be. Genre is a French word meaning "kind" or "type." Used in drama, it refers to categories that plays can be divided into based on the writer's point of view towards his subject. That point of view will then determine the form of his work, the type of characterization, and the nature of the dialogue. We should be familiar with the different genres and the special demands they make upon interpretation and rendition for performance. Though there are genres of literature, such as poetry and prose, with their sub-categories of epic, lyric, novel, short story, etc., we will just consider the genres of drama. Drama, like prose and poetry, is a form of literature. Unlike prose or poetry, however, it is always acted out by performers.

There are two chief genres of drama: tragedy and comedy—both of which are characteristically represented in the classic drama mask. These two genres were first created in Greece in fifth century B.C. The essential difference between the two is that in a tragedy, the protagonist (or hero) suffers a tragic end, while in a comedy, the protagonist overcomes all obstacles and attains his heart's desire.

Tragedy deals with the serious or solemn issues of life—issues of social, political, religious, or grave personal significance. A tragedy always ends with the suffering and/ or death of the protagonist so that he does not achieve his objective. He is overcome by obstacles, either from within or without. Despite this, the protagonist can learn and grow from his suffering. The spirit of the tragic play can ultimately be uplifting.

Comedy also offers a realistic portrayal of life and its problems, but the writer presents those issues in a humorous way—the comedy growing out of the character himself, the situations in which he finds himself, or the dialogue he speaks. The comedy writer sometimes makes light of life's challenges, or offers up for scrutiny and ridicule the effects of these challenges upon men and women. In terms of action and conflict, the comedy play has the same kind of story structure as the tragedy, but at the highest point of crisis or dramatic tension, a surprise element is introduced that allows the hero to overcome all obstacles, thereby forestalling any serious or "tragic" consequences. With the exception of *black comedy*, the hero attains his objective and lives happily ever after.

All plays are divided into either tragedy or comedy. These two major genres can be further subdivided into subgenres. Subgenres are artificial classifications, since many plays overlap several subgenres. However, they do offer some guidance to the actor. The main dramatic subgenres are the following:

Tragedy

1. *Classical (or ancient) tragedy.* Invented by the Greek playwrights Sophocles, Euripides, and Aeschylus, these plays deal with the downfall of an exalted hero or heroine, who is the protagonist of the play. Greek heroes provide some of the most sought-after acting roles because the hero is of such grand moral stature. He or she must be of noble birth, virtuous by nature, and desirous of doing good. He must also suffer greatly and die a tragic death because of either a flaw in his character, an error in judgment, the possession of a too-virtuous nature, or the overpowering influence of fate. *Oedipus Rex* by Sophocles is one of the most famous and oft-performed classical tragedies, in which the hero (and the audience) experiences what Aristotle termed *catharsis*, or a purging and cleansing of the spirit as a result of the hero's struggle and suffering.

2. *Renaissance (or Elizabethan) tragedy.* The most famous tragedies in this genre are the plays of Shakespeare, such as *Hamlet, King Lear,* and *Othello,* and the plays of Jean Racine (*Andromaque, Phèdre,* and *Bérénice*). In the Greek tradition, the hero of the Renaissance tragedy is

of a noble nature, though not always a King or a prince. The audience feels deeply with the hero and shares a tragic pity for his suffering and fate. Shakespeare's tragedies are beloved for their noble pathos and spiritual hope, while Racine's plays are recognized for their depth of characterization and clear, simple beauty. Just as Hamlet is considered the most coveted male acting role in theater, Racine's Phèdre is the greatest dramatic heroine.

3. *Modern tragedy.* Unlike Greek or Elizabethan tragedy, modern tragedy shares little with its predecessors. The main character is neither virtuous nor does he aspire toward anything noble. He is self-focused, and represents a slice of disaffected man acting out his life within a narrow domestic arena. He is generally the victim of the (perceived) corrupting influences of society or of dysfunctional relationships with those close to him. He dies without having transcended his own human condition. In some contemporary tragedies, the hero not only lacks the dignity and virtue of the traditional hero but is an anti-hero, who is supremely self-absorbed, petty, and his own worst enemy. Modern authors of this genre of modern tragedy are Henrik Ibsen (*A Doll's House*), Eugene O'Neill (*The Iceman Cometh, Desire under the Elms,* and *Long Day's Journey into Night*), Arthur Miller (*The Crucible*), and Tennessee Williams (*A Streetcar Named Desire*).

4. *Romantic drama.* This category tends to combine the most appealing elements of the three previous subgenres. It deals with the serious issues of love (human and divine), and sometimes ends in tragedy for the protagonist. However, there is enough relief in adventurous action, suspense, and humor, to preserve the romantic drama as its own classification. Examples are Goethe's *Faust*, Victor Hugo's *Hernani,* and *Camille (La Dame aux Camilias)* by Alexandre Dumas Fils. In these plays, there is a robust use of emotion rather than rationality to persuade the audience, as well as an appeal to something better and higher. A large percentage of Hollywood movies, especially from an earlier era, are based on this genre.

5. *Historical romance.* Works in this genre share similar elements to those found in romantic drama, including subject matter and the through action of the hero's pursuit of a grand love or an honorable goal. Historical romances, however, are based (if only loosely) on real individuals or events throughout history. They also incorporate the

ideals of honor and chivalry, love of God, king, and country. These plays are generally adapted from great historical romance novels, such as *The Three Musketeers* and *The Count of Monte Cristo* by Alexandre Dumas, and *Ivanhoe, Rob Roy,* and *Quentin Durward* by Sir Walter Scott. Stirring epic poems, such as Tennyson's *Idylls of the King,* and even lesser poems, such as the *Charge of the Light Brigade*—also by Tennyson, have provided continued inspiration for dramatic adaptation both for stage and film.

6. *Realist drama.* This kind of drama covers many types of serious plays dealing with realistic portrayals of man in situations that bring about personal conflict. This genre includes social dramas like Henrik Ibsen's *An Enemy of the People,* which shows one man's failed but heroic attempts to stand up against the citizenry of his community, and Lorraine Hansberry's *A Raisin in the Sun,* which portrays a black family struggling to escape the ghetto. Historical dramas come under this category, as well as docudramas that dramatize an actual event and use real names and dates to tell the story. An example of a docudrama is Robert E. Lee's *Inherit the Wind.* Many modern realist dramas, in their writing style, set décor, and world view, attempt to present reality in its raw, photographic state, untouched by any poetic appeal to the higher ideals of life. Henrik Ibsen is considered the father of realist drama. Though his play *A Doll's House* is classified as a tragedy, it is also the supreme example of the realist drama in its purpose to expose the injustices of society, without offering a solution to fix them. The world view of the realists tends to be depressing and cynical. Anton Chekhov was one of the original realist writers. *The Cherry Orchard,* though often classified as a macabre comedy, represents all the elements of this subgenre.

7. *Naturalist drama.* This style grew out of realism, but went much further in its sordid portrayal of man and of society, dealing almost exclusively with lower-class family conflicts. If realist drama depicted life in its photographic state, naturalist drama showed life at its most tortured and unheroic. Naturalist protagonists are weak and dysfunctional, such as Willie Loman in Arthur Miller's *Death of a Salesman,* though this play could also be classified as a modern tragedy.

8. *Expressionist drama.* This kind of play presents reality (ideas and characters) in a distorted, nonrealistic, and sometimes perverted way

for the purpose of creating emotional "angst." Expressionists have traditionally seen themselves as visionary prophets who would usher in a revolution against corrupt social traditions and what they perceive to be the false values of man and society. The number of cheerful expressionist works is relatively small. An example of expressionistic drama is *The Adding Machine* by Elmer Rice. The works of the German playwright Ernst Toller also represent this subgenre.

Existentialism might be classified as an extension of expressionist drama, or at least a mutant form. The existentialists rejected a higher spiritual authority, arguing that the universe contained no absolute set of moral codes, and that each individual must create his or her own order and morality. Two of the leading philosophers of this movement were Jean-Paul Sartre *(No Exit)* and Albert Camus *(Caligula)*.

Absurdist drama, which describes Edward Albee's *The Death of Bessie Smith* and *The Zoo Story*, is also an outgrowth of expressionist drama. These authors view man as lost in the world, so that all his actions are useless and absurd. Harold Pinter *(The Homecoming)* can be included among the absurdists.

9. *Melodrama.* In this subgenre, broad strokes replace the subtleties of serious drama. The conflict is usually between the forces of good and evil, so the characters tend to be "goodies" or "baddies." The more serious melodramas, such as *Witness for the Prosecution, Dial M for Murder,* and *Dracula,* are intended to arouse interest by their blood-curdling events, suspense-filled murders, and outrageous motives, such as greed or revenge. Agatha Christie's mystery plays, which center on tracking down the criminal, fit this genre. The excitement of the comic melodrama, as performed in the early days of America's West, comes through physical action: chases, fist fights, shootouts, or the attempted kidnapping of the chaste heroine. Many of such melodramas included a musical score (hence *melo*drama). Given the outrageous obviousness of the melodrama, it is sometimes classified in the comedy genre.

10. *Musical drama.* This genre represents a dramatic work that is performed through song. In opera, the story is acted out exclusively by singing. In a musical, such as we see on Broadway, the story is told through a combination of dialogue, singing, and sometimes dance.

Comedy

1. *Classical (ancient) comedy.* This kind of play shows the humorous actions of one or more characters as they attempt to solve "serious" life problems, making comments on society or famous people in society as they do so. The humor tends to be bawdy and often deliberately offensive. The plays of Aristophanes in ancient Greece and the later works of the Roman poet Plautus exemplify classical comedy.

2. *Romantic comedy.* This genre spans the literary ages. It generally deals with the adventures of lovers in love, the obstacles to that love, the outside forces trying to keep them apart, or the humorous (and often imaginative, if not fanciful) situations that occur as a result of misunderstanding between them. In a romantic comedy, the lovers always live happily ever after. This kind of play derives its comedic interest both from the characters themselves and from the unusual circumstances in which they find themselves. Examples of this subgenre cover a wide spectrum from Shakespeare's *A Midsummer Night's Dream* and Edmond Rostand's *Cyrano de Bergerac* to the modern movie scripts *Sleepless in Seattle* and *The Lake House.* Shakespeare's own words from *Midsummer* perhaps best embody the essence of this genre: "The course of true love never did run smooth."

3. *Comedy of manners* (also known as satire). Satire holds up to laughter and/or scorn the social behaviors (or misbehaviors) of mainly upper-class society. Sophisticated and witty repartee that focuses on the characters' relationships and scandalous "affairs" is common, and contributes most of the comedic interest. This genre has spread over several periods of theater history. Moliere's *Tartuffe* and *The Misanthrope*, Oscar Wilde's *The Importance of Being Ernest*, and Richard Sheridan's *The School for Scandal* are all exemplary works representing the comedy of manners. Television programs such as *Seinfeld* and *The Young Ones* best represent the comedy of manners in our modern era.

4. *Farce (low comedy).* Farce is probably the most lightweight and insignificant of the comedy subgenres. It places normal people in embarrassing or incongruous situations, where they find themselves doing something that is the opposite to how they would normally act. The plot is contrived, and the ridiculous physical action that the character finds himself engaged in is intended to elicit riotous

laughter—otherwise known as "belly laughs." The verbal dialogue is often crude or just absurd. Sometimes we find farcical characters in a play of a different genre. For example, Shakespeare's *Twelfth Night* is a romantic comedy, but the character of Malvolio, who is a pompous, self-conceited man-servant, is persuaded to wear ridiculous clothing and act like a fool because he believes his mistress is in love with him. His physical actions create the laughter of ridicule.

5. *Absurdist (or black) comedy.* This type of comedy presents a weird, if not bewildering, view of the world that is intended to make the audience feel uncomfortable. The action includes improbable events with highly unpredictable characters. Black comedy is different from other types of comedy in that it will often end unhappily. Samuel Beckett's *Waiting for Godot* and Tom Stoppard's *Rosencrantz and Guildenstern are Dead* represent the theater of the absurd. The movie scripts *Fargo* and *Pulp Fiction* are contemporary works in this genre. Though we can arbitrarily divide the theater of the absurd into comedy and drama, there is really very little difference between the two because of their torturous and maze-like introspection.

6. *Fantasy.* In this genre, the action takes place in the world of make-believe. It is divorced from reality, and settings and costumes are usually imaginative. Many children's plays and musicals fit this category, including *The Wizard of Oz* and *Peter Pan.* Maurice Maeterlink's fairy tale *The Bluebird* would be an example of a serious fantasy in the tradition of the French symbolists. This poetic and mystical story conveys spiritual truths about the search for the bluebird of happiness, and the continuity of life before (and after) death.

7. *Musical comedy.* This genre represents a play with a simple plot in which dialogue is either represented by or interspersed with songs. In a musical comedy, the emphasis is on the musical numbers, which may be enhanced with dance choreography. Franz Lehar's *The Merry Widow* and the operettas of Gilbert and Sullivan fall under this genre. America boasts the richest tradition of musicals, including those of George M. Cohan *(Yankee Doodle Dandy, 45 Minutes from Broadway)*, Victor Herbert *(Naughty Marietta, Babes in Toyland)*, Rodgers and Hammerstein *(Oklahoma, South Pacific, Carousel)*, Lerner and Loewe *(My Fair Lady, Camelot)*, and a vibrant assortment of contemporary Broadway favorites.

It is helpful to understand the genre in which a play is written so we can better interpret and therefore more faithfully represent what the author intended.

E X E R C I S E 10-29 Scene Selections From Different Genres

> *Director's Notes:* At the end of this unit is a selection of acting scenes. The first two, *A Midsummer Night's Dream* and *The Importance of Being Earnest,* represent different genres of drama. The remaining two scenes, adapted for the younger children, are identical in their subject matter, but differ in their historical setting and dialogue. Ask for volunteers to read them aloud to the class. Make sure that you have as many copies as there are characters in the scene so that each student has his or her own copy. After you hand out the scenes to the actors, review with the class the place and time period of the scene, the kind of play genre it represents, a brief story plot (where available) up to the time of the scene, and the kind of dialogue employed by the author.
>
> Read the guidelines below to the students and make sure you answer all their questions before they begin their readings. Make it clear that you are not interested in the perfect acting out of the scene. This exercise demonstrates how, by writing his play in a certain way, the author had a specific purpose in mind.

General Guidelines for Reading Study Scenes:

1. Read the scene silently.

2. Understand the meaning of all the words and note the kind of speech spoken by the characters. Is it nineteenth-century English or present day? Is it poetry or prose? Which class of people would be likely to use these kinds of words and expressions—noble born or country folk, rich or poor, old or young?

3. Which genre does each play scene represent? How does the genre influence the way the actor should interpret the scene or approach the reading of it?

4. Get a general impression of the character's personality. What are his or her character traits, goals, and motivations?

5. What is the mood of the character? How does the dramatic situation contribute to this mood? What is the setting (a forest, a living room, etc.)? What is the time of day or night?

6. Do not lose your concentration while reading out loud. Stay within the atmosphere of the scene.

7. Try to imagine yourself being there in the scene, physically, mentally, and emotionally, so that you can convey the reality of it to your audience.

Level One Action:

- Assigned actors read out loud the first two contrasting scenes, one after the other.

- How was the comedy in one scene different from the comedy in the other? Did the comedy come from the characters themselves, the situations they found themselves in, the dialogue they spoke to each other, or a mixture of the three? How did the dialogue of the two scenes differ?

- For homework, ask the students to research (on Google or at the library) the authors of the first two selections and other works they wrote that match this same genre.

Commentary:

Knowing the genre of the play can help the actor understand the playwright's purpose and point of view. For example, in reading the excerpt from *A Midsummer Night's Dream,* we are dealing with a lighthearted Elizabethan comedy of romance, in which the four lovers, Hermia, Lysander, Helena, and Demetrius, are derailed from their proper course of love by fairy enchantment. The setting of the scene is inside the magical woods of Arden. There the lovers become romantically confused under the spells of the fairy king and queen. The character portraits in this romantic comedy differ significantly from those in *The Importance of Being Earnest,* which is an example of the comedy of manners (or satire). A satire is not imaginative and fanciful. Its intent is to hold up for ridicule the well-bred silliness of upper class people in their shallow and selfish understanding of love, and the formal, ridiculous manner in which they fall in love and conduct their "love affairs."

The dialogue is also very different in the two selections. Shakespeare did not write in stiff, conversational prose, as Oscar Wilde did. He wrote in a form of poetry called blank verse, which is unrhymed iambic pentameter—five metrical feet of the non-stressed syllable followed by a stressed syllable. This kind of rhythm in the speech of his characters makes us listen to the actors more. There is something poetic and lovely about it that we do not feel when listening to Jack or Lady Bracknell talk.

Level Two Action:

- Assigned actors read out loud the last two scenes. The other students compare the setting, the characters, and the dialogue.

The last two scenes are identical in subject matter but placed in different time periods. Reading them in succession will demonstrate how our manner of addressing each other has changed radically over one hundred years. All four scenes deal with the theme of love and courtship, but the genre of each piece reveals how differently an actor is expected to portray his character and thus convey the author's viewpoint.

Summary

The human voice is the most stirring and powerful of all musical instruments because it has within it the potential for perfection. Natural and beautiful expression is the promise and harvest of every true artist. Make a painting with your words so that what you have in your mind's eye and are describing to the other character on stage playing opposite you, will be clear to him as well as to the audience.

The moving power of your voice for the stage lies first in its coherence, and secondly in its expressiveness. Anything falsely theatrical will destroy that simple coherence. Use the five dynamics of vocal production, and especially the elements of expression, to help you convey clearly and convincingly what you are thinking, feeling, and seeing. The point is not, after all, how you deliver a line or speech, but how others will hear and respond to it. That means they must know what is in the mind and heart of your character. Remember that you are the best judge of how to make your work onstage come alive with meaning, eloquence, and truth.

KEY: Getting to the heart of the issue

The voice can be the most perfect instrument when it is the dynamic resonator of the mind, the heart, and the inner spirit.

A Midsummer Night's Dream

by William Shakespeare
Abridged by Family Playhouse

Act 2, Scene 2

THE FAIRY WOOD

STORY: Our fabled story takes place in Athens of an antique time, when its surrounding woods were the enchanted domain of a fairy kingdom. The noble Theseus, Duke of Athens, has conquered Hippolyta, Queen of the Amazons, and now claims her as his bride. Our adventure occurs over the four days leading up to their nuptial ceremony. Hermia, the daughter of a wealthy Athenian citizen, refuses to marry Demetrius, the man her father has chosen. In love with Lysander, Hermia pleads her case before the Duke that Demetrius has already professed his love for her friend, Helena, and that Helena, in turn, loves Demetrius. The Duke gives Hermia four days to submit to the will of her father. If she still refuses at the end of this time, she will receive the penalty of death, or banishment to a convent. Hermia and Lysander decide to run away together and escape the law of Athens.

SETTING: A velvety woodland bank by a stream in the enchanted woods.

CHARACTERS: LYSANDER, the young man Hermia loves
HERMIA, in love with Lysander
HELENA, in love with Demetrius
DEMETRIUS, sometimes in love with Helena
PUCK, Robin Goodfellow, a mischievous elf

SCENE: After having agreed to meet each other in the woods and escape the judgment of the Duke, Lysander and Hermia find themselves lost by nightfall. Meanwhile, Puck (also known as the mischievous fairy elf, Robin Goodfellow) has been commanded by Oberon, King of the Fairies, to place a "love spell" from the juice of a rare flower in the eyes of a man dressed in Athenian garments. Though it is Demetrius to whom Oberon is referring, Puck mistakes Lysander for Demetrius and squeezes the love juice onto Lysander's eyes. When Helena and Demetrius pass by, it is Helena whom Lysander sees when he wakes, and it is she whom he now believes he loves. And so the love tryst unravels, and misunderstandings begin...

Enter LYSANDER *and* HERMIA BRAKE 2.

LYSANDER: Fair love, you faint with wandering in the wood;
And to speak truth, I have forgot our way: ['truth' substituted for 'troth']
We'll rest us, Hermia, if you think it good,
And tarry for the comfort of the day.

HERMIA: Be it so, Lysander: find you out a bed;
For I upon this bank will rest my head.
[*She crosses to* LC bower, *but* LYSANDER *follows her*]
Nay, good Lysander; for my sake, my dear,
Lie farther off yet, do not lie so near.
Such separation as may well be said
Becomes a virtuous bachelor and a maid.
So far be distant; and, good night, sweet friend:
Thy love ne'er alter till thy sweet life end!

LYSANDER: Amen, amen, to that fair prayer, say I;
And then end life when I end loyalty!

He reluctantly moves to a bower RC *and they both settle down to sleep.*

Enter PUCK BRAKE 2.

PUCK: Through the forest have I gone,
        But Athenian found I none,
        On whose eyes I might approve   [approve = prove]
        This flower's force in stirring love.
        Night and silence! [*Sees* LYSANDER] Who is here?
        Weeds of Athens he doth wear: [weeds = garments]
        This is he, my master said,
        Despised the Athenian maid; [*Looks about him*]
        And here the maiden, sleeping sound,
        On the dank and dirty ground.   [dank = damp]
        Pretty soul! She durst not lie
        Near this [*Kicks him*] lack-love, this [*Kicks him again*] kill-courtesy.
        [*Takes the flower and squeezes its juice over* LYSANDER'S *eyes*]
        Churl, upon thy eyes I throw   [Churl = someone who has no manners]
        All the power this charm doth owe.   [owe = own]

When thou wak'st, let love forbid
Sleep his seat on thy eyelid!
So awake when I am gone;
For I must now to Oberon. [*Exit* BRAKE 1]

Enter DEMETRIUS BRAKE 2, *followed by* HELENA, *running after him.*

HELENA: Stay, though thou kill me, sweet Demetrius.

DEMETRIUS: I charge thee, hence, and do not haunt me thus.

HELENA: O, wilt thou leave me? Do not so.

DEMETRIUS: Stay, on thy peril: I alone will go. [*Exit* BRAKE 3]

HELENA: O, I am out of breath in this fond chase!
The more my prayer, the lesser is my grace.   [grace = favor or good fortune]
But who is here? Lysander! On the ground!
Dead or asleep? I see no blood, no wound—
Lysander, if you live, good sir, awake.

LYSANDER: [*Waking up as though to a heavenly vision of loveliness*]
And run through fire I will for thy sweet sake.
Where is Demetrius? O, how fit a word
Is that vile name to perish on my sword!

HELENA: Do not say so, Lysander; say not so.
What though he love your Hermia?
Yet Hermia still loves you: then be content.

LYSANDER: Content with Hermia! No; I do repent
The tedious minutes I with her have spent.
Not Hermia but Helena I love:
Who will not change a raven for a dove?

HELENA: Wherefore was I to this keen mockery born?
When at your hands did I deserve this scorn?
Good troth, you do me wrong, good sooth, you do,
In such disdainful manner me to woo.

But fare you well: perforce I must confess
I thought you lord of more true gentleness.   [= the spirit of a gentleman]
O, that a lady, of one man refused,
Should of another therefore be abused! [*Exit* BRAKE 3]

LYSANDER: She sees not Hermia. [*With disdain*] Hermia, sleep thou there:
And never mayst thou come Lysander near!
And, all my powers, address your love and might
To honor Helen and to be her knight! [*Exit* BRAKE 3]

PUCK *enters* BRAKE 2 *and scratches his head in confusion when he sees that* LYSANDER *is no longer there, and that* HERMIA *lies alone. He then wakes up* HERMIA.

HERMIA: [*Waking as from a nightmare*] Help me, Lysander, help me!
[*Recovering*] Ay me, for pity! What a dream was here!
Lysander, look how I do quake with fear:
[*She sees that* LYSANDER *is not there*]
Lysander! What, removed?

PUCK: [*Mockingly echoes her words, imitating her voice*] What, removed?

HERMIA: No word?

PUCK: [*Echoing her words*] No word?

HERMIA: [*With sobbing tone*] Gone?

PUCK: [*With mocking sobs, wiping away imaginary tears*] Gone?

HERMIA: Then I well perceive you are not nigh:
Either death or you I'll find immediately. [*Exits* BRAKE 3]

PUCK *somersaults backwards, slaps his knees, laughing, then exits* BRAKE 1.

NOTES: Puck is the ever-present reminder that this is a fairy world and that we should not take the changing passions of humans too seriously. Just as we find ourselves moved by the sorry plight of Hermia, this magical elf steps in to remind us that we are experiencing but a dream.

The Importance of Being Earnest

by Oscar Wilde
Abridged by Family Playhouse

Act 1

JACK'S PROPOSAL

STORY: The plot deals with the problems two young men have in seeking to marry the women they love. Cecily loves Algernon (Algy), while Gwendolen loves Jack. However, each has said that she could only love a man with the first name of Ernest. So Jack and Algernon have both claimed to be named Ernest.

SETTING: England, 1890s. Algernon's fashionable city flat.

CHARACTERS: JACK WORTHING, wealthy English gentleman
GWENDOLEN, who loves Jack
LADY BRACKNELL, Gwendolen's eccentric mother

SCENE: The scene takes place in Algernon's flat. Jack [Ernest] has come to propose to Gwendolen, who is Algy's cousin, and who believes that Jack's name is Ernest, but it really isn't. Lady Bracknell has retired to the music room with Algernon. Jack and Gwendolen remain in the sitting room.

JACK: Charming day it has been, Miss Fairfax.

GWENDOLEN: Pray don't talk to me about the weather, Mr. Worthing. Whenever people talk to me about the weather, I always feel quite certain that they mean something else. And that makes me so nervous.

JACK: I do mean something else.

GWENDOLEN: I thought so. In fact, I am never wrong.

JACK: And I would like to be allowed to take advantage of Lady Bracknell's temporary absence.

GWENDOLEN: I would certainly advise you to do so. Mamma has a way of coming back suddenly into a room that I have often had to speak to her about.

JACK: [*Nervously*] Miss Fairfax, ever since I met you I have admired you more than any girl...I have ever met since...I met you.

GWENDOLEN: Yes, I am quite aware of the fact. And I often wish that in public, at any rate, you had been more demonstrative. For me you have always had an irresistible fascination. Even before I met you I was far from indifferent to you. [JACK *looks at her in bewilderment*] We live, as I hope you know, Mr. Worthing, in an age of ideals. The fact is constantly mentioned in the more expensive monthly magazines, and has reached the provincial pulpits, I am told: and my ideal has always been to love some one of the name of Ernest. There is something in that name that inspires absolute confidence. The moment Algernon first mentioned to me that he had a friend called Ernest, I knew I was destined to love you.

JACK: You really love me, Gwendolen?

GWENDOLEN: [*With exquisite coolness*] Passionately!

JACK: Darling! You don't know how happy you've made me.

GWENDOLEN: My own Ernest!

JACK: But you don't really mean to say that you couldn't love me if my name wasn't Ernest?

GWENDOLEN: But your name *is* Ernest.

JACK: Yes, I know it is. But supposing it was something else? Do you mean to say you couldn't love me then?

GWENDOLEN: [*Glibly*] Ah! That is clearly a metaphysical speculation, and like most metaphysical speculations has very little reference at all to the actual facts of real life, as we know them.

JACK: Personally, darling, to speak quite candidly, I don't much care about the name of Ernest...I don't think the name suits me at all.

GWENDOLEN: It suits you perfectly. It is a divine name. It has a music of its own. It produces vibrations.

JACK: Well, really, Gwendolen, I must say that I think there are lots of other much nicer names. I think...Jack, for instance, a charming name.

GWENDOLEN: Jack?...No, there is very little music in the name Jack, if any at all, indeed. It does not thrill. It produces absolutely no vibrations....I have known several Jacks, and they all, without exception, were more than usually plain. Besides, Jack is a notorious domesticity for John! And I pity any woman who is married to a man called John. She would probably never be allowed to know the entrancing pleasure of a single moment's solitude. The only really safe name is Ernest.

JACK: Gwendolen, I must get christened at once—I mean we must get married at once. There is no time to be lost.

GWENDOLEN: Married, Mr. Worthing?

JACK: [*Astounded*] Well...surely. You know that I love you, and you led me to believe, Miss Fairfax, that you were not absolutely indifferent to me.

GWENDOLEN: I adore you. But you haven't proposed to me yet. Nothing has been said at all about marriage. The subject has not even been touched on.

JACK: Well...may I propose to you now?

GWENDOLEN: I think it would be an admirable opportunity. And to spare you any possible disappointment, Mr. Worthing, I think it only fair to tell you quite frankly beforehand that I am fully determined to accept you.

JACK: [*Ecstatic*] Gwendolen!

GWENDOLEN: Yes, Mr. Worthing, what have you got to say to me?

JACK: You know what I have got to say to you.

GWENDOLEN: Yes, but you don't say it.

JACK: Gwendolen, will you marry me? [*Gets down on his knees, as an after-thought*]

GWENDOLEN: Of course I will, darling.

JACK: My own one, I have never loved anyone in the world but you.

GWENDOLEN: Yes, but men often propose for practice. I know my brother Gerald does. All my girlfriends tell me so. What wonderfully blue eyes you have, Ernest! They are quite, quite blue. I hope you will always look at me just like that, especially when there are other people present.

Enter LADY BRACKNELL.

LADY BRACKNELL: Mr. Worthing! Rise, sir, from this semi-recumbent posture. It is most indecorous.

GWENDOLEN: Mamma! [*He tries to rise but she restrains him*] I must beg you to retire. This is no place for you. Besides, Mr. Worthing has not quite finished yet.

LADY BRACKNELL: Finished what, may I ask?

GWENDOLEN: I am engaged to Mr. Worthing, mamma.

LADY BRACKNELL: Pardon me, you are not engaged to any one. [*She makes a sign for him to get off his knees, which he does*] When you do become engaged to some one, I, or your father, should his health permit him, will inform you of the fact. An engagement should come on a young girl as a surprise, pleasant or unpleasant, as the case may be. It is hardly a matter that she could be allowed to arrange for herself... And now I have a few questions to put to you, Mr. Worthing. While I am making these inquiries, you, Gwendolen, will wait for me below in the carriage.

GWENDOLEN: [*Reproachfully*] Mamma!

LADY BRACKNELL: In the carriage, Gwendolen! [GWENDOLEN *goes to the door. She and* JACK *blow kisses to each other behind* LADY BRACKNELL'S *back.* LADY BRACKNELL *looks vaguely about as if sensing something amiss. Finally turns fully around to catch* GWENDOLEN *about to send another kiss to* JACK] Gwendolen, the carriage!

GWENDOLEN: Yes, mamma. [*Goes out, throwing a last adoring glance at* JACK]

LADY BRACKNELL: You can take a seat, Mr. Worthing. [*Takes from her handbag a notebook and pencil*]

JACK: Thank you, Lady Bracknell, I prefer standing.

LADY BRACKNELL: [*Notebook in hand*] I feel bound to tell you that you are not on my list of eligible young men. However, I am quite ready to enter your name, should your answers be what any affectionate mother might require. Do you smoke?

JACK: [*Reluctantly*] Well, yes, I must admit I smoke.

LADY BRACKNELL: I am glad to hear it. A man should always have an occupation of some kind. There are far too many idle men in London as it is. How old are you?

JACK: Twenty-nine.

LADY BRACKNELL: A very good age to be married at. I have always been of the opinion that a man who desires to get married should know either everything or nothing. Which do you know?

JACK: [*After some hesitation, and with chagrin*] I know nothing, Lady Bracknell.

LADY BRACKNELL: I am pleased to hear it. I do not approve of anything that tampers with natural ignorance. Ignorance is like a delicate exotic fruit; touch it and the bloom is gone. The whole theory of modern education is radically unsound. Fortunately in England, at any rate, education produces no effect whatsoever. If it did, it would prove a serious danger to the upper classes. What is your income?

JACK: Between seven and eight thousand a year. [*She makes a note in her book as he tries to peer at what she is writing*] I have a country house with some land, of course, but I don't depend on that for my real income. In fact, the poachers are the only people who make anything out of it.

LADY BRACKNELL: A country house! A girl with a simple, unspoiled nature, like Gwendolen, could hardly be expected to reside in the country. You have a town house, I hope?

JACK: Well, I own a house in Belgrave Square.

LADY BRACKNELL: What number in Belgrave?

JACK: 149.

LADY BRACKNELL: [*Shakes her head*] The unfashionable side. I thought there was something. However, that could easily be altered.

JACK: Do you mean the fashion, or the side?

LADY BRACKNELL: [*Sternly*] Both, if necessary. Now, to minor matters. Are your parents living?

JACK: I am afraid I have lost both my parents.

LADY BRACKNELL: To lose one parent, Mr. Worthing, may be regarded as a misfortune; to lose both looks like carelessness.

JACK: The fact is, Lady Bracknell, it would be nearer the truth to say that my parents seem to have lost me...I don't actually know who I am by birth. I was...well, I was found.

LADY BRACKNELL: Found!

JACK: The late Mr. Thomas Cardew, an old gentleman of a very charitable and kindly disposition, found me and gave me the name of Worthing, because he happened to have a first-class train ticket for Worthing in his pocket at the time. Worthing is a seaside resort in Sussex.

LADY BRACKNELL: Where did the charitable gentleman who had a first-class ticket to a seaside resort find you?

JACK: [*Gravely*] In a hand-bag.

LADY BRACKNELL: [*Shocked*] A hand-bag?

JACK: [*Very seriously*] Yes, Lady Bracknell—a somewhat large hand-bag, with handles to it.

LADY BRACKNELL: In what locality did this Mr. Thomas Cardew come across this somewhat large hand-bag with handles to it?

JACK: In the cloakroom at Victoria Station. It was given to him in mistake for his own.

LADY BRACKNELL: The cloak room at Victoria Station?

JACK: Yes. The Brighton line.

LADY BRACKNELL: The line is immaterial. Mr. Worthing, I confess I feel somewhat bewildered by what you have just told me. To be born, or at any rate, bred, in a hand-bag, whether it has handles or not, seems to me to display a contempt for the ordinary decencies of family life that reminds one of the worst excesses of the French Revolution. And I presume you know what that unfortunate movement led to? A cloakroom at a railway station might serve to conceal a social indiscretion, but it could hardly be regarded as an assured basis for a recognized position in good society.

JACK: May I ask you then what you would advise me to do? I need hardly say I would do anything in the world to ensure Gwendolen's happiness.

LADY BRACKNELL: I would strongly advise you, Mr. Worthing, to acquire some relations as soon as possible, and to make a definite effort to produce at least one parent before the season is quite over.

JACK: Well, I don't see how I could possibly manage to do that. I can produce the hand-bag at any moment. I really think that should satisfy you, Lady Bracknell.

LADY BRACKNELL: Me, sir? What has it to do with me? You can hardly imagine that I and Lord Bracknell would dream of allowing our only daughter—a girl brought up with the utmost care—to marry into a cloakroom, and form an alliance with a hand-bag? Good morning, Mr. Worthing.

LADY BRACKNELL *sweeps out in majestic indignation.*

JACK *collapses on the chair in dejection.*

Master William's Courtship

An Original Scene
by Family Playhouse

SETTING: New England, 1902. The entrance gate outside William's estate home

CHARACTERS: MARY BELMONT, aged 18-20, William's governess
                     MASTER WILLIAM, aged 7-10
                     BONNIE JOHNSON, aged 7-8 years

SCENE: A young boy is waiting at the gatepost for his governess. When he sees her coming up the path, he boldly speaks to her.

WILLIAM: Miss Belmont?

MISS BELMONT: Hello, Willie. What are you doing here this late? It's almost dark you know.

WILLIAM: I've been waiting for you to come back. There's something I want to ask you. I've wanted to ask you for an awfully long time. Whenever I had the opportunity I never had the courage. Whenever I had the courage, I never had the opportunity. But now I've got both.

MISS BELMONT: [*Intrigued*] What is it, Willie?

WILLIAM: [*Builds up bravely to say it*] Well, first, I think it only appropriate that you call me Master William from now on and not Willie.

MISS BELMONT: [*With serious respect*] Very well, if that is what you wish, Master William. And now, what is your question?

WILLIAM: [*With gravity, falling on one knee, and removing his newsboy cap*] Miss Belmont, will you marry me? [MISS BELMONT *is stunned to silence*] I don't expect you to give me an answer right away...

MISS BELMONT: [*Stumbling*] But Willie...I mean William...Master William...

WILLIE: [*Eagerly…getting up off his knees*] It isn't as if I just met you. I remember the first day you came to be my governess. You were wearing a blue gown with silver lace. And you had a matching hat and parasol. I remember my very first spelling lesson when you taught me that A was A.

MISS BELMONT: William, I think you're the sweetest, dearest child…

WILLIE: Miss Belmont, you musn't think of me anymore as a child. After all, even father said at my birthday party last week that I was a young man now, and had to think about my future.

MISS BELMONT: Yes, indeed. And your father is quite correct, but…

WILLIE: Oh, I know I'm not the handsomest lad in town, well not as handsome as Billy Wildes maybe. But…I'll always love you and I'll be true to you and I won't send flowers to other girls or go out with them, not even Bonnie Johnson, though she is pretty.

MISS BELMONT: Willie…Master William, that's the very nicest thing anyone has ever said to me. And I'm very honored, but don't you think you're just a bit young to be thinking of getting married?

WILLIE: Well, father said he was betrothed to mother when she was only 12, and you're nearly twenty! Of course, I'm not in any particular hurry, though I *am* almost nine…[*She looks at him as though to correct a fib*]…well, I'll be nine next birthday, and I *have* finished my third Reader.

We hear offstage the voice of a little girl calling WILLIE'S *name.* BONNIE JOHNSON *enters with an excited look on her face.*

BONNIE: Willie! [*Runs to him*] Oh, Willie! You'll never guess what! Alice Keith is giving a Valentine's Party next week and all the girls may invite a partner. I'm going to go as Queen Guinevere. Will you be my knight, Willie?

WILLIE: [*Excitedly*] Will I! [*Turns to* MISS BELMONT] Miss Belmont, will you make a costume for me? Maybe I could go as Sir Lancelot.

MISS BELMONT: [*Ruefully*] But, Master William, aren't we engaged?

WILLIE: [*After just a moment's hesitation*] Well, I've been thinking it over. A fella has to see the world a bit before he makes up his mind about getting married. You'll just have to wait, Miss Belmont. 'Sides, all girls got to have a broken heart some time.

MISS BELMONT: Yes, you're quite right. I'll try very hard to get over my disappointment.

BONNIE: [*Sweetly and coyly*] It's getting dark and I'm a little scared. Will you take me home, Willie? I'd feel safer with you.

WILLIE: [*Emboldened*] Sure. [*Gives her his arm*] I'll be right back, Miss Belmont. Tell Mother not to wait dinner, though. [*They exit where* BONNIE *entered*]

MISS BELMONT *looks after them, bemusedly, shakes her head, then exits.*

Willie's Courtship

An Original Scene
[A modern adaptation of Master William's Courtship]
by Family Playhouse

SETTING: Modern-day. The babysitter's backyard

CHARACTERS: MARY, aged 12-14, Willie's babysitter
           WILLIE, aged 7-10
           BOBBY, aged 14-16 years, Mary's older brother

SCENE: Twilight. A young boy enters the backyard of his babysitter and next-door neighbor, who is reading a book.

WILLIE: Mary?

MARY: Hello, Willie. What are you doing over here this late? It's almost dark.

WILLIE: There's something I just got to ask. I've been wanting to ask it for an awful long time. I was nearly going to ask you a couple of times, but I got nervous and chickened out. I mean, it's a pretty important question.

MARY: [*Puts her book down*] Well, what is it, Willie?

WILLIE: [*Builds up bravely to say it*] Mary, will you marry me?

MARY: [*Stunned*] Huh?

WILLIE: I don't expect you to give me an answer right away...You could tell me tomorrow when you take me to the movies.

MARY: But Willie...

WILLIE: It isn't as if I just met you. I remember the first day you came to be my babysitter. You were wearing a new pair of tennis shoes with flashing lights. I was just finishing my first spelling book. Remember?

MARY: Oh, Willie, I think you're just the sweetest, cutest...

WILLIE: Now, don't go using those kid words on me. I'm pretty grown up now. I'm in third grade and I can read just as good as Bobby. Oh, I know I'm not the best lookin' guy in town. But...I'll always love you and I'll be true to you and I won't go out with other girls.

MARY: Willie, that's the nicest thing anyone's ever said to me in my whole life. And I'm very grateful, but I'm much too young to think about getting married.

WILLIE: Of course, I'm not in any particular hurry. We could have a long engagement.

MARY: Willie, how old are you?

WILLIE: [*Enthusiastically*] Eight, nearly nine.

MARY: [*Looking at him dubiously*] Willie, you know you only had your eighth birthday a couple of weeks ago.

WILLIE: Well, I'm going on nine.

MARY'S *brother,* BOBBY, *enters with a baseball glove and ball in his hand.*

BOBBY: Hey, Willie! Your mom just phoned and wants you to go home right away. She said dinner's ready.

WILLIE: [*Looking dejected*] Ahh, just when a fella's doing important stuff!

MARY: [*Sweetly*] Good night, Willie.

She kisses him on the cheek—a kiss that he immediately wipes off with his hand, just out of habit. WILLIE *looks up at her then starts to walk off dejectedly.*

BOBBY: Say, Willie. You wanna play catch tomorrow? I want to try out my new glove.

WILLIE: [*Brightening up*] You really want to play with *me*? [BOBBY *throws ball at him.* WILLIE *catches it*]

BOBBY: Uh, it's okay to play with amateurs sometimes. [*They continue back and forth with the ball*]

WILLIE: Gee, thanks Bobby.

MARY: [*Pretending to be hurt*] But Willie, I thought you wanted me to take you to the movies tomorrow and discuss...[*After a pause*]...you know what.

WILLIE: [*Looks at* BOBBY] Girls! They just don't understand about baseball.

BOBBY: [*Sympathetically*] Yeh! [*He puts his arm around* WILLIE *and they both go out happily as* BOBBY *talks about his new glove and the game he won that day*]

MARY *smiles bemusedly at them as they leave, shakes her head and walks out.*

The Story of an Actress

A Romance

Her first portrait

The seed of ambition

Preparing for her first audition

Her ingenue role and first bouquet

Gaining a reputation…

Her triumph!

Their first meeting…

His morning greeting…

Sharing her art with him…

After a performance…

Losing her presence of mind…

The theater or him…

He won!

Unit

Study

Eleven

The Art of
Characterization

11

The Art of Characterization

Instructions: The art of acting holds no greater challenge for the young actor than the successful creation of a character. This unit provides a complete and classic how-to guide, beginning with a detailed history of acting throughout the ages. You may wish to summarize key points that suit the interest and age level of your class, or you can distribute excerpts for discussion in small groups.

All the information in this unit is relevant to starting a professional career in acting. Make sure you cover the major concepts discussed under each of the subtitles. If you run out of class time, assign the material as homework. The little children should be given at least a summary of the essential points.

All students should be given the handout *Golden Rules of Character Study.* Allow enough time to discuss each of the guidelines so that even the little ones clearly understand what to do and how to apply the rules to real scenes.

Acting Throughout the Ages

The word *acting* conjures magic because it is a creative process that has the power to enchant and transform. As such, acting is a modern form of alchemy. The actor takes imaginary life, imbues it with the essence of real life, and makes it live, vividly and intensely, in the imagination of his audience. Portraying a character so that it is both convincing in its truthfulness and beautiful in its artistic form is the work of an actor. It constitutes his art of characterization. *How* he creates his character is a mystery that he alone must ultimately solve. Throughout the ages, actors have evolved various theatrical styles. These different approaches to their craft directly reflect the social and political dynamics of the era and the aesthetic expectations of the actor's audience.

The Golden Age of Greek Theater [circa 500 B.C.–300 B.C.]

Theater had its birth in Athens of fifth century B.C. At the civic festivals of Dionysia (in honor of Dionysus, the god of wine and fertility), dramatic exhibitions were written and performed to reflect the grandeur of piety and patriotism. Drama was considered a sacred ritual. From its beginnings of tragedy to the days of late comedy, it remained a part of religious ceremony. The performers, producers, and playwrights were all honored members of Athenian society, in which life and art were perfectly integrated. Though the theater of ancient Greece spanned two centuries to include the comedies of Aristophanes (448–338 B.C.) and Menander (342–291 B.C.), its greatness is concentrated in the tragedies of Aeschylus (525–456 B.C.), Sophocles (495–406 B.C.), and Euripides (480–406 B.C.). These plays embody the essential beauties of dramatic art—structure, unity, high theme, and noble characterizations—establishing traditions that have continued to the present.

Since the dominant theme of Greek tragedy was man's destiny set against the greater will of the gods, the actor's purpose was to invoke reverence and awe for the deities. The vision the actor was asked to impart was man moving to the inexorable hand of fate on an inexorable ascent to the Gods—an ascent that required purging of the soul through suffering. Life was viewed as an initiatic path toward self-perfection in the image and likeness of the divine. Simple stateliness of movement and beauty of speech, cultivated solely with a view to rhythm, constituted the art of acting. Actors wore masks and played in amphitheaters that held upwards of thirty thousand spectators. Thus they had to raise their voices majestically in order to be heard.

Rich, voluminous costumes—later refined to long, flowing robes with shoulder mantles—were worn to suit religious convention and meet the requirements of established standards of aesthetic beauty. The male actors themselves had a physical strength and manliness (or *thumos*) that preserved the Greek spirit of beautiful living. The actors of this age could not therefore bring any personal emotion into their parts, as they were the speaking trumpets of the poet-dramatist. It was the job of the chorus to express the soul and sentiments that animated the different characters. The Greek actor-tragedian was a magnificent living and talking puppet.

The theater of ancient Greece was all about man seeking the experience of God. For one century, playwrights and actors reminded men that they could be gods, that the beauty of divine living was theirs to discover, and that the purpose of the drama was to help artist and spectator alike make contact with the mystic creativeness of their own souls and so find immersion in the spirit. For one century, Athens was an imperishable sanctuary for the theater of the divine. The beginnings of drama were majestic and never to be forgotten. Greek tragedy died a slow death for eight centuries and disappeared altogether by the fifth century A.D.

The Roman Theater [240 B.C.–533 A.D.]

The Roman stage was born out of the tragedies and comedies of ancient Greece (or more specifically, Athens) through the translations of Livius Andronicus, a Greek sold as a slave in Rome and then made a freedman. Since Athens was also called Attica, these dramas are known as Attic tragedies or comedies. Andronicus' plays were first acted in 240 B.C. at the Ludi Romani (Roman games)—the festival in honor of Jupiter. From that year onward they were performed as secular side shows to all Roman festivals. These models of the Greek tragedy, adapted by Andronicus and later by Lucius Seneca (5 B.C.–65 A.D.), were less crafted for the dramatic stage than the originals. The tragedies of Seneca, though read and studied later by the Elizabethans, were ponderous with poor characterization and tedious dialogue unsuited for acting.

For several centuries, dramas were performed in thoroughfares and marketplaces, with no patronage from the noble class. Freeborn Roman citizens were deeply prejudiced against the profession of acting. The manager of the theatrical troupe was usually a freedman and the majority of his actors were slaves. The first permanent Roman theater was built 54 A.D. About 100 more were added in the next 500 years, during which time the comedies of Titus Plautus (254–184 B.C.) and the tragedies of Seneca continued to be performed, along with mime and pantomime (solo dance with music and chorus). Needless to say, these art forms had to compete for popular favor with the life-death spectacles of animal baitings, chariot races, and gladiatorial combats in the amphitheater. Regular drama of any kind had been all but obliterated by the middle of the sixth century A.D., by which time the Lombards in Italy had outlawed all theatrical entertainments in Rome.

Medieval Theater [870–circa 1540 A.D.]

Drama essentially disappeared from western Europe for the next several hundred years. It was, in truth, the Dark Ages of theatrical art. It was not until the end of the ninth century that Catholic Christendom provided the beginnings of a new kind of drama. Like Greek theater, it sprang from religious devotion and ceremony, though that was about the extent of its borrowings from the classical tradition. Episodes of the life of Jesus were dramatized in Latin and incorporated as part of the liturgy of the Mass—thus the name, liturgical drama. When the subject matter expanded to stories outside the Bible, these miracle (or mystery) plays moved from the church to the marketplace, where they served as a secular amusement for the public. As the guilds took over and the vernacular language replaced Latin, the acting became more dramatic, with emphasis on characterization and not merely the progression of religious events. During this time, the actor was considered an undesirable by the

Church. He lived and worked in poverty and rarely rose above the low expectations put upon him.

By the thirteenth century, the miracle plays were a popular lay institution, and for the next three centuries they remained an essential part of the life and entertainment of medieval Europe. Though the quality of the acting and the method of staging (either bare platforms or carts) was crude, the ready imagination of the spectators transformed these miracle plays into splendid exhibitions of dramatic art.

The Age of Shakespeare

By the early years of Elizabeth's reign (1558–1603), plays had moved from the marketplace to the inn-yard, and the artistic standard rose accordingly. By the end of her reign, the world had witnessed an intellectual and aesthetic flourishing unparalleled in the history of the world theater. The revival of classical learning at the beginning of the sixteenth century, which gave to Europe the Renaissance, brought to England a study of Italian poetry, with its blank verse (later adopted by Shakespeare) and the Italian novelli (tales) and romances. It was from these tales that the early Elizabethan romantic comedies were adapted. In addition, the plays of ancient Rome were resurrected as classical models of both story plot and form. But all would remain mere resources until William Shakespeare clothed them with the new beauty of the English language, and animated them with his noble genius.

Theater was redefined in the Elizabethan era by the splendor of the Bard's language. His matchless poetry in drama thrilled the boisterous crowds that filled the inn-yards. There was magic in his words; the actor needed only to speak them clearly and expressively. Shakespeare introduced plays with classical and patriotic themes written and acted in English. Their purpose was not merely to entertain but to educate the populace in a new and rich flow of everyday language. Theater was how the Renaissance in England took root and flourished, transcending all class boundaries. It was in the spoken word that the audience looked to find the action of battles, murders, and intrigues and the imagery of storms, ghosts, and madness. It was in the heart-thrilling eloquence of the poetry that they would experience the complexity of human nature, the struggle of the soul through adversity, and the triumph of virtue over evil.

Since little or no scenery was used on the Elizabethan stage, the audience had to rely on the characters' lines to define the time and setting of the various scenes, as well as to paint the beauty of a dawn, the despair of betrayal, the torment of conscience, or the ecstasy of love's first kiss. They learned a zest for words, which made the theater experience one of intrinsic enjoyment and erudition. Shakespeare's plays and sonnets set the standard for moral beauty in the dramatic arts and they continue to illumine our hearts centuries later. Moreover, every actor who spends part of his training

A panoramic view of an early Greek Theater, modeled after the Theater at Epidauros, fourth century B.C.

The Scene House of the Theater. This artist's rendering shows the building used by the actors that stood in the ruins behind the Temple circle shown above.

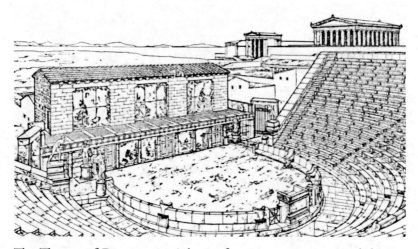

The Theater of Dionysus at Athens after it was reconstructed during the Roman period. This explains the raised stage and semi-circular orchestra instead of the full round dancing circle typical of the Temple theaters of the fifth century B.C.

A Roman theater at the time of the Roman comic poet Plautus, whose plays are the oldest surviving drama of Rome. Circa third century B.C.

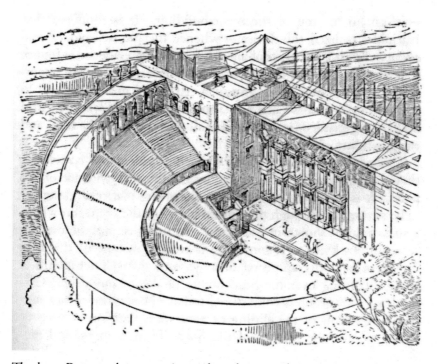

The later Roman theater at Aspendus, showing the true Roman bowl-like design. Note the contracted orchestra, raised stage and decorated stage wall. Pantomime, favored by the emperors, was performed here.

An exciting substitute for the popular theater forms of the Roman post-Christian era was chariot racing in the Circus Maximus, as shown in this painting by C. Ademollo.

A scene on a wagon stage in an English Miracle Play.

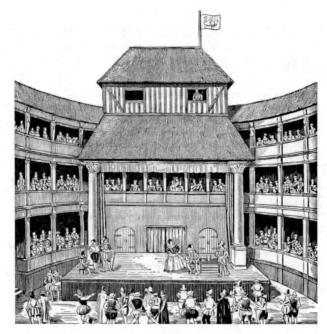

Elizabethan Swan Playhouse

performing Shakespeare on the stage gains a competence and grit that cannot be earned in any other medium of acting. Commenting on this very point, Ben Kingsley stated: "I think that the stamina, the marathon stamina that you required of your actor, I probably developed on great texts during my Shakespeare tenancy."

The Eighteenth Century

Eighteenth-century theater was known as the era of great actors, especially in France. The template of acting style for both comedy-in-verse (Molière) and heroic tragedy (Racine and Corneille) was strutting elegance, grandiloquence of delivery, and stilted gesture. This was the prescription for actors across Europe. The most famous artists of the time were Mlle. (Mademoiselle) Champmeslé and Mlle. Duclos, both of whom paraded the majestic declamatory style—considered to be the true sign of tragic art.

Michel Baron and the beautiful Adrienne Lecouvreur represented those who broke from this mannered recitative and chose to act from the heart, as distinguished from displaying "passion only in the mouth." Their characters had a fire and humanity that the audiences felt and understood. Other actors seemed melodramatic in comparison. The performances of these two great artists embodied the classic refinement for which the Comédie-Française gained even greater fame. After their deaths, France's royal theater reverted again to artificiality, despite the efforts of Voltaire, Lekain, and later Talma—who was still fighting for naturalness on the stage, both during and after the fall of the Bastille. It would take the charm and interpretive genius of Sarah Bernhardt in the last half of the nineteenth century to return French theater to something of its former glory.

At the same time, David Garrick of Drury Lane Theater in England revolutionized the English stage by introducing mobility and natural expressiveness to his acting parts. The actor-manager chose to revive the plays of Shakespeare instead of staging the standard Restoration comedy and heroic tragedy—a step, as Sheldon Cheney wrote in *The Theater,* "toward a more dignified and nobler stage." As a result, actors enjoyed an "equality and consideration" among other artists and in respectable society. Garrick's enormous popularity, and the new respect accorded actors during his reign, was proof that he pleased and touched more hearts by his sincerity than the ablest performers with their pompous rhetoric. He approached genuine acting with real character depth rather than hollow type impersonation. As Cheney wrote, "Garrick brought mimicry into touch with life." At the same time, he got rid of the fops who liked to sit on the stage and sacrificed his own need to be the shining star by giving other company players the chance to be the lead. In this way, he helped acting along the course toward the ensemble ideal, which gained such wide acceptance in the twentieth century.

The Nineteenth Century

Despite the brief flare-up of the true comic spirit with Oliver Goldsmith and Richard Sheridan, the nineteenth-century English stage was ruled by sentimentalism. Actors were timid about breaking away from type characterization. The period was an elegant and proper one, wherein real feelings were concealed, both on and off the stage. Since people did not express their emotions or their spiritual longings honestly and freely, actors were hardly expected to venture any deeper in the practice of their art than the portrayal of surface sentiment.

Fortunately, one stage artist did find that chord of true feeling and sincerity. Her name was Sarah Siddons, and she held the undisputed title of queen of the English stage for the first two decades of the century. The style of acting she brought earned the description of classic—not the stilted French classic style, but one which actors adopted in the following century to their merit. The dominant traits were simplicity and restraint. Though the outward stately appearance was still marked, Mrs. Siddons managed to personalize that noble and elevated presence with her own passion, fire, and imagination. Her heart flame thrilled audiences accustomed to the tame and extravagant conventional acting. She played the great Shakespearean heroines with a romance and idealism that jump-started the march toward Romanticism.

The motto of the poets and savants of the Romantic age was "To dream, to hope, to aspire!" Yet, with the exception of the mystical music dramas of Richard Wagner in Germany and the stirring operas of Giuseppe Verdi in nationalist Italy, stage drama lacked the true Romantic essence. Where it hoped to humanize and search the deeper life of the spirit, it failed because drama on the stage—unlike the poem, essay, or novel—was not an activity of intensifying or ennobling life; it was an escape from life. The spectator in the playhouse wanted to be taken out of his ordinary world, but not to a realm outside his own experience. He wanted the action and the characters real enough so that he could identify with them. Thus the imagination of the playwright had to be honeycombed with the familiar limitations that one found in real life. This was especially true in the American playhouse, where characters and story plots had to be plausible. There could be no deepening of the human experience, only a heightening in colors through the touch of the melodramatic.

Only in the staging of the Shakespearean plays did theater rise above the sentimental and melodramatic. The greatest actor of the Romantic era was Edmund Kean, renowned for his range of tragic emotion and depth of characterization. Even so, his reputation was built upon his Shakespearean performances. His Shylock, Othello, and Richard III are the parts for which he is most remembered. Samuel Coleridge wrote that "to see Kean play is like reading Shakespeare by flashes of lightning." His greatest successor later in the century was Henry Irving, who, like Garrick a century before, raised the actor's credibility in the community and brought acting to an eminence on par with the other arts. Irving was the first actor knighted at the English Court. Like his predecessors, his most famous roles were Shakespearean—Hamlet and Shylock the most notable. His leading lady was Ellen Terry, who became the idol of the English public with her portrayals of Ophelia and Portia. That everlasting glow of Shakespeare hallowed the actor time and time again, bestowing upon him (or her) immortality.

Edmund Kean's counterpart in Germany was Ludwig Devrient, who had those same qualities of volatility and vividness that characterized Kean's style. In Italy, Tommaso Salvini thrilled audiences with his passionate and very physical Othello. In France, Frédérick Lemaitre was the chief actor of the Victor Hugo plays. Like the dramas of the time, however, none of these players could incorporate the serenity and repose onstage that the Romantic poets and novelists had achieved so gloriously in their verse and in their fiction. There was one other player who deserves an honorable mention: the great Charlie Chaplin of that era, Joseph Grimaldi. He brought his authentic buffoonery to the English stage, and became a favorite of English audiences—adult and child alike. He was called the "Michelangelo of buffoonery."

As the nineteenth century progressed, the English stage found itself defaulting more and more to a lower theater of melodrama and bawdy vaudeville to satisfy the public fare. The musical operettas of Gilbert and Sullivan brought respectability back to the stage and seemed to express the trend across Europe to capture the lighter pleasures of the stage with the lingering fragrance of romance. The operetta form delighted in all things English but lacked greatness.

The unfortunate reality by the 1890s was that drama was nothing more than amusing, mechanical play making. Actors played their fixed character types caught up in stock situations. Nothing more was expected of them. The subject matter was predictably sweet and sentimental, and the dialogue clever and skillful, unfolding a neat little plot with a nice, happy ending. The plays had no spiritual merit, but the form itself worked theatrically. Henrik Ibsen would later base his social dramas on that same "well-made-play" that Eugene Scribe mastered so well in this era.

Drama had indeed made a significant descent from the dramatic struggles in Greek plays between men and gods. The heroic Electra was now replaced with Pinero's Iris, who slipped down to moral and social ruin because she could not resist her weakness for ease and luxury. There was no longer tragic pathos because there was no profound insight or high poetry to communicate character conflict in the striving toward something nobler. The emergence of the sparkling and witty comedies of Oscar Wilde (*Lady Windermere's Fan, The Importance of Being Earnest*) contributed perhaps the only real ingenuity of the late English romantic period.

Over time, with nothing of true feeling or beauty, the stage bred a certain stagnancy and lifelessness. The acting itself remained stylized to suit the conventionally correct

David Garrick of Drury Lane Theater, London

Edmund Kean as Richard III

Henry Irving as Shylock

American actor, Joseph Jefferson, as Rip Van Winkle

mold of the theater experience. Occasionally an actor of the mark of Eleanora Duse in Italy made drama live nobly and intensely on the stage, transcending the shallow play material by the revelation of her own fire and clear, personal expressiveness. She would be the forerunner of the tragedienne Rachel and the brilliant Sarah Bernhardt, whose crystalline voice and poetic spirit gained for her the greatest international following of any actress of the nineteenth century.

Up through the last half of the nineteenth century, England furnished America with most of her plays and players. At a time of great westward expansion, the new nation seemed generally disinterested in the stage as a cultural enterprise. The first notable American playwrights were Bronson Howard, with his native *Saratoga* and *Shenandoah;* Clyde Fitch, with his social comedies *Beau Brummel, The Climbers,* and *The Truth;* and William Vaughn Moody, with his religious folk play, *The Faith Healer.* Except for the invention of local themes, their craftsmanship was not any more original than what was playing in conventional theaters throughout Europe.

Edwin Forrest was the first native-born star of the New York stage, but even he found his greatest tributes in his Shakespearean interpretations. Other actors were Edwin Booth, Joseph Jefferson, and the first American-born actress, Charlotte Cushman. Booth brought an intellect and spiritual insight to his roles—most notably Hamlet, which he performed in New York at one hundred consecutive performances. Jefferson, on the other hand, excelled in kindly native character portraits. His greatest part was Rip Van Winkle—a part he had personally adapted and developed for the stage and played for decades to much happy applause.

The Twentieth Century

The twentieth century dawned with the revelation by directors Gordon Craig and Max Reinhardt that theater is a place of seeing, with the stage cleared for acting. The whole theatrical process—acting, setting, and staging—became more imaginative and sensuous. A new aesthetic theater, borrowing from the simplicity, physical beauty, and harmony of the Greek stage, began to emerge. It aimed to enchant the senses and beguile the emotions yet not distract from the action. The usual flapping, painted scenery used to stage the average drama was replaced by simple hangings with long, graceful lines. Masses of light and shade contributed to a more tasteful, decorative effect, lifting the senses of the spectator to new poetic heights. Theater was beginning to resurrect the seed ideals that underlie all true dramatic art: it touched upon the restful and beautiful, and through the physical senses, appealed to the spiritual faculties.

It was during this time that the Russian ballet blazed its way across the dramatic horizon with its gorgeous dance-dramas like *Scheherazade* and *Petrouchka.* Classical ballet boasted the ethereal Pavlova, while Isadore Duncan held her audiences spellbound

Molière and his troupe playing before King Louis XIV and Cardinal Mazarin in 1658.

Two paintings by Watteau, typical of the decorative French
theater of the 17th century.

(Above) The ballroom theater of the King. The group of spectators includes Louis XIII, Anne of Austria, and Cardinal Richelieu—a great patron of the arts. By this time, the proscenium frame has been made permanent. (Below) A painting by Lancret, titled *Scene from an Opera.*

Adrienne Lecouvreur, the most popular actress of the 18th century, known for her natural actions and true passion on the stage. She is here seen in the role of Cornelia, from Corneille's play, "La Mort de Pompee." She seemed to the spectators to "live" her part as no one before her had done.

Talma, the leading French actor of the 18th century, rebelled against artificiality and declamation in acting. He carried on his fight during and after the fall of the Bastille.

Sarah Siddons bridged the 18th and 19th centuries with her "classic" acting style, characterized by simplicity, nobility, and restraint. She became the greatest actress on the British stage, thrilling audiences with her portrayal of the Shakespearean heroines.

Actors at Drury Lane Theater performing *The School for Scandal* by Richard Sheridan. The bookshelves, windows, and landscape are painted on the backcloth.

The Little Theater in Haymarket, London, in 1815. From this perspective we can see the proscenium doorway, audience boxes, and the uncomfortable pit seats without backs for the less wealthy playgoers. Notice also the gas footlights.

As the 19th century progressed, so did the march toward Romanticism. Above is a photograph of the San Carlo Opera House in Naples, with its elaborate horseshoe design for ballet spectacles.

to her dramatic dance form. The theater experience they offered seemed to unify all the elements—actor, music, dance, costume, lighting, setting—into a rich, theatrical form that spoke directly to the spirit through the physical senses. It was not the same kind of ecstasy, however, that one would feel watching a Greek tragedy—there one is purged and taken beyond the world and left with a deeper awareness of the reality of life that clarifies the soul and spirit. Here the appeal was more sensual—belonging to the world, but still uplifting and refined in its effect.

In direct challenge to this kind of theater were the plays of Henrik Ibsen, August Strindberg, Leo Tolstoy, Anton Chekhov, Bernard Shaw, and John Galsworthy. These writers had been working their way into the playhouse since the closing decades of the nineteenth century. By the beginning of the twentieth century, the drama of social realism had arrived. These dramatists were impatient with the conventional "prudery" of nineteenth-century theater and what they perceived as romantic or sentimental escape from reality. They wanted their work to ring true to life, to the deeper, more complex motives of human nature, and to the underlying issues of society. Their new dramas of social purpose also rebelled against the pure, sensuous appeal of aesthetic theater and its move toward ideal beauty. It was not the aim of Chekhov to provide spiritual restfulness with the suicide of Constantin in the closing scenes of *The Seagull* or to make a statement about the overcoming spirit of man in his danse macabre, *The Cherry Orchard.* His plays expose, with a morbid irony, the decadence and decay of a Russian gentry dispossessed of home, ideals, initiative, and redeeming love.

Ibsen's *A Doll's House, The Wild Duck, An Enemy of the People, Hedda Gabler,* and the horrible *Ghosts* were torturous for their characterizations of protagonists who seemed to delight in suffering mental and emotional anguish and in inflicting that same torment upon the spectator without relief. Because of their complex psychology, however, these characters were challenging from an acting point of view, which is why the plays still remain popular. Even Stanislavski believed Ibsen's plays to be elusive and confused in their inner content, requiring great intellectual effort on the part of the actor to "decode" them. Strindberg's *The Father, Creditors,* and *Miss Julia* were realism at its most bitter. These intense psychological dramas gripped the emotions and compelled the audience to experience the (unheroic) feelings of souls in crisis.

The Realist writers asserted that imitation was the first aim of art and that the stage picture needed to be a photograph and not a painter's ideal conception. Theirs was a protest against the idealization of life as found in novels. They scorned it as pretense. The purpose of play making is to create the perfect illusion of reality; however, their reality was explicit and selective. They chose only slices of human existence that fit their idea of life in its anguished state, and they found it necessary to pry into dark and hidden motives of abnormal human behavior. Consequently, the drama of realism was characterized by pathological, criminal, or sexual-psychoanalytical components—with an obsessive amount of shocking or sensational revealment. Gone was that subtler motive of self-sacrifice clothed with nobility, or that rare sweetness that we had grown to love so well in Shakespeare's portraits.

No doubt these fathers of modern drama brought a psychological intensity to the stage, but their message was generally depressing and left one feeling ignoble. The cynical view that life is nothing more than an inglorious black-and-white photograph of injustice and folly remains with the spectator as the last curtain falls. Much of realist drama was simply not clear. It was neither instructive nor even theatrical.

The realist-idealist dramas of the French dramatists Eugene Brieux *(Les Bienfaiteurs, Blanchette, La Foi, La Robe Rouge)* and François de Cure *(La Fille Sauvage)* stood apart from other realist drama in their bold and powerful penetration. Society is vigorously scourged and social hypocrisy is laid bare, but their work, unlike the rest of realist drama, had an idealism and dramatic sweep that wrought a more favorable conception of humanity. George Bernard Shaw's plays *(Saint Joan, Candida, and Pygmalion)* were also an exception to the rule. They were written at a purer intellectual plane and glowed with more warmth and humanity.

Except for Shaw and the realist-idealist dramas, the plays of the social dramatists were essentially humanist manifestos—intense, introspective studies of man's dysfunctional qualities. As grim social studies, they could be viewed as forerunners of the Marxist movement to come. Just as deep calls to deep, so discontent calls to discontent. Unlike the wide reaches of Elizabethan drama, these new plays had no purging elements. They offered no renewal of the spirit or divine faith to illumine suffering and allow for transmutation and transcendence. Shakespeare could probe the darkest human condition and so clothe it with poetic beauty and spiritual light that its ultimate form was noble and uplifting. Reverence for the eternal mysteries was beautifully woven into the life of his characters and into his very play structure. *Hamlet, King Lear,* and *Othello* immediately come to mind. If Shakespeare performed heart surgery on his characters, they all recovered, or at least prepared for a better resurrection, and the audience left the theater similarly cleansed and healed.

The Realists, on the other hand, were focused on the microscopic society that seemed to breed life's miseries. As they made this one societal groove their study, their plays became wearisome—a litany of man's worst complaints. Though they congratulated themselves that they were exposing men's iniquities and society's ills, they actually achieved nothing redemptive. They had not the single eye on the enduring ideal. They wished to be sincere, but they were unwilling to seek truth and love outside the limited, relative, and secular social context. They reveled in a spiritually sick human condition. Such misery justified their plays, and their plays justified the misery. If they considered themselves heart surgeons, it is fair to say that all their patients died on the operating table (or committed suicide), and with them, every hope for the rest of us who were looking in through the proscenium fourth wall.

It is not surprising that, with the exception again of Shaw, the social dramatists also lacked humor. And without humor, there can be no freedom from the ever-serious, self-conscious ego—as Aesop so masterfully reminded us. They came to a theater that was overdosed with sweet sentimentality and artificiality, where all life is pleasant. They fought the good fight to make it represent what they believed to be "real" life. Realism became their battle cry, but it also became their religion. With an almost fanatical devotion, they insisted that the first test of theater as art was honest portrayal of the common man—down to the last bitter detail of motive, feeling, and thought. If anything in their plays was celebrated, it was death, because death was the end of life which, after all, was nothing but misery and injustice.

In many ways, these bleak world dramatists were the forerunners of the social engineers of today who view life as a clinic. Finding nothing redeeming in man (and not willing to acknowledge God), the social engineers feel compelled to continually dissect and probe the diseased components of man and society to justify the need for correction, while viewing themselves as the priests and mentors of that correction. The Realists refused to comprehend that reality has precious little to do with art, especially reality that is a clinical slice of morbid, disillusioned living. The purpose of theatric art, as Shakespeare and Sophocles understood supremely, is to present to man his higher reality, to show him a form of deeper, finer living that is movingly expressive and alive to his spirit. For only in the spirit—in union with the divine spirit—is the solution to all human problems.

As Jaques tells us in *As You Like It,* all the world's a stage, life is a play, and we are all players. What matter the part one is assigned? What matter the misery and suffering? To play the part well, with joy and courage, humility and faith—that is the essential thing, whether the player wear a crown or motley. Too many of the characters born of the social dramatists were like candles blown by every wind of emotion—until the very violence of the emotions snuffed out the flame. In the end, the flame had shed no light on others, but served only to provide a shadow for itself.

Meanwhile, back on the American frontier, theater was sustaining itself with native and homely plays, Indian dramas, Negro minstrelsy, and local romantic melodrama. The stage provided entertainment—sentimental and shallow, it is true—but amusing and vigorous. The trenchant realism of Europe did not find such a deep rooting in American soil, though Eugene O'Neill *(Anna Christie, The Hairy Ape, Desire Under the Elms)* was expressively somber and psychoanalytical like his European colleagues. *Strange Interlude* (1928), his third Pulitzer Prize-winning play, was a Freudian study of a neurotic woman's sex life. His *Mourning Becomes Electra* (1931) was, as one critic wrote, a "modern psychological approximation of the Greek sense of fate." His version,

Drury Lane Theater, London, in 1842 with the romantic and picturesque setting for the wrestling scene in *As You Like It*.

This realistic setting for *Tribut de Zamora* is typical of theater staging during the Romantic period.

These three illustrations were taken from the souvenir program of Henry Irving's production of *Dead Heart* at the Lyceum Theater in London, 1889. Note the realistic settings typical of the late 19th century. In the middle picture, the central figures are Ellen Terry as Catherine Duval and her (real life) son Gordon Craig as Arthur de St Valery. In the bottom picture, Henry Irving plays the leading role of Landry.

set during the Civil War period, offers a Freudian interpretation of a deeply conflicted New England family, whose members commit murder, incest, and suicide. The epic drama earned him the Nobel Prize in Literature in 1936, though in its starkness and ugliness, it betrayed everything of the beauty and spiritual exaltation of the original Electra by Sophocles.

Though the brooding and discontented O'Neill was the toast of the theatrical crowd of Greenwich Village and the Theater Guild players, American audiences generally preferred something more cheery and poetically lovely. It was hard to convince a naturally romantic and optimistic people—even in the riotous 1920s and sexually-abandoned 30s—to embrace his brutish and unheroic protagonists. What was true then is still true today. Americans are practical romantics, who put commitment behind making their dreams come true. Other more representative dramatists of this time were Susan Glaspell, Maxwell Anderson, and Sidney Howard. By his own admission, "weary of plays in prose that never lifted from the ground," Maxwell Anderson turned to playwriting in poetry. Though his first successful venture, *What Price Glory*, was a realistic play, his verse tragedy *Elizabeth the Queen* (1930) realized the idealistic model he desired. Later followed *Mary of Scotland, Valley Forge*, and *Key Largo*.

In a preface to his play *Candle in the Wind*, Anderson wrote that he viewed theater as "a religious institution devoted entirely to the exaltation of the spirit of man." Theater's aim is to "find and hold up to our regard, what is admirable in the human race." He condemned O'Neill's drama as "a low opinion of the race of men" and affirmed that man had a dignity and destiny, that "man is not perfect, but seeks perfection." Along the lines of the Shakespearean and Wagnerian formula, his tragedies centered about the struggle of an exceptional though not flawless character. "The man in the street simply will not do as the hero. The hero must not be a perfect man....He must learn through suffering....He suffers death as a consequence of his fault or his attempt to correct it, but before he dies he has become a nobler person." When Mary says to Elizabeth in *Mary of Scotland*, "I'll win men's hearts in the end," she represents the heroic personality triumphant in defeat—reminiscent of those high concepts of tragedy that the Greek playwrights introduced in ancient Athens. Anderson believed that poetry is the only language of the stage that can impel the audience toward a higher vision of life. "Dramatic poetry is man's greatest achievement on earth so far.... Without at least one [great poet] we shall never have a great theater in this country."

Aspiring toward richness and depth of feeling through poetic speech is our ancient tradition of theater. In the midst of realistic prose drama, Irish playwrights J. M. Synge *(Playboy of the Western World)* and William Butler Yeats *(The Land of Heart's Desire)* tried to restore the poetic intention. The Irish Players, who made the works of these dramatists famous, were respected for their beautiful speech and simplicity of acting. They reminded audiences that on the stage one must have joy and not just reality.

T. S. Eliot was already stirring England with his *Murder in the Cathedral* (1935), a religious play about St. Thomas Becket that was suggestive, in its choral passages, of the Greek drama. The greatest drama in history was born in poetry, whether in the Greek tragedies of Athens, the plays and poetry of Shakespeare, or the gorgeous imagery of Romantic German playwrights, Goethe and Schiller. Poetry was always chosen as the highest medium of elevated thought. Our best dramatists sought to mirror not what man does think and does say but what he would think and would say if he could express the beauty and nobility of his true self. They sought to present not what man is, but what he dreams of being.

How were acting styles being affected during this period? By the 1930s, the "star" of the old school had lost ground to the repertory or ensemble player. As Irving, Terry, Booth, Jefferson and Bernhardt died or retired, a younger generation of players—more youthful and self-assured—took to the stage. London theater, in particular, excelled in subtle and beautiful stagecraft based on classical training, absent the stylistic cliches and prescribed elocution of the past. Actors like Laurence Olivier, Edith Anderson, John Gielgud, Ralph Richardson, Leslie Howard, Gladys Cooper, and Ronald Colman dominated the stage and contributed an artistry that was skilled, expressive, and dignified. The same actors would be lured across the ocean to jump-start the presence of authentic and classically trained actors in the movies of the major American studios. Soon, the overdone faux English accent of American actors had relaxed into a more genuine American speech, as audiences became critical of the imposter. On the American stage (and later film), there was John Barrymore, Ethel Barrymore, Helen Hayes, and Katherine Cornell.

Actors now saw themselves as ensemble players working together under a single director, who would unify all the theatrical elements—actors, lighting, dialogue, movement, setting, costumes—into one form. The art of the theater was being seen as a whole, with the director commanding the complete vision of the performance instead of being the slave of the whims and idiosyncrasies of a leading actor or actress. "The Show" had become the important thing and the director, not the actor, was the man of the hour. No more was this change apparent than in the masterful work of Stanislavski and his Moscow Art Theater. In the tradition of the Comédie-Française—the original repertory company—Stanislavski's aim was to present a play well performed by all members of the cast. At no time was the whole to be sacrificed to a part, however brilliant the part (or the star who played that part). Under his direction, using a more introspective approach to acting, his players became adept at carrying the spectator to deeper planes of character revealment and understanding of the author's intention. His system would have lasting effects on American film acting.

In the years leading up to and during World War II, the American people were unified in their support of the war and of our military troops abroad. They rejected the cynical bleakness of the realist playwrights and their lack of faith. To deal with the crises associated with the war effort, both on the home front and wherever our soldiers fought, Americans needed to resurrect the enduring value of faith in our country's ideals, for which so many had sacrificed their lives—or the best years of their lives. They discovered, as their forefathers had also discovered, that the golden shaft by which man climbs out of darkness is faith. The film industry, also united behind the war effort, made hundreds of movies that reflected this unity and idealism.

The 1950s saw an explosion of Americana in the musical stage plays of Rodgers and Hammerstein. Though Ziegfeld and the major studios in Hollywood had staged grand musicals and operettas throughout the 1920s and 30s—making the music of Victor Herbert, Sigmund Romberg, Irving Berlin, George M. Cohan, and Jerome Kern as popular as Coca Cola—they were not as well-constructed or as theatrically sweeping in their story drama (with the exception of *Showboat*) as those produced in the post-war period.

With all its sparkling facets of dance, bouncy tunes, witty dialogue, and a live orchestra, the American musical remained popular throughout the 1950s and early 60s. The Hammerstein favorites are occasionally revisited on Broadway and are still an integral part of high school and community theater repertoire. The musical play differs from the earlier operetta form by its emphasis on characterizations of real people in real situations, and by its American content. Nearly every musical play uses song and dance to further the storyline rather than distract the audience from it. The stars in a musical play have to sing, dance, *and* act well.

During this same post-war period, Americans were being introduced in their living rooms to a feast of wholesome family television shows, including *Father Knows Best, Leave It to Beaver, Daniel Boone, The Lone Ranger, Lassie, The Rifleman, The Roy Rogers Show, Combat, The Gallant Men, Bonanza, Disneyland, Wagon Train, Dr. Kildare, American Bandstand, Gunsmoke, Dragnet, Hogan's Heroes,* and *The Mickey Mouse Club,* to mention just a few. All these shows promoted American values of home, family, faith, integrity, self-sacrifice, the rule of law, our country's heritage, and patriotism.

By the late 1960s, the realist playwrights, riding on the back of the anti-Vietnam war movement, gained ascendancy—this time with a grittier and more strident edge. They have continued to hold dominance and to foment their own political and cultural agenda through this first decade of the twenty-first century. As realism has progressed to hedonism, acting styles have followed suit. Today, less and less works of dramatic art express noble intention or reverence for traditional values, let alone provide a gateway to the spirit. Even fewer actors are capable of bringing to their characters a clarity and erudition that can generate a theatric current to the hearts of the audience. Though many of the great literary classics have been adapted into modern movies, their dramatic rendering is stark and lacks respect for the author's original intention.

We have to look to the British-made films to salvage some semblance of trueness and authenticity in the characterization of historical figures.

As the trendsetter for our nation's dramatic art, Hollywood has become mired in its own muddied fiction of life. The art of acting has followed a similar descent. It can be said that our world of art is steeped and soaked in eroticism and ignoble intention. What is dearly needed, both on the stage and on the movie screen, is true art—the drama of life that concentrates the best of man and is artistically revealed and presented. Hollywood, alas, is intolerant of poetic characters of delicate sensitivities who might suggest the romantic ideal. They prefer instead the palpitating actuality of men and women who riotously celebrate their liberation from the moral and ethical moorings that have long proven the making of the true hero and the true heroine.

The authority that Hollywood exerts over the American public (and the world theater) is waning. Television ratings for the annual Academy Awards have fallen to all-time lows, while most of the movies that Hollywood anoints with the unholy oil of its "progressivism" receive the lowest box office returns. Even so, Hollywood's influence is ever-present. Thanks to our current television and cinema fare, our youth have developed a dependency upon the narcotic of sex. Even PG-rated movies are inflamed with more of *The Sorcerer's* "wooing and undoing, sighing and suing" than the R-rated movies of the 60s and 70s. It is a deadly seduction. We must create a more worthy alternative, if only in our local community. As Shakespeare himself used the dramatic arts to lift the hearts and minds of the people out of ignorance and moral turpitude, so those who love what is true and beautiful must forge a new renaissance of theater that will restore beauty, purity, and dignity once again to our artistic life.

Approaching a Character Role

An actor's working goal is to give a clear and convincing portrayal of his role. His artistic goal is to present his character in an expressive, meaningful, and aesthetically pleasing form—contributing something of enduring beauty and worth in the process. I have listed below certain guidelines that can help the actor achieve these twin goals that make up the art of characterization.

1. Be true to the author's intention

Know the intention of the author and be true to it, for the author is the only authentic voice for his play. This will allow you to portray the character as the author conceived it. To honestly comprehend the author's view and the characterization of life he intended, the actor needs to research the life of the author, his political and religious beliefs, the social class in which he moved, the men and women who directly provided the inspiration for his art, and the culture of morality, ethics, and philosophy that shaped how he lived and what he wrote.

The actor also needs to make a comprehensive study of the character he is to portray, following the same guidelines that he used to come to know the author—that is, the epoch in which the character lived, his class, manners, and address, etc. This is especially true when studying the classics, where the characters have a vastly different deportment and spiritual content from those depicted in modern realist dramas. The actor is ill prepared if he does not approach his role with a true historic sense. He cannot play his character with any meaningfulness if that character is "out of joint" with the times in which he moved and lived in the imagination of the author.

A good play, like any good work of literature, has an integrity that makes it its own interpreter. It needs only to be performed skillfully and with faithfulness to the author's purpose and meaning. Unfortunately, in their feverish attempt to "suit the play to the age," many modern directors and actors have coarsened the rendering of even the great classic works—sweeping away all things of grace and noble intention. This is no more apparent than in the staging of the Shakespearean plays.

It is rather the exception today to experience "Shakespeare" as it was originally conceived and staged. Actors often lack the careful and polished stage technique and poetic spirit to perform it fittingly, while many directors lack the reverence and modesty to allow the greatest author of all time to speak to his audience without an interpreter. The spiritual vibrancy of the Plays has been diminished in favor of a more sensually edgy composition that sacrifices poetic cadence to dull, prosaic rhythms that grind out a sexual subtext that was not there in the original writing. Even renowned English troupes prevent the audience from reaching the loftier heights that the verse inspires by grounding the Plays in a dense sexual magnetism, framed by dissonant music and anachronistic costuming and sets.

The Royal Shakespeare Company's production of *A Midsummer Night's Dream* at Stratford-Upon-Avon during the 1999 season exemplified this trend. Despite a distinguished cast and celebrated director, the play bore little resemblance to the romantic comedy that parents read to their children as an introduction to the works of William Shakespeare. Titania paraded before us as 'The Great Whore.' Her fairies, one of whom bawdily seduced Puck in the opening scene, were sluts of differing preferences. Oberon, his bald head and open breast marked with cultist symbols, wove a dark, satanic presence as he performed mudras over the players and the audience—all this to a voodoo music score that throbbed out its frenzied beat while spotlights crisscrossed the room, casting a luminescence that simulated a speakeasy or a red light district.

Oberon and Puck both made their entrances from beneath the stage floor, emerging out of a red smoke that reminded one of the "mist and murk" of Hell's maw from which the conjuring Lemurs rose in Goethe's *Faust*. Hermia and Helena, with their shortened hems and high heeled shoes, made their respective appearances as ladies of the night, while their two lovers, Lysander and Demetrius, wore gangster trench coats and carried machine guns.

The spectacle of scantily clad Bottom and Titania in her fairy bower (a double bed lowered from the ceiling) fit an R-rated category of public exhibitionism. Throughout the play, but especially in the scenes featuring the rustic actors, every conceivable sexual and homosexual meaning was insinuated into the verse. While most of the audience were on their feet at play's end offering an enthusiastic ovation, others stumbled out of the theater incredulous at what they had just witnessed. The director lacked seriousness in his conception of the play, for his rendering of it was a lie.

Stanislavski believed that faithfulness to the author's dramatic purpose is the most sacred obligation of the director and actor. In the RSC's production, the director flagrantly ignored Shakespeare's intention. By choosing to set up his own personal through line, he dishonored the author, who could never have conceived so debased an interpretation of this, his sparkling gem of all comedies. A source of fanciful joy for children and adults alike for 400 years, this magical play was pillaged by a company of players who should have been its most revered guardian. To superimpose a meaner and coarser relationship between the gracious spirits that make up Shakespeare's most beloved fairy creatures was an act of cynicism, reflecting a jaded perception of romance and of the higher good that Shakespeare's art embodies. The director and cast used their exceptional talents and most privileged reputation to hoodwink their audience, duping them into believing that this was "enlightened" Shakespeare, or Shakespeare as it should be performed in these progressive days. In fact, the audience experienced nothing that spoke to the heart at all, nothing that brought the beauty of the verse into the soul's keeping.

The vocal technique of these hallowed players was unimpeachable. Where else can you find Shakespearean verse spoken with such perfect clarity, precision, and cadence? Yet the actors did not achieve truthful and convincing characterizations, since their characters were not the same dramatis personae that Shakespeare himself had conceived in his imagination when he penned the play. The actors used the original words and storyline of the play, but they invented their own characters and created a discordant and alien setting. There was no unity, coherence, or dramatic development of the characters along the lines Shakespeare had indicated. Nor did the performance meet high aesthetic standards. The staging was original and arresting—even creatively innovative, but it was not artistically pleasing or tasteful. It failed to represent the beauty and worth of dramatic art.

The 2006 Complete Works Festival demonstrated this growing trend of the RSC to give the Plays a modern face-lift in the hope of drawing in a younger audience. While *King John* and the trilogy of *Henry VI* plays were respectfully treated and masterfully staged, *Romeo and Juliet* and *The Tempest* were tampered with to the point of being almost unrecognizable. In reviewing *Romeo and Juliet,* the Sunday Times promised that "the world will love these lovers…" Many a school teacher would have strongly disagreed after seeing their young students exposed to the "erotically charged" encounters of cartel-crossed lovers in Mafia Sicily. Instead of the innocence and spiritual beauty that we have long associated with Juliet's character, we were shown a slip of a girl for whom, as one reviewer wrote, "sex and death became inseparable." Replacing rapiers with long wooden poles, which the Verona hotheads bashed against the stage floor, was an absurd abstraction for street fighting, while a scaffolding cage separating Juliet from Romeo was a sterile replacement for the traditional rose-garnished balcony.

The Tempest was even more radical. The setting of the Bermudas (intended to conjure the ancient magic of the West Indies and provide a fitting stage for Prospero's mystical powers) was changed to the icy and barren wastes of Antarctica. This transplant of the story ruptured the play's coherence and the emotional life of the characters. The play opened with a large screen movie of a modern-day shipwreck in hurricane waters. Inserted into this moving image was the action of the crew making desperate SOS radio calls. Once the ship sank, Prospero appeared center stage in a gruesome animal skin that looked suspiciously like the one Mick Dundee wore in the Aussie pub in *Crocodile Dundee*. Miranda, dressed like a 7th grader in a school tunic, Eskimo coat, short sox, and rock-climbing boots, was a cipher-like presence of utter stupidity from the first scene to the last. Patrick Stewart, in the role of the visionary Prospero, diminished the noble mien of his character by making him cower before Ariel—an interpretive twist that is nowhere hinted at anywhere in the (real) play.

Though Ariel is androgynous, Shakespeare addresses her as "delicate Ariel." We therefore imagine a feminine sylph of the air, who embodies the grace and enchantment of nature's fairy kingdom. The Ariel of this production was a disembodied male spirit. He wore a black robe, set off by white face and greasy, slicked-back hair to enhance his spectral, ghostlike appearance. Julian Bleach's portrayal of Ariel created a nightmarish effect, best described by Gordon Parsons in his August 9th, 2006 review for the *Morning Star* daily: "With a chainsaw voice, [Ariel] rises like a death's head from a burning brazier and later from a ghastly cannibalised hamper as a blood-soaked skeleton." Apparently, the director intended to showcase the principal influence of this "enlightened" dark spirit over Prospero—thus ignoring Shakespeare's conception of Prospero as an innately wise and masterful alchemist, who has the spiritual attainment to ameliorate his own destiny. Rupert Goold's production of *The Tempest,* despite the gravitas of Patrick Stewart, failed to be true to the author's intention.

These performances by the RSC prove that not even the purest and most innocent of roles from the classic past are safe from corruption. Few women's roles in our modern theater inspire toward the kind of womanhood honored by earlier generations. Even fewer men's roles project masculinity in all its traditional gallantry, strength, and courage. Swashbuckling, chivalrous depictions of clean-hearted heroes are ridiculed today or mixed in with enough moral usury to deny a real hero's claim. The 1998-1999 Broadway presentation of *The Scarlet Pimpernel* demonstrated that the characterization of high manly spirits, long associated with Baroness Orczy's splendid romantic hero, can easily be played down to wanton and unabashed feminization and trite melodrama in this politically correct culture.

If we do not respect the intention of the greatest of our authors of the world's dramatic literature, then we lose the ability to pass on to successive generations the most heavenly expressions of the ideals of truth and beauty, which is the high purpose of art. In her book *Memoirs of Sarah Bernhardt,* the famous actress wrote that the actor's first task when interpreting a role is to define the intention of the author, then to identify himself with that intention. "I have never played an author false with regard to his idea. And I have always tried to represent the character role according to history, whenever it is an historical personage, and as the novelist describes it if an invented personage."

In the last book she authored, *L'Art du Theatre* (The Art of Theater), Bernhardt spoke of the actor being a messenger of the genius and aspiration of the dramatist. She wrote:

> It is our mission [as actors] to stimulate the minds and move the hearts of men. The poets and dramatists entrust us with the finest products of their art. They place in our...hands the quintessence of their minds, the flesh of their flesh, their long-meditated utterances, the generous thoughts they would sow in the heart of crowds, the lesson they would teach society in an entertaining manner....
>
> And we are the advocates in these proceedings. We alone may communicate instantaneously to the public the ardent faith of the author...he who has so much at stake, his future, sometimes even his daily bread, his glory, his all. It is we who must, with one hand, snatch away the tares, and with the other sow the good seed....
>
> Once the curtain is raised, the actor ceases to belong to himself, he belongs to his character, to his author, to his public. He must do the impossible to identify himself with the first, not to betray the second, and not to disappoint the third.

She spoke passionately about assimilating the quality of the author's imagination through which his genius is expressed, and rendering that genius with exactitude to the public. By his art, the actor must "vivify the thoughts of the poet or dramatist," not just because the author is the author, but because his genius must be felt and heard at the same level of beauty, perfection, and charm at which it was first inspired and written down. She believed that the author (and not the actor) held the master key to the character's interpretation and that the actor could only unlock the perfect interpretation by searching out the author's intention. She wrote: "Let the dramatist enlighten you with the rays of psychology appropriate to each [historical] character. Through him, you see them developing, living, and thinking." Bernhardt's most acclaimed role was the tragic Phèdre. She believed she was successful in that role because she was able to render with obviousness "the pure and touching art of Racine."

"It is the faith of the actor, holding the torch handed him by the poet, that illumines every mind, every soul, and every sensibility," she wrote. Bernhardt was intolerant of actors who were "feebly endowed with the historic sense" of the roles they impersonated. "The character of Caesar, or of Hamlet, or of Augustus cannot be improvised. If the actor is totally ignorant of history, if he cannot fit characters into their environment, if he is incapable of investing them with the sentiments that were common to their epoch, their generation, their class, even their party, he will never be anything but a second-rate actor."

So great was her belief in the power of theater to incarnate the labor and genius of the author that she refused to play parts written by authors whose plays did not possess the "boldness, penetration, and luminosity" that could move and uplift the audience "toward the conquest of the beautiful." It was for this reason that she chose not to act in the plays of Pierre Corneille, whose female characters she described as "heavy, ludicrous, far-fetched, and commonplace....They declaim, but their heart is not in their breast, it beats in their head." Speaking of the character of Chimene, the heroine of Corneille's *Le Cid*, she wrote: "I could not interpret a character so false, so changeable, so defective in humanity." As strongly as she felt the actor was obligated to serve the author's intention, she also believed the author had an equally sacred obligation to achieve, through his art, the "evocation of the ideal." It is why she took to the Greek and Shakespearean tragedies so intensely, and with such exaltation.

When we consider the works of the Greek tragedians—Sophocles, Euripides, and Aeschylus—we have to take into account that these men were priests as well as consummate poets, who not only understood the unity of play structure but conceived of theater as a religious institution. It would never have occurred to them to write of anything less than revered gods, legendary kings and heroes with their stirring deeds, hereditary sins, and purging expiations. Such high subject matter, with its piteously courageous struggles and crushing dooms, lent a magnitude of emotion and solemnity of purpose to Greek drama that must never be brought low.

When an actor betrays the noble intention of the greatest of our authors, he cannot carry in himself every joy and every beauty that these dramatists had hoped to inspire. Many artists not only take the classics hostage to their own audacious intention but use their art to advance personal belief systems and political viewpoints that undermine the finer spirit of man. When they do that, when they confine theater to the subject of man as he is rather than what he can be, and thereby diminish the value of life, they destroy the hope of transcendence, which is what the stage is all about.

2. Be true to your highest calling

When we ignore the author's intention, the actor's purpose is also compromised. Instead of helping his audience forget their sorrows and fears for a time, he sorely rubs them in. Does it not seem a more profitable use of the proscenium and its players to calm a fretting conscience, to soothe an aching heart, to relieve a tired mind—in short, to lift the audience to a higher revelation of life than they possessed when they first entered the theater? It is the actor, after all, who has the power to refresh and strengthen our spirits—to remind us, by his acting magic, of a beauty and light that may be invisible to our eyes but will always be felt by our hearts. This is the ancient magic behind the twin masks of tragedy and comedy—a magic that can only be accessed when the actor rises to the level of the spirit, for that is his highest calling as a dramatic artist.

Where there is a lack of high conception in the creation of character or a desire to tear down all that is beautiful and true, the actor is nothing more than a stand-in for a photographic recording of life in its temporal and corrupted state. You cannot work at the top of your craft when you are not able to lift your character out of common life and into a setting of hope, of faith, of some rainbow hue of heaven. Actors fail themselves and their profession when they espouse lewdness and condemn purity, when they scorn life's opportunities and embrace cynicism, when they mock love and forget the beauty of the divine.

Sarah Bernhardt was talking about this when she wrote: "The labor of our art must only be the quest of truth." She then added, "But it is always the artist who is closest to reality in the ideal, who will triumph." In other words, the actor's comprehension of the character he impersonates should always be ideal, but the art with which he expresses that ideal should convey the true and deep feelings of the character. Yet that naturalism had its boundaries. "The actor must not shock the modesty of those who listen to him. All art whatsoever presupposes an enlightened choice (*un choix éclairé*), and no purpose is served by being brutally natural. To be natural does not mean that an actor should exhibit the passions in the manner they are lived in his own time in all circumstances and on all subjects."

She fervently believed that the stage should not accommodate any form of vulgarity. She admired actors who had a love of the beautiful and the good (*l'amour du beau et du bien*) and who could, by their art, transfer that beauty and idealism to the stage. She spoke of Henry Irving as a great artist because he accomplished such a transfer. "The staging of his plays was marked by a breadth of study, a taste, and accuracy. The Englishman guided his public to the Past with a wealth of research and idealism.... Thanks to him, the English theater gained a great reputation around the world." She was also intolerant of any show of vulgarity by an actor in his personal life. Of all the turpitudes that the press accused her of during the course of her long career, the accusation of vulgarity, she stated in her *Memoirs,* had no grounds.

Sometimes an actor has to do battle with the powers that be, or the prevailing bias of the public and media in order to bring something of beauty and reverence to the stage or screen. Sarah Bernhardt told the story of how she fought to have religious works performed in the theater. When she announced her intention to stage Edmond Haraucourt's verse play *La Passion* (The Passion), she was met with rebuffs, cowardly attacks, and a press blitz accusing her of propagandizing religion on the stage. At the same time, pastors of all denominations preached against her and the play for a different reason: they believed that religious subjects were too sacred for exhibition in a public theater officiated by "courtesans."

A year after starting her crusade, she was able to arrange a reading during an interval at a concert at the Cirque d'Hiver (Winter Circus)—a venue for musical and dramatic events. The hall was packed, but not with well-meaning souls. The spirit was hostile and enemies were planted in the audience to create a disturbance and to turn the event into a scandal. Close friends came backstage to implore Sarah not to go through with it. The rest of the story is best told by Bernhardt herself:

> I started to read this work in front of a frigid audience. The most beautiful lines were accompanied by malicious whisperings. Being a woman, I had the advantage of not being interrupted. But when it was the turn of the actor who had to read the lines ascribed to Jesus, there was an outburst of cat-calls, shouts, and roars.
>
> The public, tired of yelling, burst into laughter, suddenly realizing that laughter causes greater discomfort to the artist than hissing. I thought the cause was lost, when Edmond Haraucourt jumped up from his seat and turned on the audience, his face white with anger.
>
> "You came here knowing that a play in verse entitled *Le Passion* would be read. You have paid for your seats, you will hear the play, or you will depart."

And kissing my hand [he said]:

"Thank you, Madame, thank you!"

The effect was withering; the public, curbed by this logic and intimidated by this faith, became silent and listened without any demonstration. The ice had been broken, and this daring attempt caused great discussion. People argued against this new tendency, but the work was splendid and powerful, and was suffused with grandeur and reverence.

Three years later, *Le Passion* was performed in a theater, with scenery, lay figures, and costumes. At the same time Edmond Rostand's *La Samaritaine* (The Samaritan), a gospel in verse in three tableaux, was triumphantly and gloriously launched. The day of the first performance was a day of unforgettable emotion. Christian love filled the theater with a joy of infinite purity. I felt myself transported to the beyond as I recited the beautiful words, and other hearts beat in my heart as I wept tears devoid of bitterness, those pure tears that lave, remove, and wash away for ever the dross of our souls, of our lives too long for the wrong that we do, too short for the good that we could do. The audience was transported and irradiated, and applauded all the lines. This day was especially memorable for me, as it plunged me for a moment into memories of my early infancy, when, mystical and ignorant, I had visions of the little Jesus; it demonstrated to me more than ever the powerful influence of literary works performed in our temple: the Theater.

On the following days I received numerous letters, and I quote a passage from one of them, written by a priest:

"Madame—I was present at your performance of *La Samaritaine.* I will not conceal from you the fact that I went there...to write a vigorous attack upon M. Rostand, for I deplored this attempt to enthrone religion in the theater. I returned completely converted, for sitting by my side was a poor man with a tortured soul. During the performance he could not refrain from speaking to me and confiding to me his doubts and indecisions, and at length he exclaimed with a joyful and transfigured face that he felt better and restored. I am happy, Madame, that all that remains of my aggressive suspicions against you and M. Rostand is a touching and grateful recollection."

These few lines made me very happy....It was God Himself who inspired the work of M. Rostand. This work resembles Samothrace's [Winged] Victory [marble sculpture of Greek art found on the island of Samothrace around 190 B.C., now in the *Musée du Louvre*)], which bears in its outspread wings and fluttering tunic the immortal cry of glory of the ages that are past, to the ages that are to come.

How can a young artist fulfill his highest calling when he himself does not comprehend the high beauty of his art? In today's theatrical life there is no longer any true standard either in play structure or subject content, let alone inspiring characterizations. Movies tend to draw maximum attentiveness and emotional responsiveness not by the fine directness of story progression and appeal to the heart-true instincts, but by crude and prying exploitation of the senses. The widespread use of graphics in films, in the media, and on the World Wide Web has ushered in a revolution of self-expression that has pushed the envelope of "art" to the raw edge and done much to discredit former standards of symmetry, unity, and beauty.

The breakaway from true artistic conception and execution is so violent in our modern art that romantic tradition lies a-bleeding. Once-cherished codes of personal address, self-restraint, and plain gallantry between men and women have been replaced with profligacy and the expectation of instant self-gratification. The preponderance of R-rated movies and Reality TV testifies to a culture that is careless—even derisive—of what is pure in heart, high in faith, and perfect in intention. If our civilization is to survive as we know it, art must return to the aesthetic landmarks of the pure, the beautiful, and true, which seem so lost to us in today's art, and can only be found in the well of the classics. A golden rule for young actors in choosing their first audition piece is to avoid modern authors and their generally depressing cavalcade of tortured, self-absorbed, emoting souls, and embrace, in the words of Albert Einstein, the "worthy pursuit of beauty and truth" in the great roles of classic drama.

To achieve his highest calling, the actor needs to honor the high purpose of the great authors *and* infuse that same faith and noble intention in every role he portrays. And what is noble intention but the moral clarity, intelligence, and dignity that the actor brings to his character every moment he is onstage. Whenever the ideal is appealed to in art, we have noble intention. By it, the actor lets his audience see the struggle of the soul to be true, not false; to strive after good, not evil (or suffer the consequences of that evil and grow as a result); and to have faith, not despair. Why do these intangibles matter? Because life is all about striving toward what is free and pure and good, no matter the personal price to be paid. In life, the ideal is greater than the reality because the ideal is what endures and gives life its meaning, romance, and preciousness.

Imbued with noble intention, acting can be beautiful and complete in its magic. Nothing illumines the actor's presence more than his own high sense of the ideal, for it carries with it a hope and joy that lends breadth and sweep to the acting of the role. In actresses, noble intention can be identified by an imaginative intuition, a purity and grace of deportment, a spiritual strength and inner loveliness. We saw it in so many of the actresses of an earlier era: Norma Shearer, Greer Garson, Carole Lombard, Deborah Kerr, Irene Dunne, Gladys Cooper, Ingrid Bergman, Russian-born Eugenie Leontovich, and Croatian-born Alida Valli. (Who can forget Valli's luminous

Ellen Terry

Eleanora Duse

Lily Langtry

Sarah Bernhardt as Joan Pucelle (Henry VI)

Sarah Bernhardt
(portrait in the Théâtre Français)

…as Hamlet

…as Andromaque

role within a role of Saint Joan of Arc in *The Miracle of the Bells?*) Though some modern actresses, such as Meryl Streep, demonstrate powerful instinct, imaginative introspection, and lyrical power in their roles, the qualities of simple dignity and spiritual purity are not those that most actresses today aspire to.

The playgoer knows the sparkle of the true stone and will inevitably respond to it. It is to the authentic light that the audience bring the candles of their own hopes and dreams to be lit. It explains why Turner Classic Movies is so successful. The gems of the past are never forgotten, but revisited time and time again in our hearts and imaginations because they embody noble intention and fulfill the soul's yearning for the divine ideal.

Shakespeare's protagonists, like the heroes of Greek drama, are wrought with the impulse of noble intention, which is why so many of his characters, from Hamlet to Juliet's nurse, have the touch of immortality. The stage is ill served by fitting such characters into the puny frame of the modern-day mindset of psycho-intensity, cynicism, lewdness, and lack of faith. Prospero told us that "we are such stuff as dreams are made of." For what are our dreams if they are not the dreams God dreams for us? And what is faith but giving God the benefit of the doubt, instead of man.

Shakespeare understood that human nature is not the model of art, no matter how truthful and deep the rendering of that human condition. True art finds its inspiration in the dreams of the spirit, for only in the spirit can we know true life and not merely material existence. As in life, so in drama, it is always the spirit that brings man his triumph, even in the face of suffering and tragedy, as Sophocles taught us so richly. Great artists, like great art, make a martyrdom of the things of the spirit, not of man. This is the noble task of the actor.

A true artist is one who sees with the eyes of the eternal. He does not need to go through psycho-technics to arrive at the place of creative inspiration. He merely responds to the pure and irresistible impulses of the spirit as it carries out its mandate to bring heaven on earth.

3. Put your role first and yourself second

The first principle that Stanislavski laid down for his actors was to "love art in yourself and not yourself in art." He criticized actors who adapted all their roles to their own personalities—building their reputation exclusively on their personal charismatic appeal—and thus loving themselves in the part more than the part in themselves.

Had he lived longer, Stanislavski would have delighted in the work of an actor of the range and versatility of Alec Guinness, who was the prototype of the self-effacing, unpretentious actor, totally lacking in vanity and therefore capable of transforming himself into an amazing variety of roles—each demonstrating brilliant flashes of physical and vocal mimicry that defined each character to the core. One of the old-school acting knights of the twentieth century, he himself denied having any technique at all, yet his art was extraordinarily inspired and his technique completely wedded to trueness.

This kind of virtuosity in characterization is so uncommon in Hollywood today that few actors play "out of type." Movie roles are written specifically to showcase the personal qualities of a particular idol. It is the actor, and not the role he plays, that fans go to see. Acting is all about *him*—the star, the celebrity.

Stanislavski went on to say that "in spite of my great admiration for individual splendid talents, I do not accept the star system. Collective creative effort is the root of our kind of art." He was ardent in his belief that an actor should embody the highest ethics in his professional and personal behavior. He preached that narcissism, or the exploitation of art for personal celebrity, is the poison that cripples the actor as a human being. In *Building a Character* he wrote:

> There are a lot of bacilli [aerobic bacteria] in the theater, some are good and some are extremely harmful. The good bacilli will further the growth in you of a passion for what is fine, elevating, for great thoughts and feelings....Meantime...the dangerous, corrupting bacilli of the theater... breed in an actor the sense of craving for constant, uninterrupted titillation of his personal vanity. But if he lives only on that and similar stimuli, he is bound to sink low and become trivial. A serious minded person could not be entertained for long by such a life, yet a shallow one is enthralled, debauched, destroyed by it. That is why in our world of the theater we must learn to hold ourselves well in check. We have to live by rigid discipline.
>
> If we keep our theater free from all types of evil, we, by the same token, bring about conditions favorable to our own work in it. Remember this practical piece of advice: Never come into the theater with mud on your feet. Leave your dust and dirt outside....
>
> An actor, by the very nature of the art he serves, becomes a member of...the theater. Under its emblem and hallmark he represents it daily to thousands of spectators....In the mind of the public his artistic and his personal life are inextricably linked together....This, therefore, obligates an actor to conduct himself worthily outside the walls of his theater and to protect his good name both on the boards and in his private life.

The theater was a magical other world to Stanislavski, where theatrical life had a meaning, a glory, and a resolution that transcended even real life. If a young actor understands from the very start that his first obligation is to serve art and not his personal ambitions, then he can bring to his roles that transparency and authenticity that marks the great artist. Because the star system promoted narcissism, Stanislavski encouraged the concept of theater as an ensemble enterprise, where the motto, "One for all, and all for one" had real application. He saw the actor as a co-creator with the playwright and everyone else who is working to make the production happen.

Sarah Bernhardt agreed. She warned young actors against "all those ideas of brilliance, mirth, and flattery which are suggested by our art. How many charming people have I seen floundering in the mud of the stage, how many pure young girls lost for ever through compromising situations veiled by hope. Poor little victims, so easy to catch in the clumsiest trap, and for whom the poachers of love who hover around theaters have no pity at all." She believed that young artists who get caught up in the whirlpool of the glamor, the compliments, the adulation, the applause, the awards, and the fame follow a "false star."

If an actor does achieve stardom, it behooves him to use his "charmed" gifts with prudence and modesty and not trade on them for his own gain. Actors need to think of what they can give to their profession, not what they can get out of it, or how they can exploit it to further their own agendas. Every actor should approach his art with perspective, seriousness, and good judgment, knowing that he is a role model for millions of young people—in some cases, for generations to come.

Stanislavski went even further in his concept of the responsibility of the actor. He believed that an actor should serve his art with the same sense of sacredness that a priest embodies when celebrating Mass at the altar. Theater is an act of faith. The relationship between the actor and his audience is one of trust, as it is between the priest and his congregation. An actor should fulfill that act of faith and bond of trust by delivering to them, with a humble heart, the full value of his gift of inspiration. In *Building a Character,* he wrote: "A true priest is aware of the presence of the altar during every moment that he is conducting a service. It is exactly the same way that a true artist should react to the stage all the time he is in the theatre. An actor who is incapable of this feeling will never be a true artist!"

It is hard to imagine how far the celebrity star system of today's theatrical industry has departed from Stanislavski's ideal and from the high purposes expressed by Bernhardt. Never before in the history of theater has such tenacity, personal ambition, and media power been on display to achieve such puny purposes—namely, the mere continuance of the celebrity life of our modern actors, rather than the education and upliftment of the public toward the good and the beautiful. Fans gaze upon their idols—enthralled by the "chimera." But cultivating a life of chimera, as the great artists of the past keep reminding us, is not the high road of acting, nor the purpose of art.

If young actors see their profession merely as a ticket to stardom and wealth and life on the fast track, without obligation to the profession they serve or to its aesthetic and altruistic purposes, then dignity and high-mindedness become things of the past.

During World War II, when our soldiers were fighting Nazi Germany and the Axis Powers of Italy and Japan on several continents, it was Hollywood and its stars who united America and her allies on the home front. Basil Rathbone, who had received the British Military Cross for outstanding bravery during World War I, tried to re-enlist when England declared war on Germany in 1939. He was turned down by the British War Office because of his age. Undeterred, he spent the war years serving as President of the Los Angeles chapter of British War Relief and the War Chest Executive Committee. He also founded the RAF (Royal Air Force) Benevolent Fund and helped organize the United Nations War Relief. Rathbone entertained troops in California, visited army hospitals, and volunteered his help in the Hollywood Canteen.

John Garfield and Bette Davis created the Hollywood Canteen—a place for soldiers to go and spend quality time with pretty Hollywood starlets under crystalline lights and be served coffee and donuts by famous matinee idols. It was Betty Grable, Rita Hayworth, Ann Sheridan, Judy Garland, Jeanne Crain, and Donna Reed who were the pinup girls on the nose of bomber aircraft and who inspired the ideal of wholesome American womanhood in the hearts of our fighting men. (Remember the character of "Animal" in the movie *Stalag 17,* holding a tattered picture of Betty Grable and professing undying love for her?) It was Bob Hope, Mickey Rooney, Bing Crosby, and the Andrew Sisters, along with a host of other big-name celebrities, who traveled tirelessly to bring laughter, good cheer, and a touch of Hollywood glamor to American soldiers, flyers, sailors, and marines serving in the war. At the height of her film career, Carole Lombard was killed in a plane crash while on a war bonds tour.

Leslie Howard, a veteran of World War I, directed, produced, and starred in motion pictures that upheld the idealism of England under attack by fascism. These films included *Spitfire, Pimpernel Smith, 49th Parallel,* and *The Gentler Sex.* He also made radio broadcasts and wrote numerous articles. Not long after World War II began, he returned to his native England to help the war effort. He was shot down in June 1943 by Nazi Luftwaffe fighter planes while flying from Portugal over the Bay of Biscay on a secret mission for the British government.

Established box office stars, such as Clark Gable, Tyrone Power, Jimmy Stewart, Eddie Albert, Alan Ladd, Glenn Ford, and Ronald Reagan enlisted in the Army, Navy, or Marines, while Frank Capra, Alfred Hitchcock, Billy Wilder, and William Wyler were just a few of the top directors who churned out war films designed to remind Americans that we were the good guys and that we deserved and needed to win. Hollywood fought the war on the screen. Our sense of the enemy, our sense of ourselves, our sense of commitment, and our sense of victory came from Hollywood.

Sixty years later, Hollywood no longer promotes confidence in our country. In partnership with the political left, the entertainment elite belittle those who espouse self-sacrifice, simple duty, or love for this United States of America. Our servicemen are treated with condescension, if not outright derision. When Hollywood does attempt to take on an inherently compelling subject, such as America at war, there is the sense of merely an external show, where the costumes and makeup look painted on, and the dialogue sounds trivial, as though written by people who either don't believe what they're writing or simply don't have a clue. The 2001 movie *Pearl Harbor* is a typical example. The facts of the story are not historically correct, and the emotions portrayed by the main characters lack seriousness and pathos. We never believe for a moment that these people really lived during a time in our history when unity and patriotism bound all Americans. *Pearl Harbor* conveyed no spiritual essence. First-rate special effects and a gripping historical backdrop cannot sell a movie to an audience if there is no real heart or soul to the protagonists, or any real pulse of the spirit of the times.

Young actors need to transcend the present attitude of Hollywood and take up the torch passed to them by the great actors and entertainers of an earlier golden era. Only by putting your profession first and feeling its noble obligation, can you serve yourself, your craft, and your profession with integrity and honor.

4. Demonstrate control and commitment

The actor must be ready and willing to commit his physical, mental, and emotional energies to a role if he wants it to be convincing. Commitment takes many forms. As we discovered in an earlier unit, Patty Duke demonstrated the commitment of "staying in character" at all costs so that "the show" could go on—literally. Commitment also describes the preparation an actor will undertake to make himself ready for his part. In order to prepare for the role of Shakespeare's Othello to a young Peggy Ashcroft's Desdemona in the London production of *Othello* in 1930, African-American singer Paul Robeson moved to England and spent nearly a year studying the full script of the play and its historical context. He was also painstaking in his adoption of the precise British pronunciation so that his voice would not conflict in either its accent or cadence with the rest of the cast.

Sensitive to the prevailing racial tension of an American black man playing love scenes with a beautiful white actress, Robeson centered himself in the era and social (pre-slavery) context in which Shakespeare framed his character of the warrior Moor. As he explained in his own words in a May 18, 1930 *New York Times* article, he went about "approaching the part as Shakespeare wrote it...a noble figure, a man of singleness of purpose and simplicity with a mind as direct as a straight line." He found Shakespeare's superb sympathy for the underdog to be "wonderfully real and true and beautiful" and sought to convey it in his performance. Robeson's commitment to his role paid off. He was acclaimed for a characterization possessed of majesty and power, poetry and passion.

In his desire to give his character his all, the actor should not lose sight of the fact that his role is, first and foremost, an artistic creation. As such, the actor needs to remain in control of that creation every moment he is onstage. That means he should not get his own personality confused with the role itself, or vice versa. On the contrary, he must consciously remain a spectator to his own creation, even as he is also the living heart and soul of that creation.

The level of commitment needed to give a role psychological truthfulness may require the implementation of rigorous disciplines, comprehensive study, and time-consuming preparation, but it is not dependent on the actor *substituting*—a term used to describe the process of tapping into one's own subconscious records of emotional and physical experience and living that memory again in order to make what he is doing on the stage real and meaningful to himself. Another word used to describe this practice is *personalization,* whereby the actor sensorally creates a memory of more real value to him—something in which he has more personal investment—than what is available to him onstage to react off.

Substitution, the founding principle of modern method acting, was adapted from Stanislavski's original idea of "emotion memory." An actor would think of an experience in his own life when he had felt the same emotion that his character requires and then replay the memory of that emotion in his role in order to achieve a more genuine characterization. It was one of the techniques he developed for his actors early in his career. In later years, however, he de-emphasized emotion memory and wrote of "physical action" as the key to draw forth true feelings. Though emotions may be brought to conscious awareness via emotional memory, Stanislavski realized that there is not a direct line to emotions in performance, since emotions do not adhere rigorously to logic or consistency, while physical actions do. If the actor cannot bring his role to life spontaneously and intuitively, it is necessary to build its physical life first and reach its spiritual life reflexively through the physical actions created. It is an approach from the exterior to the interior.

He wrote in Chapter Five of *Creating a Role:*

> If a part does not of its own accord shape itself inside an actor [intuitively] he has no recourse except to approach it inversely, by proceeding from externals inward....Physical life is something material, tangible, it responds to orders, to habits, discipline, exercise, it is easier to handle than elusive, ephemeral, capricious feeling which slips away....The spirit cannot but respond to the actions of the body, provided of course that these are genuine, have a purpose, and are productive....
>
> The physical approach to a part can act as a kind of storage battery for creative feeling....Fill up the physical life of your part with feelings, and the emotions aroused will become rooted...in your deeply felt physical actions.

> They will seep in, be soaked up, they will gather up feelings connected with each instant of the physical life of your role and in this way lay hold of the ephemeral sensations and creative emotions of an actor....
>
> An actor on the stage need only sense the smallest modicum of organic physical truth in his action and instantly his emotions will respond to his inner faith in the genuineness of what his body is doing.

Sarah Bernhardt had an even simpler explanation of why physical action is one of the keys to the art of acting. Presuming of course that the actor has natural intuitive ability, he should merely "think" the character—that is, visualize it intensely. And it is through this "thinking" that he will slide into action. In *The Art of Theater,* she wrote:

> Whatever I have to impart in the way of anguish, passion, or of joy, comes to me during rehearsal in the very action of the play.
>
> There is no need to cast about for an attitude, or a cry, or anything else. You must be able to find everything you want on the stage in the excitement created by the general collaboration....Each action of the actor on the stage should be the visible concomitant of his thoughts....
>
> It is only action that arouses the emotion of the public....The actor must never forget that action is the supreme mistress.

Stanislavski's conclusion was this: "When you reach the moment of creation, do not seek the path of inner stimulation—your feelings know what to do better than you can tell them—but stick instead to the physical being of your role." Despite this wealth of good advice, emotion memory asserted itself (and remains to this day) as the centerpiece of the Actor's Studio—the first American method studio—headed by Lee Strasberg and director Elia Kazan. Stanislavski's insights about physical action were dismissed outright by Strasberg, which prompted Stella Adler, the only American to study with Stanislavski, to state about Strasberg that "he got it all wrong."

Since the late 1950s, Hollywood "method" has evolved into something of a sacramental ritual by which the actor must pay dues to the gods of psychological realism in order to achieve emotional authenticity. It has been adopted as the popular interpretive approach to modern realist scripts, though it is rarely successful when applied to classic stage roles, which carry their own intrinsic emotion. Because of its intrusive nature, method acting can trespass an actor's personal integrity by tapping into unresolved memories. When a director assumes the role of psychoanalyst and has the actor recall painful or deeply hidden experiences in his life, he goes where "angels fear to tread" and risks stripping the young actor of the constraints and inhibitions that are in place for the balance and dignity of his soul.

The same concern applies to directors who demand that actors be willing to experience (or feel sympathetic towards) the full spectrum of human realities, whether the actor morally approves of them or not. It is true that part of being a good actor is the ability to demonstrate an instinctive and compassionate understanding of the human condition, just as a painter is familiar with his palette of colors and knows how to combine them to achieve the desired effect. Nevertheless, the end result is always more worthy if the actor's understanding of human nature is enlightened—that is, informed with an intelligence, faith, and noble intention.

An actor should never forget that he is acting. He only needs to imaginatively think or intuit an emotion (even a complex one) and through controlled technique *personify* that emotion in order to give it theatrical life. The soul of the actor remains separate and apart, even as it is the soul of the actor that breathes life into the character. The most important element in any characterization is the humanity with which an actor imbues it. This can be achieved without obsessive self-analysis or psychoanalysis, which encroaches upon the soul—in fact, assumes a tyranny over it. When an actor believes that his subconscious is the one true resource for inspired acting, he is placing his faith in the process of exploring his own pent-up thoughts and feelings as the only path to revelatory truth on the stage (or screen). Though method acting schools espouse this approach, it is simply false.

Acting is always theatrical and thus requires theatricalized emotion—that is, emotion that fully *indicates* the real emotion the character is experiencing. An actor does not have to personally re-create real emotions to convey theatricalized emotion onstage. We employ theatrical means to convey theatrical life: heightened sense awareness, concentration, intuition, physical grace, and skilled vocal technique. Acting is not real life. Bette Davis made this very point when she said on the 1971 Dick Cavett Show, "We all have life 24 hours a day. Sometimes we want to forget life and have something a little bit theatrical." In a 1983 BBC television interview, she further went on to say, "The terrible thing about acting today is that it's all so real. You can sit on a street corner and see real people....Acting is larger than life. You should be aware that you are acting, not be caught up in the reality."

This is not to say that an actor's emotions should be artificial or superimposed. What you bring to your character must be sincere, with every seam perfectly stitched. Because your character is using your body, your heart, and your emotions to live theatrically, you are obliged to give that character all of who you are—every bit of your inspiration and skill—and not some hammy counterfeit. The point Ms. Davis makes is key: it is a theatrical life and not a real life that you, the actor, are portraying. Yours is the only real life, and real life is not lived on a stage; it is lived in the arena of your own personal experience. The actor is real; the character is not. The actor must know the difference.

Control and commitment are necessary components of a competent technique. They ensure that the interpretive feelings conceived by the playwright are given proper deference and are not eclipsed by the excessive emotion or subjective interpretation of the actor. The actor, above all, should be a transparency, not a pollutant. To achieve this kind of lucidity as a performer, he should never lose contact with his own soul or his own intelligence.

5. Never stop studying to perfect your technique

The only way an actor can give artistic form to his inspiration is to have a skilled technique. In his book *My Life in Art,* Stanislavski stated that the more talent the actor has, the more he should care about his technique. Many of the great nineteenth-century actors, including Eleanora Duse, Tommaso Salvini, Ellen Terry, and Sarah Bernhardt, were endowed with a natural genius for inspired acting, yet all their lives they sought the technical perfection of their art. A serious actor should feel a similar obligation to master all the acting "essentials" that makes up his craft.

Technique is not a cookbook where the actor turns to the right page and finds the recipe for a role. Technique is a rigorous discipline of applying all the principles upon which good acting is based until they become second nature—a feat that takes hard work and years of practice. As we learned in earlier units, a skilled technique is based on natural laws. Writes Stanislavski:

> Technique follows logically, admiringly on the heels of nature. Everything is clear, intelligible and intelligent: the gesture, the pose, the movement. The speech too is adapted to the part; the sounds are well worked out, the pronunciation is a joy to the ear, the phrases beautifully shaped, the inflections musical in form, almost as though they were sung to notes. The whole is warmed and given a basis of glowing truth from the inside. What more can anyone desire? It is a great satisfaction to see and hear such acting. What art! What perfection! Alas, how rare are actors of this kind! They and their performances leave behind wonderfully beautiful, esthetic, harmonious, delicate impressions of forms completely sustained and perfectly finished....It is towards this goal that we should strive.

Stanislavski was adamant that nothing of theatrical pretense, nothing that was untrue would ever take the place of inspired actions onstage, for only such actions could justify the inner life of the character. The very purpose of technique is to search out and nurture inspiration (or the creative state) and then set it forth in a compelling theatrical form that invites the audience's approval and belief. Stanislavski quoted S. M. Volkonski from his book *The Expressive Word* when he said that with an accomplished and practiced technique, "the difficult should become habitual, the habitual, easy, and the easy, beautiful."

The goal of all technique is to produce beautiful external expression that matches the inner action of the character. "You should develop your bodies, your voices, your faces into the best physical instruments of expression capable of rivaling the simple beauty of nature's creations." If the body of the actor is the musical instrument upon which the melody of the character is played, the instrument needs to be finely tuned, or discordance will be the result. Stanislavski described it this way:

> The bodily incarnation of a part, of a passion, should be not only exact but also beautiful, graceful, sonorous, colorful, harmonious. How can one manifest what is exalting by trivial means, or what is noble by vulgar means, what is beautiful by what is deformed? A street player does not need a Stradivarius; a simple violin suffices to convey his feelings. But for a Paganini, a Stradivarius is a necessity. The more substantial the inner creativeness of an actor, the more beautiful his voice should be, the more perfect should be his diction, the more expressive should be his facial movements, the more graceful his body, the more flexible his entire physical equipment. Embodiment on the stage, like any other artistic form, is only good when it is true and at the same time executes in artistic form the inner substance of the work. The shape [physical form] must conform to the inner substance... the inner score of the part...its essence.

We begin the process of embodying a character by first creating its physical life. The actor constructs with his imagination all the outer aspects of his character—his way of walking, moving, and gesturing, his deportment and manner of expressing himself, his personal idiosyncrasies, etc. He searches in his memory for anything he can recall and recreate that will help color in these external details, such as people he personally knew, observed in real life, or read about in books. He can borrow qualities from numerous sources and then combine them into a coherent form.

Years ago, a stage actor had to be knowledgeable in the application of his own makeup, wigs, and costume wardrobe for the role. Modern theater companies and television and movie studios have makeup, hairstyling, and costume specialists as part of their resident staff, who provide these services for the actor. Even so, it behooves the actor to study the history of costume and makeup so that he can make creative suggestions and feel integrated with the process of transforming a character in fiction into a living, breathing creation on the stage. The more involved he is in creating the outer role, the easier it will be for him to release the inner spring of his character's emotional and spiritual life.

Once the actor has created the lifelike dots of an external form for his character, he then begins the discovery process of the heart and soul of the character. He starts by charting the structure of the play, the points of conflict, crisis, climax, and resolution, as well as every step the character makes in his journey from the first scene to the last. The actor might also set up "what if" scenarios of circumstances that preface his character's first appearance onstage. The actor should define his character's goal and the obstacle (whether another person or a situation) that he must triumph over to achieve that goal. He should create a running flow chart of the attitudes his character displays and the changes he goes through as he encounters and overcomes (or is overcome by) those dramatic events that engage his will. As soon as he has this working biography in hand, he can choose to improvise his scenes in their proper story sequence, using his own everyday speech, then working his way up to the real text.

In *Creating a Role,* Stanislavski uses the example of Shakespeare's Othello to teach his students how to develop and chart the emotional life of their role:

> Human passions do not usually have their inception, develop, and reach their climax at once, but gradually and over a long period. Dark feelings imperceptively and slowly change into brighter ones, and vice versa. So, for example, Othello's heart is radiantly full of all joyous, bright, loving emotions [toward Desdemona], like burnished metal reflecting the rays of the sun. Then here and there dark spots are suddenly discernible; these are the first moments of doubt [Desdemona has already deceived her father, why not Othello?]. The number of the dark spots increases [the flirtatious laugh], and the shining heart of loving Othello is mottled over with evil emotions. These shadows lengthen, grow [the loss of her handkerchief], and finally his shining heart becomes darkened, almost blackened [he strikes her, calls her a strumpet]. In the beginning there were brief hints of growing jealousy, now only a few moments recall his tender, confident love. Finally these moments are gone and his whole soul is enveloped in complete darkness [he kills her].

The through line, which Stanislavski called the spine of the play, represents not only what the protagonist is doing (his objective) at any point of time in the dramatic action, but how the overall objective (superobjective) of the play impacts the character's objective and pushes him forward. Using the model above, we might take the role of the ill-fated Desdemona and chart a similar through line of change. Desdemona first appears as the innocent and pure beauty whom Othello falls madly in love with. She returns that love in full measure and consents, against her father's wishes, to secretly marry him. Nurtured by Othello's love, she grows into a confident, radiant, and self-possessed wife. As Othello falls victim to the suspicions planted by Iago and jealousy darkens his behavior towards her, she grows perplexed at his questioning, then incredulous at his accusations of her infidelity. This culminates in her panic as the cornered victim of his unjust jealousy. Finally, just before she dies, she comes full circle in demonstrating the trueness of her character. In her final act of loyalty and devotion to her husband, she does not reveal to Emilia who has killed her. Her love for Othello is pure and virtuous, and never waivers.

In order to portray a human passion, the actor does not need to personally recreate the actual passion but to have an enlightened understanding of it—that is, comprehend the feelings and thought processes that go into its makeup. "The better the actor knows the psychology of the human soul and nature," wrote Stanislavski, "the deeper he will be able to penetrate the spiritual essence of human passion and therefore the more detailed...and varied will be the score of any part he plays."

How the actor transfers that understanding to bring his character's emotions theatrically alive for his audience is the alchemy that every actor must discover for himself. It is an evolving and highly personal process. But it takes work, a lifetime of work. In his last chapter of *Building a Character,* Stanislavski expressed his frustration with the "scandalous slovenliness" of the "overwhelming majority" of actors toward their technique and, above all, in the domain of their speech. He wrote:

> Look at the way musicians study the laws, the theory of their art, the care they take of their instruments, their violins, cellos, pianos. Why do dramatic artists not do the same? Why do they not learn the laws of speech, why do they not treat their voices, their bodies, with care and respect? Those are their violins, cellos, their most subtle instruments of expression. They were fashioned by the greatest genius of all craftsmen—the magician Nature.
>
> Most people in the theater are unwilling to understand that accident is not art, that you cannot build on it. The master performer must have complete control of his instrument, and that of an artist is a complex mechanism. We actors have to deal not just with a voice the way a singer does, not just with hands like a pianist, not just with the body and legs like a dancer. We are obliged to play simultaneously on all the spiritual and physical aspects of a human being. To gain mastery over them requires time and arduous, systematic effort.

Even Stanislavski was not satisfied with his own system, believing it to be incomplete. He also never meant it to be an end in itself. He clearly stated that his system is a "companion along the way to creative achievement, but it is not a goal in itself. You cannot act the 'system': you can work on it at home, but when you step out onto the stage cast it aside, there only nature is your guide." His final statement was "Create your own method. Don't depend slavishly on mine. Make up something that will work for you! But keep breaking traditions, I beg you."

The most accomplished and successful actors are naturally intuitive. They only have to think the feelings of their character, and that character's warmth and brightness are immediately reflected in the voice, the movements, the facial expressions, and the simple presence of the actor. Others who are less intuitive will need to either search deeper into their sensory experience and memory bank of emotions to find something they can tap into, or work the external physical actions of the role to find their way to the inner essentials. Still others are so technically skilled that they can turn a phrase, lift an eyebrow, or create a breathless pause, and the character comes magically alive to the onlookers.

Whatever it takes, we have to remember that technique is an integrated skill. Though its application is subjective, its content is objective, following natural laws that need to be mastered if the actor is to be successful in his characterization. Acting is a discipline, not a whimsical form of self-expression or a public psychotherapy session. Once the component elements of his technique are internalized, the actor still has to bring that noble intention to his characterization if the spirit of his character is to transcend the external form and kindle the imagination of the audience.

Stanislavski believed the actor's primary duty to be the transmission of the superconscious, or what he defined as "the radiations of the spirit" from the soul of the character to the soul of the audience. He believed these "invisible inner currents" to have a direct, immediate, and powerful effect on the stage, conveying that essence which neither words nor gestures are capable of doing. He wrote:

> Does everything that passes through our soul lend itself only to words, sounds, gestures and movements? The irresistibility, contagiousness, and power of direct communion by means of invisible radiations of the human will and feelings are great. It is used to hypnotize people, to tame wild animals or a raging mob; the fakirs [of India] put people to death and resuscitate them; and actors can fill whole auditoriums with the invisible radiations of their emotions.

In the pursuit of such acting excellence, our passion must be equal to the task, but a passion that is ennobled by what Sarah Bernhardt called "a love of the good and the beautiful…[and] an appreciation of life that is fairer and truer." The actor must be the instrument of the "evocation of the ideal." She wrote:

> Permanent success cannot be achieved except by incessant intellectual labour, always inspired by the ideal....Whatever may be the play that is performed, of whatever type may be the action, wherever the place may be where the incidents happen, there is always an ideal, towards which the chief efforts of the actor should be directed. To create a character, however contemptible it might be, the actor must seek for the flame that illumines it.

Since theater and dramatic art develop the love of the good and the beautiful, actors, according to Bernhardt, have the obligation as the theater's first devotees, to "guard the sacred fire of art, art which in all its manifestations is the most beautiful creation of the human spirit. Without art, what would life be?...And of all the arts, that of the theater is the most complete. It employs all the others. Just as each soul feels the need of prayer, so each mind needs to evoke dreams, to create legends, and to conjure up the glory that has disappeared." If the actor does not embody this ideal, then his technique is for naught. He is merely a workman following a trade, who has "no conception of the beauty of our art, nor of the mission of its apostles."

In discussing the role of Hamlet, Bernhardt spoke of the interpretive art of discovering the "flame" within the soul of the character, allowing that flame to "illumine the whole being" of the actor, who then sends forth its radiance to the audience. That can only happen, however, if the artist is able to join her soul to the soul and genius of the dramatist and represent that genius with perfect truth, as did Bernhardt. She understood what was needed in her art to set her audience on fire with the inner flame of her character.

When an actor plays a character that has depth and subtlety such as any of Shakespeare's tragic heroes or heroines, or a compelling role such as Racine's Phèdre, the actor is literally playing with fire—the sacred fire (infused by the dramatist) that is inherent in the spirit of the character and which the actor must search out and transmit to his audience. The very atmosphere of the live performance, energized by the anticipation and excitement of the crowd, serves as a powerful animating force for an actor's creativeness, which, in turn, invites a profound response from the audience.

When an actor portrays a character that reflects the beauties of the poet's genius, the role will ignite the actor's inspiration and living response to it, which then electrifies the enthusiasm of the audience and "increases the flow of inner currents" that Stanislavski spoke of between the actor and his audience. It is the consummation of the love affair—irresistible, subtle, and powerful—that every artist yearns for. The performance of the actor inspires the audience to a higher love. The actor, in turn, receives that love and is elevated by it. Bernhardt wrote that the love she received from the audience while performing onstage felt like being "touched by the wings of a god," multiplying the strength and beauty of her characterization a hundredfold.

When great artists of the brilliance and vitality of Stanislavski and Bernhardt describe the stage as a place of intimate, even sacred, communion between actor and audience, they are tapping into the ancient alchemy of the art of acting and its power to transform not only the actor, but everyone in the audience who is part of the theatrical experience. What they are talking about is acting magic!

Romantic tradition…

...with its irresistible appeal...

…lies a-bleeding.

How to Create a Character

Technique is the master key that unlocks the art of characterization. Until the fingers are supple and the scales, arpeggios, and trills flow easily from the pianist, it is useless for him to attempt Chopin. To bring any true work of art to life on the stage requires skill in execution and sensitivity of interpretation that can only be wrought through schooled and practiced technique. The actor's "playing" is always conditional, always limited, if his technique is self-conscious and half-mastered.

Technique is the handmaid of successful characterization. A lot of actors in the beginning of their careers believe their own natural gifts to be adequate to the task of creating a character, just as the person who plays the piano by ear thinks he plays well but, in fact, plays badly compared to a skilled musician who demonstrates real execution and artistic rendering. In both cases, it is technical training that makes the difference. Technique alone will fill in the body and soul of the character.

How, then, does an actor go about studying a role? How does he make his fictional character come alive in the imagination of his audience? Students inevitably ask, "Do I use my own personality to create the character?" Part of the answer is yes. Drama is the most complete and expansive form of creative self-expression. As actors, however, we also have to portray characters that are unlike us. The theatrical life we create onstage may indeed borrow from our own personal life experience but it should not be dependent on it. That is why technique is the actor's best asset. With an assured technique, an actor can create the inner and outer life of *any* character. Technique elevates acting to an artistic discipline, making it far more than merely an outlet for expressing one's own personality.

Just as the painter brings his artistic product into objectified form, so does the actor. This implies that the actor does not "become" his role but stays in control and apart from the "artistic product" that his role represents. Keeping that product separate and impersonalized from the actor's real self does not mean that his characterization is any less sincere, intense, or powerful in its truthfulness. The acting role simply represents something larger than life, and certainly larger than the actor himself. The actor's role is his medium to take his audience to a higher plane of thought and aspiration. He can only do that if the life he creates onstage remains theatrical—that is, bigger and more concentrated in its essence than everyday life. Theater is all about framing life and its essence, if not its mystery. If we destroy the theatrical frame in favor of something more reality based, we destroy the essence and thus the true purpose of theater.

If you watch one of the great stage-trained actors of the twentieth century play a character role that is totally unlike himself or "out-of-type," you will see how that actor is able to externalize his role yet be totally invested in it every moment he is onstage or on the screen. An example is Laurence Olivier's portrayal of Ezra Lieberman, a semi-retired Nazi hunter, in the movie *The Boys From Brazil*.

Lieberman is as wise as the prophets of old. He is bright in heart, quick in humor, and full of conviction about what is "morally right." Pitting himself against a demonic Nazi geneticist trying to clone more Hitlers, he represents a wonderfully animated presence of hope, which is the real victory over the evil he confronts. Olivier plays the role with superb objectivity. He remains outside the character, visualizing not just the outer man with all his quixotic Jewish idiosyncrasies, but the vibrant inner soul.

It is Olivier's pertinent characterization that lifts the movie out of its intolerable grimness and sense of menace. You can almost see him smiling as he adds the subtle brush strokes to the role, even as he is acting it. Not for one of those magical moments on the screen does he sink into his character, working it from within his own psyche, as modern method actors are wont to do. He achieved the same kind of delightful freedom in his characterization of Mr. Creakle in the 1969 NBC Television production of *David Copperfield*. Olivier is like an architect carefully monitoring the construction of his artistic product. Because we feel his perfect control, we take joy in his art.

The same can be said of Peter Ustinov's portrayal of Agatha Christie's peerless Belgian detective, Hercule Poirot. There is not a moment in *Death on the Nile* that Ustinov does not masterfully create some exquisite nuance of vocal inflection, facial grimace, or body gesture to fully delight us and fasten our attention, very much at the expense of other notable stars who share scenes with him. Ustinov plays Poirot with such a disarming absence of guile that we are utterly charmed.

The deft characterization of Inspector Clouseau by Peter Sellers displays the same infallible instinct for the apt moment, the ideal look and tone, the canny working from the outside in to achieve classic credibility. British actress Margaret Rutherford, originally a teacher of elocution, left her mark on the stage and screen with comedic characterizations highly developed through the instrument of her voice. Her incorrigible Miss Marple—yet another Agatha Christie creation—established her as a genius in character construction.

Alec Guinness is another amazing architect of character design. Each of the roles he portrayed in his numerous films is brilliantly individual, yet copyrighted with the same logo of technical artistry. In the tradition of the famous French comic actor Coquelin of the Comédie Française, Guinness played each of his parts in a different key. Once he embarked on a role, it was fully sustained, so thoroughly did his training make that role obedient to his will. Not one of his characters can be identified as the real Alec Guinness. His acting in the supremely elegant black comedy *Kind Hearts and Coronets*, in which he plays eight different members of the D'Ascoyne family, is a microcosm of the lifetime career of this distinguished "wizard of disguise."

Olivier, Ustinov, and Guinness were stage-schooled technicians, which is why they were able to be master builders of a vast gallery of out-of-type characters. To be the pulsing heartbeat of your character *and* the observer looking on is the highest form of acting artistry, born of an accomplished and proven technique. We might call it "the Tao of the actor." The acting virtues of these marvellous artists glowed warmly and brightly both on the stage and on the cinema screen during their long and distinguished careers.

The same classic control and possession of character can also be observed with many stage-trained actors who play roles that perfectly suit their own temperament. In the movie *The White Cliffs of Dover,* Irene Dunne plays Susan Ashwood, a warm, witty, practical American (much like Dunne herself), who marries a British soldier during World War 1. Her husband is killed on a combat mission and she raises her son, John, in England. Much like Herzeleide, the mother of Parsifal, who feared that her son would grow up to be a soldier like his father and be slain in battle, Susan is haunted by the same apprehension. In fact, when World War II comes around, John does join the Regiment of his father and goes to war.

In the final scene of the movie, Susan's wounded son lies in a hospital ward in London, where she is a nurse. She knows that he is dying and spends the last few moments with him. They hear a marching band outside his window and she tells him that the Americans have arrived in England to join the fight. He asks her to describe how they look, how they march. She opens the window and looks down to a scene of thousands of soldiers, British and American, marching in time to *The Stars and Stripes.* "Can you see them yet?" he asks. And she answers: "Yes, John. Your people and my people. Only their uniforms are different. How well they march. How well they march together. There's a look of greatness about them. All the strong young boys, beautiful and proud with dreams, just like you, John. They'll help bring peace again....You know, we must never forget what that [dying] American boy said to you: God will never forgive us if we break faith with our dead again."

There is acting magic in this scene. With a restraint and grace of bearing, Susan steels her broken heart to face what she has dreaded most—"the day when he—my son—would tread the very same path that his father trod and die for England, too." When Dunne speaks, she lets the words themselves convey the tragic pathos of her character. She does not soak them with her own personal pain conjured from her subconscious memory; she merely renders them with clarity and beauty so that we can respond to this excruciating moment in our own way. The calm and self-possessed spirit of Susan Ashwood passes through Dunne's heart to ours, as we are reminded, in the words of Longfellow, "how sublime a thing it is to suffer and be strong." In that moment of transfer, our spirits are brushed by the subtle fire of heaven. The healing is complete, consummate—and we, like the character, are made stronger.

Dunne's art conveys the glorified (and thus eternal) essence of Susan's character, of what Longfellow describes as "the unconquered will,/ Serene, and resolute, and still." As John closes his eyes in death, our souls (and his) are lifted to a scene of hope, of American and British soldiers marching together to continue the fight—and the sacrifice—for something greater than all of us, and therefore worthy of all we have to give. Like the White Cliffs themselves, Susan embodies the moral strength to stand against all that would destroy that hope. Dunne's acting, like so much of the acting in this movie, is compellingly beautiful and fulfills its highest purpose as dramatic art.

That same refinement is present in the acting style of Deborah Kerr—no more movingly so than in the 1957 blockbuster romance *An Affair to Remember*. The movie is a love story about two people, each engaged to someone else, who fall deeply in love while on a ship cruise. Cary Grant plays Nicky Ferrante, a playboy and dilettante painter; Miss Kerr's character, Terry McKay, is a successful nightclub singer. They are playful, sophisticated people who do not consummate the affair on the ship but give each other six months to disengage from their respective fiancés and prove their newfound commitment to one other. A rendezvous is set at the end of that time.

As she makes her way to the Empire State Building six months later to meet Nicky, Terry is hit by a car and is paralyzed as a result. Not wanting him to be saddled with a cripple, she resolves not to contact him unless she can walk again. Disappointed that Terry did not turn up and believing that she no longer feels the same way about him, Nicky applies himself to his painting. After running into her at the ballet, and still very much in love, he visits her on Christmas Eve at her apartment, where she is lying on the sofa, a blanket over her legs. He is unsuccessful in finding out why she didn't make the rendezvous and is about to leave when he remembers the gift of a lace mantilla that his grandmother wanted Terry to have. He tells Terry that he painted a portrait of her kneeling in prayer with the mantilla draped around her shoulders and that the painting was given to a "woman in a wheelchair who had admired it." As he speaks the words, the revelation that *she* might be that woman suddenly dawns on him. While continuing his casual banter, he surveys every room in her apartment. It is when he opens the bedroom door that he sees the portrait hanging over her bed.

His awakening to the truth—to the comprehension of what had happened to her, of the reason for her silence and its eloquent expression of her love for him—is a cathartic moment. Both actors conduct the tender poignancy of the scene with the utmost delicacy and respect. They let the moral beauty of the moment stand and play itself—suspended at the level of the spirit so that we might enter its pure space and experience it, too. Both actors rendered the scene with the noble intention it required. They held back with a contained passion so that this magic moment, left still and empty, could be filled in by a million different viewers in a million different ways. This acting magic was entirely lacking when Annette Bening and Warren Beatty repeated the scene in a later remake of the movie. Not comprehending and therefore not bringing to their acting that same noble intention, they grounded the scene with their own surfeit of personal emotion. We experience only what Beatty and Bening defined that moment to be for themselves. That "moment" never rose above the level of human sentiment because it was self-sufficient unto the actors. There was simply no space left for us to enter in and experience its true (and thus eternal) magic. Excellent actors though they be, they could not convey the higher magic of their craft.

Because of their perfect restraint, without compromising the fire within them, Grant and Kerr captured that moment of ideal romantic love in all its purity and transforming power. When he says, "If it had to happen to one of us, why did it have to be you?" we experience the tender humility of the lover as he bends before the woman whose selfless love for him makes her sacred—a love that he recognizes can bring completeness to his life. A selfless love is the gift that brings us nearest to heaven, and therefore nearer to happiness. This magic moment holds out the hope to us that an exalted emotion is possible in this world when lovers see higher than their own self-gratification. It is only at the level of the spirit that we, both as actors and as audience spectators, can experience the beauty of the heart and soul of love.

We only have to watch the great romantic classics of the 1930s and 40s to discover similar moments—the selfless parting of Rick Blaine (Humphrey Bogart) and Ilsa Laszlo (Ingrid Bergman) in *Casablanca*; the fragile intensity of Julie Eden (Carole Lombard) in the 1939 romantic drama *In Name Only* as she tries to instill in her lover, Alec Walker (Cary Grant), the will to live; that aching, tearful moment in the 1941 masterpiece *Penny Serenade*, when Julie and Roger Adams (Irene Dunne and Cary Grant) lose their little adopted daughter, Trina, but find each other again through the spirit of their child's love; the sobbing sense of absence in the end scene of *Love Is a Many Splendored Thing*, when the beautiful Eurasian Dr. Suyin (Jennifer Jones) walks up the hill where she used to meet with her lover, Mark Elliott (William Holden), who now can only speak from the grave with words that make love, even in its terrible loss, a thing of beauty forever. Who can forget his heartrending words: "We have not missed it, you and I....We have not missed that many splendored thing."

There are similar "magic moments" in many films that uphold a noble intention and give us characters that have a life of their own, in which every audience member can share. These are the moments that endure because they fill our lives with hope, even amidst heartache and loss. Sometimes they leap off the screen despite a poorly-written script. An example is the sassy 1935 musical operetta *Naughty Marietta*, starring screen sweethearts Jeannette MacDonald and Nelson Eddy. In the scene at the Governor's ball when Princess Marie (Jeannette MacDonald) sings "her" song to Captain Warrington (Nelson Eddy), the chemistry between them is radiant. The beautiful melody, *Ah, Sweet Mystery of Life,* takes us into another sphere, where we feel the deep yearning for oneness with the beloved. The soul's desire for this union is fully expressed by MacDonald and Eddy, as though heaven itself passed the radiation of a perfect love through their hearts and into ours, uniting us at the level of the spirit in the remembrance of love's divine essence. It is a glorious moment on the screen—pure acting magic. The same moment is repeated by them in *Rosemarie* and *Maytime,* when it seems that not even death can separate twin flames in love.

Many people wonder why there are so few films made today that can carry to our hearts that same kind of magic. The answer is simple: most of our modern movie makers don't share the same perspective of the earlier big studio directors and producers. Films made in the golden years of Hollywood were invested with a faith in the spirit of man and not merely his mortal existence. There was a message of hope and idealism, especially in the hundreds of movies made about the war. There was a persuasion to do what is right and good and decent. On the other hand, today's movie directors focus almost entirely on the hard-core realism of life, without any appeal to the intangibles—faith in God, love of country, selflessness and sacrifice—that were honored in the old movies. Therefore there is nothing that speaks profoundly to our hearts. *Saving Private Ryan* proves this point.

Saving Private Ryan has been acclaimed as the greatest war film ever made, a film that accurately and movingly records the sacrifice of our soldiers who participated in the Normandy invasion of World War II. Though true-hearted Americans are always thrilled to see a director of the renown and talent of Steven Spielberg take on a subject dear to their hearts, Spielberg did not render the true glory of this historic event or the fitting heroism of the men who fought on those consecrated beaches. At best, the film is a shadowed silhouette.

The sacrifice of the real soldiers who gave their lives to liberate France from Nazi fascism was hallowed by their simple faith and plain duty. Spielberg presented a film that was not conceived out of simple faith, or plain duty, or any principle rooted in the love of freedom. There was nothing exalting or redemptive in the film because Spielberg intended to keep the whole conception of war earthbound, mired in its own blood, violence, and humanness. These were the images that dominated the screen, not the sense of victory over death or the triumph of the spirit.

There was a nihilism about Spielberg's conception of war, an inevitability and fatalism that made the soldiers look like puppets rather than the doers and makers of history. Even his lighting was harsh to the eyes, over bright and intense, as in an overexposed photo. This was especially marked in the opening scenes showing a soldier's arm that has been blown off and blood-drenched water soaking the beach. The effect created a visceral kind of discomfort. The cinematography was textured in a kind of monotone color scale that reminded one of an astral underworld rather than the green fields of France or, as in a flashback, a farm house in middle America.

Spielberg's point—the message of *Saving Private Ryan*—was that man is only noble by virtue of his willingness to give his life that another may live (to grow old). Thus the title, *Saving* Private Ryan. Duty, honor, love of country, love of God are irrelevant. The one good feeling we came away with was that a soldier, Captain John Miller, had been "dutiful enough" to follow orders to rescue a Private Ryan—orders that he really didn't agree with and which he obeyed without passion, heart, patriotic pride, or even a sense of caring about the man he was sent out to save. His character was more like a cipher than a real person with a soul.

If Captain Miller cherished any faith at all, it was a faith in and reliance upon his own platoon of men. At the end of the day he got killed, and the life of Private James Ryan was saved, or perhaps "preserved" is a better word. And though the hero's death was redemptive, the action of giving his life was passive and did not pierce the heart with any tragic pathos or sense of glory. As he lay dead on the bridge, there was no lifting of his spirit (or ours) to something higher. Even the scene of the now elderly Private Ryan at Normandy kneeling before the grave site of his benefactor did not rise above the white marble cross itself. The spirit of sacrifice remained earthbound, imprisoned in the dead body of the soldier who gave his life. It could have been consecrated to something higher—it should have been, but it wasn't.

When human tragedy is not set against the backdrop of faith or any enduring principle, there can be no true pathos, and thus no transcendence. The soldiers in *Saving Private Ryan* hardly seemed like the simple and manly American GI's that we came to know in the films produced in the 1940s. Spielberg's soldiers had no authentic character. They lacked youngness of heart; they were old and cynical and whined a lot—even scorned their officers and a soldier's duty. In their actions and interactions with each other, they never let us forget the landscape of bloody war.

In contrast, even in the midst of fierce and lethal battle, *We Were Soldiers* accomplished transcendence with tender and honorable pathos. Emerging as a lotus from the swamp of loathsome propaganda Vietnam films, *We Were Soldiers* seized the day. Based on the true story of Lt. General Harold Moore, who led the first American soldiers into battle against the Vietcong, it is perhaps one of the most meaningful and eloquent movies of our time. The character of the film was the character of one nation under God—of American men of all colors and creeds, simple in faith, simple in service, who went to war because their country called them to that duty. It is the character of the women who loved them and who bore the burden of their sacrifice in the same full measure. Their heroism was plain, dignified, and pure. Its essence was conveyed everywhere in the film—in the characterizations, the dialogue, the storyline, the music score, and the cinematography. The stunning action sequences focused not alone on the epic struggle of a small contingent of soldiers against their overpowering enemy, but the inner life of the man who, when all was said and done, was "glad he could die for his country."

The movie accomplished all this not by denying moral authority, but by affirming it; not by ignoring God, but by invoking His presence, naturally; not by exploiting realism, but by giving it legitimate and principled context. The movie redeemed the sacrifice of the 58,000 dead, and the suffering of so many veterans who returned from that war only to experience the ache of rejection by their countrymen and crucifixion by a self-righteous press. Where *The Green Berets* cheered and justified the call of duty of our bravest and best in Vietnam, *We Were Soldiers* took every Vietnam veteran off the cross. It opened a painful wound in our history and gave a new generation of Americans the opportunity to heal that wound with the gratitude and honor long overdue to those who "were soldiers once...and young."

Spielberg's conception of war was dark and unforgiving, as the bloody spectacle of artillery guns blowing apart human bodies graphically portrayed. His film painted a picture of war doing violence to men, and the soldiers being nothing more than victims of that violence or mere end results of the lots of war: Captain Miller just happened to get the short straw. We were left with a profound sense of meaninglessness. In fact, war can be a hallowed stage, drawing out of men and women the most valorous of actions that leave behind a glow of something brighter for the rest of us.

The 2001 movie *Black Hawk Down*, which dealt with America's disastrous military action in Somalia, reminded us that soldiers don't go to war to be heroes. It just happens that some of them end up being heroes by the action of their simple duty. With theatrical grace, honorable intention, and a belief in the goodness of America, *We Were Soldiers* rendered the even greater truth that no human life is ever lost, no sacrifice ever forgotten if men serve their country and their fellow soldiers honestly and well, for such service consecrates their lives as intensely and worthily lived.

Though the 2006 movie *The Guardian* did not deal with our military servicemen in war, it did contribute the same uplifting message that those who are selfless and compassionate, who dedicate their lives to a principle of simple duty, achieve transcendence for themselves and for the rest of us who are inspired by their sacrifice. "Greater love hath no man than this, that a man lay down his life for his friends." The elite rescue swimmers of the United States Coast Guard, as depicted in *The Guardian*, gave these words of Christ profound meaning and the power of truth.

A movie that celebrates good people, nice people, who are not self-centered, and who love their country with an old-fashioned pride, is a rarity in Hollywood today. Unless film, as an art form, can rekindle the hope and romance that earlier actors understood, and encourage Americans to fall in love with their country once again, we will have little of faith or glory to pass on to future generations. The limited, humanistic approach of method acting schools is not up to the task. Actors are programmed to believe that acting is all about them because they are told that life is all about them (what's in it for me, what can I get away with, what feels good). Thus their roles stay on the surface of reality and cannot transcend the boundaries of their own thinking and feeling world. The characters they play become nothing more than stencils of their own too-often jaded social and political beliefs. When the actor's serious and self-conscious ego controls the heart and mind of every character he plays, the real spirit of the character is snuffed out, and there can be no magic, no transcendence.

Bette Davis said: "Without wonder and insight, acting is just a trade. With it, it becomes creation." Sarah Bernhardt called acting "*la joie prestigieuse de la creation.*" Though no English translation can ever quite capture her original way of saying things, the words mean "the enchanting joy of creation." Both of these artists are telling us that acting, when executed with true joy and true integrity, exalts the soul of the actor and the soul of the audience.

Is there any one of us who doesn't want to experience wonder and joy and hope—the same kind that Lucy in *The Lion, the Witch and the Wardrobe* experiences when she steps back into the clothes closet only to realize that she is suddenly standing in a magical snow forest? Isn't the inner child in all of us yearning for that "Deep Magic" that can only be discovered when the spiritual imagination is kindled? It is the purpose of theater and all art to lead us to that enchanted realm of great spiritual quests, where we can become all we dream to be. True art is larger than life. True art is transcendent. That is why Leonardo da Vinci said: "In life beauty perishes, but not in art." The theater can frame, as no other art can do, the comedy and tragedy of life, as well as much of its unfathomable mystery. Though all drama cannot treat of a noble theme, it can and should strive toward it and not away from it.

How can an actor create a character so that it lives outside and beyond him? The first step is to separate out from those in the acting profession who delight in disenchanting us with their fixation on life's unhappy realities. There is no magic in their world because they have lost the sense of wonder. They have neither the child's faith nor the pure heart to enter the enchanted realm. Moreover, they would banish all magic from our world, or at least our belief in the magic. If a young actor enters the profession of acting with pure ideals, sadly it is not long before he hardens his heart to the radiant images of the spirit. Aspiring actors, then, must look to the examples of the great stage-trained actors and the idealism of classic Hollywood to find their inspiration and set their course straight and sure. They should also follow Ben Kingsley's advice to actors not to lose touch with the child inside of them, but to hold onto it "because it is so precious to us and it's such an extraordinary part of our lives."

Viewing a character role as separate from himself is asking a lot of a student actor. In most film and television shows the role is made to suit the actor, not vice versa. Indeed, we usually identify the role *as* the actor. Moreover, the actor's job is not as impersonal as that of an engineer or a tradesman or even a fellow artist, such as a sculptor or pianist. In contemporary roles, where the student actor finds more familiar ground with his character, he essentially plays himself. Where else is his primary reference point? Personal traits are expected to steal their way into his interpretation until he learns the control and emotional freedom that a well-schooled technique guarantees. Even if he portrays a character close to his own nature, however, he should still think of that character as something separate and apart from himself, just as the painter would view the canvas image he is creating to be separate from his real world.

Acting roles performed in the first year of drama instruction should be simple and easy to interpret. Straightforward and upbeat characterizations are fun and allow the actor to concentrate on practising his basic skills and developing his confidence. There will be ample opportunity later on to tackle roles with gravitas.

Numerous collections of acting scenes line the drama shelves of the major bookstores. Because so many of the selections are laced with immodesty and cynicism, it is better to draw on the classics for the younger children, even if the teacher must adapt and write his own scenes. You don't want the young actor to think that theater is all about looking for the worst in man and society. Too many already do.

The popular classics of the nineteenth and early twentieth centuries provide a bountiful quarry of material for both children and adults. Apart from Shakespeare and the Greek playwrights, the best authors for dramatic adaptation are Louisa May Alcott, Charlotte Bronte, Charles Dickens, Jane Austen, L.M. Montgomery, Frances Hodgson Burnett, Sir Walter Scott, Alfred Lord Tennyson, Robert Louis Stevenson, Rudyard Kipling, and Alexandre Dumas Sr. Classical operas, especially those of Wagner, Verdi, and Puccini, are also a good source for dramatic adaptation. On the lighter side, the Gilbert and Sullivan operettas offer delightful comic studies in English stereotypes—a great way for student actors to experience their roles as larger than life. (The song lyrics are naturally great tongue twisters, too!)

At the same time, it is important not to force material upon children that is pretentiously or sentimentally preachy. Drama is not meant to be religious liturgy dressed in a more expressive format. As an established discipline of the arts, theater must have an independence and life of its own. The children need to be given the freedom and trust to try on the moccasins of different characters and experience the consequences of right and wrong choices in life. It is the nature and purpose of religious doctrine to package the end result. It is the nature and purpose of drama to allow the actor (and audience) to discover that end result. If used joyously and with noble ends in mind, drama can provide children with the opportunity to experience, in a safe, virtual reality, the struggle and conflict that is at the heart of and gives meaning to every virtuous choice in life. The lessons learned by the young actor will have immediacy and permanency. What more can we ask of art?

The Role of the Director or Acting Teacher

Drama is a discipline, like singing, ballet, or any musical instrument. Just as a piano student knows better than to come into his teacher's music studio and start thrashing away at the piano without applying the careful theory he has learned, so the child in the drama classroom does not romp freely with his untrained instincts, no matter how talented he is or how original his ideas are about the character he is playing.

Your role as a director is to guide and nurture the actor. Since it is the actor who brings the character to life on the stage, it is his responsibility to do his own background study of the part and offer his thoughts about interpretation. If you jump in too soon with your ideas, you can put a damper on his enthusiasm to work out the character for himself. If the student cannot "find" his character, set up a number of questions to help him search out insights. Discuss the role with him, but don't impose an arbitrary interpretation without listening to his ideas first. This would be the same as the algebra instructor telling his student the answer before he has had a chance to reason through the problem himself. A good director shows the way for the student to discover the character on his own.

That being said, it is the director who is the objective eye and sounding board for the actor, especially the beginning actor, who has little idea of what theatrically works. In children's theater, it is the director who should shape the nuance of each characterization. This does not mean that the director creates the character for the actor, just as the conductor does not play the instrument for the musician; rather, he gives feedback to everything the actor produces onstage, drawing out what is truthful and engaging, and discouraging what is insincere or overly intense.

Each character is only one component of the play. The director's job is to bring all the components together so that they fit like pieces of a puzzle, making one coherent and aesthetically pleasing picture. Harry Andrews, the author of *Acting and Play Production*, refers to the director as the czar of the stage. Like most rulers, he will be wise not to micromanage his realm but to encourage each actor to feel free to suggest and create. It is then up to the director to bring into unity the inspired efforts of all the players, both onstage and behind the scenes, for the ultimate benefit of "the show."

The director keeps a running commentary on the effectiveness of each character as that character grows in the actor's imagination and is rendered by his technique. A character is never static. The evolving role needs the constant attention and creative inspiration of both the actor and director during rehearsal and up until the opening performance. After that, the actor is on his own. You might play the same role for three years on Broadway, but with practiced technique, you can bring to each performance a freshness and immediacy that makes it an opening night for every new audience.

Frequently Asked Questions

Question: Can an actor play a role convincingly if he hasn't personally lived the emotions he is portraying?

Answer: This question goes to the heart of the difference between "method" acting and the classical or stage-trained approach. The traditional stage actor relies on his fundamentals to guide his art. Method schools require actors to search within themelves to find the character—thus their emphasis on actors having firsthand experience of behaviors they portray. In other words, the actor needs a living record of emotional memory to draw from to make his character real. To the method actor, empathy is a sacred virtue. He is expected to be tolerant and nonjudgmental so that his identification with the mental-emotional formation of his character is authentic, or at least comes across that way. He may be encouraged to lose himself entirely in his role, especially if it is a complex role involving intense and deeply conflicted feelings. Since the method actor is not supposed to "act" but to be himself, he is expected to do whatever it takes to fit himself to the character or vice versa.

Many known method actors take their psychological preparation for a role very seriously, even to the point of obsessiveness. Before filming the scene in *Marathon Man* in which his character is tortured by a Nazi war criminal, Dustin Hoffman went off alone for several days, depriving himself of sleep and living like a homeless. It is reported that when he turned up on the set, he asked Laurence Olivier, who was playing the Nazi criminal, if he knew any other way he (Hoffman) might prepare himself for the scene. A stage-trained actor to the core, Olivier musingly replied: "Why don't you just try acting, my dear boy? It's much easier." Therein lies the difference between the two approaches to acting!

It is true that the actor needs to thoroughly understand all the complex nuances of his character. He cannot engage the imagination of his audience without making that inner connection and conveying it through his art. Emotion memory, however, is only one aspect of training. Even if the actor can be transported by physical immersion, sympathetic feeling, or memory thought to a deeper sphere of revealment, technique is still necessary to give fitting expression to the fruit of that inspiration *and* to provide the necessary space around the character where the audience can enter in and experience the magic. Moreover, the great artists of an earlier era, including Stanislavski, chose roles that reflected taste and moral integrity and executed them with the intent to uplift their audiences. What they brought to the stage and screen was not only meaningful but elevating. Without noble intention, memory recall can become an excuse to probe and even sanction the basest human passions in all their expressed perversity, which is antithetical to the true aesthetic goals of theater.

When an actor develops a skilled technique based on the fundamentals of stage performance, he can very ably "act" any role convincingly. As long as he can imaginatively visualize the outer life of his character, he will inevitably follow the treasure map to the inner life of motive, thought, and feeling. After all, that's the reason for his training: to create a a convincing and artistically pleasing *theatrical* life, not a real life.

The actor always uses theatrical training to achieve a theatrical goal. He never "becomes" the role because the character role is a theatrical life, completely separate from the actor's real life and real identity. Once the actor merges his own identity with the role he is playing, his character no longer lives theatrically in the imagination of the audience. Every role must be framed theatrically if it is to find its way into the hearts and minds of the spectators. Acting magic is not possible when reality replaces theatrical illusion. Every moment he is onstage, the actor is *playing* a role. When the play (or shoot) is over, the actor needs to remove not just his physical makeup and costume but the whole psychic makeup of the character that he has created. This ensures his own integrity as well as the integrity of the role.

The very art of acting constitutes the ability to create a theatrical life that is imbued with true feeling, without the actor losing his own presence of mind. When the actor tries to "live" the role, he forfeits his presence of mind, for he takes upon himself the psychic reality of his character. When that character is complex or evil, the psychic pain that the actor absorbs can cling to him for years without the actor even being aware of it, since he believes it to be part of himself.

Question: How is modern method acting different from the original "system" that Stanislavski introduced?

Answer: There are two ways modern method advocates differ from their first mentor. Firstly, they have not implemented the high ethics and aspirations he demanded of his actors. Stanislavski was a lover of humanity and an idealist and expected his actors to be also, both in their professional and personal lives. Theater, for him, could not exist as a viable aesthetic art form unless it was established upon altruistic principles. For the most part, Hollywood has rejected that position.

Secondly, because Stanislavski's concepts are philosophical and have never been easy to apply in the classroom, they have been open to misinterpretation. In his books, he does not lay out practical exercises. His writings are descriptive, in which conversations take place between a fictional director (who is really Stanislavski) and a fictional company of acting students (who are really his own Moscow Art Theater players). Later disciples cherry-picked his ideas and then altered them to suit their own underlying personal viewpoints, so that "method acting," as we know it today, scarcely resembles its point of origin.

Perhaps no other concept has been more abused than that of emotional memory recall. Stanislavski desired his actors to develop a rich imagination so that they could visualize sensorial experience and directly apply it to their building of a character role. In addition to being able to recall the feelings associated with personal or imaginary life experiences, he also believed in developing the actor's powers of observation through watching people, reading a lot, traveling, visiting art museums, or simply being more attentive to the immediate sensory environment. The actor would then use these heightened powers to construct his character and convey its living spirit to the audience. Stanislavski did not intend that actors immerse themselves in endless psychoanalysis, develop it as an end in itself, and call it a "method."

Although Stanislavski believed that the source of inspiration for true creativeness lay in the subconscious, he spoke of the subconscious as though it were the inner spirit of man—the same indwelling spirit where man's thoughts intersect with God's. Certainly he did not conceive of it as a storage barn of perverse fantasies that the actor indulges, unchecked by moral impulse. He presumed a moral conscience that would act as a kind of correcting or purifying sieve. His system was designed to create a characterization that was noble in intention and aesthetically beautiful in its form and thus could touch the chord of truth and beauty in the hearts of the audience.

Modern method schools, on the other hand, start with the premise that all human desires and passions resident in the subconscious are fair game for exploration and that the less idealized they are in their artistic form, the more organic, and therefore truthful, they must be. This quest for organic truth tends to be the overriding justification for almost any improvisational exercise. As a result, the process of seeking out and examining every excruciating nuance of feeling and thought has become something of a golden calf for method proponents.

Nowhere did Stanislavski say that intense psychological excavation of the psyche, whether the actor's or someone else's, was the way to get in touch with truth. On the contrary, he was adamant that proper training in all the elements of stagecraft was the only sure means to gain access to the creative state and draw forth living emotion. In other words, he acknowledged the preeminence of classical technique in both guiding and formatting inspiration.

Question: When did method acting become popular in America?

Answer: The 1956 movie *On the Waterfront,* starring Marlon Brando and directed by Elia Kazan, introduced method acting to American theatergoers. Brando's character in the movie was Terry Malloy, an ex-prize fighter struggling against union corruption along the New York waterfront. To help him tap into the explosive, volatile nature of Malloy, Brando applied the theories suggested by Kazan. Kazan had been a founding member of Lee Strasberg's Actor's Studio, which had experimented with Stanislavski's system. Brando's "method" was not so much an authentic application of Stanislavski's concepts as it was a style that suited the gritty realism of the movie's storyline.

On the Waterfront was a defining moment in changing the way American schools taught acting, just as the hearings of the House Un-American Activities Committee was a defining moment in changing the way Hollywood thought politically. The 1960s saw a darker, more cynically minded movie and television industry begin to take shape as producers, actors, directors, and screenwriters retreated from the principle that their work should serve the interests of their country first. Forty years later, and with an almost breathtaking audacity, Hollywood proudly embraces a worldview that holds even less love for its country. Method acting, with its surgical realism, has evolved hand in hand with the political-noir landscape. With high profile performers such as Jack Nicholson, Montgomery Clift, Geraldine Page, Paul Newman, Robert De Niro, Shelley Winters, Warren Beatty, and Sean Penn touting its remarkable results, method has continued to corner the market, so to speak, of American acting schools.

A film review by James Berardinelli posited the suspicion that, had *On the Waterfront* been made two decades later, the ending would have been more cynical than the upbeat one that was chosen, in which right prevails over wrong and Terry Malloy seeks and achieves redemption for his part in causing a man's death. The same reviewer also pointed out Brando's capricious penchant for "inspired" improvisation and his painstaking (and time-consuming) attempts to achieve the "perfect mood." This comment inadvertently underscores the principle weakness of method acting. Highly effective as it can be in enabling profound reaches of emotion, this very introspective style of acting can also lead the actor to practices that are both narcissistic and obsessive—qualities that are rarely identified with a practiced stage artist.

Question: What is the difference between method acting and the classical approach?

Answer: Many method trained actors believe that they must "live" the character they play, coloring in every detail of the part until there is complete immersion of self with the role. Psychological truth is the goal of the method actor, especially in the film medium. The classically trained artist, on the other hand, is content to use the resources of his art to give "theatrical" rather than "actual" life to his character. While his goal is also to render sincere and true emotion, and to bear within himself all the passions and sensitivities that his character requires, he does not feel compelled to "become" the character he plays or to shape that character to his own personality or celebrity persona. He always grows to his task by means of technique.

The stage-trained actor remains separate from his artistic creation, just as a painter stands apart from his canvas or a sculptor from his bronze. At the same time, he intuitively works the components of his technique to theatrically embody his character's life. In this way, he provides the live, theatrical dots that form the theater mask of his character and lets the audience connect those dots and thus bring the mask to full life by using their own imaginations. In other words, by projecting their own emotions, their own hopes and dreams onto the character, the audience themselves play an active role in creating the "acting magic" that they experience in the theater.

At no time does the classically trained actor lose himself in the character and thus marginalize the audience in the theater experience. He is able to use the proscenium to frame the role so that it remains larger than life in its theatrical presence, and thus large enough to invite the infinite responses of his audience. Restraint and control are part of his practiced craft. The repose that one always identifies with such an artist is the very quality that draws the audience nearer to the truth of his character. That truth, being unique for each audience member, should not be limited by the parameters of the actor's own personality, which is what happens when the role becomes solely identified with the actor playing it. The spirit of the character being portrayed must transcend the actor himself. The actor achieves this transcendence only through the expert application of his technique—his voice, his movements, his emotional power, his intuition, will, and intelligence.

The nineteenth-century American actor Joseph Jefferson described this style of acting when he wrote in his autobiography, "I act best when the heart is warm and the head is cool." Tommaso Salvini, much quoted by Stanislavski in his books, also endorsed this same perspective of the actor as both inspired participant and restrained observer. This approach to acting is not "representational" in that the actor does not assume theatrical pretense or apply mechanical stereotype so that he is "putting on an act" on the stage. Rather, it is a complete artistry that rests on an integrated technique to accomplish beautifully vibrant characterizations.

The loud cry in the 1920s and 30s for realism (both on the stage and on the screen) made a villain of the "old school" of stage technique. While there were some (especially in Europe) who still employed the declamatory approach to acting, with all its cultivated clichés and exaggeration—against which Stanislavski complained bitterly—the great actors of the nineteenth century did not. Their technique was never formal, never artificial, and never without the inspiration of rich, assured emotion. In her memoirs, Ellen Terry wrote of Henry Irving's opening night performance of Hamlet at the Lyceum Theater in London in 1874: "The new Hamlet was so simple, so quiet, so free from the exhibition of actors' artifices....The cardinal qualities of his Prince of Denmark were strength, delicacy, distinction...never a touch of commonness. Henry Irving did not go to the audience; he made them come to him."

When the actor is masterful in the use of integrating the components of his theatrical technique so that we are unaware of how he is bringing forth the life of his character and find ourselves inevitably drawn into that life, then we are witnessing the magic of his art. "If anything inspires an actor to do his best," Terry wrote, "it is the audience knowing what we intend, what we do, and what we feel [onstage]. The response from such members of the audience flies across the footlights to us like a flame."

Sadly, this is not the case with many of our modern actors. Not only do they present their characters in an overexposed state, disdainful of the theatrical frame, but far too many use their roles to promote their own celebrity or provoke controversy and angst. Stanislavski called such actors the deadliest enemies of art. He wrote: "You must make up your mind, once and for all, did you come here to serve art, and to make sacrifices for its sake, or to exploit your own personal ends?"

The very concept of the theater has lost much of its traditional sparkle and romance because many actors view the proscenium as a picture frame around their own portraits. The self-absorption, intrinsic to method acting, promotes this kind of narcissism. Factor in the highly sexualized or irritatingly banal content of a lot of modern plays and movies, and the theatergoer finds little relief from the grim and humorless worldview of our art makers. Neglecting the spiritual dimension of life, they assign an untoward importance and seriousness to the things of this world. Too many have forgotten what both Aesop and Shakespeare taught us, that we are merely players on the stage of life. When the spectators in the house are forced to view life through the harsh glare of a searchlight rather than through the gentle washes of an idealism, laughter, and noble pity, we must question if the "ship of the stage" has veered too far from its classic origins of beauty, grace, and simplicity.

Every actor must decide what approach to acting best suits his temperament and aspirations. Whatever he chooses, whether classical or method, or a blend of the two, he should seek first and foremost the highest and most radiant expression of the dramatic arts, where "spiritual light illuminates human living."

Question: Should I play roles that portray evil?

Answer: Firstly, an actor should not attempt the role of an evil or darkly conflicted person until his technique is automatic and assured and he himself has a steady grip on who he is when he's not performing on a stage. Secondly, the role should only be accepted if it has a redemptive purpose in the play—that is, a purpose of dissuading others from the deadly magnetism of such a life course. Thirdly, as long as the intention of the author and director support your own values and you construct your character through the lens of your own moral clarity—thus presenting evil in a principled context—you can play almost any character role.

While the method actor can get caught up in the minutely-examined psychological detail of his character, the stage actor more often chooses simplicity and clarity of line. In an age that celebrates the anguished performances of method actors like Marlon Brando and James Dean, it is seldom understood that an actor who is less intense in his approach to his character can reflect life more clearly and compellingly than one whose mind seeks out the more complex and tortured aspects of human psychology. Just as truth finds its way more quickly through an open and pure heart, so theatrical truth can be rendered with higher resolution through an artist whose mind is a clear pool. As Stanislavski believed, nothing should clog up the channel through which the flow of the character's life is revealed.

Evil has always been best understood by the virtuous—else, how could they have conquered its temptations? When we submerge ourselves in evil, we lose all objectivity and understanding of it because it has now become part of ourselves, our thoughts and feelings, desires and passions, as well as the very process of how we reason and rationalize. In convincing young artists that they must muddy the waters of their own soul to achieve realism onstage, much harm has been done. Many have lost their spiritual bearings and their understanding of the grander truths that await to be told.

Moral clarity is the only clear lens through which to view life and to render that life theatrically in all its truth and simple pathos—and yes, even darkest despair. Such a view, however, is out of tune with these times of Reality TV and the manic hunt for the "extreme" experience, which is why the modern artist must go back to what has worked in the past, and set the events of life against the backdrop of more lasting values. Great art teaches that when the mind is closely attuned to the inner spirit, all great inspiration, power, and wisdom can flow. The clearer the transparency, the purer and more authentic the picture image of life, as that life resembles the divine intent. The actors and actresses who have held power over our hearts and imaginations for generations, such as Paul Muni, Robert Donat, Leslie Howard, Ronald Colman, Claude Rains, Greer Garson, and Irene Dunne, prove the point convincingly.

Question: What is the greatest weakness of method acting?

Answer: The greatest weakness of method acting is what makes it so appealing in the first place, and that is its emphasis on the actor himself. The "actor" is our modern-day Narcissus—that is, he who admires his own reflected glory. The danger of approaching acting from the starting point of the actor's self image is that every role can become a means to enhance that sense of self. A role that is merely a makeover of the actor is a role that cannot expand beyond who the actor believes himself to be. Therefore, the role cannot have a theatrical life of its own because it is limited by the actor's ego.

Characters are created for the audience, not for the actor, nor for the actor's glory. Character roles that are charged with a light and spiritual power exert an influence far beyond the actual lifetimes of the actors who made those roles famous. Unfortunately, it is the actor and not the role he plays that gets the spotlight today. In many cases, the role serves merely to draw attention to the actor instead of the actor serving the role—a subtle but alarming attitude change in Hollywood.

Question: What does "presence of mind" mean?

Answer: An actor has presence of mind when he can hold intact the theatrical life of his character. To accomplish this, he must create a space between himself and his character, even when he is in the midst of acting out the role. In this space, the actor is alert and intensely present with all his trained faculties and spiritual senses as he carefully guides the construction of his role. We refer to this inner space as the magic circle. The audience must enter into this magic circle before they can share in the life of the character. Once the actor crowds that circle of presence with his own thoughts and emotions, the role loses its theatrical frame and the audience become merely bystanders, instead of participants in the creative experience.

This luminous space that encloses the character exists at the level of the spirit, for only at this level can true communion between the character and the audience take place. The job of the actor is to broker such a communion, which is why Stanislavski compared actors to priests. From the moment they enter the theater house, the audience are keenly alive to all that uplifts and enriches their perceptions. The actor, by his art, leads them to this pure space, where the character's life is more deeply felt and understood. It's like a safe zone. Here, uncontaminated by the ego, the theatergoer can open up his heart and soul in complete trust. Indeed, one of the most magical aspects of theater is that the audience will often feel the "reality" of what happens to the theatrical character more deeply and more profoundly than if the same thing were to happen in real life.

When an actor colors the role with his ego, there can be no communion of the audience with the character at the level of the spirit because the actor's ego sucks up all the spiritual oxygen, so to speak, of the space where the character lives. The role loses its theatrical altitude and becomes grounded in the magnetism of the actor's own patterns of reacting and interacting, which are framed by his ego. The intrusion of the egoic mind always cancels out that space of clarity and creative stillness, wherein all magic is possible. The role inevitably becomes an inflated image of the actor himself rather than a "life" that can be transcendent and meaningful to the audience.

Sarah Bernhardt used the term *presence of mind* to describe the process by which the actor can animate his character with the full measure of emotion—and thus sustain the illusion of life on the stage—yet retain the awareness, at all times, that his own personality is separate and apart from the role. The actor "works" on the stage to play another person. "The artist's personality," she wrote, "must be left in his dressing-room." She told the story of how she once had an Italian chambermaid who, returning one evening from seeing her in Jean Racine's play *Phèdre,* said: "Oh! Madame was so lovely that I didn't recognize Madame!" Bernhardt wrote, "No compliment ever went more direct to my heart." The soul of the actor and the soul of the character are distinct, even as the soul of the actor breathes the life of sensibility into the role, making it come alive with "the sentiment of truth" and the "revelation of thought," and thereby "preventing the audience from recognizing it to be illusion," though the actor never loses sight of the fact that the life he creates on stage is *only* illusion. In other words, presence of mind allows the actor to sustain the illusion of theatrical (and not real) life on the stage.

Never let a characterization take over your own identity, either onstage or after the curtain has fallen. When that happens, you are no longer a working actor; you are merely a sponge that absorbs into its open pores the full weight of the character's fictional life, which, for the actor, then becomes real to him. Gaining presence of mind may take years, simply because an actor is not always aware of how much of his own personality is invested in a role, or how much of his ego is attached to playing that role. But if he begins his training with a view to watching himself act, as he would watch himself in a dream, that "presence" will come to him in time.

Having presence of mind empowers both the actor and the role, so that there is the true and deeper coming together of the character and the audience. Bringing about the oneness of your character and the audience is true artistry. We are not after oneness of the character and the actor, which can only serve the actor's ego and not the theatrical life of the character. When you have presence of mind, a spiritual essence and joy will flow into and transform what you do. There will be quality and power in your characterization. Only with presence of mind can the actor find the deeper perfection of his role and share it with his audience. That deeper perfection is the true magic of the role, for it charms the spirit. And only what charms the spirit lives on and makes a difference. The actor's ability to bring it forth describes the art of acting magic.

Question: What are the ideal qualities of a good actor?

Answer: The qualities Alec Guinness claimed to most admire in an actor were "simplicity, purity, clarity of line." We might also add those attributes that Guinness himself embodied both in his performances and in his private life: intelligence, grace, dignity, a noble trust, modesty, and perseverance toward perfection in his art. Like most of the stage-trained actors of his time, he taught us to enjoy our art, to enter enthusiastically into each role, without taking ourselves (or our egos) too seriously.

Sarah Bernhardt wrote extensively of the qualities she believed an actor should possess. They include a natural (intuitive) talent, a poetic imagination, a strong and melodious voice, a retentive memory, a firmly tempered soul, a resolute will, a love of the beautiful, a keen historic sense, a comprehensive study of the human soul, and presence of mind. She also gave particular emphasis to sensibility of feeling. She described it in a way that exquisitely characterized her own art: "The artist must be

PRESENCE OF MIND ON THE STAGE

An original illustrated cover for The Saturday Evening
Post, March 1, 1902 issue. The artist is Harrison Fisher.

like one of those sounding discs which vibrate to every wind, and are agitated by the slightest breeze." To accomplish this state, an actor must lose his ego or sense of self during the time he remains on the stage. She wrote: "*Il perd son 'moi'*—he must lose his 'me.'" Only then can his consciousness be a transparency that "skips from age to age, from one people to another, from one hero to many heroes."

Bernhardt also spoke about being true to who you are. She told the story of how, as a new student at the Paris Conservatoire, she idolized the tragedienne Maria Favart and desired to imitate her art. When the elder actress heard of Sarah's adulation, she arranged a private meeting so she could share with Sarah some of her "artful" devices. Bernhardt records that she was immediately disillusioned by Favart's pretentious acting style. The famous artist had built her "tragic effect" on what Sarah called "gross and ignoble sensibility." From that day she resolved to form an ideal for herself. "I no longer wanted to resemble anyone else, and said: 'I will be myself.'" The unrivaled command she demonstrated in all her acting roles and the captivation of her stage presence was proof that she followed her own advice and fulfilled her own ideal—an ideal that clearly set her apart from her contemporaries. Everything about her acting was authentic. She was not called the "divine Sarah" lightly.

The great stage and screen artists, though different in the execution of their art, shared one infallible quality: they each brought artistic distinction to their profession. An actor should believe in beauty and truth—a beauty that is informed by intelligence, and a truth that finds itself at home in a wide-awake mind that conceives endless possibilities for creating meaningful and uplifting characterizations. For it is only the actor who, on the wings of his imagination, can pass through the ages and bring to countless others the glories of the past and the hopes and dreams of the future. The actor who fulfills this noble obligation is a master alchemist. The purpose of the actor, after all, is to breathe into the hollow masks of comedy and tragedy the breath of life and to animate them by his inspiration and genius.

The actor in today's world has the privilege and opportunity to influence millions of people every time he performs a role. When the Olympian enters the center of the ring and competes before his worldwide audience, he carries on his shoulders the hopes and aspirations of his countrymen. When an actor shares his role with the audience, he bears an even greater burden: the hopes and dreams of humanity.

To bring magic to the stage is a rare gift and an act of love. When the audience enter into communion with the life of the character, it means that they recognize the character's struggle as their struggle, his overcoming as their overcoming, his triumph as their triumph. Through the art of characterization, the actor can help others strive to become better, and so discover more of the beauty of life. When, as an actor, you inspire in others the desire for self-transcendence, you have fulfilled the ancient art of theater in all its profound revealment and transforming magic.

Golden Rules of Character Study

Below is a condensed list of the practical steps or *golden rules* of character study that are helpful to the actor's art of creating a character.

1. *Read through your selection piece or play several times* so that you understand the dramatic context. Take notes on the main theme, storyline, points of dramatic conflict, climax and resolution. This will provide an external road-mapping to guide your characterization. Also note the setting of the play, the social and intellectual background of the men and women who people it, their costume and deportment, social manners, and mode of personal address. Make sure you understand the nature of the scene and the reason for the character's actions. If you are staging a play from an earlier period, use old periodicals and magazines to research the era. Peterson's Magazine and Godey's Lady's Book are ideal for the Civil War era, while Ladies Home Journal, Harper's Weekly, Cosmopolitan, and Saturday Evening Post provide a pictorial window into the Victorian era through World War II.

Director's Notes: If you are staging an entire play, provide a summary of the story and of each character when the scripts are handed out to the cast. Briefly discuss the historic era, the central theme and message of the play, as well as the kinds of costumes and sets that are being designed for the production.

2. *Identify the genre of the scene or play*—whether Greek tragedy, Elizabethan romantic comedy, English comedy of manners, modern realist drama, French farce, etc., and the style of writing, whether it is written in blank verse (Shakespeare), period narrative verse (Tennyson), or contemporary prose. The type of literary genre often determines the tone of the acting, approach to characterization, and delivery of the lines.

3. *Define the physical action of your character, as well as his outer and inner life* by answering the following questions:

Physical action of the character:

a) What is the goal of your character in the scene—that is, what does he or she wish to accomplish? Who or what is the obstacle to his goal?
b) What is the nature of the conflict that your character must overcome? Is it an outer struggle (physical events) or a struggle from within?

Outer life of the character:

a) What does your character look like? How old is he? How does he dress? How does he walk, sit, or move around the stage?

b) Is there any unusual physical characteristic about your character? For example, the role of Helen Keller in *The Miracle Worker* is that of a blind mute. The role of Colin in *The Secret Garden* is that of a crippled child who learns to walk.

c) Is the character poor or well-to-do? How does his level of poverty or wealth affect his character—that is, how he perceives himself and acts toward others? What is his class or social background? What religious beliefs does he have, if any?

Inner life of the character:

a) What are three adjectives that describe your character? Does your character maintain the same attitude throughout? If not, what are the reasons for his change? What is the nature of the conflict that makes him change? Does he grow as a result of these changes?

b) Does the dialogue use images of nature? Does it express faith or some internal psychological state? Do the images evoke a loving, thoughtful, or violent mood? Is the character a romantic or a realist? What do the images tell about the mental, emotional, or spiritual state of the character?

Director's Notes: Each student can optionally prepare an oral or written biography of the imaginary life of the character he is portraying. If there is little information available on which to base a believable characterization, the student should make up the missing facts but keep it consistent with the historical time indicated.

4. *Improvise the scene* (make up your own lines) with the other actors after becoming familiar with the script and your character. Stay close to the same storyline and the author's intention. Do not use improvisation to insert your own personal attitudes, thus making the character something he was never intended to be. Apply your inspiration to what is given in the text.

5. *Learn your lines as quickly as possible.* Have all your lines memorized no later than the run-through rehearsals—that is, one to two weeks before the opening performance. (Sarah Bernhardt memorized all her character's lines

before the first rehearsal.) The quickest way to memorize your part is to highlight all your character's lines and have another actor (or available sibling or friend) read the dialogue leading up to and immediately following yours. Do not learn your lines in isolation. You should be thoroughly familiar with the lines of other actors in the scene so that there is dramatic continuity and a pace that you and the other actors in the scene are used to working at. Use whatever method will work to increase your memorization skills.

6. *Mark your script with the proper stage directions* learned in Unit Study 2, including Cross in, Cross out (X in, X out), the playing areas (DL, DR), and body positions (Quarter Right, Quarter Left).

7. *Your character lives every moment he is onstage* in front of the audience. Get into character before an entrance and continue the characterization until the curtain falls. Backstage discipline is just as essential as onstage behavior, since the actor needs to be able to concentrate and "energize" his role before making his entrance. Your "magic presence" begins before you enter and continues until you have made the final exit. Your character's presence is revealed in:

a) *action.* Action is descriptive of the total character attitude. It is usually expressed by movement from one stage area to another; a change in body position of the actor—for example, sitting to standing or turning from full front to quarter; body gestures; spoken dialogue or emotional utterances—for example, crying; and facial expression. Action is always preceded by motive and moves the storyline.

b) *reaction.* Reaction encompasses the total deportment of the character in response to another character's actions and spoken words. This reaction may be registered by dialogue, body language, or facial expression alone.

c) *interaction.* Interaction (inter action) refers to the mutual or reciprocal actions between two actors, each cueing off the other.

d) *non-action.* Non-action refers to the silent action of the character or the continuous flow of thought and feeling in the absence of dialogue, movement, or apparent facial expression. You are the character at all times onstage even when you are not doing anything active. You must listen and react to everything that is done and said by other characters whether you have lines to speak or you remain silent. Onstage, silence can be eloquent. Your character may speak his thoughts or merely think them, but he is always engaged with the total stage action because a theatrical character lives in the theatrical world. The ability to listen to another character's words and be thinking the natural thoughts that his speech provokes is just as important a part of characterization as the assigned spoken dialogue. When several people are onstage, only one character can speak at a time; if any of the others are not listening and reacting, there will be *blank spots* in the stage picture. A blank spot (empty inactivity) is the opposite to non-action. A blank spot will distract the audience from the character who is speaking. There should never be a blank spot on the stage because a blank spot is a void. It is like punching a hole in a painting or leaving out a few bars in a musical composition. The whole is affected adversely and the magic is destroyed.

8. *The theatrical cue is the building block of character* just as it is the building block of every scene in a play. The first rule in the actor's character notebook should read: do not act, do not speak, do not think, do not feel without a reason. Every piece of stage business must be motivated; it must grow out of the life or 'reason to be' of the character. Doing or saying something unnecessary or inappropriate onstage is just as bad as being a blank spot.

Director's Notes: The imaginative actor with a keen dramatic sense and strong powers of concentration will think through the whole scene and stay in it from entrance to exit. If a student loses concentration or is a blank spot, you should stop the scene and say: "I can't tell what your thoughts are yet." Then ask the following questions: "What is your character thinking right now? What does your character feel about what the other character just said? Do you agree with what the other character is saying? What would you say at this point in the scene if you had a line of dialogue? Even if you don't have a line, how will you let your audience see your thoughts?" A question or two usually brings the actor back into the action, reminding him that he must think the thoughts and feel the feelings of his character and stay in character every moment he is onstage.

9. *Choose character roles that are sufficiently simple and age-appropriate.* In early training, the student will inevitably draw upon his own personal traits to color in his role. Once the roles become more challenging, encourage the students to do background research. If the character to be played is a real

life historical figure, the actor should get photographs and diaries or any written records of that person and become intimately acquainted with his life and times. Even statues and paintings can reveal invaluable insights. An actor can look at a sculpture or a portrait of someone and immediately tune in to the inner quality of soul informed by their life experience. It is why Stanislavski urged his players to visit museums and historical landmarks. In Augustus Saint-Gaudens' statue of *The Puritan*, for example, we learn much about the spiritual nature of the Puritan. The Pilgrim hat, the severely buttoned-up coat, the clasped Bible and cane, and the strong, masterly presence, all capture the stern rigor and moral strictness of the inner man. In Michelangelo's statue of *Moses*, we are aware of a powerful man of courage and integrity, who became the patriarchal leader of his people, struggled on with them, and died without being able to follow them into the promised land to which he had led them. Something of his transcendent strength is represented in this magnificent sculpturing of him. In *David*, we have the artist's conception of the perfect man—warrior, poet, and king. The sculpture would be a prophecy in art of the spiritual God-man who would later incarnate as Jesus. Then there is the immortal *Pieta*, which imprisons a mother's divine love for her son in a marble statue that remains unchanged by the ravages of time.

Author's Story: Before I mounted our theater's production of *Saint Bernadette*, I visited Lourdes, France, where the child, Bernadette Soubirous, received the heavenly visitations. In the grounds of the Grotto there is a white statue of Bernadette as a novice nun. There could not have been a more revealing and eloquent picture of the young girl's simplicity and purity than this piquant statue. The image was used as a principle source of inspiration for the student who played the role of Bernadette.

10. *The essence of interpretation is imaginative understanding.* Imagining yourself in the role is half the work of creating the role. The physical references (looking, dressing, and speaking like the character) guide you to the deeper levels of your character's inner life. You must discover this inner life if your character is to ring true to the audience. Every line of dialogue should be spoken as though it comes right from the character's heart. The unit study exercises in mime and improvisation are designed to teach you to build real human thoughts and emotions around imaginary cues until they look and sound like real life. To do his job well, the actor needs to cultivate some special qualities: an artistic temperament—that is, a nature that is

responsive to things of the heart and the soul and to the beauties of the natural world around him; a searching theatrical instinct that makes him eager to delve into the possibilities of his role; and dramatic intelligence, which is the power to reason out the multi-layered growth that his character undergoes from the first scene to the last.

The golden rules of character study are only guidelines. The actor must study and analyze his part well and think it through thoroughly until he can visualize a living person inside it. He should explore whatever is within his means to cultivate his imagination and his subtle powers of interpretation, while recalling Stanislavski's words that "Artistic emotion is weighed not in pounds but in ounces." The actor's challenge is to reveal, in the clearest and most compelling way he can, a certain spectrum of life experience that comes alive in the imagination of his audience, even as he retains awareness that it is only illusion. In mastering the art of characterization, the actor can stretch the boundaries of what has already been accomplished by the great artists of the past. In the footsteps of those visionaries, he too must sail by the compass of the Spirit of God within, wherein the true fires of inspiration, aspiration, and endeavor are kindled. From that pure center, all enlightened understanding will come!

It often happens that an actor has all the fine, subtle, deep feelings necessary to his part and yet he may distort them beyond recognition because he conveys them through crudely prepared external physical means. When the body transmits neither the actor's feelings to me nor how he experiences them I see an out of tune, inferior instrument....The more complex the life of the human spirit in the part being portrayed, the more delicate, the more compelling and artistic should be the physical form which clothes it.

This makes an enormous call on our external technique, on the expressiveness of our bodily apparatus, our voice, diction, intonation, handling of words, phrases, speeches, our facial expression, plasticity of movement, way of walking. To a supreme degree sensitive to the slightest twist, the subtlest turns and changes in our inner lives while on the stage, they must be like the most delicate barometers....

Train your physical apparatus to the limits of your natural, inborn capacity. You must still go on developing, correcting, tuning your bodies until every part of them will respond to the...task of presenting in external form your invisible feelings. You must educate your bodies according to the laws of nature. That means a lot of complicated work and perseverance!

—Constantin Stanislavski, *Building a Character*

Making the Body Expressive

Many of the matinee idols who graced the movies of the 1930s and 40s were remarkably well trained in all areas of the gymnastic use of their bodies. It was an essential part of the art of characterization. When we think of Douglas Fairbanks Sr., Douglas Fairbanks Jr., John Gilbert, Errol Flynn, Tyrone Power, Basil Rathbone, Cornel Wilde, Gene Kelly, and Louis Hayward, to mention just a few, we think of actors who could portray real men—swashbuckling heroes who knew how to handle a sword in defense of their own honor or the honor of any woman who sought their protection. These same actors also knew how to dance the perfect waltz, quadrille, galliard, minuet, or occasional tango. Cornel Wilde and Tyrone Power actually started off their careers as fencing champions. Cornel Wilde, a member of the U.S. Olympic fencing team, quit the team just prior to the 1936 Berlin Olympics in order to take a role in a Broadway play. He was hired in the dual capacities of fencing choreographer and actor (in the role of Tybalt) in Laurence Olivier's 1940 Broadway production of *Romeo and Juliet*. Hollywood signed him soon after.

Very few of our modern actors are trained in the art of fencing, dance, or the kind of all-round physical athleticism that would allow them to leap over tall walls or across rooftops in the pursuit of villains (or to escape returning husbands). The actors of an earlier era had bodies that responded with strength, agility, and grace to any physical challenge or ritual of romantic courtship.

In our contemporary Hollywood, stunt men are used on a regular basis when the physical tasks are even slightly menacing to the star's physical well-being. Expert masters and choreographers are brought in to teach the actors the bare necessities of looking like the genuine article. Camera angles and editing are more concerned with close-ups and eye play than capturing a grand theatrical spectacle. There are, however, some actors who had extensive training in classical fencing before beginning their movie careers. These include Cary Elwes, Mandy Patinkin, Catherine Zeta Jones, Orlando Bloom, and Viggo Mortensen—all well known for their screen portrayals of swordsmen and swashbucklers.

It is a lamentable fact that most modern actors do not make the best use of their physical apparatus. Few develop it as a complete instrument or maintain it in excellent working order so that it can meet all artistic requirements. We see far too many flabby muscles, hunched shoulders, sagging chests, and shuffling walks. We have become so accustomed to realism in the movies, that there is no longer a standard of physical beauty or manliness. The audience has learned not to expect anything better and therefore does not mind if an actor displays poor posture, walks like a slob, or lets a woman outdo him with a sword or an archer's bow.

Michelangelo stands by his sculpture of Moses and the great love of his
life, Vittoria Colonna

Many modern actors are simply undertrained. Unless a specific role calls for it, there is no physical culture required of the star, with the result that he does not convey the mobility, proportion, subtlety of movement, or flexibility of action that characterized actors of an earlier era. If physical training takes place at all, it is usually confined to weight lifting and powerful body building, which many people do not find particularly attractive. Moreover, a muscular body often typecasts an actor in one kind of movie genre—the violent action film, such as the series of *Die Hard* movies, featuring Bruce Willis as the tough-guy cop, and the *Terminator* films, which have starred the iconic action hero Arnold Schwarzenegger. Bulging muscles have never looked good in the form-fitting costumes of medieval Venice or the snug Renaissance doublet, which is why we may never see Mr. Willis or Mr. Schwarzenegger playing Shakespeare.

Being fully instructed in all the physical components of stage performance can only improve the quality, expressiveness, and range of the actor's characterizations. Some form of gymnastic sport, therefore, should be a necessary part of acting training. With the exception of martial arts, the most common and easily adapted sport for theatrical purposes is fencing. What production of *Hamlet* or *Romeo and Juliet* can be successful without actors who know something of the use of a rapier?

The Art of Fencing: (To touch without being touched)

Basil Rathbone, considered the greatest swordsman in Hollywood, made many adventure films during the 1930s. In most of them he played the villain, who happened to be a deadly swordsman. One of his best-known roles was Sir Guy of Gisbourne in *The Adventures of Robin Hood.* In the final fencing scene, he and Errol Flynn (Robin Hood) actually fight each other on the screen with real (untipped) swords in hand. Because of the accomplished skill of both actors, the scene stands as the quintessence of what actors had to do for the sake of their art in the golden years of the cinema. In *Castle of Frankenstein,* 1969 issue, Rathbone explained why he enjoyed swordsmanship more than any other recreation. He thought it was a wonderful exercise but refused to put it under the category of a sport. He believed fencing to be a discipline of the arts because it required tremendous skill *and* wrought a beautiful theatrical form.

Instruction in the classical use of foil, épée, and sabre is one of the best gymnastic and aerobic forms of physical training that an actor can undertake. Fencing is an ancient art with a wonderful history. It has evolved over 800 years from being man's first defense in combat to a complete and modern sport. When Baron Pierre de Coubertin revived the Olympic Games in Athens in 1896, fencing was chosen as one of the premier events. Though it cannot compete with mainstream attractions like gymnastics, track, and swimming, the art of swordfighting still retains a glamor and excitement that is uniquely its own.

The art of fencing offers diverse benefits, including improved coordination, speed, physical strength and stamina, sharpened reflexes, agility of movement, increased self-discipline, control, and confidence. Because of the necessity to analyze the opponent's game and to develop intricate strategies of defense and attack, fencing is also a sport of the mind. The action of making a touch on the opponent without his sword touching you first addresses man's first instinct of self-preservation. Even if the swords are blunted, as they are for practice foils, the student still experiences the thrill of the theatrical illusion: What if the sword were sharp? The answer, of course, is that the touch would be deadly. Therefore, the student is mentally as well as physically alert to a degree not manifest in any other sport.

Working with swords—even the blunted, bated blades designed for modern fencing—requires self control, precision of movement, presence of mind, and mental discipline. Training in the art of fencing nurtures these qualities, which is why fencing has been used as a form of physical therapy, as well as a rehabilitative tool for troubled teenagers. But even more importantly, the art of fencing is essentially improvisational, in that the player must make on-the-spot decisions that achieve his goal. He has to learn to think clearly under pressure, to understand the relationship between mind, body and emotion, and to maintain balance and equanimity.

The elegant and flowing techniques of the fencing masters of the classical Italian, French, and Hungarian schools have largely disappeared from the modern sport of fencing, where participants are more concerned with scoring points than displaying finesse and grace. The emphasis has shifted from the quality of the touch to who can touch first. This hit and run approach sacrifices the fine art of beautiful line and restraint of action in favor of speed and power. As in the art of acting, this degradation of the finer and nobler aspects of the art has upset those who wish to preserve the beauty and refinement of the time-honored forms.

Classical French foil is the best fencing weapon to introduce to the actor because its forms retain the ancient rituals of the art and have theatrical application. The foil has a rectangular cross-section blade and a small bell guard. French foil is quiet, precise, and accurate. The forms are executed with balance, harmony, and smoothness. The style is fluid and continuous. The weapon hand exhibits very fine movements in circular, lateral, and diagonal actions, while the legs make subtle postures that include crossing (an advance or retreat by crossing one leg over the other), balestra (forward hop or jump, usually followed by an attack such as a lunge or fleche), gliding (an attack or feint that slides along the opponent's blade), passing (an attack that involves moving past the opponent), lunging (an attack made by extending the rear leg and landing on the bent front leg), passata-sotto (a lunge made by dropping one hand to the floor), and fleche (an attack in which the aggressor leaps off his leading foot, attempts to make the hit, and then passes the opponent at a run).

To execute these moves well, the fencer's mind must be quiet and focused, and his emotions calm. Moving with a smooth, fluid line also prevents the body from becoming rigid or tense and makes the muscles more resilient and adaptable. Strength is dynamically focused because smooth movement requires perfect physical and mental control, as well as equanimity of spirit.

Concentration is one of the most important elements of the French foil technique, as it is for successful acting. In order to effectively execute a touch, the mind cannot be anywhere but on the present action, as the strategy of coordinating a quick and decisive hit demands total attention. To lose concentration or slacken the pace can mean a quick defeat, just as failing to stay in character on the stage can destroy the theatrical illusion for the audience.

The personal benefits of fencing impact every area of the participant's physical and intellectual being. The intensity of the demands it places on the mind and body makes it a perfect adjunct to the skills learned in acting. Both as a sport and as a form of art, fencing offers the most complete union of thought and action. A successful fencer must be capable of mounting both powerful driving attacks and subtle and cunning defenses, all within the space of one or two seconds. The coordination must be so finely developed that the fencer can adapt all movements to many different opponents of widely varied strength, skill, body proportion, and speed. The fencer must also possess a keen and alert intellect with a concentration powerful enough to focus lightning-fast execution of his strategies.

Like many of the martial arts disciplines, the French foil technique has intrinsic courtesy and ceremony, owing much to its noble heritage. The spirit of fair play, good sportsmanship, and honor—integral to fencing—is expected both on and off the fencing strip. A gentleman's consideration is always observed while competing with others. Indeed, fencing is as much a character attitude as it is a sport, and those who practice the art find that it can bring erudition and refinement to their own personal and professional conduct.

Children love to fence because each fencing play has a clear and defined goal with precise results, determined by who has the quickest hand and brain. Simple. It is also a very effective way for women to learn self confidence in confronting an aggressive opponent. As far as the boys go, fencing is just a great way to provide an outlet for the aggressive, competitive instinct. But even more useful in relation to theater is the practical training that actors get in knowing how to fence when swordfighting is a part of their characterization. Many of Shakespeare's plays feature men with swords, which therefore requires the actors to work with the sword as part of their costume and deportment. *Romeo and Juliet* is a perfect example. There are very few scenes in that play where the male characters are not required to either wear or use their sword.

Introducing Fencing (En Guarde, Ready, Fence!)

If you are not an experienced fencer yourself, follow the guidelines below:

• Contact a local fencing academy or a teacher of fencing at a nearby university or community college, where swordsmanship is sometimes included as part of the theater program. Arrange a time for him to either give a presentation at your studio or bring the students to his place of instruction. Because the players need to be dressed in full protective equipment from head to foot, practice on special fencing mats, and use properly blunted and bated practice swords, it is better to use an instructor who has all of his own safety regulated gear, mats, and electrical equipment (if electrical scoring is used).

• Though classical French foil is the most desired technique to be taught, the basic principles of fencing can be imparted using any form, as long as the instructor emphasizes the importance of graceful lines and finesse. The three weapons are the foil, the épée, and the sabre. In modern fencing, each has its own rules, attacks, and parries (or blocks). In any case, students should learn foil first, since the foil provides the basis for épée and sabre techniques.

• Though the swords used will have buttoned tips to render the points less dangerous for practice, the student should still be dressed for maximum protection. This means he should wear two thick sweatshirts or a thick jacket under his "whites." Long pants and closed shoes with good traction are also required.

• If possible, have each student experience at least one competitive bout— an assault (also known as a friendly combat), at which the score is kept.

• All fencing masters require their students to do special stretching exercises before they practice with a sword. If time (or budget) does not allow you to set up regular fencing instruction as part of the weekly curriculum, try and incorporate the stretching exercises in your pre-class warm-ups.

• Find scenes from older movies that show actors swordfighting. Turner Classic Movies offers a wide selection of classic movies, while many of the most popular are now available on DVD. Two of the best choices are *Captain Blood* and *The Adventures of Robin Hood,* both starring Errol Flynn and Basil Rathbone. Other fun choices are *Romeo and Juliet,* starring Leslie Howard, the silent movie version of *The Three*

Musketeers, starring Douglas Fairbanks Sr., the later MGM Technicolor version, starring Gene Kelly, and *Cyrano de Bergerac,* starring José Ferrer. Beautifully acted, *Cyrano* sets the art of fencing against the backdrop of a poetic and chivalrous age. More modern movies that feature excellent swordplay action are *The Princess Bride* with Mandy Patinkin, *Duellists* with Keith Carradine (though brilliant play, it is a bit bloody), *Ladyhawke* with Matthew Broderick, *By the Sword* with Murray Abraham, and *The Count of Monte Cristo* with Jim Caviezel.

- Have your class attend a live theater production of a play that features extensive swordplay. If possible, get permission from the choreographer or fencing director to witness a rehearsal. Though actors can get away with minimal preparedness in the art of fencing for a movie scene, the theater exacts its physical toll. The Royal Shakespeare Company's staging of the ten-hour *Henry VI* trilogy during their 2006 Complete Works Festival exemplified near-heroic virtuosity on the part of the 29-strong ensemble cast. Not only did most of the actors (who played over 90 different roles in true repertory fashion) engage in constant swordfights on the stage, but many of them spent time hanging or swinging on ropes—with swords in hand—sometimes spilling blood midair. Moreover, as the straight sword was part of the costume of all but the courtly female characters and the pious King Henry, ascending and descending the ropes and steel ladders, that were set at the corners of each of the three-level seating tiers, was a masterful effort in timing and coordination. The battle scenes between the House of York and the House of Lancaster were mesmerizing, with the respective troops making entrances hoisted from high-roofed rafters or swinging on harnesses—reminding the spectator of SWAT teams or trapeze artists in swift motion. The three-part production was a spectacle of exhilarating action and, as one reviewer wrote, "unrelenting physical vigor." It proved, beyond a doubt, that live theater is the only true conservatory for complete training in the dramatic arts.

> Movie magic is movie magic and acting magic is acting magic....I'm very much in love with the fact that the camera is revolted by acting and loves behaviour. The camera does not like acting. The camera is only interested in filming behaviour....I think if I were to go back on stage I might be in great danger of acting.
>
> —Ben Kingsley

Winifred Emery and Lyn Harding in *Sir Walter Raleigh* by W. Devereux. Theater Royal, Portsmouth, August 15th, 1910.

"In five minutes, three were slightly wounded, one on the wrist, another on the chin, and the third on the ear, by the defender of the stair, who himself remained intact."
—*The Three Musketeers*

Unit

Study

Twelve

Staging the Play

12

Staging the Play

Creative Play Acting

The weeks that have been devoted to pantomime and improvisation will have laid the foundation for creating playlets and short plays. The goal for the end of the first quarter is to stage an informal presentation of material that you have worked on, developed, and refined in class. You will choose one or more of the improvisations with which you are already familiar, polish and rehearse them, and perform them before your classmates and family members as an acting exercise. The purpose of such a presentation is to show what you have learned and internalized as actors up to this point in your training. This first performance will also help prepare you for a formal recital at the end of the second quarter in front of a public audience.

Many of the Unit Study 6 change-of-mood pantomimes on which the longer speech improvisations in Unit Study 7 were based contain the fundamental elements of good drama, and thus provide very workable material for creative play-acting.

Playlet (ages 4 to 7 or ages 8 to 12)

Instructions: You should prepare as many different playlets for the older group as there are actors to fill the roles. The youngest children like to imitate each other and may wish to play the same role in the same scene rather than try a new playlet. It may seem unusual for the audience of friends and parents to watch the same playlet performed two or three times by different students, but this is very common and is perfectly fine when working with the smallest of the actors. Children who are shy or lack confidence will be willing to take more emotional risks if they see other children in their group play-acting the same role. The older children, on the other hand, tend to be more independent and enjoy the challenge of creating their own unique character in their own unique scene. Needless to say, the adult students will need a separate rehearsal space and extra class time to work up their scenes, as more is expected of them.

Making the Playlet

Director's Notes: You may read aloud to the class the information below, or simply summarize the key points before they start on their project of making a playlet. Though the playlet is to be performed by the younger students, you can invite the teens and adults to participate in helping to script it.

A *playlet* is a miniature drama in which all the action takes place in a single scene. A playlet lasts up to three minutes for the littlest ones and three to five minutes for the age 8 to 12 group. The playlet consists of only one scene, though that single scene will be divided into several acting units based on the complexity of mood changes and the dialogue that develops between the characters.

To demonstrate how to develop a simple idea into a playlet for performance, we will use the Mime with Character Attitude pantomime in Unit Study 6 of Billy at the mailbox, later expanded in Unit Study 8 as Exercise 8-3: Billy's Birthday Gift.

In its earlier form as a pantomime, we had no real beginning point in the story. The exercise was only dramatic play in which Billy checked the mailbox and showed his disappointment when he did not find a birthday present. Now, according to the rules of good drama, we need to create a storyline from the idea, starting with a proper *beginning*. What would be a way to start off the scene and get the audience's interest? Remember that you don't have to tell the whole story in the opening shot, just create interest in the character. *(Let children suggest some ideas.)*

Sample Playlet: Here is an example of how the playlet could unfold.

- The porch of Billy's home could be the setting. We might open the scene with Billy running downstage to the mailbox. To let the audience know where he is, Billy might call out to his mom as he runs onstage that he'll get the mail. With a big smile on his face, he opens the lid to the mailbox, where he sees a couple of letters but no package. He takes out the letters, quickly checks the mailbox again, then looks all about him in case the parcel was too big to put in the mailbox. Nothing.

- What would Billy be thinking and feeling right now? What spontaneous words would he speak? (*Make sure you let the younger children make their suggestions before you and the older students decide on the dialogue that will be used.*) Billy might say something like: "Gosh, it didn't come. My box didn't come!" If he was expecting a particular object, he might name the object, such as a remote-controlled car. Hearing these words, the audience immediately understands Billy's cause of disappointment. He was expecting a special package and it didn't arrive.

- What is Billy's expression now? How has his mood changed since he first ran onstage? Does the audience sympathize with Billy at this point? Is our interest stirred as to why Billy was expecting this particular package or why he didn't get it? If the answer is yes, then we have defined the first conflict in the scene: Billy's goal in checking the mailbox was to find a box meant for him that he fully expected to arrive that day. That goal was not achieved. The mailman brought no package for him.

- Still hopeful, Billy might think that the mailman just forgot to leave the box and that soon he will discover it in the back of his truck and return to give it to Billy. Billy strains to see if the truck has gone to the next street yet. No, it's just two houses down. And the mailman is getting out of his seat and going to the back of his truck. Billy might yell out: "Mr. Mailman, is there a big box in your truck that you forgot to give me?" Imagine the mailman smiling, checking inside his truck as he tidies up his packages, then shaking his head. He gets back into his truck and drives away into the next block. This is more action with conflict. What would be some clear statements and facial expressions that Billy could make to convey to the audience the progression of the thoughts he is thinking as he interacts with the imaginary mailman?

- Looking dejected, Billy slowly walks back to the porch. Grandma must have forgotten all about what day it was. Billy's mom comes out, sees his disappointment, puts her arm around him and tries to convince him that maybe the package will come tomorrow and that grandma must have just mailed it too late to arrive on his special day. It will certainly arrive tomorrow. Billy is too let down to be cheered by a promise of the package turning up tomorrow. It just won't mean the same getting it tomorrow.

- The audience's sympathy is increased. Could today be Billy's birthday and was he expecting a birthday package from his grandma? Meanwhile, Billy's mom looks at the mail and tells Billy that one of the letters is from Uncle Frank. Maybe it's a birthday card. Uncle Frank writes in the letter that he is coming for a visit today and should arrive by 3 pm. She looks at her watch. It's almost 3 pm now. Perhaps Uncle Frank will bring Grandma's package! Billy feels a flicker of hope. His mom suggests that he wait on the porch for Uncle Frank. Billy agrees, but he doesn't want to get too hopeful. After all, Grandma may have forgotten all about his birthday.

- With this new element of suspense, Uncle Frank arrives on the scene. (Since we are dealing with an outside setting, Uncle Frank can make an entrance from the back of the house or classroom). Billy jumps up when he sees his uncle and is filled with anticipation as he watches him approach. We might hear Uncle Frank call out a hello as he strides up the path. Billy sees his uncle walking toward him, but there is no package under his arm—nothing! This is the moment of crisis. What words would best show Billy's utter disappointment?

- Billy feels like crying, but he summons his self-control as he doesn't want to act like a baby in front of his uncle. Do you think Billy believes that Grandma did forget his birthday after all? Is this what makes him sad, or is it simply the thought of not getting a present from her? Or does Billy think that Uncle Frank doesn't even know that it's Billy's birthday?

- Billy's mom greets Uncle Frank, but Billy is so dejected that he can't even look up at him. His mom urges Billy to shake hands with his uncle. Reluctantly, Billy does so but without any spirit. Uncle Frank greets Billy and winks at Billy's mom. Then he tells Billy that he has to get something very special out of his car and needs his help. With hope in his eyes, Billy goes back out with Uncle Frank.

- Within seconds we hear an excited voice calling from the back of the house: "Mom, it's from grandma. It's my present. She didn't forget!" He runs to his mom, pressing the package to his chest. He reads aloud to her the writing on the package: "To Billy from Grandma." This is the happy climax. With both arms firmly wrapped around his present, Billy exits the stage—the picture of a perfectly contented birthday boy.

Instructions: As in the example above, once you have established the storyline, defined the structural elements of beginning action, suspense, crisis, climax, and denouement, described the characters, and fleshed out the action with dialogue, you will have a scene playlet for the little ones that is ready for casting and dramatization. It will include entrances, exits, blocking, dialogue, costumes, a set, and stage props. Through their class discussion about this scene or any of several different story improvisations in Unit Study 7, the children soon begin to identify the dramatic elements that make up a workable acting scene. Each improvisation or change-of-mood pantomime that you develop for the end-of-quarter playlets must contain these structural elements. Scene episodes developed along proper lines can be transformed into good drama. Do not write the scenes *for* the children. The objective is to stimulate them to think spontaneously and creatively so that they will feel a certain ownership of their work. There will be plenty of opportunity down the line to work with ready-made scenes and plays. This is the time to draw them out of themselves, encourage lots of ideas, and get them looking forward to performing in front of a real audience.

Building the Playlet

To act out your characters better, you can break down the playlet into individual acting units, or scenelets. In the sample story, "Billy's Birthday Gift," we can identify eight individual acting units:

1. Billy's opening words and pantomime as he enters the stage feeling happy and excited and looks inside the mailbox

2. Billy's disappointment as he discovers that there is no package, his checking again, and then his searching on the ground

3. Billy's hope that the mailman forgot about the package, followed by his questioning of the mailman before he leaves the neighborhood

4. Billy's conversation with his mother about the letter and his uncle's visit

5. Uncle Frank's arrival and Billy's new hopefulness

6. Billy's utter disappointment as his uncle approaches without a package and Billy's dejected behavior in front of his mother and his uncle

7. Uncle Frank's wink at Billy's mom and his dialogue about something he forgot in the car

8. Billy's receipt of the gift and his very joyful exit.

Director's Notes: Work on each unit of this miniature drama separately and in order of story sequence. If the whole scene is worked as one long unit, many of the subtle turns in the thoughts and feelings of the characters will be overlooked, the storyline will appear shallow, and the dialogue will be sketchy.

Improvising the Playlet

Director's Notes: The same instructional guidelines below can be used for both the age 3-7 and age 8-12 group.

Instructions for the Director

- Starting with the first scenelet or unit, assign two or three of the boys to play Billy, performing only the first scenelet.

- Allow a lively group discussion to follow each improvised playing of the scenelet until everyone decides on the best dialogue, movements, etc. (The second and third actors who play Billy will generally be more convincing, having profited from the constructive criticism of the performance of their earlier colleagues.)

- Have the teens write down the blocking directions, body movements, and dialogue as the group decides on them for the working script.

- Complete the working script for each scenelet before going on to the next unit. (As the students get more involved with the creative process, you can ask for volunteers to play the roles, instead of assigning the parts.)

- Use different actors for each unit until every section of the playlet has been thoroughly worked through and scripted.

The improvisations should be worked out in the proper story sequence and without interruption. Only after the actors have completed acting out a unit, should the group or director offer their suggestions. By the time all the units have been constructed, every child will have become familiar with the three characters and will likely be excited about playing a role. This entire procedure may take up to four class periods for the little ones and one to three classes for the 8-12 age group, depending on the length and difficulty of the story being dramatized.

Casting the Playlet

Instructions for the Director

- Have a meeting with your teen students (and helping-out moms) to (1) cast the playlets to be performed by the two younger age groups; (2) make plans for extra rehearsal periods if needed; (3) ask for volunteers to obtain the necessary set pieces and props; (4) decide whether you wish to use physical set pieces and props to help create a more realistic scene setting or if you want the actors to pantomime everything (a more difficult task).

- If there are more children in your age 4 to 7 group than roles to play, you can create multiple casts for the same playlet, so that each child has a chance to play one of the roles. For those aged 8 to 12, you may be willing to develop and rehearse more than one playlet, especially if you have the support and participation of several other parents who can donate time and resources to supervise extra practices, make sets and props, and help out with costumes (if any are needed).

- You want to make the class's first performance a successful acting exercise for each participating child, not merely a public spectacle to please the audience.

Other Ideas for the Director

- If you have an enthusiastic and creative class of students in the age 8 to 12 group, you may wish to have some of them suggest their own stories for dramatization. It may be something they write themselves or a favorite idea they borrow from existing written material. This is not something you want to try with the little children, however, since they do better making a play out of something they are already familiar with.

- A child, whose idea you accept as the seed for a playlet, will be your proudest actor. Even so, make sure that the idea can be adapted into an interesting storyline with characters the children can easily take to. The story idea must also be developed to clearly show the proper elements of structure. There is no better way for young actors to become good writers and discriminating judges of good dramatic form than to start with an original idea and fashion it into a playable stage piece.

- If the class is made up of more girls than boys, you may wish to adapt a story like Billy's Birthday Gift with a girl in the title role—that is, a Jenny or an Olivia instead of a Billy. If you have no boys at all in the class, Uncle Frank can become Aunt Nancy (or whatever name you prefer).

- The priority for this preliminary class presentation is that every child plays a role. Each child should equally contribute to the successful achievement of the group's learning and performance goals.

Short Play (ages 11 to 13 and teens)

Director's Notes: You may read aloud to the class the instructional information below, or simply summarize the key points before they start on their project of making a short play.

The playlet is the simplest and briefest kind of creative play-acting, which is why it is a perfect choice for the younger children. For the older students, the improvisations can be developed into short plays lasting anywhere from five to fifteen minutes, with emphasis on building a more sophisticated storyline with character conflict.

All the vocal and improvisational exercises in the previous units have been geared towards building a character in a dramatic setting and making that character appear real and convincing to an audience. This is always the ultimate goal of performance and the focus of the short play exercise. The actor's importance in a short play is not how many lines of dialogue he speaks or how long he remains in front of the audience, but how believable he is in his role during the moments he *is* onstage.

The optional scenarios listed in Unit Study 6 as well as the advanced improvisations suggested in Unit Study 7 provide excellent short play-making material. Although the same procedures for the building and casting of the short play are the same as those suggested for the playlet, the short play will require not just several miniature units making up one scene, but multiple units making up multiple longer scenes. A short play also needs a thoroughly structured storyline, more complex characterizations, and increased action with conflict to heighten the overall dramatic value of the piece.

Some guidelines for preparing the short play are listed below:

- Assign a student the responsibility of jotting down workable bits of dialogue that the actors come up with during the improvisations of the scene units. Don't rely on your memory or the memories of your students, especially with a whole week to separate class periods.

- Have another student take notes from the group's discussions that follow each improvisation. This will provide the resource material for developing the script.

- Assign a third student (or ask for a volunteer) to act as the script writer. This person will write down the final dialogue decided on as the storyline evolves. The final play will be typed from this working manuscript.

- The director should always collect the manuscript at the end of each class session. Depending on the size of the group, not all the students may get the chance to portray the role of their choice or try out every acting unit in improvisation, but all should take an active part in deciding the final format of the play, including storyline, characterizations, and dialogue.

Sample Short Play: As an example, here are some ways you could expand upon the original storyline in Exercise 7-9, Older Teens and Adults #4, concerning the girl with the wet hair who greets the new neighbor boy.

Scene One Setting: Kitchen by back door

- You are reading a magazine or finishing up some schoolwork. On her way out to do some chores, your mom tells you that she invited the new teenage boy up the street to drop by after school and introduce himself to you. What is your first reaction? Indifference? Curiosity? Panic? Have you seen this boy before? If so, what did you think of him? Is he someone you would like to meet or avoid? If he was someone you thought was really cool, you may react with words like: "Oh, mom, how could you invite him without warning me? I'm not dressed properly and I don't have any makeup on—and, worst of all, my hair's dirty!" Your mother could casually mention that she didn't think of that at the time and just wanted to be friendly. She tells you that he'll be by in five or ten minutes. She leaves before you have a chance to complain any further. You look at your watch and mentally figure out the options you have available to make yourself look presentable.

Scene Two Setting: Same setting

- You are convinced that you won't have time to both change into another outfit *and* make your hair look decent. You look down at your t-shirt and jeans. You definitely have to put something over that grape-juice stained t-shirt. You look at the dry cleaning bag hanging over the kitchen chair. Your mom picked it up on your way back from school. It has your new purple silk sweater in it. You tear off the plastic bag and put the sweater over your t-shirt. You jump up and down trying to see how you look in the kitchen window. Yes, the sweater does the trick. Now for the hair. Using the window glass again as a mirror, you try different hair arrangements, but you aren't happy with any of them. Your hair is just too lank and greasy.

- Frustrated, and checking your watch again, you decide that you simply have to wash your hair. Impulsively, you put your head under the kitchen tap, then reach for the shampoo bottle. Suddenly you realize that this is not your bathroom sink, and there is no shampoo bottle nearby. You spy the bottle of dishwashing detergent and figure that it's better than nothing. You madly start scrubbing your scalp (all pantomime). When you rinse, however, the suds won't come off so easily.

- The next series of actions can follow the developments described in Exercise 7-9 #4: the conflict of not being able to find a towel, frantically searching all over the floor as you try to wipe the detergent out of your eyes, panicking when you hear the knock at the door, then making your way from the kitchen with eyes squinting from the stinging suds and arms outstretched, feeling your way like a blind man, as you make your exit from the stage.

Scene Three Setting: Foyer by front door

- You enter the stage in the same way you exited. Groping for the door, you open it but can't see a thing in front of you. After a moment of obvious silence, the new boy says a cheerful hello. You invite him in and stretch out your hand but miss him by at least a foot. Squinting involuntarily, you explain—as though it's the most common thing in the world—that you have dish detergent in your eyes and can't quite see him. Bemused, he immediately pulls out a large clean handkerchief and places it in your hand to wipe your eyes with. You gratefully use it to clear your eyes of the stinging suds. When you look up, blinking furiously, you can't believe how wonderfully good-looking he is.

- As you stare at him, you notice that he is grinning as he scans your pants (or skirt). You look down and see that your jeans are stained with unseemly blots of dye—the same bright purple color of your silk blouse. As you look, large drops of water from your dripping hair are still falling on the blouse creating continuous color bleeds. You are mortified and beg to be excused. But, with a true gentlemanly grace, he laughs cheerfully and says that he's glad you're just a normal girl. Then he tells you that he saw you earlier at school and thought you were kind of standoffish, so he was reluctant to come by and meet you. He says he'll check back later after you've gotten yourself together, and maybe you'll feel like going out for some pizza or perhaps catching a movie. He leaves with a big, good-natured smile on his face before you can even say goodbye to him. You stand at the door, looking ridiculous and staring absentmindedly at him as you wave a goodbye.

Director's Notes: This is just one possible scenario. The students will spontaneously think of many other ways to develop the storyline and create some fun dialogue. This kind of co-ed scene is a good way to introduce the dynamics of the teenage boys and girls working together as actors. It acknowledges the awareness of this sensitive period in their lives, but resolves it in a respectful and lighthearted way. It also prepares them for the comedy courtship scenes that are offered as part of the recital program for the next quarter.

Fun Alternatives

If the students really enjoy putting their play together and developing their characters, you might give them the option of adapting their performance piece to an historical period, which is always a fun thing to do. The playlet, *Billy's Birthday Gift*, could take place in 1900 New England or in the Old West, or in any period that sparks the imagination and interest of the children.

If a different historical time and place is chosen, the students would have to make appropriate adjustments in the dialogue and change the references to objects, such as cars, that did not exist in an earlier period. They might also like to try on a Texan accent if they choose an Old West setting, or a British Standard dialect if they choose a setting in Victorian England. All dialogue, deportment, and personal address must suit the times. As a creative twist, the students could perform one version of the play or playlet in the modern day, and another version (with a different cast) in an earlier period. The last two sample scripts included at the end of Unit Study 10 demonstrate how the same subject matter, characters, and dialogue can be adapted to different historical periods.

Similarly, if the teenage play were to take place at the end of the nineteenth century or the beginning of the twentieth century, the new neighbor would call on the young lady in his best striped suit and boater hat, and the young lady might try more drastic measures to avoid opening the door to let him in, considering the strict rules of courtship that existed between young men and women those days. Students could present both versions of their play—the contemporary and the historical— and experience firsthand in a fun and picturesque way how very differently teenagers courted each other in an earlier and more formal time.

Helpful Hints

For these playlet and short play presentations, it's best to downplay sets, costumes, and props and concentrate on the acting experience. When performing the scenes in modern times, there should not be any need for costumes, since the actors can wear everyday clothing. If the students choose to play their scenes in a different time, signature costume pieces are all that is required—for example, a newsboy hat for a boy in the 1900s, a cowboy hat for a Western boy, or a bonnet for a prairie girl. Some students may wish to wear full costumes, which is fine.

If you do not have an actual stage platform or proscenium theater, shutters or room dividers work well as an artificial back wall or backdrop to hide the backstage area from the playing area and from the audience. The actors can also make their entrances and exits from UR and UL of these shutters. To add an even more formal effect, you may wish to drape some velvet curtains over the shutters. Make sure the actors have, as a minimum, a playing area of twelve feet in depth and fifteen feet in width.

Formal Recital (Second Quarter)

Director's Notes: You may read aloud to the class the information below, or you can summarize the key points and prepare a summary of them as a handout.

Procedure

The recital is a very special event. It marks a formal presentation of real acting scenes. For most of the students, this will be their first theatrical role and the joyous opportunity to show off their acting skills to family and friends. If you have a lot of students participating, you may wish to stage two recitals—a matinee for the younger children and an evening show for the teens and adults. Try and use adults to play adult roles in scenes from classical plays or novels such as *Jane Eyre, Huckleberry Finn* or *The Secret Garden.* If your student body is small, mount only one recital. A recital should be no longer than one and a half hours with a ten-minute intermission.

Performance pieces should be introduced no earlier than six weeks before the scheduled recital. Though a professional actor may spend months working on a particular role, and enjoy every minute of it, beginner students tend to get very bored if they are given too much time to rehearse and they have to share that rehearsal time with twenty or thirty other children waiting to practice their roles.

If you are using selections from our *Golden Treasury of Acting Scenes*, each student should be assigned one dramatized Aesop fable and one scene. Some of the fables for the children aged 3 to 7 (for example, *The Wolf and the Lamb* and *The Fox and Mistress Crow*) require two or more children playing different characters in the same fable. Most fables, however, are designed to be performed by one actor. When the class is preparing for the recital, begin by taking as much time as you need to read each fable selection out loud. If they choose, the students can take turns reading them. After all the fables have been presented, ask the children to make their individual choices for which fable they want to perform. Once you have given each student a copy of their fable, the students do the following:

- Neatly circle the musical consonants *(m's, n's, and ng's)*, the plosives *(t's, d's, and p's)*, and the fricatives *(f's and v's)*. The circles will remind the students to consciously make these (usually weak) consonants clear and strong. The *n's* and *m's* in the middle of words should also be circled, as in the word *and*.

- Draw a squiggly line under all the verbs. Every verb is a description of action in the fable and should have an added emphasis of expression by the speaker.

- Place a slanted bar after every comma and three slanted bars after every period. A slanted bar represents a one-second sense pause. This sense pause does not necessarily mean a breath pause. A breath pause always occurs after periods, indicated by the three slanted bars.

Director's Notes: These mechanical guidelines are meant to aid personal expressiveness by reminding the student what he learned about diction, resonance, and phrasing, etc. Until these technical components become second nature, and the interpretive sense more highly developed, the guidelines should be reinforced, especially for the younger children.

Casting of Scenes

Your selection of recital scenes should be introduced only after all the fables have been allocated, and copies handed out. By this time, you will have a good idea of the personality and skill level of each student, and can make your casting choices for the scenes without requiring the children to audition. The students do not choose their own scenes; the director casts them. Before the session in which you will give role assignments, make sure that you have a list of the roles and the names of the children assigned to play them. It is always possible that after hearing another child read a part, you may change your mind, but generally this will prove the exception to the rule. Do not wait until the day of class to cast. Rarely are actors (even in professional theater) cast at an audition. A good director knows well ahead of time which actors he would like to play the major roles in the drama he is to direct.

Talk about the scenes, have some of the children read them to the class, and let the group know that you will cast the roles, and that you have already made some preliminary choices. If you use scenes from our *Golden Treasury* collection, expect that half the girls will want to play the popular heroines, Sara Crewe and Heidi. Explain that every role is important in a scene and that sometimes it is the smaller or less familiar role that outshines the titled role.

The casting process for scenes (and later plays) is not based on democratic principles but on your best judgment as to who can carry the scenes (or play) best. Casting decisions take into account age-appropriateness and the vocal skills demonstrated by each student during the quarter. Remind the children that the actor is the servant of the role and not vice versa. The needs of the role must come first. Do not assign a difficult role to a child who has consistently proven timid. Such a role might prove overwhelming and undo the progress already made. Roles that require a force of imagination and intensity, such as Jane Eyre and Helen Burns in the scene at Lowood Institution from *Jane Eyre*, should be given to children who can bring to those roles a natural altruism and dramatic energy.

Unlike the playlets and short plays, do not double cast fables or recital scenes. A recital is a showcase for each child. Each child should, therefore, have his own special role—a role that is his alone. He is the star in that role and that star can only shine its brightest when it stands alone. Remind the children that every role in every scene is equal in importance because every role is necessary for the success of the scene, and each and every scene is a unique part of the tapestry of the whole recital.

Ten-Step Script Preparation

1. Make sure each student has his own personal copy of the scene that is assigned to him. Send a note home to parents advising them to Xerox the material. At least two or three students always manage to leave their scripts in the classroom, so a home copy is good insurance against all kinds of accidents. Make sure you have at least one extra copy of each script with you when rehearsing, just in case a student leaves his folder at a friend's house or in the car (a common occurrence). Don't ever give out your director's (marked up) copy or you may never see it again.

2. Before a scene reading, explain the storyline of the play or novel from which the scene is taken. Summarize the context of the scene—that is, where it fits into the play or novel. If the scene takes place in a different historical period, give the students a brief idea of life and manners in that era, especially as it relates to the way the character thinks, feels, stands, sits, or addresses the opposite sex. Define the expectations of a gentleman or a lady in that era. You may also wish to assign this kind of background research as homework. Expect, however, that not all the students will do the preparation required. You, as the director, will need to know this information yourself.

3. The actors should take turns doing a line reading of their scenes. For this first reading, have them sit on chairs in the playing area. There should be no impromptu movement or blocking. You want the students to become familiar with the dialogue and their individual characters. It is not a time to direct. After the read-through of each scene, ask the actors if they have any questions. Is there anything about the scene or the characters that they do not understand?

4. After a scene has been read and discussed, ask the players involved to go to another part of the rehearsal room (or a different room in the building) and (a) work out the goal and obstacle of each character in their scene; (b) assign two adjectives that best describe each character; (c) do several readings of the script with each other.

5. Encourage the children to read through their handout *Golden Rules of Character Study* and follow it as a road map to study their new roles. They can do a lot of their own preparation at home. Remind them to start memorizing their lines. The quicker the actor gets off his script, the quicker he will "find" his character and feel comfortable with his dialogue.

6. By the second week of script rehearsal, start blocking the scenes. Keep the actors' movements to a minimum and block most of your action in the center and downstage areas of the stage. The actor should mark down on his copy of the script all blocking directions he is given, including entrances and exits, even those that do not apply to him directly.

7. Discourage unnecessary gestures or personal habits that some children have, such as rocking back and forth on their feet, shifting weight from one foot to another, playing with their hair, or saying "Um" when they forget a line of dialogue. Beginner actors are very self conscious on the stage, so give them as little to do as possible, and remind them that they are speaking to the other character in the scene and not to you.

8. Wait until the third week of rehearsal before you give the students personal notes about vocal delivery and character interpretation. The children need

some time to work into their roles and make them their own. Give line readings (saying the line as you think it should be said to best express the meaning and mood of the character) when you observe a pattern of flatness in an actor's delivery or when he shows little imaginative sense. Work off what the student gives you before imposing how you think the character should say his or her lines. You don't want the children to parrot the way you, the director, would act out the scenes. These are not elocution exercises but discovery classes in character study and interpretation. As such, they require the student's own inspiration and imagination.

9. Remind the students that their goal is to create a theatrical presence. This means that everything they do and say onstage must be larger than life. They have to heighten their normal level of expressiveness and vocal projection, without appearing artificial. We do not "underplay" an emotion on the stage. That is something a director may request of an actor when he is performing in front of a film camera.

10. Be sure the class completes breathing and voice exercises before every rehearsal to keep both relaxation and vocal performance at an optimal level.

The Order of the Recital

If you make up a recital program using selections from our *Golden Treasury* set, it's best to alternate a fable with a scene in the order of presentation. Ideally, as in the sample "Welcome" piece included in the collection, you should have two of your youngest (and brightest) littlest players open the recital. Showcase the little ones as much as possible. Their spontaneity and natural enthusiasm are endearing, and never fail to set a joyous mood for the event.

If you are mounting only one recital, place the teenage scenes last in your program. The first half should contain most of the younger children's scenes. The second half can be a mix of the teen and adult pieces. This way, the little ones can join their families after intermission and watch the older students perform. Having the little children complete their scenes in the first half also allows the parents who cannot stay for the full length of the recital (or whose smaller children are getting restless) to leave gracefully after intermission. Only those students who have completed all their scenes should sit in the audience. The rest of the cast should remain backstage, unseen by the audience. This is part of the discipline of maintaining the magic of theater. The students who are sitting in the audience will need to return backstage after the last scene is completed to get in place for curtain call. At no time should any student (or audience member, for that matter) cross the stage area to get backstage.

Sets and Props

This is a formal recital. If you do not have a real theater stage, set up the playing area as you did for your first quarter presentation with a backdrop curtain, shutters or room dividers separating the stage area from the backstage and dressing room areas. Without wings or curtain legs, the room dividers provide a facsimile back wall as well as upstage entrance and exit positions. For the convenience of the actors, create dressing room space behind (or to the left and right of) the stage so that the cast have a closed off backstage area to enter from and to make an exit into.

For set pieces, I advise using lightweight chairs, fold-up tables, and individual props that can be removed quickly between scenes and without a lot of fuss. If you stage a recital where all the scenes take place at the same time in history, as in our Victorian Christmas collection, *Christmases of Long Ago,* it is best to create a permanent set that provides a picturesque background suitable for all the individual scenes making up the program. All you need to add to a permanent set are particular hand props that the actor uses for his scene and which he can carry on and offstage himself.

Stage Management

The stage manager is the person who runs the production, and is in charge of both cast and technical crew. He or she is responsible for everything backstage—the timely and ordered entrances and exits of the actors, the lighting, costumes, sets, props, and all other technical aspects affecting the performance onstage. If anything goes wrong with the production, the stage manager is the one who makes the emergency decisions. It will make things a lot easier if you can get one of your adult students (or a parent) to be stage manager and one or two of the responsible teens to be assistant stage managers. An adult has the presence of mind and authority to keep order backstage.

When staging a children's theater recital or play, the director may choose to help the stage manager backstage. As productions become better managed, the stage manager can take over and the director can position himself in the back of the house where he can gain the best perspective on the performance, write notes to give to the actors later, and communicate with the stage manager by means of a walkie-talkie or intercom headphones that operate on short-range radio frequencies. A formal recital is a good opportunity to get acquainted with the mechanics and flow of an intercom system before the full technical webbing of a play production is upon you.

Ideally, the stage manager should attend all rehearsals so that he can make up his own prompt book (in this case, a copy of each of the scenes organized in a binder in their order of presentation). The prompt book contains all cues and their precise timing, including notations for entrances and exits, blocking, any set pieces needed to be moved on or off the stage between scenes, and lighting and sound cues. One of the most important responsibilities of the stage manager in professional theater is to keep the prompt book up to date. During rehearsals, the director will cut lines and add in new ones. He will experiment with blocking directions and write character notes for different actors. The prompt book should contain a record of all of these notations. If your assigned stage manager cannot attend every rehearsal, make sure that the prompt book is kept current with any changes.

Although prompters (sometimes called prompts) are never used in professional theater during an actual performance, as the actors are expected to improvise if needed, have a prompter on hand if your players are mostly children. Some children can be devastated if they forget a line and have no outside prompt to help them get through. Make sure the prompter is familiar with any long pauses by the actors so that he does not mistake a deliberate pause for a memory loss. An actor should call out "Line" if he forgets what dialogue comes next, though children rarely remember to do so.

If you have a lighting system which enables you to darken the stage between scenes, you can mark the stage with either colored tape or iridescent tape to guide the stagehands in the darkness to place each new furniture set piece in the correct place and at the correct angle.

When the youngest children are performing their scenes, have the teens dress in black and serve as assistant stage managers and stagehands. Somewhat like understudies, they should be willing to know all the duties and responsibilities of the stage manager. For a recital, the assistants may divide up their duties between keeping the little children quiet and in their proper places backstage (which means having lots of games), operating any lighting and sound systems, helping to dress the actors and keep the costumes in order, organizing the props backstage, being responsible for getting the actors lined up for their entrance cues, or simply running last-minute errands to secure tape or needle and thread, etc. Assistant stage managers should have initiative, pay attention to details, and respond quickly and cheerfully to the needs of the production. What they do during a recital will be good training for the technical management of a full play production.

The principal duty of the stagehands is to strike (or remove from the stage) the scenery, set pieces, and small props between scenes and acts. When you stage a production in a commercial theater, one of the stagehands will have to act as the fly operator who operates the machinery that raises the backdrops. Stagehands are also responsible for clearing a place backstage to store, organize, and conveniently access stage scenery, furniture, and props. A recital will require very little change in set furniture, especially if you have one permanent set. Even the little that is performed by the stagehands in a recital, however, is good practice for the full play ahead. The most important function of stagehands is to facilitate the quickest possible changing of stage sets and properties. Stagehands should work in tandem, with one crew removing the old set while the second crew is replacing it with the new.

Final Rehearsal Schedule

When dealing with amateur theater, the final rehearsal schedule refers to the two weeks prior to the recital. The second to last week should be devoted to at least two complete run-throughs of the recital program. During a run-through, the recital scenes should be rehearsed in the order they will be performed. At this rehearsal, the stage manager confirms with the director the final line cuts, blocking, entrance and exit positions, and any technical (mainly lighting or sound) cues that need to be integrated. This is also the time for the stage manager to assign duties to the stage assistants and stagehands. Because scenes are rehearsed out of performance order during regular class time, it is often not until the run-throughs that a conflict, such as insufficient time for an actor to make a costume change, is discovered.

Actors need to have all lines memorized by the run-through or the director and stage manager cannot get a proper idea of the overall timing of the scenes and the length of the recital. The purpose of a run-through rehearsal is to get a handle on the flow of the recital and make the necessary adjustments before the dress rehearsal.

Performance Week

The final week, known as performance week, should be organized to allow for two concurrent days of rehearsals—a technical rehearsal and a dress rehearsal. Professional theaters may have several tech rehearsals, but there are time and labor restrictions with community theaters, children's theaters, school and homeschool enrichment programs, since the schedules of many families and volunteer workers have to be coordinated when organizing additional rehearsal time.

Technical rehearsal takes place during performance week and is supervised by the stage manager. The purpose of the tech rehearsal is to ensure that (1) all technical cues are set and properly sequenced and notated in the prompt book; (2) that these cues are integrated smoothly into the performance; and 3) that all the assistant stage managers and stagehands know exactly what duties they have to perform. If there are any problems with costume or set changes, lighting or sound cues, this is the time to fix them. By the tech rehearsal, the stage manager should have assigned a house manager (or main greeter) who will let him know, prior to the program beginning, if the audience are seated, or if a short delay is required.

The needs of the crew—the stage manager, stage assistants, and stagehands—are foremost during a technical rehearsal, even if the actors are inconvenienced. Expect many stops and starts as adjustments are made by the costume assistants, broken light bulbs are changed, and the lighting plot is finalized as the director decides the exact placement of cast and furniture to secure the most advantageous audience perspective. The stage assistants may double as lighting, sound, and curtain technicians if the production is not held in a real theater, which normally has its own house crew consisting of a stage carpenter, a property man, and an electrician as well as possible grips (or stagehands) who handle the theater's scenery and properties.

Be advised that when you rent a real theater house, you will have to contract their house crew. The technical rehearsal is geared toward giving the stage (and house) crew the "rehearsal" they need to cover all their bases and get their timing down for the "real" thing. At the end of the technical rehearsal, the stage manager should have a meeting with the crew and give them notes. Additionally, he should make sure that the actors know where their dressing rooms are, where their costumes will be hanging, and who will be doing their hair and makeup for the dress rehearsal.

Dress rehearsal essentially functions as a practice opening night performance. The director, stage manager, and technical crew execute the staging of the show exactly as it will be on opening night. They can observe the production for the first time as a complete unit from beginning to end and spot any last-minute flaws. The purpose of a dress rehearsal is to allow a seamless, uninterrupted performance; however, its very nature as a "rehearsal" may necessitate stops to refine some aspect of the staging. Even during the final dress rehearsal of an opera at the Metropolitan Opera House, the conductor or stage director will often have the singers re-do a song or begin a musical unit again to correct some staging problem.

Because the final dress rehearsal functions as a real performance (even with stoppages), many professional companies, such as the Metropolitan Opera, invite full paying audiences to attend. A "dress," as it is often called, is an ideal show for school groups, senior citizens, special needs children, foster home organizations, the disabled, etc., to watch and enjoy. You may wish to ask family and friends who cannot make the public performance to come. It's also the perfect show to get lots of photographs taken of the cast. The audience don't appreciate flashes going off on opening night.

The successful running of the dress rehearsal rests on the stage manager's shoulders. The aid of competent assistants and reliable stagehands will greatly ease his burden. In professional productions, there may be more than one dress, depending on how big the production is. In amateur companies, which rely largely on volunteer help, one dress rehearsal is generally all that can be arranged.

Opening night normally takes place the day after dress rehearsal or after a preview performance.

Opening Night

Opening night (even if it takes place in the middle of the day) is always an exciting event. If the backstage duties have been organized during the technical and dress rehearsals, the stage will already be set for the actors to play their parts. When the technical crew are doing everything right, the actors have no excuse for not performing their best, and moving the play at its optimal tempo. Competent help backstage enables a smooth running show, and a smooth running show is one that keeps waits between acts and scenes to a minimum, which translates into a contented audience.

Make sure you have the programs set out at the foyer entrance or front door to your theater auditorium. Ask siblings of students to act as ushers to hand out programs or to direct people to their seats. Make sure they are nicely dressed. Do not use any of your actors as greeters. None of the actors should be exposed to the audience before they are seen onstage in character.

In professional theater, the director plays no role in the performances of the show that follow opening night. The stage manager takes on the entire production responsibilities. This is not the case in children's theater, amateur community theater, or school presentations, where the director remains in charge of all artistic and technical aspects of the show from opening night until the final performance.

Below is a list of activities to do and the times at which they are to be done on opening night and during all subsequent performances:

- If the performance begins at 8:00 pm, all actors should be in their dressing rooms one hour prior. Members of the cast who need their hair and makeup done should arrive at the theater even earlier. Actors Equity rule requires that all actors be checked in a half hour before curtain, no matter how late their entrance is in the play. When dealing with children in a recital program or amateur production, you would be wise to extend that preparation time.

- The stage assistants and stagehands should make sure the cue sheets are posted, lights work, the sound system (or CD player) is plugged in, small props are accounted for, set pieces are organized and placed conveniently, and the stage has been swept and preset properly for the first scene. No lights should be on at this time except the work lights and, of course, the house lights. The stage manager or his assistants should enforce the rule that no actors be on the stage, even if there is a curtain to hide them. The stage may be the home of the actor, but only when he is in character before an audience. At all other times, the stage is home to the stage management crew.

- At 7:30, the assistant stage manager should report to the dressing room and call "Half hour to curtain." At 7:45, he calls "Fifteen minutes to curtain." Then he should do a final check on the set and props onstage, making sure that the furniture pieces are placed on the proper tape marks and that the small props are accounted for and situated correctly. At 7:55, he visits the dressing rooms again and calls out the first three scenes (if it is a recital) or "Act 1" if it is a play. At that call, all the actors in the first three scenes or Act 1 should go to the wings and be checked in by the stage manager or his assistant. It is important that the stage manager knows that they are there. Any actors who are preset on the stage when the curtain opens, take their places at this time. The assistant will then line up the actors at their appropriate entrance positions, and the prop master will personally check if any hand props need to be assigned.

- The stage manager, via headsets, signals the lobby (house manager) and the director that the performance is ready to begin. In a professional theater, the house manager will give the final okay to begin based on how many people are still waiting to be seated. In a children's theater, the director may choose to make that decision. The stage manager then gives the cue to the lighting assistant to turn on the stage lights. The stage manager now awaits word from the director (or house manager) as to when to actually begin. The maximum delay is usually ten minutes after the scheduled time. An audience won't have any patience after that. When the final word is given, the stage manager calls "Places," though the actors should already be in their places.

- The stage manager signals the lighting technician, who lowers the house lights. At this cue, there will be a recorded message played or the house manager will announce (directly in front of the closed curtain) that all cell phones are to be turned off. It is up to the director if taking pictures is permitted. (Flashes and clicking sounds can be distracting to actors. You can always invite parents to bring their cameras to the dress rehearsal.) After the announcement, the production is ready to begin. The stage manager starts to "call" the show, beginning with a signal to raise or open the curtain, unless there is a pre-curtain music or sound cue that takes precedence, such as an overture.

- The recital or play begins. The stage manager marks down the actual curtain time, and later when the curtain falls for intermission, rises again, and so forth until the final curtain. If a play is performed, he will also record the beginning and ending time of each act. This will give him the actual playing time of each act and provide a guideline to the actors as to whether the show is "slow" or is moving well. He may also make notes regarding late entrances by actors, missed technical cues, etc.

- As each recital scene is completed, the assistant stage manager takes the actors back to the dressing room and calls the next group of actors to the stage. This action is not necessary during a play as all the actors who appear in each act are called to assemble at the wings before the act begins. The exception to this would be if a crowd of little children were in one particular scene late in the act. To avoid the exuberant disturbance that little children always bring to the wings, it is smart to keep them in the dressing rooms or in a play area as long as possible. Most directors of children's theaters recruit extra adult help to keep things quiet backstage.

- The assistant stage manager makes sure that the actors are in their correct places to make their entrances. When working with little children, it is necessary to stand with them and tell them when to go on. If a child is a main character in a play and has multiple lines in multiple scenes, he will need to be reminded what scene is coming up and, in some cases, what his lines are.

- The props are organized on two property (prop) tables, set up on either side of the wings. They can be situated either downstage or upstage depending upon where most of the entrances and exits of the actors take place. One table holds the props that are to be placed stage right and the other table holds the props that are to be placed stage left. The hand props to be carried onstage by the actors are also placed on the side from which the actor makes his entrance. The prop master should have a cue list of what props go with what actor in what scene. It is his responsibility, as much as the actor's, to make sure the actor goes onstage with his proper prop. It is also his responsibility to take the prop from the actor once that actor exits the stage.

- The stage manager pays close attention to timing the lighting fade-outs at the end of scenes as well as the curtain closures at the end of acts. A late curtain or light cue can hold an actor in an awkward position, reducing the dramatic value of the scene. Once the curtain cue to end the act or the first half of the recital is given, the stage manager signals the lighting technician to fade out all stage lights and bring up the house lights for intermission. If necessary, have the house manager announce intermission and the time allotted, or simply use a recording.

- When the curtain is lowered to indicate the end of the act or first half of the recital program, the stage manager has the stagehands strike the set (if a new one is needed) and prepare the stage for the first scene after intermission. If he needs to supervise the strike, the stage manager goes to the down center of the stage just behind the curtain. All actors should leave the stage. If there is no curtain, the stage assistants still strike the stage and set up (preferably in the dark).

- During intermission, the stage manager or his assistants should visit backstage and make sure that all costumes are picked up and that the set pieces and stage properties that are not to be used again are safely stored away. If some of the children are keeping their costumes on right through to the curtain call, make sure they do not eat or drink anything that could stain the costumes.

- Intermission should last no longer than ten minutes. Not even Broadway theater extends its intermission beyond this limit, despite the long bathroom queues! This is a necessary discipline of theater. Audiences are not the first consideration—the play is.

- Two minutes before intermission ends, the stage manager should visit the dressing room and call "Places for Act 2," or name the first three scenes to be performed, as he did before the first half of the performance. Again, the stage manager signals the lighting technician and the house manager (or director). He may also have the house manager announce in the lobby that the show is to recommence.

- The stage manager checks that the stage is clear of crew and set properly, and that the technicians and actors are ready to go. If certain actors are to be preset, this is the time they should get into position. He then signals the lighting technician to bring up the stage lights and lower the house lights. When he gets the go ahead from the house manager, he signals for the curtain to open and records the start time. The second half or second act begins.

- The same steps as above are followed for the transition to the final curtain in a recital program or for the transition from the second act to the third act in a play (longer if it is a five-act Shakespearean play).

- At the end of the performance, the cast should immediately line up in the wings for their curtain call. A curtain call should never be left to chance, but choreographed with as much artistic care as any other part of the play. Learning to bow in front of the audience can be an art in itself.

Curtain Call

The curtain call takes place at the end of the performance, when the actors come to the front of the stage and take their individual and group bows. The bow is the traditional gesture that graciously acknowledges the audience's approval for "the show" and for each actor's contribution to its success.

The curtain call is the victory lap for actors. This is the moment they have worked so hard for—the reward of jubilant applause and heartfelt appreciation from an audience who loves and cherishes each "starry" performance. There is no more priceless gift for the actor, whether she be a 3 year old reciting a poem for the first time in front of a public audience, or a veteran of many year's hard-won triumphs. Both have achieved the dream of all who step behind the footlights—the glory of acting magic!

We climb to the stars by the long ladder of an infinite patience.
The mountaintop of the Ideal is never shaken.

—Francis Bacon

Epilogue

*Never be afraid, Chips, that you can't do anything you've made up your
mind to. As long as you believe in yourself you can go as far as your dream.*

—Katherine Chipping to Mr. Chips, *Goodbye Mr. Chips*

Acting is among the most evocative of the arts. It has an unequaled power to conjure up ideas and images and make them soar in the imagination. The art of acting vests the actor with the master alchemist's key to create life out of illusion, and not just any life. The life he creates onstage is a magic presence that he can use to imbue everything he thinks and does with a higher beauty and a higher love.

The actor's indispensable virtue is faith. He must believe in himself, in his art, and in the nobility of life. His faith must also be a belief in beauty and truth—not just for their rightful place in dramatic art, but for their own sake, so that he can use them and inspire others to use them as guides for personal growth and erudition.

When an actor miscomprehends the high purpose of theater, he cheats himself of its true magic. Sarah Bernhardt wrote, "If the sacred fire burns in you, you will succeed." Bernhardt spoke a remarkable truth. The actor who discovers the divine fire within himself can illumine the hearts of millions with the inspirations and aspirations of the great poets and dramatists of all time. Only when the artist becomes a transparency for the sacred fire, which is the spiritual essence of life, can acting magic be achieved. If the actor, on the other hand, squanders this inner fire in pursuit of the intoxicating pleasures that surround his career, then he surely tumbles from his high position of what Bernhardt described as "apostle and guardian of his art."

The arts should be an expression of the noblest and purest of human sentiments and a tribute to lives beautifully lived and fully given. Acting, the most intimate of the arts, is a discovery and a sharing of the God-given beauty we all can experience. The goal of the actor is to find that beauty within and, through his artistry, touch the beauty in the hearts of his audience, leaving his indelible forget-me-not in their lives.

In Sonnet 65, Shakespeare asked the eternal question: "How with this rage [the ravages of time and man's inhumanity] shall beauty hold a plea,/ Whose action is no stronger than a flower?" He answered the question with his own solution: "O, none, unless this miracle have might,/ That in black ink my love may still shine bright." In other words, art that is suffused by the sacred fire, art that glows with the beauty of the divine—the source of all true inspiration—will live forever. As the prophetic words of Leonardo da Vinci proclaim: "In life beauty perishes, but not in Art."

Unit
Study
Handouts

To Be a Star!

Please circle Yes or No to the following questions:

1. Is going to a theater and watching a play one of your favorite activities?　　Yes　No

2. Do you think you have a vivid imagination?　　Yes　No

3. Do you like to talk to people and make new friends?　　Yes　No

4. Do you laugh a lot?　　Yes　No

5. Do you imagine you are the characters in the books you read?　　Yes　No

6. Do you like to express what you are thinking and feeling?　　Yes　No

7. Do you like to entertain your family and your friends?　　Yes　No

8. Do you like to mimic or act out characters you see on television or in the movies?　　Yes　No

9. Do you like making up imaginary stories?　　Yes　No

10. Have you ever written your own play?　　Yes　No

11. When you make up a story or a play, do you cast yourself in the star parts?　　Yes　No

12. When you watch a play or a movie, do you find yourself caught up in the characters' emotions?　　Yes　No

13. Do you feel it when other people are happy or sad?　　Yes　No

14. Are you a good listener and observer?　　Yes　No

15. Would you like to play a tragic hero or heroine?　　Yes　No

Count up all the Yes's and all the No's and put the scores in the boxes. ☐ ☐

Handout: *To Be a Star!*

507

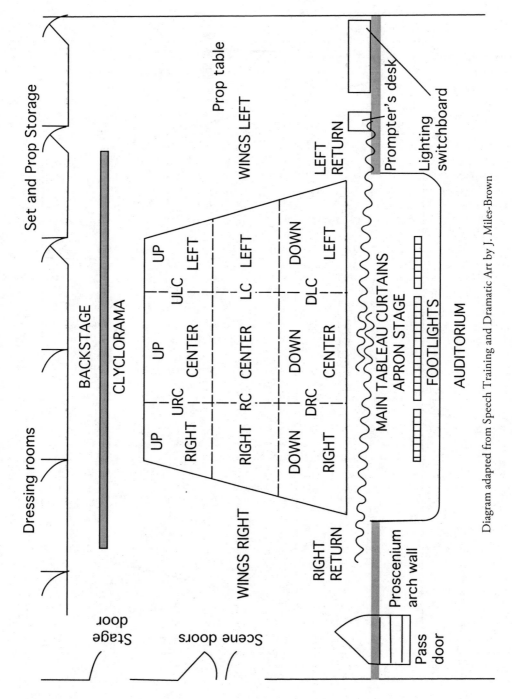

Diagram adapted from Speech Training and Dramatic Art by J. Miles-Brown

Handout #2-1A *Stage Geography*

508

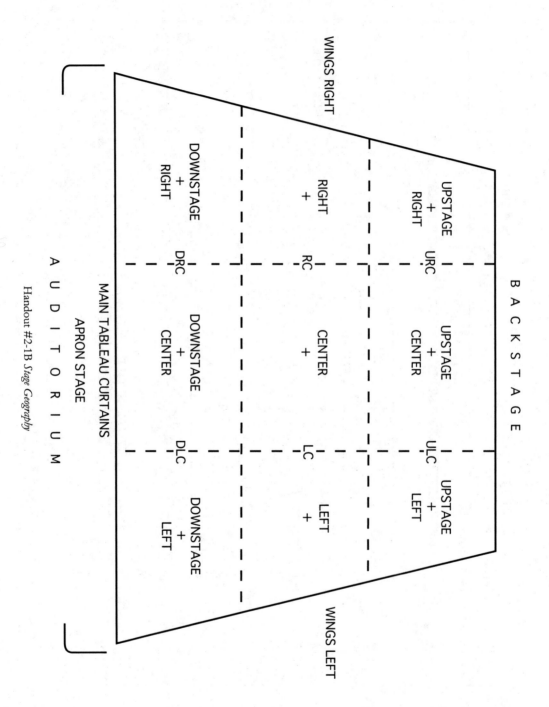

Handout #2-1B *Stage Geography*

DO NOT THINK...
DO NOT FEEL...
DO NOT ACT...
DO NOTHING
WITHOUT A

THEATRICAL CUE

Handout #3-1 Theatrical Cue

510

UPSTAGE

DO NOT

DO NOT

DO NOT

DO NOT

DO NOT

DO NOT

DO NOT

DO NOT

DO NOT

DO NOT

DO NOT

Handout #4-1 *Stay in Character*

512

Drama Is Conflict

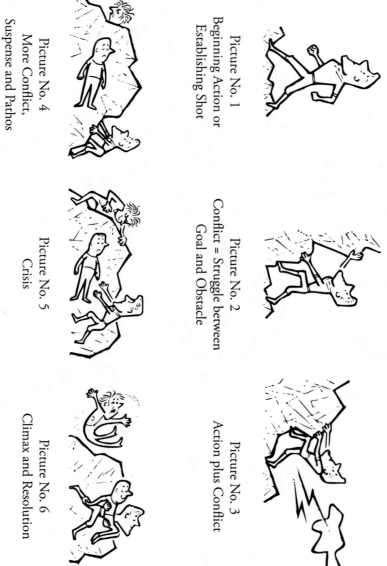

Picture No. 1
Beginning Action or
Establishing Shot

Picture No. 2
Conflict = Struggle between
Goal and Obstacle

Picture No. 3
Action plus Conflict

Picture No. 4
More Conflict,
Suspense and Pathos

Picture No. 5
Crisis

Picture No. 6
Climax and Resolution

Golden Rules of Character Study

1. *Read your selection piece carefully several times.* Read the play or novel from which your scene is taken to understand its dramatic context. Study the life and times of the author.

2. *Identify the genre or type of writing.* The literary genre determines the tone of acting, demeanor of character, and interpretation of the lines.

3. *Define the physical action of your character, as well as his outer and inner life.* What is your character's goal? Who or what opposes that goal? What is the conflict that your character must overcome? Is it an outer struggle (physical events) or a struggle from within? What does your character look like? How does he dress, walk, sit, and move around the stage? What are two adjectives you would use to describe your character?

4. *Improvise the scene* (make up your own lines) after becoming familiar with the storyline and your character.

5. *Learn your lines quickly.* Be off book no later than two weeks before opening night. The quickest way to memorize is to highlight all your lines on the script and have someone else read the dialogue leading up to and immediately after yours. Do not learn your lines in isolation.

6. *Mark your script with the proper stage directions* learned in Unit Study 2, including Cross in, Cross out (X in, X out); the playing areas (SL, DR) and body positions (Quarter Right, etc.).

7. *The character lives every moment it is onstage.* Get into character before you make your entrance. Your character's presence is revealed in *action, reaction, interaction,* and *non-action.* Never be a *blank spot* on the stage.

8. *The theatrical cue is the building block of character.* The first rule in the actor's notebook should read: do not think, do not feel, do not act, do nothing without a theatrical cue. There is always a reason behind everything you do onstage. Remember to follow the golden rules of magic.

9. *Character roles for beginner actors should be simple and age-appropriate.* Complex characters require a practiced stage technique.

10. *The essence of interpretation is imaginative understanding.* Imagining yourself in the role is half the work of creating the role.

Unit

Study

Voice

Handouts

Making Music

Hum Hum Hum Hum Hum Hum
Hum Tram Hum Tram Hum Tram

Bumble bees humming
Summer is coming

Merry merry month of May
The mavis sings her roundelay
Marsh marigolds embroider the meads
Where streams go murmuring 'mid the reeds

How the trumpets sound
How the hills rebound

Merry are the bells and merry would they ring
Merry was myself and merry could I sing
Merrily, merrily, shall I live now
Under the blossom that hangs on the bough

Evening red and morning grey
Send the traveler on his way
But evening gray and morning red
Will bring down rain upon his head

Nine brand new ninepins down in the line
One ball knocked eight pins down of the nine
Eight ninepins gone
That left only one
Ninth ball knocked ninth pin
Then there was none

Have we clean knees?
Yes, these knees are clean
No one has ever seen knees
Cleaner than these clean knees

Romeo stands alone watching the winter moonbeams
Have you seen at autumn time vines of wild bryony adorn the fair morning?
Autumn's banquet of mountain ash hung with wondrous September charm

Voice #1 *Making Music*

Making Consonants

Word	Consonant (how it sounds)
pet	p
bat	b
tin	t
deed	d
kind	k
good	g
men	m
new	n
king	ng
loot	l
will	w
when	hw
full	f
very	v
those	th
think	th
six	s
shirt	sh
pleasure	zh
zebra	z
around	r
his	h
chin	ch
joke	j
year	y

Meeting Point of Organs	Consonant Produced
Lip-lip	p b m w
Teeth-lip	f v
Teeth-tongue	s, z, th (thick) th (the)
Hard palate-tongue	t d j ch (choice) n l r sh zh
Soft palate-back of tongue	k g ng
Vocal cords	h (hit) hw (as in when)

Voice #2A *Making Consonants*

Making Consonants

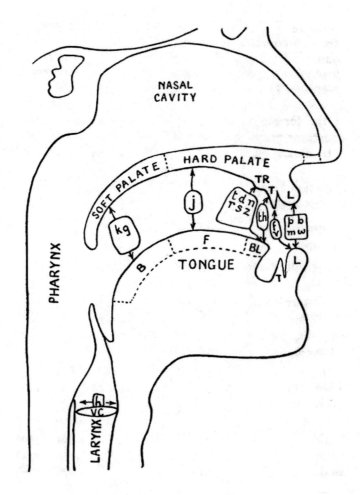

Sectional Diagram showing points of contact of the organs of speech to make consonant sounds. TR = teeth ridge, T = teeth, L = lip, B = back, F = front, BL = blade of tongue, VC = vocal cords. Diagram adapted from *Speech Training* by A. Musgrave Horner.

Voice #2B *Making Consonants*

Vowel Expansion

Preset each consonant. Visualize the contact point for each consonant and the particular organs of speech involved, whether the lips, teeth, tongue, hard palate, or soft palate. Execute each contact vigorously. A strongly articulated consonant is the springboard for a fully projected vowel.

Follow the vowel through its course. Imagine you are standing on one side of a mountain gorge and wish to send the sound across to the other side in a circular arc. Visualize the vowel tone traveling with the same trajectory as a rocket. Your goal is to expand the vowel tone to its fullest potential of carrying power. The mouth should be stretched and open, and the vowel tone placed in the back of the throat, where it receives its optimal resonance and can be projected without strain on the vocal cords.

Words are living sounds. Respect each letter in a word for each letter contributes to the full life of that word. Every word that is spoken is a unique chalice of meaning and emotion. Like a firecracker, the inner content of a word needs to be ignited before it can be released. Its proper release depends on the bold and firmly controlled contacts of the lips, teeth, tongue, hard palate, and soft palate.

Hah hah	Father said Hurrah! when the baby said Dah! Dah!
Hah lah	
Hah nah	The audience sighed Ahhh! when the magician said Te-Dah!
Hah tah	
Hah dah	Rah! Rah! Rah! cheered the All Stars from afar
Hah rah	

Hah hay	Each day they say they pay their way
Hah lay	
Hah nay	The grey clouds break; they sail away
Hah tay	
Hah day	The rain in vain stays mainly on the pane
Hah ray	

520

Hah hee	Each league we see the angry sea green with its fury
Hah lee	
Hah nee	The green team was seen to be lean and mean
Hah tee	
Hah dee	Please leave me the key for the house we need to see
Hah ree	
Hah haw	At dawn we saw beside the lawn the lame jackdaw
Hah law	
Hah naw	That old jackdaw has an awful Hee-Haw!
Hah taw	
Hah daw	The small ball falls from the wall to the water
Hah raw	
Hah hoh	Herds low, flowers grow, winds blow, stars glow
Hah loh	
Hah noh	Old folks go strolling, O so slowly
Hah toh	
Hah doh	A pageant slow, a nation's woe, the mourner's grow, a lord laid low
Hah roh	
Hah hoo	Youths who choose to do so prove the rule
Hah loo	
Hah noo	When wars loom and cannon boom
Hah too	
Hah doo	The soldier's doom is oft a tomb
Hah roo	

Speech Drills

He's a seer of visions and a dreamer of dreams
They came from far and near, from near and far
It's the North wind that blows from the country of snows
Our kites are flying high in the sky
His broad clear brow in sunlight glowed
On burnished hooves his war-horse trode
There is sweet music here that softer falls
Than petals from blown roses on the grass
Music that brings sweet sleep from blissful skies

Voice #3 Vowel Expansion (Page 2)

More Vowel Expansion

Marm	Mam	Meem	Mawm	Mohm	Moom
Narn	Nan	Neen	Nawn	Nohn	Noon
Larl	Lal	Leel	Lawl	Lohl	Lool

Roll on thou deep and dark blue ocean, roll

On and on the angry billows roll

Farewell, a long farewell to all my greatness

The league long rollers thundering on the reef

Ring out wild bells to the wild sky

The bells, bells, bells, bells, bells

When all the world is young lad
Laugh and the world laughs with you

Blow, blow thou winter wind
Freeze, freeze thou bitter sky

Tongue Twisters

Betty Botter bought some butter, but she said this butter's bitter. If I put it in my batter it will make my batter bitter, but a bit of better butter will make my bitter batter better. So she bought a bit of better butter than the bitter butter and made her bitter batter better. So it was better Betty Botter bought a bit of better butter and made her bitter batter better.

Billy Boggs blew back the blackboard.
Did Billy Boggs blow back the blackboard?
If Billy Boggs blew back the blackboard,
Where is the blackboard Billy Boggs blew back?

Billy Bluster blissfully blew blue balloon bubbles in a blinding blizzard. Blue balloon bubbles burst. Billy Bluster blubbered. Blubbering blindly, Billy Bluster blew more blue balloon bubbles in a blinding blizzard.

Charlotte's shaggy Shetland pony shied at the sheep in the shrubbery and shot Charlotte out of the chase into the shrubs.
Did Charlotte's shaggy Shetland pony shy at the sheep in the shrubbery and shoot Charlotte out of the chase into the shrubs?
If Charlotte's shaggy Shetland pony shied at the sheep in the shrubbery and shot Charlotte out of the chase into the shrubs,
Where is Charlotte's shaggy Shetland pony that shied at the sheep in the shrubbery and shot Charlotte out of the chase into the shrubs?

She sells sea-shells by the sea-shore. The shells she sells are sea-shells I'm sure.

It seemed like the theme of a dream in the glittering gleam of a stream.

Fanny found some fine flesh of freshly fried flying fish.
Did Fanny find some fine flesh of freshly fried flying fish?
If Fanny found some fine flesh of freshly fried flying fish,
Where is the fine flesh of freshly fried flying fish that Fanny found?

The duke paid the money due to the Jew before the dew was off the grass and the Jew, having duly acknowledged it, bade adieu to the duke forever.

Theodore Threshly thoughtfully threaded thirty-three thousand thick thistles.

Any noise annoys an oyster but a noisy noise annoys an oyster most.

Crispy Consonants

Pap-a-pap	pap	pap	pep-a-pep	pep	pep
pip-a-pip	pip	pip	pop-a-pop	pop	pop
pup-a-pup	pup	pup			

Bab-a-bab	bab	bab	beb-a-beb	beb	beb
bib-a-bib	bib	bib	bob-a-bob	bob	bob
bub-a-bub	bub	bub			

Dad-a-dad	dad	dad	ded-a-ded	ded	ded
did-a-did	did	did	dod-a-dod	dod	dod
dud-a-dud	dud	dud			

Faf-a-faf	faf	faf	fef-a-fef	fef	fef
fif-a-fif	fif	fif	fof-a-fof	fof	fof
fuf-a-fuf	fuf	fuf			

Gag-a-gag	gag	gag	geg-a-geg	geg	geg
gig-a-gig	gig	gig	gog-a-gog	gog	gog
gug-a-gug	gug	gug			

Tat-a-tat	tat	tat	tet-a-tet	tet	tet
tit-a-tit	tit	tit	tot-a-tot	tot	tot
tut-a-tut	tut	tut			

Sas-a-sas	sas	sas	ses-a-ses	ses	ses
sis-a-sis	sis	sis	sos-a-sos	sos	sos
sus-a-sus	sus	sus			

Mam-a-mam	mam	mam	mem-a-mem	mem	mem
mim-a-mim	mim	mim	mom-a-mom	mom	mom
mum-a-mum	mum	mum			

Nan-a-nan	nan	nan	nen-a-nen	nen	nen
Nin-a-nin	nin	nin	non-a-non	non	non
Nun-a-nun	nun	nun			

Voice #6 *Crispy Consonants*

Double Do Consonants

P.P.   Hop poles, sharp point, limp paper, ripe pear, deep pond, steep place, plump pony, bump proof, top prize, lamp post

B.B.   Herb broth, cub bear, crab basket, crib blanket, cube base, superb beauty

T.T.   Fit time, trite truths, rat trap, hot tea, soft tufts, quiet time, abstract truth, apt teacher, sweet thyme, russet tresses

D.D.   Good day, mad dog, horrid din, muffled drums, second division, loud derision, timid deer, wild delight, candid debate

K.K.   Book case, black cat, dark chasm, public care, rustic cottage, heroic conduct, domestic concern, bleak country

G.G.   Big gorilla, vague guesses, fig groves, dog growls, nutmeg grater, dig ground, pig grunts

F.F.   Tough food, rough fight, brief fortune, safe foil, leaf fibre, chief foe, reef fish

V.V.   Native vales, brave votary, drive vehicle, plaintive voice, extensive views, active vessel

S.S.   Fierce strife, dense smoke, sleepless sorrow, precious stone, pious saint, boundless space, close scrutiny, reckless sinners, injurious slanders, tempestuous seas

Z.Z.   His zeal, summer's zephyrs, these czars, praise Zeus

TH.TH.   Sixth theme, fifth thrust, truth thrives, warmth thaws, health theory, eighth thought, Corinth theater, ninth theme

THE.THE.   Soothe them, sheathe thy dagger, both thee with thee

Inflection Exercises

Did he say arm or arm?

He said arm not arm.

Did he say all or all?

He said all not all.

Did he say air or air?

He said air not air.

Did he say eel or eel?

He said eel not eel.

Did he say men or men?

He said men not men.

Did he say her or her?

He said her not her.

Did he say eye or eye?

He said eye not eye.

Did he say old or old?

He said old not old.

Voice #8 *Inflections*

Unit Study

Voice Handouts

For Little Children

The Music Makers

Hum Hum Hum Hum Hum Hum
Hum Tram Hum Tram Hum Tram

The moonbeams gleam with a shimmering sheen

The merry men were muttering
The wooden shoes were clattering
The children's feet were pattering
The baby hens were scattering

And he himself was tall and thin,
With sharp blue eyes, each like a pin,
And light loose hair, yet swarthy skin,
No tuft on cheek, nor beard on chin,
But lips where smiles went out and in,
There was no guessing his kith and kin.

—*The Pied Piper of Hamelin*, Robert Browning

Child's Voice #1 *The Music Makers*

Vowels and Consonants

Once there was a little rose
Rosy, posy, nosy little rose

Bow, wow, wow
Whose dog are thou?
Bow, wow, wow

Once there was a little owl
Owly, prowly, howly little owl

Ouch! Pouch! Couch!

Shoo! all you birds!
Shoo! Shoo! Shoo!
Winter is coming
It's time you flew

Says the crow in the cornfield
Caw, caw, caw
He's a very bold robber
He fears no law

Our kites are flying high in the sky
Tiny and white like a butterfly

Child's Voice #2 *Vowels and Consonants*

Rat-a-tat-tat-tat-tat
Whose knock is that
Every morning at eight
At the garden gate
He is never late

He was bang-bang-banging on his Big Brass Drum,
And the regiment went marching with their
Thrum-thrum-thrum.
They came marching up the garden with their firm
hard tread,
A line of Yankee soldiers with a drummer at their
head.

Send an Echo

Helloooooooo

Helloooooooo

Hiiiiiiiiiiiiiiiii

Hiiiiiiiiiiiiiiiiii

Tongue Twisters

(For Little Children)

Bashful Bobby bounced a big brown ball beside beautiful Bonnie's baby bunny

Mollie merrily meowed for Mommy
Mommy merrily meowed for Mollie

Friendly Fanny found a fine fresh flying fish that flipped and flapped in the frying fat

Caroline crunched a crispy cracker while cradling a cuddly cute koala

Shy Shelley said she saw some shining seashells on the shimmering shore

The wild and wintry weather worried weary General Washington

Harry, the happy hairy horse, hoofed his way up the high, hard hill

Child's Voice #3 *Tongue Twisters*

Magic Dust Letters

Words that begin with the sound "wh" are magic dust letters. We always need to blow air through the lips when we bring "w" and "h" together.

*Wh*ere	*Wh*ack	*Wh*ence
*Wh*en	*Wh*enever	*Wh*ale
*Wh*y	*Wh*ammy	*Wh*isker
*Wh*at	*Wh*ite	*Wh*eat
*Wh*ich	*Wh*ither	*Wh*istle
*Wh*ile	*Wh*im	*Wh*ee

*Wh*y and *wh*at do you want?

*Wh*ere and *wh*en are you going?

The *wh*eat is growing wild

*Wh*ither are you going?

With *wh*at joy we learn to *wh*istle! *Wh*eeeeeee!

Child's Voice #4 *Magic Dust Letters*

Unit
Study
Sample
Recitations

Sample Recitations

#1 Where the pools are bright and deep,
    Where the gray trout lies asleep,
    Up the river and o'er the lea
    That's the way for Billy and me.
    Where the mowers mow the cleanest,
    Where the hay lies thick and greenest,
    There to trace the homeward bee,
    That's the way for Billy and me.
                    (A *Boy's Song*, James Hogg)

#2 When can their glory fade?
    O the wild charge they made!
    All the world wonder'd.
    Honor the charge they made!
    Honor the Light Brigade,
    Noble six hundred.
            (*Charge of the Light Brigade*, Tennyson)

#3 Color is a lovely thing,
    Given to soothe the sight;
    Blue for sky, green for grass,
    And brown for roads where tired folk pass.
    Silver for moon, for sunset red,
    And soft cool black for night.

#4 And slowly answer'd Arthur from the barge;
    "The old order changeth, yielding place to new,
    And God fulfils himself in many ways,
    Lest one good custom should corrupt the world.
    Comfort thyself: what comfort is in me?
    I have lived my life, and that which I have done
    May He within himself make pure! But thou,
    Pray for my soul. More things are wrought by prayer
    Than this world dreams of."
                    (*The Passing of Arthur*, Tennyson)

#5 Once more unto the breach, dear friends, once more;
Or close the wall up with our English dead.
In peace there's nothing so becomes a man
As modest stillness and humility:
But when the blast of war blows in our ears,
Then imitate the action of the tiger;
Stiffen the sinews, summon up the blood,
Disguise fair nature with hard-favour'd rage;
Then lend the eye a terrible aspect....
Hold hard the breath and bend up every spirit
To his full height....
I see you stand like greyhounds in the slips,
Straining upon the start. The game's afoot:
Follow your spirit; and upon this charge
Cry "God for Harry! England! and Saint George!"
(*Henry V*, Shakespeare)

#6 The Assyrian came down like the wolf on the fold,
And his cohorts were gleaming in purple and gold;
And the sheen of their spears was like stars on the sea,
When the blue wave rolls nightly in deep Galilee.
(*The Destruction of Sennacherib*, Byron)

#7 I stood tiptoe upon a little hill. The air was cooling and so very still that the sweet buds had not yet lost those starry diadems caught from the early sobbing of the morn. The clouds were pure and white as flocks new shorn and, fresh from the clear brook, sweetly they slept on the blue fields of heaven.
(*I Stood Tiptoe*, Keats)

#8 To every thing there is a season, and a time to every purpose under the heaven;
A time to be born, and a time to die; a time to plant, and a time to pluck up
    that which is planted....
A time to weep, and a time to laugh; a time to mourn, and a time to dance....
A time to rend, and a time to sew; a time to keep silence, and a time to speak;
A time to love, and a time to hate; a time of war, and a time of peace.
(*Ecclesiastes* lll)

Sample Recitations (Page 2)

Sample Recitations
For Little Children

#1   We are little holly fairies
Messengers of Christmas cheer,
Before it's time for Santa Claus
You'll see our bright-faced holly here.

#2   We are very little creatures,
All of a different voice and features;
One of us in *glass* is set,
One of us you'll find in *jet*.
The other you may see in *tin*,
And the fourth a *box* within.
If the fifth you should pursue,
It can never fly from *you*.

#3   Folks call me a snowflake,
When they see me dancing by,
But I'll tell you a little secret
I'm a winter butterfly.

#4   The world's a very happy place,
Where every child should dance and sing,
And always have a smiling face,
And never sulk for anything.

#5   If the evening's red and the morning gray,
It is the sign of a bonnie day;
If the evening's gray and the morning's red,
The lamb and the ewe will go wet to bed.

#7   Thirty days hath September,
April, June, and November;
All the rest have thirty-one;
February twenty-eight alone –
Except in leap-year, at which time
February's days are twenty-nine.

Child's Sample Recitations

#8 January brings the snow
Makes our feet and fingers glow.
April brings the primrose sweet,
Scatters daisies at our feet

#9 Nothing is so quiet and clean
As snow that falls in the night;
And isn't it fun to jump from bed
And find the whole world white?

#10 "Will you walk into my parlour?" said the Spider to the Fly,
"'Tis the prettiest little parlour that ever you did spy;
The way into my parlour is up a winding stair,
And I have many curious things to show when you are there."
"Oh no, no," said the little Fly, "to ask me is in vain;
For who goes up your winding stair can never come down again."
(*The Spider and the Fly*, Mary Howitt)

#11 The polar bear will make a rug
Almost as white as snow:
But if he gets you in his hug,
He rarely lets you go.

#12 A child should always say what's true
And speak when he is spoken to,
And behave mannerly at table:
At least as far as he is able.
(*Robert Louis Stevenson*)

#13 Good little boys should never say
"I will," and "Give me these."
O, no! that never is the way,
But always, "Mother, if you please."
And, "Yes, sir" to a gentleman
And, "Yes, ma'am" to a Lady.

#14 A sunshiny shower
Won't last half an hour.

Selected Bibliography

Andrews, Harry Lee and Bruce Weirick. *Acting and Play Production*. New York: Longmans, Green & Co., 1925

Bernhardt, Sarah. *L'Art Du Théâtre*. Paris: Editions Nilsson, 1923

Bernhardt, Sarah. *The Art of Theater*. New York: Dial Press, 1925

Bernhardt, Sarah. *Memoirs of Sarah Bernhardt*. London: William Heinemann, 1907

Burger, Isabel B. *Creative Play Acting*. New York: A.S. Barnes and Company, Inc, 1950

Cheney, Sheldon. *The Theater*. New York: Tudor Publishing Company, 1929

Cooper, Morton. *Modern Techniques of Vocal Rehabilitation*. Illinois: Charles C Thomas Publisher, 1973

Dean, Alexander and Lawrence Carra. *Fundamentals of Play Directing*. Fort Worth: Holt, Rinehart and Winston, Inc, 1965

Horner, A. Musgrave. *Speech Training*. London: A & C Black Ltd., 1963

Herbert-Caesari, E. *The Alchemy of Voice*. London: Robert Hale, 1965

Herbert-Caesari, E. *The Voice of the Mind*. London: Robert Hale, 1951

Miles-Brown, John. *Speech Training and Dramatic Art*. London: Sir Isaac Pitman & Sons Ltd., 1963

Pickering, Ken. *Key Concepts in Drama and Performance*. London: Palgrave Macmillan, 2005

Prophet, Mark L. *The Science of the Spoken Word*. California: S.U. Press, 1965

Traynor, H.W. *The Art of Speech*. Melbourne, Australia: Whitcombe & Tombs Pty. Ltd., 1957

Stanislavski, Constantin. *An Actor Prepares*. Translated by Elizabeth Reynolds Hapgood. New York: Theater Arts Books, 1936

Stanislavski, Constantin. *My Life in Art*. Translated by J.J. Robbins. Little, Brown, and Company, 1924

Stanislavski, Constantin. *Building a Character.* Translated by Elizabeth Reynolds Hapgood. New York: Theater Arts Books, 1949

Stanislavski, Constantin. *Creating a Role,* Translated by Elizabeth Reynolds Hapgood. New York: Theater Arts Books, 1961

I have gathered here an offering of other people's flowers, bringing to them of my own only a thread to bind them with.

—Michel de Montaigne

About the Author

Deslie McClellan was born in Sydney, Australia. She completed studies in speech and drama, graduating with a teaching degree from the Trinity College of Music, London. She also received the coveted Exhibition Letters from the Trinity College for performer excellence in drama.

While attending the University of Sydney for her Bachelor of Arts degree, Deslie pursued a professional career as a nightclub singer with appearances on national television variety shows. With the dream of all young artists, she moved to Las Vegas, Nevada, in the mid-1970s, where she started the entertainment capital's first professional acting school and repertory company, winning rave reviews from Variety and Hollywood Reporter. The school became a hub for professionals working on the Las Vegas Strip as well as wanna-be performing artists. The theater soon evolved into a leading agency for photographic, film, and convention jobs in the city. Deslie also enjoyed frequent television and radio appearances and she freelanced as a journalist, writing articles on celebrity entertainers for national magazines.

Feeling the need to explore theater outside the commercial glamor track, Deslie sold the school and accepted a position as a drama teacher at a California high school for the next four years. During this time, she became convinced that theater can be used as a magical tool to help children develop a genuine love of what is noble and good in life. Tending the garden of childhood through drama has remained her life's goal. She strongly promotes live theater as the best training ground for the young actor and has, herself, played a variety of stage roles including Shaw's Joan of Arc, the Irish heroine Pegeen, Catherine from *Wuthering Heights,* Christopher Fry's Jennet, and Shakespeare's Puck, Viola, Queen Katherine, and the ever tragic Juliet.

Deslie now lives in Emmaus, Pennsylvania, with her husband, Jim, an airline pilot, and their two children. Before taking a sabbatical to write and publish, she staged highly successful plays from the classics and Shakespeare with her theater, Family Playhouse. The theater represents the fourth of such successful acting schools that she has mounted as she followed her husband's military and later airline career around the world.